URBAN GROWTH AND INNOVATION

Ashgate Economic Geography Series

Series Editors:
Michael Taylor, Peter Nijkamp and Tom Leinbach

Innovative and stimulating, this quality series enlivens the field of economic geography and regional development, providing key volumes for academic use across a variety of disciplines. Exploring a broad range of interrelated topics, the series enhances our understanding of the dynamics of modern economies in developed and developing countries, as well as the dynamics of transition economies. It embraces both cutting edge research monographs and strongly themed edited volumes, thus offering significant added value to the field and to the individual topics addressed.

Other titles in the series:

The Emerging Economic Geography in EU Accession Countries
Edited by Iulia Traistaru, Peter Nijamp and Laura Resmini
ISBN 0 7546 3318 7

Urban Growth and Innovation

Spatially Bounded Externalities in the Netherlands

FRANK G. VAN OORT
Urban and Regional Research Centre Utrecht (URU), Utrecht University
and
Netherlands Institute for Spatial Research (RPB), The Hague

ASHGATE

Published by
Ashgate Publishing Limited
Gower House
Croft Road
Aldershot
Hants GU11 3HR
England

Ashgate Publishing Company
Suite 420
101 Cherry Street
Burlington, VT 05401-4405
USA

Ashgate website: http://www.ashgate.com

British Library Cataloguing in Publication Data
Oort, Frank G. van
Urban growth and innovation : spatially bounded externalities in the Netherlands. - (Ashgate economic geography series)
1.Cities and towns - Netherlands - Growth - Econometric models 2.Urbanization - Netherlands - Econometric models 3.Industrial location - Netherlands 4.Space in economics
I.Title
307.1'416'015195

Library of Congress Cataloging-in-Publication Data
Oort, Frank G. van, 1970-
  Urban growth and innovation : spatially bounded externalities in the Netherlands / Frank G. van Oort.
    p. cm. -- (Ashgate economic geography series)
  Originally presented as the author's thesis (doctoral)--Erasmus Universiteit, Rotterdam, 2002, under the title: Agglomeration, economic growth and innovation.
  Includes bibliographical references and index.
  ISBN 0-7546-3867-7
    1. Urbanization--Netherlands. 2. Metropolitan areas--Netherlands. 3. Regional economics--Mathematical models. 4. Space in economics--Mathematical models. 5. Industrial location--Netherlands--Mathematical models. I.Title. II. Series.

HT384.N4O57 2004
307.76'09492--dc22   2003054489

ISBN 0 7546 3867 7

Printed and bound in Great Britain by Athenaeum Press Ltd., Gateshead

Contents

List of Figures   *vii*
List of Tables   *ix*

1   Introduction   **1**
1.1   The Need for Accurate Urban Modeling   1
1.2   Research Questions   4
1.3   Outline of the Study   9

2   Agglomeration in Economic and Geographical Theories   **13**
2.1   Introduction   13
2.2   The Common Factors   21
2.3   New Trade and Growth Theories on Agglomeration Economies   32
2.4   Proximity and Spatial Networks in Innovation Diffusion   42
2.5   Agglomeration Economies in the New Industrial Geography   53
2.6   Summary and Synthesis   57

3   Heterogeneity in Localized Economic Growth   **65**
3.1   Introduction   65
3.2   Heterogeneity in Industry Classification   66
3.3   Modeling Spatial Structure and Heterogeneity   72
3.4   Identifying Spatial Heterogeneity in Regimes   78
3.5   Firm Life-Cycle Heterogeneity   96
3.6   Summary and Synthesis   103

4   Exploratory Spatial Data Analysis   **107**
4.1   Introduction   107
4.2   South-Holland Firm and Employment Density and Function   111
4.3   South-Holland Firm and Employment Growth   120
4.4   New Firm Formation and Exit in South-Holland   124
4.5   Employment Density, Function and Growth in the Netherlands   129
4.6   Innovation Intensity in the Netherlands   133
4.7   Synthesis and Conclusions   136

5   Location-Industry Employment Dynamics   **141**
5.1   Introduction   141
5.2   Construction of Variables   143
5.3   OLS Analysis for the Netherlands   148
5.4   OLS Analysis for South-Holland   152
5.5   Spatial Econometric Models for South-Holland   158
5.6   Synthesis and Conclusions   165

6   Sectoral Employment Dynamics   **169**
6.1   Introduction   169
6.2   Sectoral Models for South-Holland   171
6.3   Sectoral Models for the Netherlands   181
6.4   Synthesis and Conclusions   190

7   Innovation Intensity   **195**
7.1   Introduction   195
7.2   Descriptive Analysis   198
7.3   Spatial Econometric Models   206
7.4   Synthesis and Conclusions   213

8   Summary and Conclusions   **217**
8.1   Research Questions   217
8.2   Research Results   219
8.3   Research Conclusions   229

Appendix A: Data on Employment Dynamics   *235*
Appendix B: Data on Innovation Intensity   *247*
Bibliography   *251*
Index   *271*

List of Figures

2.1   A framework for agglomeration economies: concepts and
       contingencies on externalities   18
2.2   Circular causality in spatial agglomerations of firms and workers   35
3.1   Municipalities with more than 20,000 inhabitants (1991)   71
3.2   The research area of South-Holland   81
3.3   Dominant occupations in urban locations in South-Holland
       (regimes, 1993)   83
3.4   Dominant occupations in non-urban locations in South-Holland
       (regimes, 1993)   84
3.5   Gravity model (macro-zoning regimes) for employment
       $(\alpha,\beta=1; 1997)$ 87
3.6   Percentage change in gravity values for employment $(\alpha,\beta=1; 1991\text{-}1997)$ 89
3.7   North- and south-wing of the Randstad (spatial regimes)   90
3.8   The 'connectedness' spatial regime (1990)   91
3.9   Components of change in South-Holland (employment 1988-1997)   101
3.10 Components of change in South-Holland compared to base year 1988
       (number of firms and employment)   102
4.1   Moran scatterplot employment density South-Holland
       (1997, n=416, w_1)   113
4.2   Moran scatterplot map employment density South-Holland (1997, w_1)   114
4.3   Moran scatterplot employment function South-Holland
       (1997, n=416, w_1)   118
4.4   Moran scatterplot map employment function South-Holland (1997, w_1)   119
4.5   Moran scatterplot employment growth South-Holland (1988-1997,
       n=416, w_1)   122
4.6   Moran scatterplot map employment growth South-Holland
       (1988-1997, w_1)   123
4.7   Moran scatterplot map new firm employment South-Holland
       (average % 1988-1997, w_1)   127
4.8   Moran scatterplot map firm-exit employment South-Holland
       (average % 1988-1997), w_1)   128
4.9   Moran scatterplot map employment function Netherlands (1997, w_1)   131
4.10 Moran scatterplot map employment growth Netherlands
       (1991-1997, w_1)   132
4.11 Moran scatterplot map innovation intensity (1999, w_1)   135
4.12 Moran scatterplot map industrial innovation intensity (1999, w_1)   137
4.13 Moran scatterplot map non-industrial innovation intensity (1999, w_1) 138

7.1 Location quotients and index intensity of industrial innovation in connected and national zoning regimes   201

7.2 Sectoral and spatial effects in the distribution of innovation intensity (n=580)   204

7.3 Provincial, sectoral and spatial effects in the distribution of innovation intensity (n=12)   205

7.4 Sectoral and spatial effects in the distribution of innovation intensity in connected and national zoning regimes (n=16)   206

A1 The research area of South-Holland decomposed by zip code (416), municipality (69) and registration area (3)   243

A2 (a) Wage levels in 40 regions in the Netherlands (average 1988-1997) and (b) change in average wage levels (1988-1997)   245

List of Tables

2.1 Urbanization economies: agglomerative implications of variety — 29
2.2 A comparison of geographical economics and new industrial geographical frameworks of analyses — 59
2.3 Stylized hypothesized relations between agglomeration circumstances and economic growth — 60
3.1 Ten largest industries represented in the Netherlands and South-Holland data (number and employment) — 70
3.2 Ten largest manufacturing industries in the Dutch (municipal) dataset on location-industries (n=1404) — 72
3.3 Observations in the regimes on national zoning and connectedness (absolute and share) — 92
3.4 Correlation coefficients of national spatial regimes (n=580) — 93
3.5 Employment and population in national spatial regimes (1997: absolute and share; 1991-1997: yearly percentage growth) — 95
3.6 Location quotients of employment in zoning and connectedness regimes (1997) — 97
3.7 Firm formation, dissolution and migration in South-Holland (average 1988-1997) — 100
4.1 Moran's I statistics for employment and firm density (South-Holland 1997, w_1, randomization assumption) — 112
4.2 Standardized values Moran's I statistics for employment and firm density (South-Holland 1997, randomization assumption, w_1) — 115
4.3 Moran's I statistics for employment function and firm representation (South-Holland 1997, randomization assumption) — 117
4.4 Moran's I statistics for employment and firm growth (South-Holland, 1988-1997, randomization assumption) — 121
4.5 Standardized values of Moran's I statistic for new firm formation, exit and employment creation (South-Holland, 1997, randomization assumption, w_1) — 126
4.6 Standardized values of Moran's I statistic for employment function and firm representation (Netherlands, 1997, randomization assumption) — 130
4.7 Moran's I statistics for innovation intensity (Netherlands 1999, w_1, randomization assumption) — 133
5.1 Definition of location-industry variables and average values for South-Holland (n=1797) and the Netherlands (n=1404) — 144
5.2 Explanation of 1997 employment levels in 7 selected industries (t-values in parenthesis) — 149
5.3 Determinants of employment growth per municipality-industry (OLS, n=1404) — 151

5.4   South-Holland regression results per zip code-industry (OLS, n=1797)   155
5.5   OLS analysis of change in employment in location-industries in
      South-Holland (n=1797)   158
5.6   Spatial lag analysis of change in employment in location-industries
      in South-Holland: spatial linkages across all industries (n=1797)   161
5.7   Spatial lag analysis of change in employment in location-industries
      in South-Holland: spatial linkages only within industries (n=1797)   163
5.8   Spatial multipliers in employment growth models in South-Holland   165
6.1   OLS and spatial lag models for employment growth in manufacturing
      activities in South-Holland (n=416, w_1)   174
6.2   OLS and FGLS models for employment growth in distribution activities
      in South-Holland (n=416, w_1)   176
6.3   OLS and spatial lag models for employment growth in producer
      services in South-Holland (n=416, w_1)   178
6.4   OLS and spatial lag models for employment growth in consumer
      services in South-Holland (n=416, w_1)   180
6.5   OLS and FGLS models for industrial employment growth in the
      Netherlands (n=580, w_1)   182
6.6   OLS and spatial lag models for employment growth in distribution
      activities in the Netherlands (n=580, w_1)   184
6.7   OLS, spatial lag and FGLS models for employment growth in producer
      services in the Netherlands (n=580, w_1)   186
6.8   OLS and spatial lag models for employment growth in consumer services
      in the Netherlands (n=580, w_2)   190
7.1   Innovation intensity in connected and national zoning regimes
      (absolute, share, intensity and index intensity)   199
7.2   Industrial innovation intensity in connected and national zoning regimes
      (absolute, location quotient, intensity and index intensity)   200
7.3   Non-industrial innovation intensity in connected and national zoning
      regimes (absolute, location quotient, intensity and index intensity)   202
7.4   OLS and spatial lag models for industrial innovation intensity in the
      Netherlands (n=580)   208
7.5   OLS, spatial lag and FGLS models for industrial innovation intensity
      in the Netherlands (n=580)   210
7.6   OLS, spatial lag and FGLS models for industrial and non-industrial
      innovation intensity in the Netherlands (n=580)   211
8.1   Summarizing results of spatial econometric analyses of employment
      growth and innovation intensity   223
A1   2-digit industries (49) in employment data and aggregation into sixteen
      detailed and four broad sectors   239
B1   BSI-technology fields (aggregated into 5 classes)   248

For Maura and Jermo

Chapter 1

Introduction

1.1 The Need for Accurate Urban Modeling

Agglomeration economies are on many people's agendas. For centuries, urban areas are the sites where innovative cultural, social and economic developments take place (Hall 1998). Urban and regional planners as well as spatial and economic scientists are interested in the forces that build up, shape and maintain clusters of economic activities. Recently, (renewed) attention is paid to economic externalities (technical or pecuniary firm-external circumstances that induce increasing returns to scale of production) and (knowledge) spillovers in urban environments, aspects hypothesized to foster agglomeration, innovation and growth that would not have occurred outside those environments. The paradox in urban economics in recent years, however, is that agglomeration economies (and diseconomies) are seen as the driving force behind explanations of geographical concentration of economic activity within cities, while remaining something of a black box (Richardson 1995, p.123). Several diverse attempts to measure these economies are addressed in this dissertation, but their precise geographical nature and economic role remains elusive. External economies of scale (both for individual firms and industries) help to explain why economic activity concentrates in cities. Spatial concentration is eventually limited by offsetting diseconomies, ranging from pecuniary diseconomies (e.g. high land rents and wages) to traffic congestion and density-related pollution. Historically, both agglomeration economies and congestion costs are generated within the central core of cities, and as the economies begin to be overwhelmed by the congestion effects, firms (and households) can escape the consequences by relocating to decentralized locations. The new locations may still be within the spatial range of some of the core location economies (Phelps *et al.* 2001) but avoid most of the congestion costs; they offer opportunities for higher profits (for firms) and higher utility (for households). These individual relocation decisions of firms and households, guided by local and regional spatial policy, gradually reshape the metropolitan landscape (Richardson 1995).

This study focuses on spatial economies (geographically determined externalities) of firm establishments in a specific urban context: that of the Netherlands. Alongside academia, spatial policy in the Netherlands by tradition shares an interest in spatial economic growth circumstances. This is worked out by guiding concentration of economic activity by planning new industrial sites near existing ones and stressing urban and localized amenities and externalities that lead to higher economic productivity. This philosophy of compact urban planning for gaining optimal benefits from spillovers and spin-offs due to agglomeration economies to some extent determines agglomeration of economic activity in the Netherlands[1]. It is assumed that this policy builds on endogenous growth forces of economic activities that shape the urban and regional economic landscapes. However, part of my argument is that not much is yet understood on causal relations in economic agglomeration forces. In economic science, (partial) equilibrium models are interpreted by their degree of spatial agglomerated outcomes that are the result of a stylized modeled interplay of agglomerating and de-agglomerating forces (Fujita *et al.* 2000)[2]. Urban and regional economics as well as economic geography by tradition pay more detailed attention to what exactly those agglomeration forces of economic activities are. Unfortunately, until some years ago economic geography and urban and regional economics were not part of the mainstream economic research agenda. But recently, more mainstream international (trade) economics as well as growth and evolutionary economics have become more urban and spatial in character. The common focus on 'urbanisation' and 'localisation' does not mean that geography and economics tackle agglomeration economies in a common accepted framework, though. The research agendas within both disciplines do not (yet) allow for that. As will be discussed in more detail later on, the theoretical nature of functional relations that determine spatial development is envisioned differently, being predominantly social and institutional in character in geographical disciplines, and neo-classical economic in economic disciplines. This lack of consistent economic frameworks still causes considerable degrees of freedom in conceptualizing within sub-disciplines like evolutionary, trade and growth economics, and prohibits an overall clear impact on urban economics. But the relevance and potential impact of the hypotheses stemming from these disciplines are becoming more and more accepted and further explored (Lambooy 1998a). In recent contributions, especially dynamic externalities modeling (Glaeser *et al.* 1992, Henderson 2003), innovation-based spatial diffusion modeling (Jaffe *et al.* 1993) and endogenous growth theory (Aghion and Howitt 1998) emphasize the spatial role of knowledge possessed by economic agents. These contributions aim at identifying knowledge spillovers between agents as crucial factors leading to external economies of scale in production (Romer 1986, Lucas 1988). Empirical tests of this theory often have looked at cities, systems of cities and agglomerations of economic activities to identify settings in which these external factors most effectively and firm-endogenously foster growth (Pred 1977).

On of the most promising recent contributions in understanding the nature and content of dynamic urban externalities is provided in the theoretical and empirical

---

[1] A more practical reason for compact urban development is the (perceived) scarcity of land in the Netherlands. This scarcity enforces a spatial policy aiming at intensification of the built environment and the combination and transformation of urban functions in their present setting.

[2] It should be emphasised that in our study agglomeration economies are treated as a means of economic growth and innovation. Agglomeration itself is not the (explained) objective of research design, as in the geographic-economic research tradition as summarised in Fujita *et al.* (2000).

framework developed by Glaeser *et al.* (1992). In their seminal contribution to the research field entitled 'growth in cities', an endogenous growth framework based on employment growth patterns in mixtures of industries in US cities is developed. Glaeser *et al.* (1992) interpret Romer (1986) as predicting that knowledge externalities will be most significant among firms in the same industry. The implied corollary is that industries that represent a high level of employment in a given city relative to that industry nationally will grow faster as they benefit from information externalities (Feser 2002). More exactly, Glaeser *et al.* (1992) use three theoretically 'contrasting' spatial causal concepts of agglomeration economies: (1) local industry-level specialisation; (2) local industry diversity; and (3) the degree of local competition. This framework builds on the well known concepts of localisation (specialisation) and urbanisation (diversity) economies from the regional-economic discipline, that differentiate between localized growth and innovation patterns (Richardson 1995, Dicken and Lloyd 1990). Missing in Glaeser *et al.*'s (1992) contribution is a proper treatment of space, distance and spatial (statistical) dependence as surfaced from the regional science and geographical literature. There is a large need for exact definitions of agglomeration economies in terms of multiple and linked alternative scales and spatial configurations (Parr 2002 p.728, Olsen 2002 p.154, Hanson 2001 p.270, Rigby and Essletzbichler 2002 p.429). It is exactly on this need that our study tries to find conclusive answers.

Using spatial econometric research methods in combination with research methods of the existing literature will do this. The former methods in general distinguishes neighbouring (contiguous) and heterogeneous (non-contiguous, functional) spatial conditions for development (growth or innovation). In our study, static (R&D) and dynamic (growth) externalities are tested for their importance on firm- and industry-level innovation intensity and employment growth, using the framework of Glaeser *et al.* (1992) as the initial starting point of analysis. This because of its initial importance (it was the first paper that systematically studied growth processes at the urban level) and frequent citation. Rather than emphasizing differences in empirical model outcomes because of a focus on a Western European country instead of the US, the research stresses on the implications of theoretical and conceptual alterations from the Glaeser *et al.* (1992) framework. These alterations are introduced (one by one) because they better capture important conceptual aspects concerning spatial scale and spatial composition when analysing firm- and industry-level growth and innovation. Generally speaking, the present literature does not acknowledge the importance of these aspects, and where acknowledged it does not make sufficient use of theoretical insights, available measurement and econometric modeling techniques.

Throughout history, the Netherlands is a highly urbanized, poly-centered and (relatively) data-rich country. Alongside conceptual and econometric research extensions, these facts impose some important research advantages that set our study apart from the (growing) US-induced research output on the subject of spatial externalities. The advantages (and hence scientific contributions) that concern the research in our study can be summarized into three closely related dimensions: (1) the given natural context of a dense and polynucleated urban environment; (2)

theoretical conceptualisations concerning spatial growth and innovation; and (3) empirical (measurement) issues. The third issue concerns a full account of possibilities and limitations of formal spatial econometric modeling, not beforehand conditioned by research traditions. Through contributions on these three issues, our study aims at improving existing insights in spatial (urban) growth and innovation externalities research. The empirical contributions in this respect aim at clarifying the nature of spatial scale and spatial composition that can be conducted from empirical observations on employment growth and innovation intensity in the Netherlands. A major point of my argument is that controversial research results in the literature concerning explanatory spatial circumstances that most favourably induce dynamic and innovative externalities, (to a large extent) can be attributed to the lack of consistent spatial research designs that allow the modeling of multiple spatial scale and composition effects. Theoretically, the lack of consistent inclusion of life-cycle aspects of firms (age and connected growth potential) in the present mainstream literature on dynamic externalities, arguably contributes to controversies in research outcomes too. The remainder of this chapter introduces and shortly discusses the research questions of our study. This then concerns three aspects of the (interrelated) dimensions considered important within the scientific literature: natural setting, theory, measurement issues and econometric modeling.

1.2   Research Questions

The spatial context of empirical analyses of economic externalities of firms is of crucial importance for understanding the dynamic processes associated with economic growth and innovation intensity. When regularities in research outcomes are found over different natural settings (e.g. over US or European urban systems), the conceptualisation wins in robustness. The international literature on spatial externalities focuses mainly on urban environments (cities) for testing spatial externalities, headed by the influential papers by Glaeser *et al.* (1992) and Henderson *et al.* (1995). In our study we find that the contradictory research results of these two major contributions to the research field might to a large degree be attributable to their respective research designs. In short: Glaeser *et al.* find evidence for a diversity-based explanation of spatial growth externalities, while Henderson *et al.* conclude on the significance of localized specialisation of economic activities as guiding principle. Using comparable spatial research units (metropolitan areas in the US), the research design of Glaeser *et al.* focuses on the composition of the largest six industries in each city, while Henderson *et al.* look at individual industry performance. The choice for six largest or individual industries for analysis, the lack of supposed (and modeled) spatial interaction within and between cities and metropolitan areas and the lack of embeddedness of local urban developments into regional (or even global) contexts appear as trivial (but relatively little acknowledged) research choices in the present spatial externalities literature. When designed according to similar frameworks as the two important papers mentioned above, respective research results are almost identical concerning the relation of dynamic externalities or agglomeration economies with growth and innovation in urban contexts. Bivand (1999) for Poland and Paci and Usai (1999) for Italy, for instance, find predominantly diversity-based research results concerning spatial externalities while using indicators and spatial research designs quite similar to those used by Glaeser *et al.* (1992). Comparable with Henderson *et al.* (1995), Combes (2000) and De Lucio *et al.* (2002) find additional evidence for the role of specialisation by investigating growth of individual industries in France and Spain. The major research question of our study concerns looking at research outcomes in the Netherlands in this respect. In short: in what respect are spatial economic externalities (agglomeration economies) related to endogenous employment growth and innovation intensity of firms in the Netherlands? In our research a substantial contribution stems from incorporating spatial scale and composition effects in consistent modeling and conceptualisation that are underdeveloped in previous studies.

The Natural Setting: an Urban Field?

The specific spatial setting of urban development and agglomeration externalities in the Netherlands deserves conceptual creditability in its own right. It is often pointed out that the polycentric character of the urban structure in the Netherlands forms an ideal spatial-economic setting for urban sprawl, urban field and urban network conceptualisations (Atzema and Lambooy 1999, Batten 1995, Hall 1977, De Jong 1987, Lambooy 1998b). While the largest cities are not present, (parts of) the Netherlands are indeed urbanized to a degree that it makes sense to define multiple forms of urbanism (Van der Laan and Van Oort 2003). In its most extreme form, the present spatial constellation provides polynuclear circumstances that make the Randstad (the economic core region), or even the country as a whole, function as an *economic* entity (labeled 'urban field' by Van Geenhuizen 1993, Vaessen 1993 and Wever and Stam 1999). This suggests that 'space' does not matter for economic activities to function more efficiently. However, the conceptualisations and metaphors should be treated carefully for at least two reasons. Firstly the relevant spatial level of analysis is important. Policy as well as research frequently uses metaphors in analysis, vision-building and policy implementation. (Too) little evidence is available at present that confirms or rejects hypotheses concerning agglomeration economies that lead to such far-reaching conclusions. Secondly, the metaphors used have long and specific histories and should be treated accordingly. Friedmann and Miller (1965) and Lamb (1975) on urban field theory, for example, developed and presented their conceptualisation in well defined circumstances, using more stringent definitions than used in most research and policy in the Netherlands today[3]. Despite this criticism concerning conceptual flaws, the polycentric layout of many small and medium-sized cities in the Dutch urban

---

[3] Friedmann and Miller (1965) and Friedmann (1978) envision the urban field (in their US definition of 1965 comprising two and a half hours travelling time or a diameter of a 100 miles) as an optimal region for spatial planning.

system connected by multiple transport routes and modes[4] does potentially make an important difference in spatial externality testing when compared to US and other Western European contributions. A lack of clear spatial dependence (both in an agglomeration and a non-contiguous, functional sense) in economic growth and innovation data, both indicators of firm performance, could arguably be regarded as provisional proof of the urban field hypothesis.

The Representative Firm versus Economic Heterogeneity

The introduction of different research designs according to age of establishments and firms is often suggested in the literature (most notably by Henderson *et al.* 1995, Harrison *et al.* 1997 and Glaeser *et al.* 1992) but not systematically explored because of a lack of adequate, spatially detailed data. From the literature review presented in chapter 2, it becomes clear that many growth and innovation hypotheses are largely connected to new and young firms that operate in niche markets, characterized by (rapid) development and innovative behaviour. On the other hand, market power that enables large firms to internalize profits and (spatial) market externalities is also believed to be an ideal economic market structure in many theories. All such theories potentially contribute to the distinction of development potentials for regions and cities. The general economic framework as developed in Glaeser *et al.* (1992) initially does not allow for a deviation from the representative firm conceptualisation (see Hamermesh 1996, Taylor and Asheim 2001). In this framework, a typology of firms according to age, sectoral composition, location or other source of economic heterogeneity does not naturally fit in the (general equilibrium) concept of economic modeling. Models presented in this dissertation however do allow for spatial, sectoral and age-determined research populations to be central foci, and hence deviates from generalized economic theory.

In our study, local economic competition (a source for economic heterogeneity) is 'captured' according to several alternative definitions. In Glaeser *et al.* (1992), local (urban) competition is measured by local average firm size. Whether this indicator gives insight in firm turbulence and niche market conditions remains debatable throughout the literature. Alternatively, a local competition indicator is introduced based on flow and survival functions of (new and established) firms, labeled establishment turnover. While potentially capturing local competitive structures better than (or at least complementary to) pure size indicators, a major difficulty in the literature remains the spatial extent to which competition influences firm- or industry-level economic performance. Many producer activities are competitive on regional or even global markets instead of local (urban) ones. The empirical literature shows that (relatively large) global operating and trade-sensitive firms still profit from localized and regional externalities (Shelburne and Bednarzik 1993, Sjöholm 1996). In the next sections

---

[4] According to Batty (2001, p.650) this is the formal (visual) definition of polynucleated urban structures.

spatial econometric modeling is discussed where this multilevel character of agglomeration indicators is captured, although international spatial linkages (concerning markets or world city specialisation) are not. Finally, it should be noted that the main focus of agglomeration externality research in the literature is on *innovation* analyses. Identical research setting for spatial *growth* patterns that capture spatial heterogeneity and contiguity-based spatial dependence are less common in research.

The main theoretical contributions presented in this dissertation are: the introduction of age-determined research populations (in contrast to representative firm conceptualisation), the construction of an alternative measure of local economic competition based on localized firm dynamics (turbulence) and the application of the agglomeration externality framework on both endogenous growth and innovation contexts. They lead to insights in the economic heterogeneity of our research populations that are important for endogenous growth and innovation models.

Spatial Scale, Contiguity and Composition

Analyses of employment growth and innovation intensity in our study are initially undertaken at low spatial levels in the Netherlands in general and in the most urbanized province specifically, South-Holland. The regional science tradition, in which our study is embedded, puts a great deal of emphasis on interactions, interrelations and composition aspects of spatial dependencies. As the appropriate interpretation of spatial externality theory and empirical research depends so much on spatial research designs (much more than the present literature acknowledges), the multilevel issues dealt with in analyses are treated as the major empirical research focus. The pioneering research by Glaeser *et al.* (1992) functions as the conceptual starting point for analyses, but it does not explicitly acknowledge any formal spatial structure, and hence does not actually conclude on spatial dependence. Their analyses are relatively space neutral. Besides copying this research design (and concluding on differences between the European and US context), additions to the spatial configuration of modeling are made according to the subjects mentioned above, with not one single spatial level a priori acknowledged as ideal in isolation. On four spatial measurement aspects (closely related to the theoretical research focus) our study clearly stands apart from the existing literature.

This first concerns the attention paid to intra-urban spatial-economic agglomeration dependency, additional to prevailing cross-sectional urban research designs. Cities are regarded as the relevant observation unit for testing spatial externality structures in theory and practice, but they are in general researched in a space-neutral, cross-sectional fashion (cities are the usually the lowest spatial level of observation). As Anas *et al.* (1999, p.1431) remark 'the distinction between an organized system of (urban) subcenters and apparently unorganized urban sprawl depends very much on the spatial scale of observation'. Part of the research design in this dissertation focuses on the region of South-Holland in the Netherlands with the intention to look for agglomeration externality circumstances *below* the city level (within urbanized, accessible, economic specialized or diverse, and working- or living-oriented neighbourhoods). It is believed that a finer spatial scale than metropolitan areas (in our case: zip codes that can be aggregated into cities, municipalities and regions) reveals insights on intra-urban spatial dependency when modeled adequately (Wallsten 2001, Cervero 2001).

The second contribution of our study that is largely induced by measurement improvements is the distinction in contiguity-based and non-contiguity-based spatial dependence. The exact definition of agglomeration is subject to much discussion in the international literature (Parr 2002). This dissertation treats spatial adjacency, contiguity and proximity of zip codes and municipalities as formal definitions of localized agglomeration, but *also* definitions of regional labor markets, national spatial zoning and (hierarchical) degrees of urbanisation that fit into spatial regimes over locations (spatial heterogeneity). Arguably, contiguous and heterogeneous spatial research designs form different sides of the same externalities coin. Proximity aspects of economic development in the latter agglomeration definition (where distance becomes more functional in character) usually are less developed in empirical research than the former (physical) accessibility aspects (Weibull 1976). The prevailing dearth of spatial heterogeneous research designs in the present spatial economic literature a priori excludes spatial network relational frameworks of analysis, as opposed to spatial clustered ones. The spatial aspect of externalities in relation to innovation and employment growth are closely related to theoretical and technical research aspects concerning scale and composition effects, as summarized in the modifiable areal unit problem (MAUP, originally developed in Openshaw and Taylor 1979) and in multilevel statistical analyses (Goldstein 1995).

A third empirical contribution of the research presented concerns the fact that models on agglomeration externalities tend to focus on one single spatial measurement unit. *A priori*, the theoretical discussion on spatial externalities focuses on cities as testing grounds for analyses. Besides intra-urban, local dependencies (discussed above), explicit inclusion of *regional* agglomeration circumstances in the spatial econometric models reveals that not one single level of analyses earns highest priority. The models presented in this dissertation are in principle designed to incorporate the spatial regimes presented in the previous section as 'explanations' (local *or* regional circumstances) that induce *local* growth and innovation. Analyses are performed using different slopes of coefficients for growth and innovation models over different spatial regimes, in fact inducing the type of models presented as multilevel in character. Multilevel models, as in random coefficient models, allow (in our case geographically) determined groups to deviate from the mean (OLS, *explained variable*) solution, either in the intercept or the slopes. Since only a few (theoretically) predetermined higher-order cross-level interactions (regimes) are defined and applied in our research designs, we prefer to speak of spatial regime analyses instead of multilevel analysis. Also, distance weighted (gravity-modeled) regional versions of agglomeration *(explanatory)* variables (specialisation, diversity and competition) are introduced in local models to test for spatial hierarchical (nested) interaction. Explanatory spatial data analyses in chapter 4 shows that these distance-transformed variables are explicitly regional in character. In the empirical framework of Glaeser *et al.* (1992) no explicit room is made for multilevel and spatial interaction research designs.

A fourth addition to the Glaeser *et al.* (1992) research design concerns the treatment of sectoral interdependencies. While their model distinguishes six largest industries per city, Glaeser *et al.* do not model any particular set of functional relations between those industries. Are relations that foster growth and innovation, intra-industry in character or are they essentially inter-industry in nature (implicitly embodied in the diversity variable)? *Explicit* modeling of these relations proved helpful in agglomeration externality contexts in the work of Alonso and Chamorro (2001). In the location-industry analyses for the province of South-Holland an explicit distinction between intra- and inter-sectoral distance weight matrices is constructed. This distinction enables us to draw sound conclusions on this subject.

1.3 Outline of the Study

Relatively recently, much attention to concepts of agglomeration economies is given by 'new' strands of theorizing within international economics (new trade theory), growth theory (spatial versions of new growth, evolutionary and innovation diffusion theory) as well as in economic geography (the new industrial geography). The insights from these evolving theories are important to understand the spatial-economic setting of the empirical research applied in our study. Chapter 2 gives an overview of the literature on economic externalities, agglomeration economies and growth theory from both economic and geographical perspectives. A simplified conceptual framework for endogenous employment growth and innovation intensity is presented, in which static and dynamic accounts of agglomeration economies are discussed alongside the concepts of localisation and urbanisation economies. Chapter 2 ends with a short description of the main theoretical hypotheses that are tested in our study. The several hypotheses proposed in the literature concerning agglomeration conditions under which knowledge externalities affect growth and innovation are conditioned on contingencies of which the most important concern the spatial scale of analysis and the industrial decomposition of the data.

Chapter 3 describes these sources of economic heterogeneity in more detail. The two main datasets used in our study are introduced. On both the South-Holland and Netherlands level of analysis, spatial regimes (non-contiguous spatial configurations) are introduced. Descriptive analyses are presented to show employment dynamics in industries in two of them: in national potential (gravity) functions (distinguishing the Randstad core region, intermediate zone and periphery, labeled national zoning regimes) and in local labor market areas (labeled connected spatial regime). Insights in components of employment change of firms (new firms, growth incumbent firms, dissolution of firms, moving firms) in South-Holland are discussed briefly in this chapter as well.

Chapter 4 concentrates on spatial dependence and correlation statistics of employment, population and innovation data on the lowest spatial level of zip codes for the South-Holland database and municipalities for the Dutch database. The relevant explained variables central in the econometric models (employment structure, employment growth and innovation intensity) are tested for spatial dependence characteristics (using Moran's *I* coefficients, scatterplots and scatterplot maps)[5]. As a result of the (initial) low spatial level of analysis, certain modeling requirements (homoscedasticity, no multicollinearity) might not be met. From theory and knowledge of the specific Dutch situation, we expect these problems to be relevant for both employment and innovation intensity data. The innovation data are used in chapter 7, the employment data in the empirical chapters 5 and 6 and the descriptive analyses in chapters 3 and 4 together provide us with necessary insights into the spatial structure of the models.

Chapters 5, 6 and 7 apply spatial econometric models to endogenous growth and innovation hypotheses described in the research questions above. If we accept from theoretical hypotheses that cities (or metropolitan locations) reduce costs of moving ideas and thus endogenously internalize externalities, then it is in those environments that employment growth as well as innovation accumulation in and between firms should be most profound. Hypotheses as introduced by Jacobs (1969), Porter (1990) and Marshall (1890), Arrow (1962) and Romer (1986) (MAR) concerning urban and regional facilitated information spillovers are translated into testable indicators in chapter 5. This chapter presents null-models as designed by Glaeser *et al.* (1992) that test the hypotheses from the perspective of endogenous growth in location industries[6] in South-Holland and the Netherlands. Separate models are presented for all firms and for incumbent firms only. As introduced above, our research then takes a few steps toward a better understanding of the relationship between knowledge and growth spillovers and agglomeration economies. Building on the framework of location-industry ('the null-model') agglomeration indicators of economic specialisation, diversity, initial levels of employment (history) and local competition[7], several model extensions are introduced in the remainder of chapter 5 and in chapters 6 and 7 to capture more systematically spatial agglomeration dependence in the growth data. Model extensions concern respectively: (1) the influence of polycentric urban structures; (2) intra-urban growth modelling, (3) a distinction in incumbent, new and all establishment-populations, (4) an alternative definition of local competition that

---

[5] Spatial dependence in population and population growth data are used as reference.

[6] Location-industries combine locations and industries as observation units in statistical analysis. This poses certain strains on the interpretation of the modeling outcomes (see chapter 3).

[7] A criticism important to keep in mind concerns the importance of industrial organisation as an explanatory framework (Glaeser 2000, p.118). Monopolies may be either good or bad for intellectual progress. Monopolies will tend to reap more of the social benefits from their innovations since they have fewer competitors who imitate them. Alternatively, competitive firms have stronger incentives to invest. Certainly, the empirical facts in the literature support the positive view of competition (more competitive areas or city-industries tend to grow faster), but the aggregate nature of this evidence means that it has many possible interpretations.

based on business volatility and establishment turnover ('turbulence'), (5) a location-industry focus on industrial sectors only, (6) estimating separate sector equations for growth in industrial, distribution, producer and consumer service activities, (7) estimating contiguous agglomeration effects by spatial lag and error modeling, (8) sectoral interrelations captured in location-industry spatial weight matrices that allow for inter- as well as intra-sectoral growth interchanges, (9) spatial heterogeneity (as non-contiguity agglomeration design) modeled by spatial regimes, forming network-based spatial research designs complementary with spatial-contiguous ones, (10) regional interactions of explanatory (externality) variables with local ones, and (11) comparison of growth- with innovation-intensity modeling in cities. These (simultaneous) model extensions arguably put the localisation-urbanisation debate in a more balanced perspective by more adequately defining its theoretical and empirical components. Analyses in chapters 5, 6 and 7 take place at the urban (Netherlands) and the subcity level (South-Holland). For the latter, data are used to analyse growth in very small areas within an already small, heavily urbanized region. This analysis offers several advantages over previous studies including natural control of location-specific attributes and the (longitudinal) identification of incumbent and new firms.

Chapter 9 presents an overall summary comprising research results from all chapters and feeds back on the research questions.

Chapter 2

Agglomeration in Economic and Geographical Theories

2.1   Introduction

The Resurgence of Agglomeration Economies as a Fuzzy Concept?[1]

The wealth of nations is not evenly spread among its regions and within regions among locations. It would be better to speak of wealth of regions and locations instead (Porter 1998). But what exactly fosters the competitive advantage of nations, regions, cities and locations? Much of the current debate in the economic and geographical literature is focused on the determination of explaining static and dynamic circumstances for this stylized fact[2]. Especially since the early 1980s the spatial configuration of the economy became of interest in mainstream western social science, including political scientists, sociologists, economists and geographers. For some, this interest was considered renewed because long traditions already exist on spatial (aspects of) analysis in their respective disciplines (Storper 1997). A central theme in this 'resurgence' of geographical thought concerns the revived value attached to the concept of agglomeration economies. This is the element most perceived as stylized fact, because clustering of population and economic activity in cities and regions is among the most common observations in every society. Discussions though exist on the exact substance and (economic) mechanisms behind these agglomeration forces. The notion of economic agglomeration has only to limited degree been perceived as a crucial factor in geographical and economic theory. And the renewed recent attention on the spatial dimension of economic activity in the mainstream literatures does not unambiguously clarify important conceptual difficulties in the agglomeration discussions (yet). Especially spatial conceptualization remains scattered and therefore often fuzzy in character (Parr 2002). This chapter is devoted to an overview of this theoretical and empirical work on spatial agglomeration economics and its aim is that it will provide the rationale for developing additional

---

[1] This title refers to an article by Storper (1995) and a critical paper written by Markusen (1999).

[2] A stylized fact in economics and geography is an empirical regularity which theorists accept as a defining feature of a given phenomenon, and then complete to explain using formal models (Clark 1997, Dymski 1996). Von Böventer (1975, p.238), in the context of agglomeration economies, describes this as something 'conomists cannot shy away from'. As will become clear, much conceptualization depends on (the acceptance of) numerous stylized facts.

and alternative empirical models on the topic in the remaining chapters of this book.

It is often argued that agglomeration economies are part of a story concerning old wine in new bottles. Indeed, as will become clear, economists and geographers used conceptualization of agglomeration economies from the early beginnings of both disciplines onward, although with different timing and intensity of use. But, as Glaeser (2000), Lambooy (1998a) and Scott (2000) clearly indicate, the recent attention given to agglomeration advantages in cities implies a fundamentally different treatment of economics and geography than traditionally was the habit. Contributions of related research fields get more and more interwoven, stimulating them to cross-fertilize economics, geography and sociology (Fingleton 2000, Plummer and Taylor 2001, Boggs and Rantisi 2003). Localized productivity gains (principally the core determinant of agglomeration economies) that were observed for a long time already, become integrated and explained in theoretical conceptualizations and empirical research, replacing and mixing old wine with new. Examples are the transformation from static to dynamic accounts of agglomeration, the integration of institutional and social theory in both economics and geography, the incorporation and explanation of knowledge and information spillovers as stylized facts in theory and empirical research, the growing acknowledging of disequilibria in economic modeling due to endogenous growth processes and dynamic externalities regarding localized factor inputs and the explosive growth and availability of (micro)data concerning geographically determined economic agents[3]. As Lambooy (1998a) concludes:

> [Geographical] agglomeration advantages have undergone refreshing conceptualizing developments. For the first time since Adam Smith and Von Thünen the urban agglomeration dimension seems to arrive home again in economics. This will change economics probably as well (Lambooy 1998a, p.18).

Although theoretical overviews of modern concepts related to agglomeration economies are widely available by now (e.g. Fujita and Thisse 2002), many questions remain unanswered after his suggestion on the potential impact on the respective disciplines. The current debate on the conceptualization and empirical testing of agglomeration economies is far from finished and will remain so for quite some time though.

---

[3] Dosi *et al.* (1997) and Rigby and Essletzbichler (2000) mention the growing availability of large micro, longitudinal databases at the firm level, as one of the three complementary reasons for a revived and innovating interest in economic modeling. The two remaining reasons mentioned are the innovations in computing resources and techniques and the dissatisfaction with existing models, theories and methodologies that have industry dynamics as their primary focus.

As mentioned, much of the central debate on conceptualization is embedded in the renewed discovered liaisons between regional economic (trade) theory and economic geography (Krugman 1993b, Martin and Sunley 1996)[4]. Although relations are confirmed from both sides, a marriage still seems far from practice. As will become clear from the discussions in this chapter, both fields of research use quite similar theoretical notions like agglomeration economies, knowledge spillovers, dynamic externalities, localized productivity gains, returns to scale, growth theory, diversity, institutions, cities, learning, urbanization and localization economies (Brakman *et al.* 2001, Ottaviano and Puga 1998, Storper 1995). An overview of the concepts of agglomeration economies therefore needs careful studying of both strands of literature. The question is whether this should be done separately for each field, as is more less the habit. Although a fruitful interplay or sense of complementary of the two disciplines seems logical to be advocated, the scientific attitude in the literature is often characterized by critical scepticism[5]. Much of the *supposed* 'controversy' is due to relatively stigmatic (views of) research traditions, of economists typically focusing on stylized facts of economic outcomes and its macro-economic foundations and geographers attaching much more significance to the diversity of economic life (Clark 1997, Button 2000). Geographers claim that the recently introduced concepts in trade theory are well-known and documented for a very long time, economists argue that the case-study-like fragmented character of much geographical research leads to (too) much diversification in research interpretations and little common accepted theoretical relations in formalized economics (Martin 1999). But this 'controversy' should not be sharpened too much: the methodological pluriformity of research traditions potentially complement each other and usually both disciplines are aware of this

---

[4] Confusingly, within the two schools of economic and geographical science different resembling labels circulate. Krugman in several contributions sharpened the analytical economic framework necessary for coping with economies of scale stemming from increasing returns, non-convex production functions, spatial monopoly and monopolistic competition. His relative renewed approach in economist traditions he therefore labeled the New Economic Geography, the emphasis being on economics. At the same time within the geographical tradition, embedded in the notions of location theory, new conceptualizations on the institutional and local-conventional embeddedness of firms were worked out, and this strand of literature became known as the New Industrial Geography. For practical reasons and in concordance with habit in the literature (Krugman 1993b; Martin and Sunley 1996) we will call the two post-modern mainstream schools concerning spatial agglomeration analysis, economic geography and new industrial geography (or just geographers) and geographical economics (or just economists) respectively.

[5] Over time, the intention to liaison of the main advocate from the geographical economic point of view, Paul Krugman (1991a, 1993b) has been considerable diminished. In more recent publications he seams to leap back toward the familiar terrain of mainstream (trade-) economics (Dymski 1996, Krugman 1996a). Martin (1999) expresses geographical worries most explicitly, when he argues that the agglomeration resurgence among economists happened without acknowledging the recent body of literature on the institutional embeddedness of agglomeration and externalities in economic geography. Exchange is not fruitful when it is one sided and deliberately not mutual: economists do not seem to worry that much on philosophical and epistemological clarity in this subject. On the other hand, it appears easy and provocative to publish one critical survey after another on this methodological issue, instead of building on the intellectual complementary achievements of both disciplines (as explicitly in Fingleton 2000 and Plummer and Taylor 2001).

nature of the work of the other. It is not as sharp a division in mainstream and institutional economic theory as is sometimes suggested. Albeit critical, most reviews on Krugman's work by geographers are at least sympathetic. But the common notion these reviews give is that Krugman's approach provides only partial insights into the origins and actual determining processes of economic growth (Isserman 1996, Martin and Sunley 1996, Olsen 2002, Pinch and Henry 1999). Untraded interdependencies and institutional relations, trust and conventions as externalities in local settings are generally regarded as unresolved explaining elements in Krugman's versions of agglomeration theory.

From a spatial planning and policy point of view, in the Netherlands and Europe a considerable tradition exists stressing the importance of spatial concentration of economic activities on city and regional spatial levels and its national institutional embeddedness (NREB 1999). The trade- and spin-offs between policy concepts like compact cities, Randstad Holland and European city-regions within recent economic and social spatial theory remain to a large extent unclear though (Lambooy 1998b). In the recent academic resurgence of agglomeration economies within economic theory, policy-makers find justification for city-development and large-scale investments in spatial configurations in the sphere of influence of large(r) cities. Especially the supposed de-agglomerating enabling aspects of information and communication technology receive attention. What exactly its sphere of influence is remains questionable throughout, but the existence of agglomeration economies (still) plays an important role in the arguments (Van der Laan and Van Oort 2003). Focusing on very detailed spatial structures, 'modern agglomeration patterns' are characterized by fragmented and splintered patterns of urbanization within larger (regional) agglomerations (Graham and Marvin 2001, Wheeler *et al.* 2000). Following this, discussions on urban field developments in the Netherlands or Western Europe are as numerous as they are diverse, with some researchers and policy-makers stressing its existence, others ignoring it. Although its implications are potentially contradictory to (planned) cumulative urban development and agglomerations, this is all little understood and thought over. Much empirical research does not value out networked urbanization and agglomeration economies at all, and if it does, not on the right spatial levels (Parr 2002). In a political context, the responsibilities for quantitative and qualitative elements of local labor market developments and economic performance of locations are distributed over economic, planning, financial, internal affairs and social ministry departments unevenly and seemingly inconsistently. A considerable extent of this focused attention is due to a semi-academic appeal of agglomeration economies in a highly institutional-oriented literature. Since governments themselves are among the most prominent institutions, their aroused attention is logical. Regional specific development trajectories based on institutional embeddedness of firms are often placed in the tradition of the new industrial geography. They leave policy-makers wondering if and to what extent successful regional examples concerning economic growth can be copied or learned from in specific (Dutch) contexts. Whether the accompanying (new) regional and institutional paradigms actually are appropriate one-to-one references for regional policy remains highly questionable (Lovering 1999).

We can conclude that the discussion on agglomeration in economic and geographical science, as well as current policy initiatives, is still far from unanimous *accepted* theory fruitful for policy and planning. Conceptualization is actually provided on numerous details and sub-questions. All are somehow associated with the notion of agglomeration economies, causing economic activity to cluster spatially and gain from (or result in) spatial variations in productivity growth in industries, especially in cities. This research wants to contribute to only a few (though to our opinion crucial) well-defined aspects of agglomeration economies, linking endogenous (industry- and firm-level) employment growth, industrial composition, spatial detail and (reach of) knowledge externalities to economic and policy implications.

Basic Concepts and Contingencies in Externalities Research

When researching agglomeration economies and intending in contributing to certain issues in it, we have to account for, or at least be aware of, some agglomeration concepts related to economic growth nowadays commonly used in the literature. Only then we are able to determine on what issues we contribute. We will use figure 2.1 as a guiding conceptual framework in this[6]. It enables us to describe and put into perspective the various directions of the agglomeration literature in several, of which two basic, dimensions. The main focus should be on internal firm- or industry-level productivity and large-scale economic growth (Isard 1956). Agglomeration economies then focus on how these firm-internal increasing returns to scale are fostered by firm-external (agglomerated) scale economies (externalities). Although we do not *a priori* want research to be data-driven, a major drawback to all research on agglomeration economies suffers from the lack of firm-level productivity information. Under certain (and rather stringent) restrictions on assumptions and conclusions, growth is most commonly measured by employment development of firms and dynamics in number of firms and/or employment in industries (Dosi *et al.* 1997, Glaeser *et al.* 1992). Two main dimensions of agglomeration economies and a set of six contingencies together potentially make up a relevant set of firm-external, localized dynamics of factor inputs, outputs and throughputs that can cause (endogenous) firm and productivity growth to emerge, complementary to firm-internal economies of scale. The first dimension concerns the distinction in general (industry-indifferent) urbanization economies and industry-specific localization economies. By tradition, economic theory on labor demand and industrial organization mainly focuses on the second set of externalities, localization economies.

---

[6] This figure has been constructed by means of some main publications on agglomeration economies discussed in the text. The main publications are: Brakman *et al.* (2001), Duranton (1999) Fujita and Thisse (2002), Glaeser *et al.* (1992), Harrison *et al.* (1997), Henderson, *et al.* (1995), Krugman (1993b), Lambooy (1998a), Malmberg *et al.* (1996), Ottaviano and Puga (1998) and Storper (1997).

Figure 2.1   A framework for agglomeration economies: concepts and contingencies on externalities

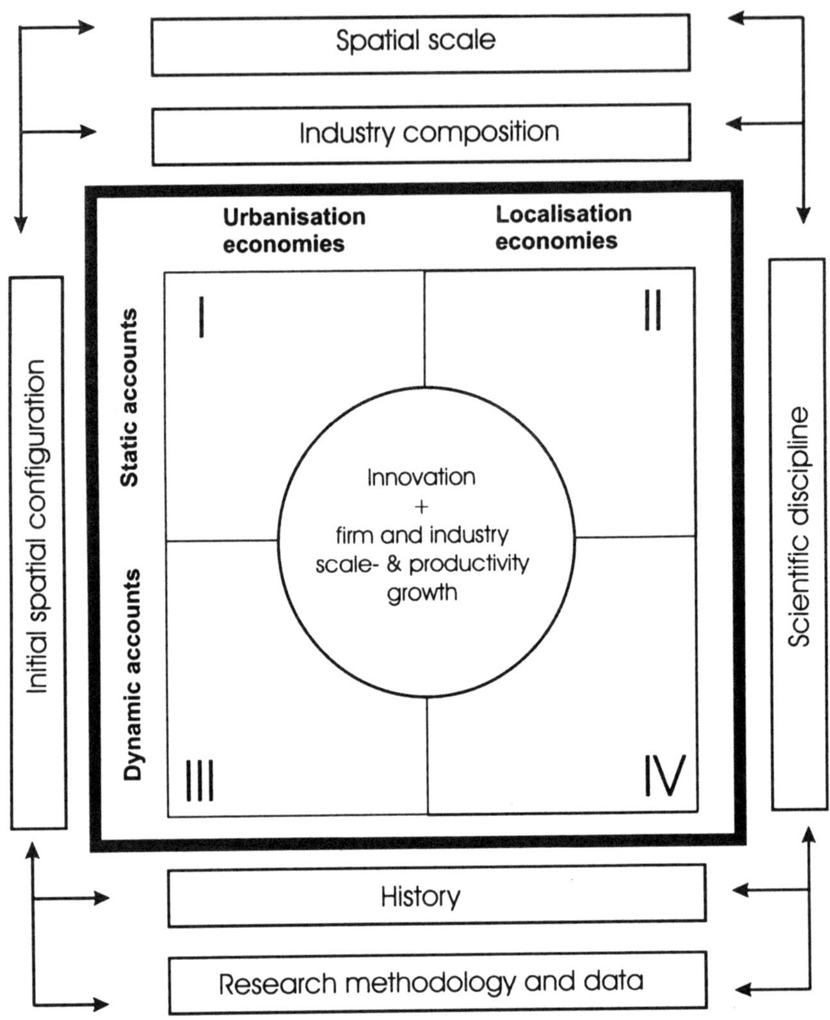

This is because it gives most natural way to extension and deepening of existing, accepted (equilibrium) theory (Feser 2002, Malmberg and Maskell 2002, Rigby and Essletzbichler 2002). But it is the more intangible type of urbanization economies that are recently found more relevant for firm and productivity growth in agglomerations (Glaeser *et al.* 1992, Glaeser 2000). The second dimension we introduce stresses the static respectively dynamic accounts on agglomeration economies applied in empirical research. This distinction is more difficult to make in practice, since much of the dynamic accounts are just time- and place-varying versions of static accounts, without changing the underlying mechanisms that are supposed to operate (Henderson *et al.* 1995). The dynamic character of externalities especially is important in new growth and trade theories, as well as evolutionary theories on economic growth. The four quadrants (labeled I, II, III and IV in figure 2.1) formed by the two distinctions cover potentially many concepts related to agglomeration economies in several clusters of theories and make them conceptually recognizable from each other. But as in all conceptual frameworks, the theory, stylized facts or empirical research designs actually applied show internal and external (contingent) variations to this framework. These make that no single theory fits exactly into one of the four quadrants. Dynamic frameworks are often extensions of or complementary to static ones and for certain stylized facts on agglomeration the general or industry-specific linkages are too unclear for justified separation. Six (mutual influencing) contingencies of the conceptualization are encircling the static/dynamic-general/industry matrix. These contingencies need to be taken into account explicitly for a proper understanding of the research context before studying any specific literature on agglomeration economies. Often they are not treated as contingencies, but as important aspects locked in theories shaping the character of the processes observed or 'stocked' in the four quadrants[7]. The six contingencies are: the spatial scale of analysis, path-dependency and historical (growth) account, the (initial) spatial configuration of a research area, the industry composition or focus in research, data availability and methodology of research and the main discipline of scientific interest. Because of the large and fragmented (though interesting) body of ongoing research in the field yet to be published, this set of (endogenous and exogenous) concepts with its respective interpretations cannot be made into a complete picture either. The scientific life cycle of research on agglomeration economies has not reached maturity yet and innovations and pragmatic applications are made instantly.

Structure of the Chapter

The remaining sections of this chapter will draw the main features of the frameworks applied in economic and geographical research on agglomeration

---

[7] Path-dependency and the initial spatial configuration of research areas and industries for instance are central objects of study in evolutionary economic theory (Nelson 1995). Not by accident, these two aspects (accidental reasoning of first nature situations and locked-in path dependency of developments) are among the most important in Krugman's new-trade models on agglomeration (Clark and Wrigley 1995, Krugman 1992, 1996b, Pinch and Henry 1999).

economies. First, the concept of firm and industry (productivity) growth and the four central quadrants of figure 2.1 are used for identifying the most commonly applied concepts in spatial-economic research in the past (section 2.2). This then concerns some key notions on agglomeration economies and proximity we want to work on empirically in remaining chapters of this study. Four early contributors (godfathers) to agglomeration theory are introduced. After this, the generally accepted notions on localization and urbanization are in depth discussed. This section ends with an outline on the importance of dynamic approaches to these concepts. The discussion then turns towards the resurgent character of space from a (geographical) economist's point of views in section 2.3. It will be argued that the frameworks of new trade and new growth theory are in concordance with dynamic externalities and endogenous growth theory in many ways, leading to common applicable and testable hypotheses of economic growth performance of firms and industries in relation to agglomeration economies. It turns out that the treatment of knowledge spillovers in inter-firm and interpersonal networks and their spatial reach are important topics for both economists and geographers. New trade theory, new growth theory and evolutionary theory are the main relevant economic theories discussed. It will become clear that as a basic building stone this literature on agglomeration concerns aspects of proximity and knowledge spillovers in relation to technology and innovation in economic structures. The relation between spatial development, technology and innovation will therefore be discussed in more detail in section 2.4. The geographical discipline, finally, does not turn to space per se in a renewed revival of course, but does treat agglomerative forces in the space economy with a relatively renewed and modern focus: this was the reason for a 'new' mainstream geography emerging from the 1980s and 1990s. From a more interdisciplinary perspective, recent applications within the 'new industrial geography' discipline, towards institutional, social and organizational theories are described in section 2.5. It will be argued that these sophisticated developments (although sometimes philosophical in character) are highly relevant and generate necessary complementary insights for understanding what really explains the current geography of enterprise. The hypotheses put forward by these theories are intuitively appealing but in general limited or difficult to test on agglomeration economies in a quantitative manner.

These theoretical overviews are all somehow connected to the question central in this thesis: how, where and to what extent does space (measurably) matter for firm and industry growth and innovation intensity in the Netherlands and what part of this is related to (current) concepts of agglomeration economies. Section 2.6 presents a synthesis of the dimensions introduced in this chapter concerning agglomeration research and makes clear where our empirical research potentially contributes to the agglomeration discussions and where not, which elements will remain fuzzy despite its resurgence and which we want to clarify more. Empirical evidence is scattered and heterogeneous in the light of the six contingencies distinguished in the present section. Most remarkable and prominent is the wide range of definitions used for sectoral as well as spatial decomposition. In our empirical analysis, we will explicitly make clear how our choices of research methods and data used refer to and are embedded in common practices of research linked to theories as discussed in this chapter. To a large extent, different interpretations of 'the evidence' are attributable to different choices concerning how to deal with the six contingencies.

2.2   The Common Factors

The discovered liaison occurring between geographers and economists is not completely unfounded in history. As Lambooy (1998a) clearly describes, the history of economic thought and agglomeration is a rather long one. He distinguishes at least four godfathers of conceptualization of agglomeration economies. As will become clear, they did not make the division between economics and geography as explicit as recently is the case. Much 'modern' agglomeration theory builds on their notions and therefore we will summarize their thoughts first. From this, we distil in the subsequent sections the notions of localization and urbanization economies respectively. These notions naturally work towards integration in cities and urban agglomerations. Finally, we focus on dynamic interpretations of these concepts as being recently adopted in economic theory.

Four Godfathers of Agglomeration Theory

The importance of Adam Smith, Von Thünen, Marshall and Weber in economic theory in general, and location and agglomeration theory especially is never to be underestimated, although their contributions are, by their pioneering nature, in general far from complete. This does not mean, as some suggest[8], that the renewed attention and research interdependencies, based on their work, is founded on old wine in new bottles. But we have to distinguish between the fact that their observations and theories are still important while at the same time these theories are triggering and leaping into qualitatively more understandable academic research. The way in which this is done in new growth and trade theories as well as evolutionary theory is quite innovative, albeit Richardson (1973b) already gave clues for filling the 'academic gap' in regional growth theory[9]. The exact placement of those four authors in either a geographical school of thought (location theory) or an economic one (trade theory) is not that easy: they were true contributors to both

---

[8] See notably Dymski (1996), Hoare (1992), Isserman (1996), Martin (1999), Martin and Sunley (1996) and Pinch and Henry (1999).

[9] Richardson (1973) and Von Böventer (1975) speak of a noticeable gap between regional growth theory and regional equilibrium theory on the one hand and the approaches taken in empirical investigations on regional growth and spatial planning in the other. This division leads them to conclude upon a pure and exact regional theory without agglomeration economies and applied regional theory that is inexact but takes agglomeration factors into account (Von Böventer 1975, p.236). Note that increasing factor return differentials that have a high degree of multicollinearity with relative agglomeration sizes and sectoral structure are among their terminology and models.

'disciplines'. As a matter of fact, they at the same time defined location theory as well as trade theory. Location theory of production then deals with the problems of where to locate production, why and where industries, firms and employment agglomerate, and what the locational effects would be of economic growth. Trade theory then is concerned with the problem of who produces what for whom in a predominant international context. That these conceptualizations are mingled now, was not *a priori* a problem in early years. As Ohlin (1933) puts it: "A theory of international trade must, therefore, be founded upon the general localization theory: indeed, it consists of a localization theory, which gives special attention to the circumstances arising from the existence of a number of countries".

Adam Smith in the eighteenth century already was concerned with equilibrium in demand and supply in labor, acknowledging that markets in which this usually takes place are characterized by a limited action-radius. Increased productivity, an important characteristic of agglomeration economies, was therefore limited to certain market places (Smith 1776). How location and trade contribute to the evolution of cities, regions and countries was described by Smith as:

> The inhabitants of a city, it is true, must always ultimately derive their subsistence, and the whole materials and means of their industry from the country. But those of a city near either the sea-coast or the banks of a navigable river, are not necessarily confined to derive them from the country in the neighborhood. They have a much wider range, and may draw them from the most remote corners of the world, either in exchange for the manufactured produce of their own industry, or by performing the office of carriers between distant countries, and exchanging the produce of one for that of another. A city might in this manner grow up to great wealth and splendor, but all those to which it traded, were in poverty and wretchedness (Smith 1776, p.406).

Clearly, location and trade concepts are mingled here. He argued that a better division of labor, made possible by (geographically segmented) market conditions, could enhance and trigger economic growth. Enlarging the spatial action radius (the 'wider range' of market potential) as described above then enhances regional and urban differentiation and growth.

Von Thünen (1842), well known for his model of land rents for varying types of agricultural production that differentiate with distance to the market, also made several statements concerning the character of this market place or city. He argued that because of a larger market potential, larger cities usually inhabit larger capital stocks (e.g. agricultural machinery). Besides that, (capital) cities contain extra advantages in the form of a reservoir of specialized labor, like scientists, civil servants and specialized work- and craft-shops. But it is predominantly trade and (agricultural) production that determines the number and location of cities in his models.

In his time, Marshall (1890) wanted to overturn the pessimistic predictions on economic and population developments made by Malthus and Ricardo by introducing some form of aggregate increasing returns for firms. He did so by introducing three notions of increasing returns that were external to any individual firm. Those Marshallian externalities are by now well known and recently summarized by Feser (2002), Henderson (2003) and Rigby and Essletzbichler (2002). The first notion concerns pooling demands for specialized labor. Industry size reduces search costs for firms looking for workers with specialized training relevant for the industry. The second notion focuses on the development of specialized intermediate goods industries. These can concern measured and unmeasured public and business intermediate inputs tailored to the technical needs of a particular industry or firm. Unmeasured inputs though correlate high on the third externality, knowledge spillovers among firms in an industry. These concepts of externalities have been used to describe a great variety of situations. In the economic and geographical literature, externalities, increasing returns to scale, spillovers or external economies of scale are used simultaneously. Carlaw and Lipsey (2002) and Brakman *et al.* (2001, cited from p.29-31) in their contributions on external and internal economies of scale, put these crucial concepts into their right perspective. As they explain, the term 'economies of scale' or 'increasing returns to scale' refer to a situation in which an increase in the level of output produced implies a decrease in the average cost per unit of output for the firm. It translates itself to a downward sloping average cost curve. To identify the source of the fall in average costs, Scitovsky (1954) distinguished between internal and external economies of scale. With *internal economies of scale* the decrease in average cost is brought about by an increase in the production level of the firm itself. The more the firm produces, the better it can profit from scale economies and the higher its cost advantage over smaller firms. The market structure underlying internal scale economies must necessarily be one of imperfect competition as the firm cannot be a price taker. With *external economies of scale* the decrease in average costs with growing output comes about through an output increase at the level of the industry as a whole, making average costs per unit a function of industry-wide output. Following Scitovsky (1954) again, it has become customary to consider at least two categories of these externalities. The first category concerns *(pure) technological externalities*, such as information and knowledge spillovers, dealing with non-market interactions. These are realized through processes directly affecting the utility of individuals or the production function of firms. An increase in industry output increases the stock of knowledge through positive information spillovers for each firm, leading to an increase in output at the firm level. In new growth theory, new trade theory and economic geography, pure external economies are assumed to exist. The market structure can then be perfectly competitive since the size of the individual firm does not matter.

The second category of external economies concerns *pecuniary externalities*, which by contrast take place through usual market mechanisms via the mediation of prices. Local markets for specialized inputs and labor market pooling are examples of these. A large industry can support a market for specialized intermediate inputs and a pool of industry-specific skilled workers, which benefits the individual firm. Contrary to pure external economies these spillovers do not affect the technological relationship between inputs and outputs of firms. Pecuniary externalities exist in the geographical economics literature through a love-of-variety effect in a large local market. Each consumer's utility depends positively on the number of varieties that they can buy of a manufactured good. The price effects crucial to pecuniary externalities can only come about with imperfect competition. This is consistent with the imperfect competition requirement for internal economies of scale in the literature[10].

Marshall was not explicitly aware of these distinctions, and his externalities turn out to be a mixture of both technological and pecuniary externalities[11]. Information spillovers, urban amenity (cities as ideal institutions for the development of social contacts corresponding to various kinds of externalities), advantages of clusters of firms with the same activity (specialization in industrial districts with vertical integrated individual firms), networks, trust and the famous 'something in the air' were described in his pioneering work. "These external effects entered into economics first were intended to preserve the analytical machinery of supply and demand curves and price taking in the presence of increasing returns: pecuniary economies. The analysis of other kinds of external effects, the smoke and bees and so on, came later" (quoted from Romer 1994). Most attention Marshall thus devoted to the advantages of proximity of firms in the same industry, and he labeled those advantages localization economies. As Marshall (1890) puts it, these externalities and economies contribute to a productivity growth in labor demand (and supply) and naturally in agglomeration in the following manner.

> When an industry has thus chosen a location for itself, it is likely to stay there long: so great are the advantages which people following the same skilled trade get from near neighborhood to one another. A localized industry gains a great advantage from the fact that it offers a constant market to skill. Employers are apt to resort to any place where they are likely to find a good choice of workers with the special skill which they require; while men seeking employment naturally go to places where there are many employers who need such skills as theirs and where therefore it is likely to find a good market. (Marshall 1890, p.225)

In summary, it is important to realize along Marshall's reasoning that spillovers or externalities are crucial for external economies. Our study sticks to the use of spillovers or externalities when we refer to external economies of scale in general. In the same manner, increasing returns to scale are discussed. From the context it will be clear if firm-level or industry-level processes are referred to.

---

[10] It should be remarked that within the geographical economic literature, external economies in models are static in character. In the case of *dynamic external economies* the average costs per unit of output are a negative function of the cumulative or growth in output of the industry. Also important are the facts that certain externalities are national instead of industry-specific and that theory usually presupposes positive externalities while also negative external economies (an increase in a firm's production leads to an increase in per unit costs for other firms) are possible (Brakman *et al.* 2001, p.32).

[11] According to Carlaw and Lipsey (2002), such a broad definition of externalities is close to real impacts of new purpose technologies and technological complementarities on economic growth.

The fourth godfather, Alfred Weber (1909), is commonly considered to be the founder of modern location theory. Location theory is concerned about place, location and geography of economic activity. Minimization of transport costs combined with the weighing of different input factors of firms and industries determine the optimal location of a firm (Dicken and Lloyd 1990). As a main principle, location theory usually starts out with an even distribution of population and by principles of central place theory, minimizing transport costs and hierarchical trade patterns ends up with (systems of) cities (Lösch 1954). This actually is the most prominent pain in regional economist's views, because this outcome directly conflicts with the basic assumption. Cities are more densely populated which affects the demand and competition structure for individual producers[12]. But, as opposed to general equilibrium models of the neo-classical trade theorists: location matters explicitly. And that is large attributable to Weber. He explicitly introduced agglomeration economies, minimum efficient scales and backward and forward linkages as concepts. New trade regional economists heavily build on these concepts.

Marshall's (1890) rich description on all possible externalities (in his time), Scitovsky's (1954) distinction in internal economies of scale and in pecuniary and technological externalities and Weber's and Marshall's emphasis of localization economies are nowadays common language in economic agglomeration theory. A second concept, of urbanization economies, is more modern but does excellently fit in the thoughts of Adam Smith, Marshall and Von Thünen on the potential service roles of towns. They contain externalities that are not directly linked to industry-specific increasing returns, but are profitable to *all* industries in an agglomeration, as well as (social) city amenities and the availability of varieties in goods for both consumers and producers in agglomerations. Scale and variety of economic activity somehow dynamically foster productivity growth of economic activity with constant factor inputs. We will focus on this pair of externalities now.

Static Accounts: Localization Economies

A broad definition of *agglomeration economies* is that it concerns those external economies from which a firm can benefit by being located at the same place as one or more other firms. Although applied like this in modern research frequently, this definition is broad because it inhabits in itself too many and too few aspects of clustering in space of economic activities to be non-exclusively clear (Martin and Sunley 2003). The economic and geographical literature therefore shows a considerable spectrum of refinements and attributions on the contents of the concept of agglomeration economies. Figure 2.1 makes two divisions: into general (urbanization) economies and industry-specific ones (localization economies) as

---

[12] A second objection of regional economists against (early) location theory is that outcomes of location models are, above, all characterized as partial equilibrium systems: demand and income levels are given and not determined within the system. New trade and growth models endogenously model and determine these variables.

well in static and dynamic accounts. By discussing the two dimensions and the four quadrants resulting from its intersections we can explore this framework further. Many standard textbooks on economic geography and urban economics have incorporated the distinction in localized and urbanization economies. They all links to a threefold classification, as made by Hoover (1948) and Isard (1956) in which the sources of agglomeration advantages are grouped together as[13]:

(1) *Internal increasing returns to scale.* These may occur to a single firm due to production cost efficiencies realized by serving large markets. There is nothing inherently spatial in this concept other than that the existence of a single large firm in space implies a large local concentration of factor employment,

(2) Whether due to firm size or a large initial number of local firms, a high level of factor employment (labor demand) may allow the development of external economies within the group of local firms in a sector: *localization economies,*

(3) Or the development of external economies available to all local firms irrespective of sector: *urbanization economies.*

Localization economies usually take the form of Marshallian (technical) externalities whereby the productivity of labor in a given sector in a given city is assumed to increase with total employment in that sector. In short they arise from labor market pooling, creation of specialized suppliers and the emergence of technological knowledge spillovers. The above classification of the sectoral range of economies cuts across Marshall's functional typology, with each of his potential sources of local externalities potentially obtaining within one or more groups of sectors, or across the whole of a local economy (Gordon and McCann 2000). The strength of local externalities is thus assumed to vary, so that these are stronger in some sectors and weaker in others (Duranton and Puga 2000, p.540). The associated economies of scale comprise factors that reduce the average cost of producing commodities. External scale economies apply when the industry in which the firm belongs (rather than the firm itself) is large. Under further assumptions on crowding (congestion costs that increase with population triggers dispersion), perfect product and labor mobility within and between locations and the influence of large agents, the urban system is composed of (fully) specialized cities, provided that the initial number of cities is large enough (Henderson 1974, Richardson 1973a)[14].

The theories on localization economies can be further enhanced by explicitly taking market form into consideration. Contradicting views emerged on that matter over time. Externalities that concern knowledge spillovers between firms in an industry that is concentrated in a location (specialized agglomeration) are generally

---

[13] This classification does not exactly coincide with Scitovsky's (1954) distinctions in internal and (technical and pecuniary) external economies of scale discussed before.

[14] Recent research on the implications of these assumptions on the rank-size distribution concerning the number and sizes of cities can be found in Black and Henderson (1999b), Dobkins and Ioannides (2001), Drennan (1999), Eaton and Eckstein (1997), Fujita *et al.* (1999) and Krugman (1996b). The stylized fact of the very constant distribution of cities ranked according to their sizes in Western society is known as (a version of) the law of Zipf (Caroll 1982, Pred 1977, Zanette and Manrubia 1997).

known as Marshall-Arrow-Romer (MAR) externalities. These spillovers are thought to be most important when there is little prevailing local competition so that rents associated with sector-specific knowledge can be internalized[15]. The MAR-theory in a dynamic context (Glaeser *et al.* 1992, Henderson *et al.* 1995) predicts, as Schumpeter (1942) did, that local monopoly is better for growth than local competition, because local monopoly restricts the flow of ideas to others and so allows innovator-internalization. This again then is supposed to speed up growth and new innovation. Porter (1990) agrees with the existence of localization economies, also arguing that that knowledge spillovers in specialized, geographically concentrated industries stimulate growth. On the ideal market form though Porter disagrees from the MAR-theory: he insists that local competition fosters the pursuit and rapid adoption of innovation. Both influential frameworks (Porter on competitive advantage and MAR on innovation monopoly and power) embrace the concept of localization economies, both in static as well as dynamic versions, explicitly. From an extensive review of Duranton and Puga (2000) it appears that a pattern of specialization in the composition of economic activities in cities has both advantages and disadvantages. The advantages are less urban crowding effects and stronger localization economies arising from the proximity of closely related producers[16]. The disadvantages are less innovation and more exposure to risk as the fortunes of specific sectors and technologies rise or fall. Overall, there appears to be a need for both large and diversified economic structured cities as well as smaller and more specialized cities (see also Henderson 1997a).

This of course mainly applies to the US-oriented literature and our study might reveal more information on the Dutch situation. The focus on cities is in general a relevant one, because the discussion of agglomeration is to a large extent shaped by the fact that clustering of economic activities often actually appears as a stylized fact and visualizes in (networks of) cities. But within the analysis of cities, localization economies are often mingled with urbanization economies. This is because much of the theory as well as empirical testing and findings are clearly related to the relevant definition of cities, regions or locations as well as industries. When is a mutual untraded benefit caused by industry-family relations, and when by general circumstances that might have attracted certain industry-family members in the first place? Large urban agglomerations in the United States that are most subject to research on agglomeration economies in the literature are practically not comparable in terms of scale and content to cities in the Netherlands or Germany (Lambooy 1998b). Also, the degree of diversity in terms of population and industry composition within large cities veils the outcome of much urban-induced

---

[15] The role of Marshall (1890) in this theorem is obvious when the previous sections are read. Arrow (1962) and Romer (1986) build on his theory by assuming specific mechanisms on human capital accumulation that internalize the growth resulting from sector-specific spillovers (see section 2.4).

[16] Henderson (1986), cited in Glaeser *et al.* (1992, p.1129) presents empirical evidence indicating that output per labor hour is higher in firms that have other firms from the same industry located nearby. Static localization externalities (on the existence of local productivity gains) can thus be regarded to account for city specialization, but not directly for economic growth.

agglomeration research (Black and Henderson 1999a), causing researchers only to conclude upon stylized facts noticed on the urban level[17]. So when it comes to the actual mechanisms that make up the agglomerative force, the distinction between localization and more general characteristics connected to the production environment (urbanization economies) are less clear (see figure 2.1). The empirical chapters following will discuss the choices on operationalization connected to this. Choices also mean different alternative outcomes. In most cases, agglomeration economies have their roots in processes whereby links between firms, institutions and infrastructures within a geographic area give rise to economies of scale and scope (Malmberg *et al.* 1996). Agglomerations economies are believed to arise when such links (whatever the family ties) either lower the costs or increase the revenue of the firms taking part in the local exchange.

Static Accounts: Urbanization Economies

Urbanization economies reflect external economies passed to enterprises as a result of savings from the large-scale operation of the agglomeration or city as a whole, independent from industry structure. Relatively more populous localities, or places more easily accessible to metropolitan areas, are also more likely to house universities, industry research laboratories, trade associations and other knowledge generating institutions. It is the dense presence of these institutions (not solely economic in character, but also social, political and cultural) that support the production and absorption of know-how, stimulating innovative behavior and (through aggregation) differential rates of interregional growth (Harrison *et al.* 1997). The diverse industry mix in an urbanized locality improves the opportunities to interact, copy and modify practices and innovative behavior in the same, related or other industries. The functional specialization of firms in heterogeneous industries in close proximity of each other is supposed to generate spatial interdependencies and generates benefits and costs for everyone in that specific location (Scott 1988a, OhUallachain 1989).

These notions on possible positive agglomerative effects from a diverse and heterogeneous (socio-) economic structure in localities (only a few are represented above) make clear that we should not veil the fact that these gains, externalities or feel-good attributes actually come in many guises, concerning both production and consumption economics. In her well-known theory on urban growth Jacobs (1969) defines diversity as a key source of agglomeration economies. Although dated, her book is still very well readable nowadays and the descriptions and daily life examples in her chapter 2 ('How New Work Begins') still produce the core for every spatial diversity-based theory.

---

[17] This is mainly because of the lack of adequate data for detailed spatial levels of analysis, or the limitations of research techniques that can not handle too much detailed information efficiently while still producing for researchers interpretable outcomes.

In a setting of dynamic externalities, Jacobs conceptual setting is often cited for being the representative of diversity-[18] and variety-based explanations why geographically proximate industries induce growth rather than specialized ones. Jacobs thus, unlike the MAR theory, believes that the most important knowledge transfers come from outside the industry. She also favors local competition in her framework because, like Porter (1990), she argues that it speeds up the adoption of technology.

Adopted from Quigley (1998) is an overview in table 2.1 of agglomerative (economic) implications of size and diversity and heterogeneity in locations (cities) that builds on the framework and arguments of Jacobs, together with that of Marshall (1890). Knowledge or human capital may be the most important example of the application of the theory of endogenous growth with increasing results on accumulation of productive activities in cities (De Liso *et al.* 2001, Eliasson 2000). Nevertheless, cities have *other* important attributes that might affect growth of the (local) economy in analogous ways, most especially their internal heterogeneity and diversity on social and cultural aspects (Quigley 1998, Glaeser 2000). Chinitz (1961) speculated that an urban environment with many firms producing heterogeneous output serves the varied tastes of consumers and intermediate producers, conducting more growth than an environment dominated by a few large firms in specialized single industries. Quigley introduces four concepts that should handle and summarize some of the massive literature he envisaged when focusing on diversity and urbanization economies. The empirical models on heterogeneity and knowledge spillovers he (acknowledging) left aside, although it is exactly that subject that receives most prominent theoretical and empirical acclaim in the debate on the geographic extent of the new growth theory.

Table 2.1 Urbanization economies: agglomerative implications of variety

Factor	Examples	
	Production	Consumption
scale economies	large plant sizes	public goods, amenity
shared inputs	business services	cultural variety
transaction costs	labor market matching	shopping variety
statistical economies	unemployment insurance	resale market, substitutes

Source: Adapted from Quigley (1998, p. 131).

---

[18] Diversity as a phenomenon should be clearly distinguished from diversification. While the former indicates a state, the latter is an indication of a process in getting more divers (O'Donoghue 1999). In the literature the two terms are often mingled without noticing the severe difference in implication (e.g. Izareli and Murphy 2003, Jackson 1984).

The main distinctive difference for the latter theory forms the explicit dynamic character of these spillovers compared to the static (or only implicitly dynamic) characteristics of the four concepts summarized in table 2.1[19]. The first factor Quigley (p.130-132) describes, scale economies or indivisibilities within a firm, are the historical rationale for the existence of productivity growth in *agglomerated* industries in the first place (Brakman *et al.* 2001, Isard 1956). Without the existence of scale economies in production, economic activities would be dispersed to save transportation costs (Fujita *et al.* 2000, Palivos and Wang 1996). In consumption terms, the existence of public goods leads to urban amenity: cities function as ideal institutions for the development of social contacts corresponding to various kinds of social and cultural externalities (Florida 2002). That is also where cities deserve credit from images and perceptions of spatial quality, amenity and well-being (Brueckner *et al.* 1999, Webber 1964). The second factor, shared inputs in production and consumption, encompasses the economies of localized industry described by Marshall, as well as in its consumption analogue. The use of shared inputs to produce more differentiated consumption goods in agglomerations (variety inducing fashion, culture and style, where seemingly identical inputs are rearranged to produce different products) is well known (Katz and Shapiro 1985). A third possible reason why a metropolitan area may provide greater economic efficiency growth arises from reductions in transaction costs (Martin and Ottaviano 1999). The Western economies in general and the Dutch economy especially develop into services-based economies. Business and consumer services make up most of urban employment nowadays, often characterized as the main stylized fact of a knowledge-based information society. A logic product of the interaction of urban economies and the larger emphasis on knowledge-based service industries is the growing importance of transactional economic explanations of local economic productivity growth (Castells 1989, Gottmann 1983). Most recent, the so-called Californian School of economic geography emphasizes transactional costs in explaining agglomeration economies. Scott (1988a) especially argues that in urban localities small and relatively powerless firms can more easily survive, because relatively low transaction costs in agglomerations facilitate vertical desintegration of economic activities within the production column of a product. Especially, lower search costs for workers with differentiated skills and employers with different requirements for labor, combined with a larger range of possibilities, lead to potential better (local) labor market matching (Helsey and Strange 1990, Kim 1987)[20]. Again analogous to production, better matching may occur in consumer functions (shopping). The fourth set of potential economies distinguished in table 2.1 is the application of the law of large numbers to the fact of fluctuations in the economy. It applies to the extent that fluctuations in purchases of inputs are usually imperfectly correlated across firms, as sales of outputs are across buyers. Less

---

[19] Some of the theories embodied and 'captured' in figure 2.1 apparently also concern manufacturing industries clustering in areas because of Marshallian (localization) externalities.

[20] Acemoglu (1996) demonstrates that in a matching-context returns to human capital accumulation can be shown to exist, even when all output in a city is produced with constant returns to scale and with no technological externalities.

inventory and pooling resources represent real savings to business firms, pooling and varied retail market supplies to consumers (Quigley 1998, p.132).

Dynamic Agglomeration Accounts

The distinction in urbanization and localization economies can be conceptualized in static or dynamic perspectives. This realization has grown in both geographical and economic frameworks of agglomeration theory. Originally, agglomeration theory was embedded in a relatively static, non-temporal framework of analysis. Industries or firms, which are related in whatever ways, tend to co-locate and thus form spatial clusters of (similar or complementary) activities. Usually it concerns patterns of concentration and location that are analyzed, not the dynamic processes of growth of agglomerated industries. It is first and foremost the increased efficiency of the transactions of goods and services that is believed to give rise to benefits for firms located in certain agglomerations. It should be noticed though that there exists a substantial geographic tradition of time relevance in observation of agglomeration economies: it is observed that once in place, the agglomerative process tends to be cumulative in nature (see for extensive overviews Von Böventer 1975 and Richardson 1973b). This not only applies to analyses concerning the 1950s till 1970s, but it concerns conceptualization that is also recently subject to observation and is incorporated in formal economic and geographical modeling (Krugman 1991b, 1993a).

Dynamic externalities deal with the role of prior information accumulation in the local area on current productivity and hence employment growth (Henderson *et al.* 1995). They simultaneously try to explain how cities form (static approach) *and* how they grow. Such accumulations are fostered by a history of interactions and cultivated long-term relationships, which lead to a build-up of knowledge available to firms in a particular local area. As in their static counterparts discussed above, there are two types of dynamic externalities. Using the terminology used in Glaeser *et al.* (1992), dynamic externalities may be Marshall-Arrow-Romer (MAR) (localization) economies, which derive from a build-up of knowledge associated with ongoing communications among local firms in the same industry. Or they may stem from Jacobs (urbanization) economies, which derive from a build-up of knowledge and ideas associated with historical diversity. Dynamic externalities can have implications similar to those of static externalities. However, dynamic externalities have broader implications concerning industrial development over time. They potentially help provide explanations for the location and growth patterns of both mature and newer industries. In theory, specialization and concentration of activities is, to considerable extent, thought to be a product of historical accident. The specific location of a particular industry is to a large degree intermediate and history-dependent (Berliant and Konishi 2000, Cronon 1991). This notion, that there is a strong tendency toward path-dependency and that 'history matters', is related to issues of (international and local) industrial inertia and sunk costs in economics (Clark and Wrigley 1995)[21]. But more important than the persistent magnitude of growth on the same locations is the notice that this cumulative process is in principle only limitedly diffusive but rather concentration-inducing in character[22].

2.3 New Trade and Growth Theories on Agglomeration Economies

Departing from common theoretical notions as developed by Adam Smith and Marshall as discussed in the previous section, trade theory developed into a more mainstream economic discipline than location theory did. It gave trade or international economics a more authoritative character than location theory (geography). Remembering the common historical background, but mainly because of its own inadequacy to explain locational patterns and agglomerations of production that appear as stylized fact all around the international trade arena, the 'resurgence' of regional economics as an extension of the so-called new trade theory was induced by economists. We will discuss the main principles of new trade theories and its implications for, and connections with (new) growth theory and agglomeration theory. A discipline connected to new growth theory concerns evolutionary theory; the potential contribution of that theoretical strand to agglomeration economies is highlighted as well. Summarizing the main concepts in this paragraph, the principal agglomerating forces in economic theory that emerge 'anew' are economies of scale, increasing returns, monopolistic competition, market size, central place hierarchy and technological spillovers. The principle spreading forces are the market size in peripheral locations, competition in the central places, penetration (transportation) costs and congestion in central places. Most extensions of the principal general equilibrium model on monopolistic competition tend to stress one of these forces.

New Trade Theory

Generally, trade theory is concerned with the problem of who produces what for whom. As location theory is concerned about place, location and geography, trade theory is with flows of commodities and its economic implications. From the point of view of trade theory, only when these flows are caused by differences in places (conceptually predominantly applied to nations) of production and use (consumption), the two mingle. The problem of explaining who produces what for who (and where) is traditionally solved by means of the principle of comparative

---

[21] Because of the long-lasting geographical history on cumulative causation from the 1950s on, geographers do tend to point at their treatment of history in order to address the 'newly' discovered nature of the subject in geographic economic literature and analysis correctly. Evolutionary economics regards path dependency and cumulative causation as its core business as well.

[22] Put into a core-periphery model explicitly by Krugman (1991a), we notice that concentration somewhere is the perpetual rule. So though apparently attentive to historical change, this model is static in its assumptions about the operation of economic-locational principles.

advantages, basically developed by Ricardo (1817). He stated that comparative advantage exists whenever there are technological differences between two countries (or regions) in the production of the same commodity. He furthermore stressed that technology can be expressed by the productivity of labor. In his model there is comparative advantage when the relative labor requirements of two goods differ between countries. Using the same line of reasoning (on comparative advantages) but replacing technological differences by capital/labor ratios in general made Ricardo's theory develop into the well-known Heckscher-Ohlin (HO) theory. According to this theory, the country that is comparatively better endowed for capital goods, exports these and imports the labor-intensive goods (in which the trading partner is specialized). The more countries (or regions) differ in their respective endowments (capital/labor ratios), the more they will trade. Unfortunately, the HO-theorem appeared to be unable to explain intra-industry trade (trade in similar products over and within countries). Furthermore, it is unable to explain welfare effects of trade based on technological spillovers or other industry-level externalities. Distances between trading partners, transportation costs, cumulative growth patterns and history were not allowed to matter in the theory. Correlated variables associated with intra-industry trade and proximity and distance between trading partners (mainly used in gravity model analyses) proved to be not very robust in measurement and limited in interpretation. These considerations forced theorists to develop the so-called new trade theory (called so because of its relatively short history since the 1970s), enabling to model just such stylized facts as intra-firm trade, welfare effects of trade based on technological spillovers and other than internal economies of scale.

The most striking differences of the conceptualization of this new trade theory concerns the assumptions of imperfect competition and increasing returns to scale. The main market form in modeling became that of monopolistic competition (Dixit and Stiglitz 1977) instead of perfect competition in the neo-classical model. Each firm is able to differentiate its product from that of competitors. The pricing strategy of firms is characterized by equality of marginal revenue to marginal costs (constant mark-up). This strategy brings about equality of output levels across firms. Consumer preferences are dealt with either as single horizontally differentiated variety or as demand on all available varieties[23]. As a result of the introduction of differentiated products (love of variety that induces an increase in welfare and well-being) inter- as well as intra-industry trade flows between locations can become the focus of analysis. In order to maintain the zero-profit assumption, firm entrants and exits establish equilibrium over the number of firms. With a combination of the neo-classical and new trade theories, international economics now became able to model inter- as well as intra-industry trade flows, under both market forms of perfect and imperfect competition and still within a general equilibrium modeling framework. The latter means that the entire structure of demand and supply is (endogenously) explained within the same consistent

---

[23] The main results of the new trade theory are not influenced by the way consumer preferences are defined.

model. Still, explicit location aspects of firms and consumers (compare location theory) were not incorporated in trade and economic theory by these models as such.

That honor has to be given to Krugman (1991a,c, summarized in Krugman 1998)[24]. He set up several geographic models of trade that produced results resembling the outcome of (geographic) central place theory or rank-size rules of the geographic distribution of economic activity. He reaches this outcome via a dynamic process reminiscent of the model of cumulative causation and growth in agglomerations and cities as described by Pred (1966, 1973). Krugman focuses on the interaction of forces that influence geographic concentration resulting from trade patterns. Contrary to most location theory, he did not ignore the interaction between market structure (monopolistic competition) and location decisions. And contrary to most of the then relevant trade literature, he did not ignore geographic mobility of labor and transportation costs. Therefore, a specific location structure is not fixed *a priori*: the central location of growth within a region or country is determined endogenously in his models. In these models, the basic aspects of geographic concentration depend on the interaction of three variables: internal economies to scale, transportation costs and local demand. In this respect, Krugman agrees with and builds on most of the (standard) location theory (Dymski 1996, Krugman 1993b).

If internal economies of scale are strong and transportation costs low, each manufacturer wants to serve the market from a single location. In order to minimize transport costs, each manufacturer chooses the location with the largest local demand. However, local demand will be large precisely there where the majority of manufacturers choose to locate. This induces a circularity that tends to keep geographic concentration in existence once established (compare Pred 1977 and Myrdal 1957 on their notions on cumulative causation). It is important to realize that both internal and external economies of scale will enable industries to offer higher real wages in the agglomerations. Industrial labor will as a result move to the concentrating region. Geographic real wage differences depend on a trade-off between the centripetal forces of the home market effect and centrifugal forces of the competition effect (Fujita 1996, Ottaviano and Puga 1998). The relation between internal economies of scale and the wage level are usually described as the home market effect. Manufacturers in the larger economic agglomeration have an advantage, since the size of local demand allows them to profit more from internal economies of scale, and hence can afford higher nominal wages. Figure 2.2 illustrates this process of circular causality. Higher demand of goods induces more ranges of variety of goods, induces real income effects that attract new workers, consumers and firms. In general, this effect will be stronger as local demand is greater and internal economies of scale higher. The competition effect on the

---

[24] The work of Krugman avoids any direct assumption of external economies: they emerge as a consequence of market interactions involving economies of scale at the level of the individual firm. The spatial version of the Dixit-Stiglitz monopolistic competition theory then is a crucial ingredient in all spatial economists models on the location of economic activities (Abdel-Rahman 1988, Fujita *et al.* 2000).

contrary refers to the advantage of producers outside the large agglomeration. Due to transportation costs they face less competition for their local demand. Producers might therefore be able to pay higher nominal wages. Forward linkages (the supply of a greater variety of goods increases the worker's real income) and backward linkages (a greater numbers of consumers attracts more firms) as pecuniary externalities create scale economies at the individual firm level that are transformed in increasing returns at the level of a location as a whole (Gianmarco *et al.* 2001). A third, and to this circular system contradicting type of effect, has been added to these centrifugal forces, being negative externalities like congestion and high land rents in the larger agglomerations (Quigley 1998). Especially for manufacturing firms this potentially leads to decreasing returns to scale in cities (Glaeser *et al.* 1995, Moomaw 1985). Geographic concentration with factor mobility in these models is determined by internal economies of scale, transportation costs and demand externalities. The local market is largest where wages are highest, which is where manufacturers want to locate. The largest local market will become larger, and the ultimate equilibrium depends on the initial point of departure. Equilibrium does not any longer automatically mean that spatial units of observation converge in terms of regional growth (Kubo 1995). Krugman in his models thus reinterprets Marshall's principles of externalities stemming from benefits of pooling labor supply and demand for specialized nontradable inputs.

Figure 2.2   Circular causality in spatial agglomerations of firms and workers

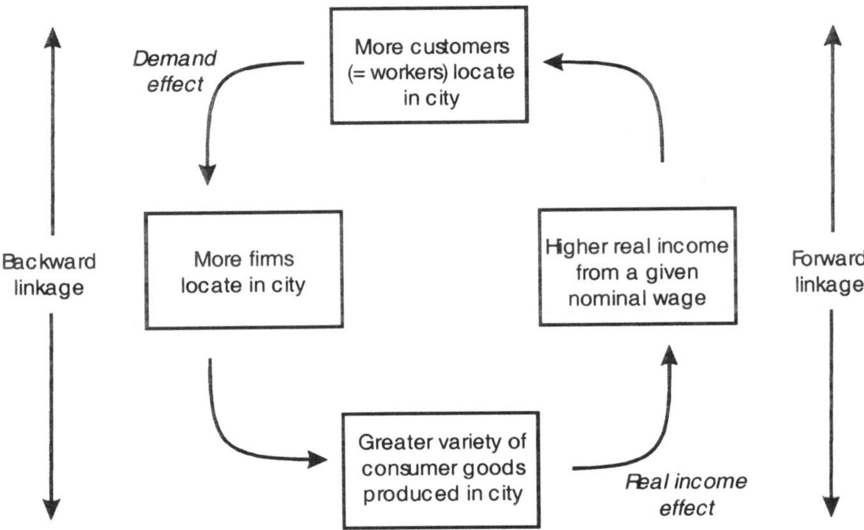

Source: Fujita (1996, p.42), based on Pred (1977, p.72) and Myrdal (1957)

He shows that if the industrial sector itself constitutes a principal source of demand for industrial products, and if transportation costs increase with distance, then firms will cluster because they produce under increasing returns. Transportation costs ensure that multiple clusters will exist instead of one monocentric city: the pull of Krugman's pecuniary externalities balances the push of transportation costs.

Several critical surveys from a geographical point of view have recently been published on especially these Krugman models in the 'new economic geography' tradition. Some critiques were mentioned along the text already, but an integral summary of the points of worry is useful for understanding further sections. Almost all critiques start with an appraisal of Krugman efforts, but finally conclude upon several major drawbacks from the geographic discipline point of view. Mainly, all critiques articulate the vague and immeasurable notions of increasing returns. This is worked out in several partial, more detailed critiques. The (too) strong distinction between what is theoretically possible and what is empirically and practically important comes to the fore. Also the fact that the models presume to capture dynamic processes while being static in their assumptions[25], the ignorance of human capital and technological spillovers (Marshall's third factor of agglomeration) and the insistence of only pecuniary economies as accepted externalities are stressed. Further, the stigmatic treatment of firms as unity, the representative firm, ignoring firm and organizational life cycle aspects of economic performance and the lack of awareness that different models give back the same mathematics, and that mathematics thus does not *a priori* dictate the model are stressed by Dymski (1996) and Acs (2002). The reliance of a whole theory on too abstract, over-simplified and too idealistic a set of assumptions on just two economic sectors, holding constant and ignoring many stylized facts to make models meaningful and (technically) applicable, is felt especially by Martin (1999, p.70) and Peneder (2001)[26]. They indicate the model's failure to incorporate (or even acknowledge) concrete institutional-social dynamics on relevant spatial scales, what is at the core of the recent geographic discipline (the new industrial geography). This gives a dull sense of déjà vu to the leading spatial mechanisms of the treatment of agglomeration economies that were deliberately abandoned by geographers on philosophical and epistemological grounds (Martin 1999, p.81, Isserman 1996 and Hoare 1992). The following sections of this chapter will

---

[25] It should be noticed that the main schools of economic geography and political economy may be criticized on similar grounds though (Martin and Sunley 1996).

[26] Fujita *et al.* (2000) acknowledge the extreme simplifying character of some of their modeling, they call them 'modeling tricks' (p.6). The most famous and unrealistic is the so-called Samuelson iceberg form of transportation costs: "Rather than modeling a separate transportation sector, we suppose that a fraction of a good shipped simply melts away or evaporates in transit. Combining this with a Dixit-Stiglitz model causes many potentially nasty technical complications simply to, well, melt away" (p.7). Extension of this two-sector model into a more sectors-model by Peneder (2001) gives substantially different results on agglomeration outcomes.

indicate to what extent other theories deal with these aspects of agglomeration economies.

New Growth Theory

A second strand of mainstream economics that shows a remarkable symmetry with modern trade theories and is mutually influenced by and influencing itself revived notions of agglomeration economies, is that of new growth theory. This theory builds on several concepts of economic growth developed in different academic disciplines (Barro and Sala-i-Martin 1995, Nijkamp and Poot 1998, Verspagen 1992). And also similar, this discipline develops an explicit spatial dimension in theory and empirical applications. That spatial aspect concerns knowledge spillovers inducing growth, which was already mentioned by Marshall as a centripetal force in clustering economic activity, hence forming an explanation for agglomeration patterns of firms and industries.

Baldwin and Forslid (1997) suggest most explicitly the link of (endogenous) growth theory with new trade theory. They suggest an alternative way of modeling in which agglomeration may occur without factor migration of employment determined upon real wages differences (as is the case in new trade theory). They show that factor accumulation can play the same role as migration in fostering agglomeration through demand linkages. The structure of their model resembles new trade models of Krugman (1991c) and Krugman and Venables (1996) with the addition of a research and development (R&D) activity that uses labor to invent and patent new manufacturers. It is shown in their model that inter-regional learning spillovers are a stabilizing (agglomeration-enforcing) force. Factor accumulation and intertemporal linkages induce endogenous growth, preventing an even distribution of firms and hence fostering agglomeration. This benefit obtained by R&D labs from input differentiation is also applied in Martin and Ottaviano (1996) and is in principle equivalent in working as labor mobility in Krugman's models and that of input-output linkages in Puga and Venables (1996) and Venables (1996). In all these models, reductions in trade costs trigger agglomeration and faster growth, making use of modeled principles of increasing returns to scale and endogenous efficiency growth in factor inputs. The latter is usually summarized as dynamic externalities.

These models all assume that the notion of increasing returns is spatially embodied in economics by the concept of agglomeration economies, which is basically about the dynamic and cumulative advantages of spatial proximity. Agglomeration economies then concern geographical explanations of locally bounded externalities or increasing returns, meaning that certain place-specific circumstances induce higher than proportional growth in productivity with a fixed amount of factor inputs. It provides thus economic explanations of variations in competitive advantage across regions (Porter 1998) and why regions are able to maintain and even reinforce these advantages over others, once certain locations have taken a lead in a particular activity (Arthur 1994, Krugman 1991c). Internal economies of scale for specialist suppliers (one of Marshall's proposed types of factor externalities) can be transferred into external economies for firms purchasing these commodities as intermediate inputs. Local external economies of scale can thus be derived from market size effects[27]. But local external economies may *not only* be associated with market-size or pecuniary external economies, like these Marshallian explanations of enlarged probabilities of increasing returns in agglomerations due to divisions of labor, specialist suppliers and commodity-based industry input-output spin-off effects. They can complementarily, and with equal plausibility, be related to information or technological externalities and spillovers (like experience, learning and knowledge diffusion) concentrated in a particular area (Englmann and Walz 1995, Krugman 1995a). As the theory of diminishing returns seems useful for the bulk-processing, smokestack economy of especially Marshall's days, the theory of increasing returns, generating instability and lasting dynamics, seem more applicable in modern, knowledge-based industries. Of course, mechanisms of increasing returns exist alongside those of diminishing returns in industry (Scitovsky 1954). But in the light of the separation of different branches of economic theory it became clear that the concept of external economies serves a purpose in different contexts, in general equilibrium theory as well as industrial organization (Von Böventer 1975).

The aspect of knowledge-based societal and industrial development is a central and crucial element in modern growth theory. Grossman and Helpman (1994) clearly state that, as it did to Schumpeter (1934) and Solow (1970), improvements in technology have been the real force behind perpetually rising standards of living. It is argued that most technological progress requires, at least at early life-cycle stages, an intentional investment of resources by profit-seeking firms or entrepreneurs. Embedded in this theorem, industrial innovation as engine of economic growth is incorporated in formal modeling in a long tradition now. Continuing output expansion outpacing population growth and the continuing divergence of growth trajectories among nations and regions gave rise to a current generation of growth theorists in which growth is identified by long-run performance reflecting structural and policy parameters of the local and global economy. Boschma and Lambooy (1999) further argue that local externalities may also be linked to the importance of selection in terms of 'fitness' of a local milieu. Specific spatial circumstances contribute to trigger technological change and related economic growth. Contrary to the neo-classical notion of rational actors selecting an optimal location, adherents of behavioral geography contest that the survival of new technology in space has hardly anything to do with rational and conscious decision making. New technology may emerge in space by accident, inducing new varieties of products (hence a clear connection to new trade theory), but is likely to expand only in those local environments that provide favorable conditions to meet requirements of new technology spread.

---

[27] Although introduced by Marshall (1890), he did so under the assumptions of perfect competition, equilibrium and diminishing returns to scale: products or companies that get ahead in a market eventually run into limitations (rising costs of scarce factor inputs). A predictable equilibrium of prices and market shares is thus reached.

With this apparent similarity of intentions, recent research efforts on economic growth have headed in two different directions. One strand of theory continues to see capital accumulation (though conceivably with a broad interpretation of capital that includes human capital) as the driving force behind economic growth. Firms continually add to their stocks of capital in a perfectly competitive environment with constant returns to scale. Perfect competition requires that the invested capital be paid its marginal product, which must stay above the discount rate for investment to remain profitable. A second approach casts external economies in a leading role in the economic growth process. According to this view, when individuals or firms accumulate new capital, they inadvertently contribute to the productivity of capital held by others. Such spillovers may occur in the course of investment in physical capital (Arrow 1962) or human capital (Lucas 1988). As Romer (1986) has pointed out, if the spillovers are strong enough, the private marginal product of (physical or human) capital can remain permanently above the discount rate, even if individual investments would face diminishing returns in the absence of external boosts in productivity. Growth can be sustained by continuing accumulation of the inputs that generate the positive externalities (Grossman and Helpman 1994). In later contributions, Romer (1990, 1994) refined and emphasized his views about the treatment of knowledge, arguing that private investments in knowledge could only take place in a market environment with imperfect competition. Here the link with new trade theory, that also embraces the market form of monopolistic competition, is again evident. A straightforward abandonment of the idea of diminishing returns to capital (thus also being interpreted as human capital or stock of knowledge[28]), the proposition of increasing returns to scale made modeling of imperfect competition necessary[29]. Because growth resulting from technological change is endogenously determined as outcome of an economic system in these models, the term endogenous growth theory became apparent (Romer 1994, Solow 1994)[30].

---

[28] Romer (1994) argues that technological advance, the main determinant of economic growth, comes from things that people do. Discovery will seem to be an exogenous event in the sense that forces outside people's control seem to determine whether they succeed. But the aggregate rate of discovery is ultimately endogenous. Endogenous growth models thus accommodate technological advances by people. Palivos and Wang (1996) and Rotemberg and Saloner (2000) in their equilibrium models build further on this principle.

[29] Chamberlin (1933) already argued this way, and introduced a model of monopolistic competition based on the notions of imperfect competition and increasing returns to scale. Internal economies of scale for specialist suppliers can be transferred into external economies for firms purchasing these intermediate inputs. Local external economies of scale can thus be derived from market size effects.

[30] Solow (1994) relativists the strict rejection of neo-classical views on the relation between technological change and economic growth. "To say that the rate of technological progress is exogenous is not to say that it is either constant, or utterly erratic or always mysterious. (...) No one could ever have intended to deny that technological progress is at least partially endogenous to the economy" (p.48). Pack (1994) in a critical article in this line argues that endogenous growth theory in principle remains a rich expansion of existing growth theory rather than being a powerful organizing framework for thinking about actual growth phenomena. Verspagen (1992) gives an overview of new growth models on endogenous innovation and calls them new neo-classical growth models.

Knowledge is thus assumed to be an input factor in production that has increasing marginal productivity. Endogenous growth is further enhanced by dynamic externalities, geographically these work out as agglomeration economies (again a similarity with the outcomes of new trade theory)[31]. Lucas (1993) emphasizes that the most natural context in which to understand the mechanics of dynamic externalities and economic growth is in metropolitan areas where the compact nature of the geographic unit facilitates communication and human capital accumulation. He argues that the only compelling reason for the existence of cities would be the presence of increasing returns to agglomerations of resources that make these locations more productive. The view of human capital as social input that induces productivity gains in cities was after Lucas further explored and examined by other scholars as in Bostic *et al.* (1997) and Henderson (1986). They argue that the microeconomic foundation of the external effect of human capital is the sharing of knowledge and skills between workers that occur through both formal and informal interaction. The distinction in tacit (implicit) and explicit knowledge bases is a crucial one in the way knowledge externalities are embodied in growth (implicit) and innovation (explicit) externalities. Intuitively it seems clear that the higher the average level of human capital (knowledge) of more concentrated numbers of agents, the more 'luck' these agents will have with their meetings and the more rapid will be the diffusion and growth of knowledge (Rauch 1993, p.381). This all points to metropolitan areas when examining productivity-enhancing effects of human capital abundance. This in a micro-economic setting explains higher wages as well as land rents in cities. The exact outcome of these externalities on actual productivity remains ambiguous and heavily dependent on historical economic context (Bostic *et al.* 1997). The distinctions in manufacturing and non-manufacturing industries as well as the degree of maturity of industries seem to be important determinants of city-based productivity growth in this respect (Moomaw 1985).

Endogenous agglomeration modeling with external effects, increasing returns, monopolistic competition and variety of products and services for both consumers and producers in a (hierarchical) system of cities is the instrumentation regional economists, both in trade and growth theory, apply (Fujita 1989, Fujita and Thisse 2002, Rivera-Batiz 1988). But, as McCann (1995) argues, there is much to clarify and good terminology is needed in order to describe the exact role of space and location in questions of growth. The spatial corollary of a-spatial increasing returns to scale is economies of agglomeration, and the spatial corollary of a-spatial decreasing returns to scale is diseconomies of agglomeration. But a lack of conceptual clarity in every research undertaken under this umbrella may lead to several definitional and comparing problems. In principle there is nothing inherently spatial about increasing returns or innovativeness of firms as far as agglomeration is concerned, unless the size of a single firm or group of firms

---

[31] Note that agglomeration in new trade theory is the geographic *outcome* of modeling, while in new growth theory it forms an endogenously determined *explanation* of growth that can be spatially related to dynamic externalities inducing increasing returns in factor inputs.

produces local external benefits for other firms. Economies of scale are one particular potential cause of agglomeration economies, along with many others, which may be historical, topographical or legal in character.

Evolutionary Economic Theory

New trade and growth theory comprises insights from evolutionary economic theory as developed and reviewed by (Nelson and Winter 1983). As Nelson (1995) puts it:

> The general concept of evolutionary theory involves the following elements. The focus of attention is on a variable or set of them that is changing over time and the theoretical quest is for an understanding of the dynamic processes behind the observed change. The theory proposes that the variable or system in question is subject to somewhat random variation or perturbation, and also that there are mechanisms that systematically winnow on that variation. It is presumed that there are strong inertial tendencies preserving what has survived the selection process. However, in many cases there are also forces that continue to introduce new variety. (Nelson 1995, p.54)

Boschma and Lambooy (1999) summarize the development of this strand of economic theory in the light of local environmental and agglomeration development. They notice that evolutionary theory in that respect is inspired and stemming from both endogenous interest for Darwinian processes of (biological) change and a general dissatisfaction with the main ideas of conventional neo-classical economic thought. The latter concerns the treatment of technological change as exogenous to the economic process, and that is also what concerns new growth theorists in general. Boschma and Lambooy (1999) describe three reasons for substantial impact of the local environment on new variety stemming from evolutionary theory, despite many stochastic events. Firstly, uncertainty provokes firms into routinized, risk-averse behavior which determines to a large extent the available options and probable outcomes of searches. This path dependency of innovative behavior is related to the accumulation of knowledge, information and experience (learning process, compare Arrow 1962 and Romer 1990). Besides human capital lock-in, physical capital investments are another source of locational inertia. History, in the form of sunk costs resulting from the operation of many firms at a site, creates a first-mover disadvantage that can prevent relocation (Arthur 1989, Rauch 1993). Secondly, increasing returns is basically about the build-up of cumulative advantages that locks in the predominant outcome and excludes the survival of other competing outcomes. Arthur (1994) shows that the notion of increasing returns provides an explanation for why technology is able to maintain and reinforce its competitive advantage once it has taken the lead in the market (originating from either superiority or coincidence and luck). Network and complementary externalities are among the most important. Increasing returns are further characterized by the fact that they can facilitate multiple potential, unpredictable, possibly sub-optimal or irreversible outcomes. Thirdly, the selection environment functions as a filtering mechanism that ultimately decides which of the innovations will thrive or fail. This selection environment consists of both a number of markets (consumer, financial) and a set of non-market institutions (regulations, values, norms, customs: see Storper (1997). Here, the link with the more institutional oriented new economic geography, Krugman's new trade model and conceptualization of cumulative causation from location theory is evident. In evolutionary theory, the combination of chance (potential centrifugal forces) and increasing returns (centripetal force) implies that there may be a multiplicity of spatial outcomes (Boschma and Lambooy 1999). In this light, evolutionary theory implies that it is hardly relevant to regard the existing (local) environment as a mechanism that determines the success or failure of regional new technology trajectories. Historical accidents do blur the balance between history (initial and proven advantage) and expectations for regional growth (Ottaviano and Puga 1998)[32].

2.4   Proximity and Spatial Networks in Innovation Diffusion

Renewed attention for agglomeration economies is also to be found in innovation-based economic research, mostly linked to (new) growth theory. We already noticed that human capital and knowledge spillovers are associated with new growth theory, and they most naturally take form as innovations (Verspagen 1992). Until the 1970s the economic literature paid attention to diffusion of knowledge mostly over time and not over space. The little attention to the *spatial* diffusion of knowledge was consequently mainly advocated by economic geographers and not by (regional) economists (Caniëls 1999). Diffusion of innovation over space was supposed to occur according to predictable, well-known proximity patterns that failed to penetrate other conceivable locations (Richardson 1973b). Siebert (1969) in an early contribution attempted to incorporate technology creation, application and spread into a neo-classical growth model. He assumed technology to be not perfectly mobile, but to diffuse slowly over time and space, first nearby and in a later stage at greater length. The empirical validity of this assumption is still among the most fundamental and most questioned elements of present spatial innovation diffusion and economic growth research. Geographers (by nature) showed more interest in spatial diffusion of innovation and knowledge and two types of approaches can be distinguished concerning technological diffusion accordingly: those stressing physical proximity and those focusing on functional linkages in hierarchically equivalent but not necessarily nearby locations. Space matters quite differently in the two conceptions. In the former theory, close neighboring proximity is important for the emergence and spread of innovation, in the latter the transactional linkages (networks) of similar and complementary firms, usually

---

[32] That historical context is extremely important in productivity and factor growth research becomes clear from several empirical papers, especially Bostic *et al.* (1997), Drennan (1999) and Rauch (1993).

found in places (cities) of similar size and with similar production structures and milieu's are crucial.

On this dichotomy of spatial implications of innovation diffusion and growth theories we will focus in this section. First, the proximity thesis turns out to have the deepest roots in economic research, embedded in life-cycle aspects of firms and industries in innovation diffusion. The spatial filtering-down theory most notably incorporates these aspects, and at the same time preludes the second diffusion approach that became more important in the 1980s: the hierarchical (network) diffusion pattern. Recently we notice a tidal return of research focusing on the proximity-thesis again, especially in relation to (new) economic growth theory. Because this implies a more explicit role for space and agglomeration, this literature is more thoroughly discussed. The conclusions of these recent contributions on proximity-based diffusion hypotheses do not contradict the hierarchical vision. Rather, they indicate that the reach of proximate knowledge spillovers is limited and that they can be complementary to network diffusion patterns.

Contiguous Diffusion Models and Proximity

Caniëls (1999, p.29-34) summarizes the evolution of the idea of diffusion of knowledge over space in the economic geographical literature. The central idea since the early 1970s is that inventions can take place everywhere across space, but that they diffuse along two types of spatial paths. The first is called the *general spatial diffusion* model. This conceptualization is embedded in and worked out with several concepts of agglomeration theory, the best known being growth pole theory embedded in the 1950s and 1960s French tradition (Boudeville 1966, Perroux 1955). Its main assumption is that economic growth (in the form of innovations) is spread throughout a growth center's hinterland to lower order (nearby) cities and localities. Innovations and knowledge are (once generated in a certain central location) expected to spread among regions from one locality to its neighbors. Richardson (1978) summarized growth pole theory as:

> A growth pole is defined as a set of industries capable of generating dynamic growth in the economy, and strongly interrelated to each other via input-output linkages around a leading industry. This industry and its interdependent sectors grow faster than the rest of the economy because of advanced technological practice and high innovation rates, high income inelasticities of demand for their products, sale to nationwide markets and the large spillover and multiplier effects on other segments of the economy. (Richardson 1978, pp. 164-165)

The French economists have introduced the growth pole theory into location theory on the assumption that the set of dynamic industries is spatially clustered. After linking this clustering to locations, the spillover effects for the surrounding are studied. Besides its obvious relevance in developing countries, the principles of this concept have been noticed and implemented in developed countries, not in the least because of a high policy relevance (Malecki 1997, Parr 1999a,b). Proximity, neighboring and nearness of the innovation- or growth center are supposed to be crucial for development. What exactly fosters the spillovers to occur remains rather unclear in the literature, suggesting either buy-out of specialized professionals, joint projects, subcontracting, learning, imitation or informal contacts.

Usually, the growth pole center in a geographical context is a larger (diversified) city, university or a (group of) large branch plant(s) specialized in an innovative activity that generates knowledge and employment spin-offs in the surrounding region. The growth pole concept has been intensively revised, extended and complemented with other modern economic geographical concepts. Depending on the nature of linkages (direct or indirect) as well as the role of spatial proximity of linked activities, the literature was consequently enriched by concepts as industrial complexes, formations, filières, industrial districts and clusters (Harrison 1991). The exact determination of the differences (in terms of spatial scale and relations between economic actors) in these conceptualizations is a complex matter (Martin and Sunley 2003). Industry *clusters and complexes* are ideally characterized as a complex of related and nearby firms with a minimum (threshold) requirement of production, being labor- and capital-intensive, containing at least one basic (specialized) industry, a degree of industrial diversification, functional linkages, spatial proximity and a strong developed (physical) infrastructure. Proximity of location is thus forced by production-technical reasons in first instance and by functional ones in second (Feser and Bergman 2000). *Formations and activity families* tend to be characterized by equal qualifications, although here the functional linkages tend to be more important and indirect in character and the spatial sphere of influence tends to be larger (compare table 2.1). Non-productive aspects of proximity, like nice living environments, shopping and labor market facilities as well as physical accessibility seem to be more important in these concepts (Lambooy 1990). *Filières and networks* leave the explicit spatial proximity even more and suppose functional linkages in principal to be neighboring independent ('connection replaces place'). All these conceptualizations in principle try to structure the complex economic specialization relations we observe in daily agglomeration life. They are supposed to foster and capture innovation and growth by perpetual interaction. Depending on definition, these mechanisms and their spatial (proximity) configuration are observable in all Western societies.

By means of the earlier discussed principles like cumulative causation and agglomeration theory, the growth pole, formation, district or cluster locality can grow further (as usually anticipated for by regional policy), potentially causing spread as well as backwash effects in relation to neighboring localities. According to these principles, there is a trend towards inequality: once an economic activity has been (innovative) successful in a certain location, that economic activity will attract new economic activities (Breschi 2000). Some locations can be interlocked in such a process; others will be left out. Hirschman (1958) in this respect distinguished two types of spillover effects associated with growth pole theory: backward linkages and forward linkages (earlier discussed in the context of figure

2.2). The former effects are associated with activities that provide inputs to economic activities, drawing towards the location where the clients are. The latter concern activities that use outputs by new activities or expanding existing activities that draws them towards locations where these existing activities are already (over) represented. This can turn into backwash effects that are usually unanticipated, occurring when the growth pole attracts so much attention and cumulative growth that it drains the surrounding areas. Migration of workers towards and concentration of investment capital in the initial center of innovation initiate the emergence of high-level urban services in the growth pole. This can then lead to a further polarization of economic growth, restricting growth elsewhere (thus a backwash effect, see Richardson 1978). The existence of spread effects is based on the belief that ongoing growth of the core location (growth center) will eventually lead to diseconomies of scale. Congesting and rising soil and real estate prices will force industries that are less dependent on urban location to move out of (central) cities. This all contributes to the actual observed patterns of spatial-economic development we observe. But what is needed for better explaining in an economic framework?

Bleichrodt *et al.* (1992), building on De Jong (1987) and Markusen (1985), argue that this selective process is determined by the phase in the (product) life cycle an industry or firm has reached at a specific moment in time. Those industries that concentrate on well established products, making use of mature standardized production processes are less dependent on face-to-face contacts and highly qualified labor present in a pooled urban labor market. Spread effects are supposed to diminish with distance from the core, specially affecting surviving firms or industries that become mature and pass a certain minimum efficient scale threshold. Moving firms locate relatively near the core location they leave, still in the influence of the larger conurbation of a city. This is empirically confirmed by research by Carlton (1982) and Chapman and Walker (1991).

An interesting theoretical framework closely related to the discussion on life cycle theorems in combination with proximity in growth and innovation transmission processes is that of the filtering-down theory, developed by Thompson (1968). This theorem leans on economic base theory, in which economic activities are classified in basic and non-basic activities. The former group of activities earns its profit and sales by trading and relations outside the region of location, while the latter is oriented and dependent on the population present in the home region. Regional economic growth and innovation creation and transmission is favored by the presence of basic industries. The incomes earned create multiplier effects by cumulative growth and industry-specific spin-off processes. Thompson (1968) describes the embedding of economic base industries of a region in terms of a regions economic infrastructure:

> This is (...) the creativity of its universities and research parks, the sophistication of its engineering firms and financial institutions, the persuasiveness of its public relations and advertising agencies, the flexibility of its transportation networks and utility systems, and all the other dimensions of infrastructure that facilitate

the quick and orderly transfer from old dying bases to new growing ones.
(Thompson 1968, p.53)

The filtering-down theory links these concepts of regional exporting basic activities
and economic infrastructure to a geographical translation of the industrial life cycle.
Phases of industrial (or firm) life cycles are linked to specific attributes of regions
concerning their economic infrastructure. In the introductory phase of products
(and related to that, industries) sales are not stable, products change constantly but
unpredictably and firm (survival) risks are high. The diversity of the urban labor,
capital services and product markets foster the function of nursery schools for
starting firms (the incubation function of cities or agglomerations, Davelaar 1989,
Leone and Struyck 1976). When firms and industries survive or last, mature firms
tend to standardize production and become more capital-intensive. The initial
advantages of the urban agglomeration core now can become disadvantages:
growth is difficult to be realized in-situ and physical movement becomes apparent
when limited accessibility and congestion can become an economic disadvantage.
Growing firms might filter down towards more peripheral locations and regions,
where land, labor and transport costs are more economically justified. More
recently, this theoretical framework has been applied in agglomeration studies of
Henderson (1997b) and Brouwer *et al.* (1999) on innovation intensity and
Henderson *et al.* (1995) on employment growth. All these papers argue that there is
an 'urban product cycle' notion that new products are developed in large diverse
metro areas with diversified skill base, but that matured products eventually
decentralize[33]. Clearly, part of the problem these papers tend to address have to do
with growth of new firms as compared to growth in existing firms. In fact they
argue that new firms essentially settle in diverse, urban regions, but that over time
those firms in diversified areas inevitably decline as they lack the benefits of
spillovers and externalities from similar firms.

Although this short description gives an ideal picture of the filtering-down and
life-cycle theorems in a spatial context, it is the economic core essence of it that is
(still) being observed as stylized fact nowadays. It therefore is treated accordingly
in industrial-organization modeling (Klepper 1997). The notion of innovative
identification of types of firms and industries initiated a large amount of spatial
econometric and geographical modeling. Once empirical setbacks concerning the
definition of new innovative industries, promising industries and growth potential
industries, as well as their relevant economic infrastructure and position in a life-

---

[33] Two studies that relatively accurately focus on spatial detailed and longitudinal testing of filtering-
down hypotheses in the Netherlands are Ottens (1976, esp. p.72) and Bleichrodt *et al.* (1992). From
these studies, the following spatial development trajectories can (simultaneously) be distinguished as
important sources of spatial heterogeneity concerning economic growth: (1) national zoning (Randstad,
intermediate flanking zone, national periphery); (2) urban-hierarchical; and (3) proximity-based
neighboring effects. The research in our study falls short in many of the ingredients necessary for
proper testing of filtering-down hypotheses (especially occupational composition and longitudinal
innovative product-group information), hence this will not formally be the case. The potentially spatial
discriminating characteristics following from filtering-down hypotheses (proximate and heterogeneous
spatial classifications) will explicitly be incorporated in growth and innovation models.

cycle context were overcome, (urban) research design in the 1980s and 1990s actually fitted quite well in modern econometric modeling. Especially new and innovative firms receive attention in modeling for their supposed growth potentials. Remarkable in all empirical work though is that the initial conditions favoring growth for new industries and firms in urban agglomerations are found to be lastingly important. Also remarkable is that both in early as well as mature phases of economic industry development, urban hierarchical connections appear and remain important.

Hierarchical Systems of Diffusion

The filtering-down theory of growth and innovation diffusion brings along hierarchical transmitting channels alongside and complementary to contiguous, proximity-based channels. The former discussion indicates that it might be theoretically and empirically fruitful to look at hierarchical system of diffusion. This second framework for diffusion processes is also generally applied and advocates that innovations and knowledge spread from the place of origin to other larger centers in the economy. Lower hierarchical urban centers will only be reached after considerable time. Richardson (1978) explains this diffusion process with the concept of urbanization economies or Jacobs-like externalities comparable to the already mentioned economic infrastructure introduced by Thompson (1968). Larger cities in their view are more likely to be receptive to innovations and knowledge spillovers because a disproportionate concentration of innovation-adopting institutes and institutions is present there, combined with a more favorable social structure and the location of decision-making centers of large corporations. In diffusion models based on this concept, the size of regions, cities or localities (in terms of concentration of population and entrepreneurs) is the most important factor determining the timing, spread and rate of acceptance of knowledge spillovers (Brown 1981). Especially Pred (1977), Gottmann (1983) and Hepworth (1989) in early stages of research on the subject stressed the role of information density for innovation diffusion. Larger cities contain larger potential reservoirs of (producer and consumer) information. The urban growth model developed by Pred (1977) explains the continuing favorable growth position of those cities that were already the largest in the first place by their popularity for headquarters of multi-plant enterprises. Complex information transmission in strategic decision-making entrepreneurial contexts, face to face contacts, specialized services and labor supply as well as the necessary 'human moments' in daily activity systems are argued to be decisive in the urban primacy of the economic landscape (Duranton 1999, Feser 2002, Gertler 2003). As was argued before, the connection between the theory of agglomeration economies and diffusion with that of transaction costs economics and network theory may be very useful in explaining certain spatial economic developments. The spatial diffusion of growth and innovation (or the absence of it by agglomeration and concentration) certainly belongs to that.

Theoretical embedding of network theory in agglomeration theory is interesting, but empirical evaluation of the hypotheses stemming from this turns out quite complex. Recent research by Oerlemans *et al.* (2001a, b) for the Netherlands for instance does not *a priori* contradict the spatial hierarchy thesis concerning the diffusion of innovation, nor the proximity thesis. The question whether innovation acceptance and spread is empirically linked to networks in 'the relevant firm environment' is positively answered, making use of and confirming the formal economic network models and frameworks as proposed by Dosi (1988). Oerlemans *et al.* suggest that the moderating effects of industry composition, managerial backgrounds, spatial scale and type and level of innovations produced are too contingent in character for general statements to evolve in what exactly is the relevant environment of firms concerning innovation. In general, it is the anti-pole of spread effects, backwash effects, that is often thought to be dominating over the other, blurring the discussion of the spatial configuration of innovation and growth transmission in its core existence. Growth impulses are then not transmitted from a core location to more peripheral ones, but the core by its initial attractiveness attracts capital and high qualified labor from the periphery, sustaining and cumulative enforcing its own favorable position. The existing city-hierarchy will remain, and growth will be transmitted within this system[34]. The similarity of reasoning with earlier accounts like Pred (1977) is remarkable. Although the weighing of effects remains suggestive and the balance of weighing does not say *a priori* something useful of the individual effects, focused attention to underlying theoretical frameworks of life-cycle concepts and structures of networks have proven useful for understanding certain 'stylized' hierarchical innovation and growth transmission facts[35].

Geographical innovation research never actually concludes upon one of the two polarized diffusion alternatives: reality (as observed in the data) does not always support a strict division between spatial neighboring and hierarchical models as described above (Hägerstrand 1966). In general it is observed that at first, knowledge spreads depending on the size of the city or region and after a short period diffusion proceeds depending on the proximity of competitors and outsourcing partners (localization economies) or potential buyers and trade fare institutions (urbanization economies). 'At first' then is related to initial stages of a combination of firm industry and regional economic life cycles. Proximate and neighboring localities with higher probability of exposure and absorption are then probably more likely to be feasible for imitation and acceptation (Robson 1973, Phelps *et al.* 2001). This being embedded in a fine working (or not negatively working) firm-specific environment and inertia partly forms the (non-push) reason

---

[34] Remark that this discussion focuses on the outcomes of transmission processes, not at transfer *mechanisms* that are left as a black box. This is a peculiar conceptuality persistent throughout our study as well.

[35] Spatial planners and social scientists though claim to have a firmer grip on this, as evidenced by their recent explicit attention to informational, network and global city-systems (Batten 1995, Castells 1989, Taylor and Walker 2001). The question to what extent spatial hierarchy and its (supposed) accompanied functional linkages, in contradiction to spatial proximity, do determine in themselves a basis for fostering innovation, technological development and economic growth has not found a common accepted answer by them.

why incumbent firms are often reluctant to leave their present location (Richardson 1995). Recently, geographically induced industrial district research even notices that neighboring *and* hierarchical equal locations can be leapfrogged by growth in and spread to seemingly peripheral and not economic history-dense locations (Scott 1988b, Storper and Walker 1989). Conceptualizing spatial frameworks for innovation diffusion then becomes a highly blurring activity when allowing different subjects, scales and processes to interact within a single framework. The role that geography plays in organizing trade interactions within a country thus remains far from clear. Esparza and Krmenec (1996, 2000), in their recent article on hierarchical city-system interaction, notice that within the US, trade interaction is consistently biased from and towards larger cities and that the size of origin cities is associated with the size of destination cities. But they also conclude that physical distance, more so than destination city size, plays the dominant role in shaping large city patterns of trade. The most important conclusion is that the geography of existing urban settlement complicates the arena of investigation clearly. Large numbers of proximate, diversified economic cities in the Midwest and eastern parts of the US create circumstances that force trade interaction to span shorter distances[36].

The Proximity Thesis Revisited?

As can be noticed from the main references in the geographical innovation diffusion literature summarized above, the 1970s were productive in conceptualization and still rather weak in empirical (economic) explaining. Relatively new geographical and economic concepts like networks, linkages and transactions were linked to the hierarchical and neighboring diffusion visions in the 1980s. Mainstream economic theory on labor demand and firm performance did not seem to be adjusted accordingly during the 1980s and early 1990s though. But from an economic point of view, a remarkable recent body of research shows (for the discipline rather innovative) interest in the geographical spread of innovations, potentially extending mainstream (growth) economics. Interesting in the light of the above painted traditions, this then concerns the proximity thesis again. The central notion in this literature concerns dynamic externalities of firms that foster knowledge spillovers, spatially determined growth of economic activity and innovation accumulation (Acs 2002). This leads to endogenous efficiency growth in factor inputs and thus locally determined economies of scale and productivity gains. Economic growth theorists have, as described in section 2.3, focused new attention on the role of knowledge capital in aggregate economic growth, with a prominent modeling role for knowledge spillovers. As Jaffe *et al.* (1993) conclude, we know very little about where such theorized spillovers go. The discussion on

---

[36] Esparza and Krmenec (2000) at the same time notice that firms based in Los Angeles and Phoenix trade over larger distances. They argue that this may be more the result of the relative sparseness and lack of diversity of cities in the western US than purely of distance.

neighboring and/or hierarchical (global) distribution systems of growth seems to undergo a rebirth:

> Is there any advantage to nearby firms in the same country, or do spillovers waft into the ether, available for anyone around the globe to grab? (...) the belief that universities and other research centers can stimulate regional economic growth are pre-dictated on the existence of a geographic component to the spillover mechanism. The existing spillover literature, however, is virtually silent on this point. In growth literature it is typically assumed that knowledge spills over to other agents within the country (...). This implicit assumption begs the question of whether and to what extent knowledge externalities are localized. (Jaffe *et al.* 1993, p. 577-78)

Acknowledging the importance of spillovers and increasing returns requires renewed attention by economists to issues of economic geography. Krugman (1991a) summarizes, revives and explores the explanations given by Marshall as to why industries are concentrated in cities (see also section 2.2): (1) the pooling demands for specialized labor; (2) the development of specialized intermediate goods industries; and (3) knowledge spillovers among firms in an industry. Krugman believes that economists should focus on the first two of these, partially because he perceives that '[k]nowledge flows, by contrast, are invisible; they leave no paper trail by which they may be measured and tracked, and there is nothing to prevent the theorist from assuming anything about them that she likes' (Krugman 1991a, p.53).

Despite this little encouraging remark, several extremely interesting results from economic innovation and growth diffusion research emerged during the 1990s. (Jaffe *et al.* 1993) argued that knowledge flows sometimes do leave paper trails in the form of citations in patents. By studying the geographic location of patent citations, Jaffe *et al.* test the extent to which knowledge spillovers are geographically localized[37]. They found that citations to patents are more likely to be domestic and more likely to come from the same state and even the same SMSA as the cited patents, compared with a control frequency reflecting the pre-existing concentration of related research activities. Their measured effects were particularly significant at the local (SMSA) level, indicating that localization fades over time, but only very slowly. The most difficult problem confronted by the effort to test for spillover localization in this research is the difficulty of separating spillovers from correlates that may be due to pre-existing patterns of geographic concentration of technologically related activities. Overcoming this by use of control samples and cohort analysis, the probit results of their analyses for matching sending and receiving patens and citations still indicate the very short distance patent-citations seem to travel. This tendency for localization, and hence a

---

[37] Implicit, the assumption of a threshold of proximity for localized spillovers within a nation has always been present in the international R&D literature. As Glaeser *et. al* (1992) describe this stylized fact: 'After all, intellectual breakthroughs must cross hallways and streets more easily than oceans and continents'.

confirmation of the neighboring proximity theses is what could be researched. Jaffe *et al.* justly remark that

> (...) what is going on is probably that knowledge spillovers are not confined to closely related regions of technology space. (...) a significant fraction of the total 'flow' of spillovers affecting firms' own research productivity comes from firms outside of the receiving firm's immediate technological neighborhood. (Jaffe *et al.* 1993, p. 596-597)

This then indicates (translated to the classical spatial innovation diffusion literature) that (spatial) hierarchy and regional or global crossing transactional linkages might be (more) important for innovation diffusion[38].

Research by Audretsch and Feldman (1996), Acs (2002) and Feldman (1994) confirms the evidence that suggests that knowledge spillovers tend to be geographically bounded within the location where the new economic knowledge was created. New economic knowledge may spill over, but the geographic extent of such spillovers in a neighboring sense is bounded. Baptista (2000) labels this finding 'the inverse link between knowledge externalities and the size of the geographic market holding for the diffusion of innovations' (p.531). Additionally to these empirical findings, it might be interesting to extend to the fore the question whether the spatial economic composition fosters innovation and technological change that then fosters growth. Feldman and Audretsch (1999), in line with previous discussions on growth theory and the spatial determinants of production externalities, tested the hypothesis whether local diversity or specialization of economic activity better promotes innovation (and hence economic change). The effect of spatial economic composition on innovation is positively related to diversity; considerably less support is found for the specialization thesis. The research found a tendency for innovative activity in complementary industries sharing a common science-base to cluster together in geographic space. Because the necessary complementary inputs and services are likely to be available from small specialist niche firms but not necessarily from large, vertically integrated producers, it is argued that cities with a concentration of this kind of competitive and diverse amount of firm dynamics attract innovation and hence (economic) growth. This research then indicates that especially diversity-based, Jacobs-like, cross-industry external economies foster especially neighboring diffusion of innovation and growth. Following the Feldman and Audretch (1999) study, Kelly and Hageman (1999) also find that the location of R&D activity in a particular place is determined more by the location of innovation in other sectors than by the location of its own production. Carrincazeaux *et al.* (2001), however, find evidence for the opposite thesis. Gersbach and Schmutzler (1999) in a theoretical model

---

[38] Jaffe *et al.* do not explicitly consider knowledge spillovers to be either across-industry or within industry specific, as Glaeser *et al.* (1992) do: '...we do not consider the industrial identity of either generators or receivers of spillovers' (Jaffe *et al.* 1993, p.579). Evidence from the R&D spillover literature (e.g. Glaeser *et al.* 1992) suggests that across-industry knowledge spillovers indeed are (more) important. In an international context this is considered explicitly in Grossman and Helpman (1994).

argue that localisation (specialisation or concentration) of employment and production determines the location of innovation activity, an argument also made by Sutton (1996). Most of these empirical papers focus on American states as spatial units of analyses. Some Anglo-Saxon research, however, focuses on lower scales of analysis. Anselin *et al.* (1997, 2000) and Wallsten (2001) use metropolitan statistical areas to analyze the spatial extent of R&D externalities and find that local spatial externalities are present and important at that level as well. A tentative conclusion of the empirical studies presented so far is that knowledge externalities (spillovers) become less important with increasing distance. Proximity matters in the transmission of innovation-based knowledge.

Complementary to the resurgence of the proximity thesis, it appears to be especially in network-dense metropolitan environments that innovation spillovers occur. Malecki and Bradbury (1992) find that quality of life aspects and city size are significant locational considerations both to professional workers and to firms conducting R&D. Frenkel (2001), OhUallachain (1999), Krugman (1995b), Roper (2001) and Rallet and Torre (1999) also emphasize city-size or metropolitan spatial distributions as a relevant spatial regime for explaining the geography of innovation. Cortright and Mayer (2001) stress high-tech employment specialization in metropolitan areas as indicative of innovative competitiveness, while Frenkel (2001) finds a negative relationship between specialization and R&D intensity. Florida (2001) finds economic diversity most crucial for technological development in metropolitan areas. Paci and Usai (1999) in a spatial-econometric framework find *both* concentration and diversity indicators of local economic structures important determinants of innovation intensity in labor market areas in Italy. On the spatial level of NUTS2 regions in Europe (109 regions), the same authors find clear relations of innovation intensity with economic concentration patterns only (Paci and Usai 2000).

Important methodological issues emerging from these recent discussion emerges as to when innovative activity can be traced to be: (1) spatially clustered; (2) whether the extent and propensity of this clustering 'outperforms' that of 'normal' economic activity and (3) the degree (distance, degree of proximity, network) of spillovers (externalities) of innovation and growth to occur. Important findings as discussed above confirm that investment in innovative investments by private organizations and universities 'spills over' for third-party firms to exploit. It can also be concluded that the interrelated definitions of spatial scale of analyses, hypothesized functional structure (proximity, urban hierarchical or combinations), research population and spillovers to a large extent determine our understanding of the geography of innovation. No clear picture arises concerning local or regional (metropolitan) specialization and diversity circumstances that are connected to innovation intensity.

2.5   Agglomeration Economies in the New Industrial Geography

Local Institutional Embeddedness

The 'New Economic geography' as emerging from new trade and growth theories has gained considerable influence and is undoubtedly appealing, as it provides solid economic reasons for local agglomeration in a globalizing economy: reduced transportation costs, economies of specialization and diversification, knowledge spillovers and innovation externalities. Economic geographers argue though, that it fails to properly investigate the real sources of these local urban advantages, which, according to a conceptual strand of literature developed largely by economic geographers themselves, lie in the character of local social, cultural and institutional arrangements (Amin 1999). More specifically, insight is drawn from institutional and evolutionary economics, sociology and culture concerning ties of proximity and association as a source of knowledge and learning (Storper 1997).

Leading exponents in these discussions are Amin and Thrift (2002), Barnes and Gertler (1999), Malmberg and Maskell (1997), Oinas (1998) and Storper (1997). They suggest that a distinctive feature of places in which globalization is consistent with the localization of economic activity: this is the strength of their relational assets or untraded interdependencies. These are assets that are not tradable, nor are they easily substitutable, since they draw on the social properties of networks in which economic agents are implicated. They include tacit knowledge, knowledge based on face-to-face exchange, embedded routines, habits and norms, local conventions of communication and interaction and reciprocity and trust based on familiarity. These relational assets are claimed to have a direct impact on a region's competitive potential or advantage insofar as they constitute part of the learning environment for firms. They provide the daily access to the relevant resources (information, knowledge, technology, ideas, training and skills) that are activated through the networks of interdependency and common understandings that surround individual firms. Many of the insights of the literature on so-called learning regions (such as Silicon Valley and Italian industrial districts) derive from analysis of the learning properties of local, industry-specialist business networks (Amin 1999, p.369). These networks of reciprocity, shared know-how, spillover expertise and enterprise support systems are supposed to be the real sources of growth. Different roles of formal and informal knowledge for economic competitiveness are stressed, suggesting that geographical proximity plays a unique role in supplying informally-constituted assets (Nooteboom 1999). Tacit forms of information and knowledge are better consolidated through face-to-face contact, not only due to transactional advantages of proximity, but also because of their dependence upon a high degree of mutual trust and understanding (Maskell *et al.* 1998, Gertler 2003).

An important, seemingly paradoxal theme in these ('newly' emerging) institutional paradigms on agglomeration economies is the local-global contradiction. As Oinas (1998, p.133) describes, the initial debate seemed to regard globalization and localization as opposite developmental directions, and therefore conflicting. A refreshing middle ground in the process is recently being articulated: globalization takes special forms in certain localized economies, in global cities[39]. These localities (or regions in which they are located) are favored by globalization effects in that they form nodes in global corporate activities and other localities are left in a dependent situation to this. In the debate we recognize concepts of urbanization economies, cumulative causation, hierarchical diffusion models (on a global scale), technological spillovers, learning spillovers and proximity diffusion models (on a local scale within the 'global' locations)[40]. Two elements are added. First, the fact that transnational corporations are usually large and powerful and are potentially more able to influence their own relevant environment (Harrison 1994). It then becomes natural to study local agglomeration effects by studying (those) individual firms or powerful (and highly concentrated) industries of firms when focusing on localized agglomeration economies. (Markusen 1994, Storper and Walker 1989). Second, the stressed importance of economic, cultural and social embeddedness in networks in this relevant socio-spatial environment (Gordon and McCann 2000). This spirals us back to (from an econometric point of view) rather intangible agglomeration forces we discussed in previous sections.

In general it is argued by geographers that this institutionalist approach offers a much richer understanding of territorial proximity and agglomeration economies than that offered by new trade and growth theories, which (as Amin 1999, p.370 puts it) 'continues to stress well-known but rather tired [location theory based] agglomeration factors'. Proximity in geographical research should be considered in ways that acknowledge the territorial parameters of the institutional and social sources of economic action (Thrift and Olds 1996). This research strand in modern geography is potentially rich in explanation, but rather poor in formal modeling. Often, case studies and successful regional examples (Silicon Valley, Third Italy) are investigated. Institutional arenas differ considerably over these regions, and it is difficult to come to general applicable stylized facts. Clearly, it does not contradict with endogenous growth, new trade and evolutionary theory as described in the previous section. Instead, learning and technological spillovers between geographic proximate locations or within the same locations is at least complementary and to a large extent the common crucial factor for local economic growth in both the new industrial geography[41] as in the discipline of the new geographical economics. And

---

[39] There is a large literature on the globalization-localization debate and global cities in planning and geography, most notably are Batten (1995), Castells (1989), Oinas (1998) and Sassen (1991).

[40] Malmberg and Maskell (1997) stress the fact that regional economic advantage is derived from the existence of various factors that prevent external competitors from imitating unique regional capabilities that underpin economic success. Competitiveness is therefore based, essentially, on the curbs to imitation of such relational assets. This defensive line of agglomerative reasoning is also common in new trade and evolutionary models theory on locked-in (and thus also -out) spatial cumulative growth.

[41] Some scholars are being uncomfortable with the continued use of the moniker new 'industrial' geography (e.g. Coe and Townsend 1998). Non-manufacturing activities remain somewhat in the background, whereas new institutional economic geography should be more sensitive to the different forms of economic activity. This applies especially to the Netherlands, not having a main industrial economic structure but having a services-based economy.

although the enlarged attention to spatial scale in order to turn it into an emancipatory and empowering academic and policy process is of course a good thing, careful consideration on conceptualization remains important.

Flexible Specialization and Agglomeration

As Martin (1999, p.79) remarks, it is not possible to review the entire field of economic geography, nor is that the goal of this section. A number of interlocking literatures and theoretical frameworks have informed and shaped this work. Central are, as mentioned in the previous section, the political, economic, institutional and social bases of regional development and industrial agglomeration. A major influencing theme in that discussion is explicitly concerned with agglomeration economies though: the spatial translation of the paradigm of flexible specialization. The initial influence was the book by Piore and Sabel (1984) with their argument that we are witnessing the emergence of flexible specialization as a new industrial technological paradigm. In their wake, two influential and mutual influencing frameworks appeared. The first is that of the French regulation political economy, stressing the contemporary transition from Fordism to post-Fordism, facilitating and supporting economic accumulation (Peck 1996). The regional setting is argued to be the most relevant scale of analysis on which this trickles down. The second focuses on the (re-)emergence of the regional setting in terms of technological learning and spillovers, neo-Marshallian agglomeration networks, regional innovation systems and industrial districts (Braczyk *et al.* 1998, Sabel 1994, Scott 1988b). It should be stressed that, as Harrison (1991) and Markusen (1996) make clear, there is no single typology for these industrial districts of flexible specialization agglomeration; rather, such districts differ considerably on origin, economic structure, social regulation, institutional organization and degree of political intervention. This diversity may well limit the ambition and success of constructing an over-arching universal model of spatial agglomeration, and in fact this lack of stylized facts is exactly the concern that withdraws geographical economists in their confidence in the agglomeration conceptualizations in the new industrial geography (Martin 1999). Citing Peck (1996, p. 121-123), agglomeration economies in the flexible specialization debate are believed to follow from the following 'perceived stylized facts'. First, forces in contemporary capitalism, captured under the rubric of transition from Fordism to flexible accumulation, are engendering a need for enhanced flexibility in production systems. Fragmentation of consumer markets and heightened levels of business uncertainty are the two key-factors behind this shift. Second, it is argued that the imperative of flexibility is stimulating a process of dynamic vertical desintegration in the production system, as companies seek to enhance their flexibility and responsiveness by externalizing many of the functions previously performed within the firm. This amounts to more than breaking up established production chains. Because flexible production systems are expansionist and innovation-rich in character, new and independent forms of specialist production will emerge. The third element in arguing is that in this deepened social division of labor, individual producers become locked into networks of extremely malleable external linkages and labor market relations. The redrawing of the boundaries of individual production units, and the concomitant downsizing and narrowing of organizational specialities, brings about heightened interdependencies in the production system as firms become deeply embedded in complex webs of inter-organizational transactions. The twin requirements of minimizing external (interfirm) transaction costs and establishing appropriate labor market relations bring about a marked agglomeration of economic activity. New industrial spaces, then, coalesce around dense networks of transactional interrelations and are associated with the establishment of new local labor market norms, based on numerical and functional flexibility. This brings about three strategies for labor market flexibility: individualizing employment relations away from collective negotiation systems, achieving firm-internal flexibility by multi-skilling and reduced job demarcation and external flexibility by hiring part-time and temporary workers.

This spatial translation of the second industrial divide, manifesting itself in localized accumulation of economic growth and local regulatory institutional development in flexibly specialized industrial districts with accompanying employment (labor demand), is not overwhelmingly accepted though by all geographers. The ideal geographical picture drawn, seeks to specify the linkages between industrialization, urban structure and the formation of territorial production complexes from a flexible labor market perspective. Labor economists, especially Peck (1996), but also Gertler (1988) and Markusen (1999), show that the flexibility claims in these theories can easily and maybe even better be accounted for by other processes than a new technological divide. Phenomena interpreted as evidence of rising flexibility are in fact manifestations of quite different processes. There is no straightforward connection between industrial structure and labor market structure, let alone between flexibility in production and flexibility in labor markets (Peck 1996, p.126). Peck and Phelps (1992) also remark that the discussions triggered by Scott *et al.* are based on several older concepts, like Marshall's classic account of industrial districts, evolutionary economic theory, cumulative causation[42], technological spillovers, transaction costs approaches (Williamson 1975) and concepts of Marxist rounds of (capital) accumulation (Massey 1984). The spatial scale of analysis (from local trajectories for flexible industrial trajectories to regulatory theories on the macro-level) is not always clearly defined.

Much researched examples of the modern industrial districts came to us by explorative case studies research on certain well-known success stories. Emilia-Romagna, Tuscany, Baden-Würtenberg, Silicon Valley, the London and Paris regions, Texas Fort Worth, Los Angeles and the M4 corridor are well-known and scrutinized examples, usually by local scholars having the district in their backyard.

---

[42] Phelps (1992) warns for cumulative causation to have the latent property to become the sole explanation of localized economic growth. Without separating divisions of labor from inter-firm linkages, ignoring the initial configuration of the spatial economic structure and the loose relationship between theory and evidence this will certainly become (and remain) the case, he argues (p. 37-38).

Industrial districts show remarkable theoretical similarities in conceptualization with older concepts: networks, production complexes, value chains, production chains, clusters of industries, related industries, development blocks, industrial systems, growth poles, innovation systems, business systems and filières (some of those were mentioned earlier in a growth pole perspective). Evidence of the agglomeration thesis because of flexible specialization often remains questionable and speculative though, or counter-evidence using the same empirical and theoretical principles is generally ignored (Martin and Sunley 2003, Coe and Townsend 1998, Curran and Blackburn 1994, Markusen 1996). Their critical view does not deny that significant changes in conceptualization can be noticed, but challenges the assertion that these changes are all-pervasive and represent a distinct break with the past and the dawning of a new era of production. Instead, it argues that the intensification and development towards an information and knowledge society is embedded in historical trends established long ago (Gertler 1988) and explains why the majority of non-successful regions has difficulties in copying supposed relevant agglomeration and innovation trajectories.

2.6 Summary and Synthesis

How Does Space Matter in External Economies?

From this chapter it becomes clear that externalities that can induce agglomeration of growing and innovative economic activities are described in the economic and geographical literature in many guises. Marshall's (1890) rich description on all possible externalities (in his time), Scitovsky's (1954) distinction in pecuniary and technological externalities that is central in modern geographic economic analyses and Weber's, Marshall's, Arrow's, Porter's and Romer's stress upon *localization economies* are nowadays common language in economic agglomeration theory. A second concept, of *urbanization economies*, fits in the thoughts of Adam Smith, Marshall, Jacobs and Von Thünen on the potential service roles of towns. They contain externalities that are not directly linked to industry-specific increasing returns, but are profitable to *all* industries in an agglomeration, as well as (social) city amenities and the availability of varieties in goods for both consumers and producers in agglomerations. Scale and variety of economic activity somehow dynamically foster productivity growth and innovativeness of economic activity with constant factor inputs.

A fundamental point is that a variety of mechanisms by which the external economies are achieved (alongside various off-setting diseconomies) operate simultaneously, often indirectly and cumulatively, in static and dynamic manners, so that individual sources of the agglomeration process cannot be isolated or individually identified (Gordon and McCann 2000). Simplifying research hypotheses always come at the cost of neglecting important, detailed aspects. Our study is predominantly concerned with spatial externalities, employment growth and innovation intensity patterns in an econometric modeling framework. The spatially oriented conclusions leave out many firm- or individual-level social or institutional explanations of agglomeration economies as presented in this chapter. Both the literature of geographical economics and that of the new industrial geography use quite similar theoretical notions like agglomeration economies, knowledge spillovers, dynamic externalities, localized productivity gains, returns to scale, growth theory, diversity, institutions, cities, learning and urbanization and localization economies. Other, less common economic theories, on evolutionary and growth paradigms, use aspects of these (spatial) externality ingredients as well. Table 2.2 compares in a polarized and summarizing form the main elements of emphasis concerning externality discussions in the geographical economic and new industrial geography literature. From this table it becomes clear that research traditions in regional and urban sciences, on which our study heavily builds, uses elements from both strands of literature to build their theoretical framework. The frameworks used by the regional and urban economists are therefore rather fragmented in character and use indirect measurements for spatial externalities, disadvantages the research in our study also faces. At the same time they are able to conclude empirically on testable hypotheses of local, urban and regional growth, something the fully theoretical models of geographical economics and the new industrial geography are not up to. In general, our study sticks to the language of spillovers or externalities when we refer to external economies of scale. Table 2.2 shows that the economic and geographical literature inhabits a considerable spectrum of refinements and attributions on the contents of the concept of (static as well as dynamic) agglomeration economies. The summarizing figure 2.1 makes two divisions: one in static and dynamic accounts and one in general (urbanization) economies and industry-specific ones (localization economies). By discussing the two dimensions and the four quadrants resulting from its intersections this framework was explored in this chapter.

The distinction between localized and urbanization economies appeared to be commonly accepted in the literature. Localization economies usually take the form of technical externalities whereby the productivity or growth of labor in a given sector in a given city is assumed to increase with total employment in that sector. Externalities that concern knowledge spillovers between firms *within an industry* that is concentrated in a location (specialized agglomeration) are generally known as Marshall-Arrow-Romer (MAR) externalities. Urbanization economies reflect external economies passed to enterprises as a result of savings from the large-scale operation of the agglomeration or city as a whole, independent from industry structure. Jacobs (1969) and Quigley (1998) are the most cited references in this respect. Our study uses (generalized) testable hypotheses concerning competitive structures of internal market organization, localization economies (specialization) and urbanization economies (sectoral diversity), see table 2.3 (in chapter 5 the hypotheses are explicitly translated into statistical indicators). In the MAR-theory focusing on localization economies, spillovers are thought to be most important when there is little prevailing local competition so that rents associated with sector-specific knowledge can be internalized.

Table 2.2   A comparison of geographical economics and new industrial geographical frameworks of analyses

Element	Geographical economics	New industrial geography
externalities	Marshallian: labor pooling, specialist suppliers Pecuniary: market size effects	Marshallian, labor market, specialist suppliers, knowledge spillovers
agglomeration	local clusters interregional center-periphery	industrial districts high-tech clusters financial clusters
competition	imperfect: monopolistic competition economies of scale	Competitive flexible specialisation economies of scope
transfer costs	Transport costs	transaction costs
technological spillovers	not typical, important in some industries	local and fundamental to innovatory success
labor market pooling	strategy of insurance (representative firm)	form of local social embeddedness
social and cultural local characteristics	difficult to formalize, assumed not distinctive *a priori*	key preconditions for successful localization

Source: Martin and Sunley (1996, p.270)

The MAR-theory in a dynamic context predicts that local monopoly is better for growth than local competition, because local monopoly restricts the flow of ideas to others and so allows innovator-internalization. This again then is supposed to speed up growth and new innovation. Porter (1990) agrees with the existence of localization economies, also arguing that knowledge spillovers in specialized, geographically concentrated industries stimulate growth. On the relevant market form though Porter disagrees from the MAR-theory: he insists that local competition fosters the pursuit and rapid adoption of innovation. Both influential frameworks (Porter on competitive advantage and MAR on innovation monopoly and power) embrace the concept of localization economies, both in static as well as dynamic versions. The third element of agglomeration externality hypotheses (besides localization and competition economies) is proposed by Jacobs (1969) and appeared generally accepted in the literature. She agrees with Porter that competition fosters growth, but contends that regional diversity in economic activity (as a measure of *urbanization economies*) will result in higher growth and innovation rates as many ideas developed by one sector can also be fruitfully applied in other sectors.

The several hypotheses proposed in the literature concerning agglomeration conditions under which knowledge externalities affect growth and innovation (summarized in table 2.3) are conditioned on six contingencies (see figure 2.1).

Table 2.3   Stylized hypothesized relations between agglomeration circumstances and economic growth

	MAR	Porter	Jacobs
Concentration	+	+	−
Diversity	−	−	+
Competition	−	+	+

Besides empirical implications these contingencies represent important theoretical conceptualizations as well. The most important of these concern the spatial scale of analyses and the industrial decomposition of the data. The advantage of the initial small spatial scales of the empirical analyses presented in our study is that inter- as well as intra-urban spatial transmitting channels can be explored in spatial econometric models (a neglected aspects of the literature). Also, the initial level of decomposition allows for multilevel designs of local and regional externality models. This enables us to test for relevant spatial circumstances embodied in economic growth and innovation (externalities) by means of spatial heterogeneity in urban or filtering-down zoning regimes, as well as spatial autocorrelation (contiguous, proximity-based spatial dependency) using combinations of spatial scales of analyses previous research has neglected. Indicators of firm dynamics and competitive firm-size structures are added to econometric analyses as explanatory variables. This is possible because of the detailed initial data-decomposition (this aspect is not accompanied in the literature that explicitly). The initial detail of industry-related data also allows for optimal clustering on relevant industry levels, as well as for individual sector analyses. Other important contingencies concern initial spatial configurations, history (previous growth patterns), the research methodology suitable for the data under consideration and the scientific discipline of analysis. Our study will focus explicitly on these aspects when relevant. Interesting for examination in the Dutch context is how growth and innovation 'transmit' (spatially coincide) in combinations of hierarchical (urban/non-urban) and (neighboring) spatial research designs of many small and medium-sized cities as is the case in the South-Holland Randstad region and the country as a whole.

Modern Elaboration: The Glaeser et al. (1992) Empirical Modeling Framework

Recently, building on the 'classic' distinctions presented in table 2.3, knowledge-based theories of endogenous growth are presented at the city level. Two recent and important papers that empirically test the hypotheses are by Glaeser *et al.* (1992) and Henderson *et al.* (1995). Both papers try to bridge the gap between geography and economics focusing on externalities and spillovers in an endogenous growth framework. We build our analyses on the empirical modeling frameworks of both papers; albeit more on the Glaeser *et al.* framework because of its pioneering position in the analytical discussion. As became clear in the previous sections, according to endogenous growth theory, knowledge and knowledge spillovers potentially give rise to external economies of scale in production. However, the recent empirical literature (using predominantly US employment data in urban contexts) does not reach a clear conclusion as to the geographical, and especially agglomeration circumstances under which knowledge is transferred most easily. Does knowledge spill over predominantly between firms within the same sector or between firms in different sectors? And what is the role of competition in the growth process? The Glaeser *et al.* modeling framework enables us (with alterations concerning spatial dependency and urban configuration) to answer these questions more adequately than other (older) analytical frameworks.

Founded on Romer (1986) and Lucas (1988), the theory of endogenous growth emphasizes the role in the growth process of both the stock of knowledge and the (planned or unplanned) transfer of knowledge between economic agents. For example, knowledge spills over between firms via informal contacts between employees, or because employees switch jobs and take their knowledge with them. Indeed, the most important type of knowledge that plays a role in the growth process is not necessarily path-breaking innovations, but may be learning opportunities for everyday people (Cooper 2001; Glaeser 1999, 2000; Lambooy 2000). Knowledge as a main resource in the process of economic growth comprises intangible entities that are available to persons, firms and countries (or populations) and enable them to produce and consume efficiently and effectively (Hunt 1997, p.60). So although intangible by nature, economic growth theory tries to measure knowledge externalities under differing economic settings. Recent empirical tests on geographic dimensions of this theory often have looked at cities to *identify settings in which these external factors most effectively foster growth and innovation.* Both papers use employment data to measure growth, but reach different conclusions, particularly regarding effects of local industrial concentration versus local industrial diversity. Because of the lack of data on sectoral output and the capital stock at the city level an appropriate measure of total factor productivity cannot be constructed. Glaeser *et al.* (1992) build a small model where output is produced with only one input, labor, under conditions of decreasing returns to scale. Then, technological progress enhances the marginal value product of labor and hence the demand for labor increases. In that model, assuming constant prices for inputs and outputs, employment growth is an appropriate indicator of output growth. This simple, highly stylized model is embedded and formalized in labor demand theory (Hamermesh 1996, p.21 and further) as follows. The relative small surface and little spatial institutional and social differentiation of the Netherlands supports the assumption that each firm in an industry takes technology, wages and prices as given[43]. With $A_t f(l_t)$ representing the firms production function of output, a firm in some industry in a given location maximizes:

---

[43] This does not mean that there are no variations in wage levels and R&D and technology intensities across the Netherlands. From appendix B it becomes clear that this is not the case, but intra-industry variations appear much smaller than inter-industry variations.

$$\pi_t = A_t f(l_t) - w_t l_t \tag{2.1}$$

where π is the profit flow, l is the amount of labor employed and w represents the wage rate. The parameter A reflects general productivity: it captures both the prices at which goods are sold and the state of the technology at time t (the latter being measured nominally). This basic production function $f(l_t)$ abstracts from capital service inputs[44]. Allowing for only one input strictly means that labor-saving technological development and innovations capturing only further accumulation of physical capital are not captured in this specification. Maximization implies that the value of the marginal product of labor should equal the wage rate:

$$l_t = \left(\frac{\alpha A_t}{w_t}\right)^{\frac{1}{1-\alpha}} \tag{2.2}$$

Productivity is determined by both local and national circumstances. Nationwide factors are technological progress, as well as the level of demand for the industry's output. Local factors are predominantly those that determine technological spillovers, such as for example proximity of similar industries, differentiation of the local industry mix or the degree of local competitiveness in industries[45]. But also local circumstances such as the issuing of new industrial sites will play a determining role. Indeed, the local or regional determinants influencing the productivity of firms embody the external and agglomeration factors (localization and urbanization economies) discussed above, whether these are tangible or intangible. Agglomeration economies have been measured and incorporated in empirical analysis in reduced form equations and relatively simple models as shift and share analysis. In terms of shift and share analysis, it represents the non-industry-dependent shift or differential part of spatial growth (see chapter 6 for a more detailed discussion). Rearranging equation (2.2) and rewriting it in terms of log growth rates gives[46]:

---

[44] As Hamermesh (1996, p.22-23) notifies, basic labor demand theories require assumptions of at least two inputs into production, the second most commonly defined as capital services. For instance, the crucial notion of factor substitution for (non-spatial) labor demand modeling, that underlies much empirical work, is impossible to discuss when only one input is assumed. Since our interest is predominantly *spatial* in character, we for simplicity use a one-input theorem, and construct testable spatial hypotheses from it. Extension to two- or multi-input models is due to data availability restricted upon our modeling and empirical testing.

[45] Recently these latter kind of competitive factors are incorporated into frameworks of carrying capacity in organizational ecology induced research as well, notably in Hannan and Freeman (1989, p.131-141) and Van Wissen (2000).

[46] This is the formulation of the growth definition on employment and population as used in chapter 4 in explanatory spatial data analyses.

$$\log\left(\frac{A_{t+1}}{A_t}\right) = \log\left(\frac{w_{t+1}}{w_t}\right) - \log\left[\frac{f'(l_{t+1})}{f'(l_t)}\right] \qquad (2.3)$$

Working towards testable reduced form equations and assuming a multiplicative relationship between local and national factors of productivity determinants, the productivity factor A (representing the level of technology) can be decomposed as:

$$A_t = A_{national,t}\, A_{local,t} \qquad (2.4)$$

The growth rate of the overall level of technology will then be the sum of the growth of national technology in an industry and the growth of local technology. The growth of national technology is assumed to capture the changes in the price of the product as well as the shifts in nationwide technology in the industry. The local technology component instead is assumed to grow at a rate exogenous to the firm but depending on the various technological externalities present in an industry in a location:

$$\log\left(\frac{A_{local,t+1}}{A_{local}}\right) = g\,(agglomeration\ forces,\ initial\ conditions) + \varepsilon_{t+1} \qquad (2.5)$$

In order to test for theories of dynamic externalities and agglomeration circumstances, the agglomeration factors should at least comprise spatial indicators of specialization and diversity (both indices of economic concentration) as well as the (degree of) local monopoly (Encaouda and Jacquemin 1980). The initial conditions account for particularities present in certain spatial units that work out (positively or negatively) for all firms in different industries at localities in the same manner.

The study of Glaeser *et al.* (1992) finds evidence supporting the Jacobs hypothesis, whereas the study of Henderson *et al.* (1995) finds evidence consistent with both the MAR and Jacobs view, depending on whether mature capital goods or high-tech industries are considered. One key difference between these studies rests on whether data from all cities in a given industry are analyzed (Henderson *et al.*) or whether only the largest industries in each city are included in the sample (Glaeser *et al.*). Consequently, Glaeser (1998, p.148) suggests that '[a] possible reconciliation of results [on this point] is that scale and concentration may have value for smaller firms; however, diversity has more value for long term growth'. Beardsell and Henderson (1999) argue that another important difference lies in the treatment of time invariant firm and/or location attributes. In particular, they state (p.449) that '... rather than the link between the present and the past representing mostly dynamic externalities, an alternative explanation is that there is a location fixed/random effect in estimation that gives rise to the role of history'. Glaeser *et al.* (1992, p.1148) counter this view by distinguishing between the role of historical factors, such as natural resource and transport advantages, in location versus the role of these factors in growth. Kim (1999) and Ellison and Glaeser (1999) provide more complete discussions of issues related to natural advantage and location. Other explanations for the differences in results from these studies are possible, too. For example, in the Henderson *et al.* (1995) study, the strategy of analyzing all cities in a given industry turned out to be problematic. Because of disclosure rules, employment data for as many as 30% of cities were censored. This problem led to estimating a Tobit model in which the log of the end-of-period (1987) employment level was regressed on the log of beginning-of-period (1970) employment level. This approach is natural given the circumstances faced; however, controlling for the fixed/random effects of history becomes difficult with only one cross-section of data for each industry. A number of explanatory variables were tried that might be components of a fixed effect, but they performed unevenly.

Glaeser *et al.* (1992), on the other hand, estimated equations to explain growth in, rather than the level of, employment for city-industries in the period 1956-1987. As the existing growth models imply that the knowledge externalities are sources of *permanent* growth, they focus on the largest (and hence often mature) industries. Therefore, data were drawn from the six largest industries in each of the US cities studied (the previously discussed city-industries), so censoring did not appear to be as serious as in the Henderson *et al.* (1995) study. Also, they drew a substantial fraction of their observations from non-manufacturing industries (about one-third came from wholesale trade, construction, and auto dealers and service stations), whereas Henderson *et al.* (1995) looked only at manufacturing industries. Recent evidence for France shows that indeed the composition of the dataset may at least partially explain the difference in findings. Combes (2000) finds that diversity tends to enhance employment growth in services whereas it tends to retard growth in manufacturing industries, but specialization does not seem to foster growth in either type of activity. Finally, in addition to variables measuring agglomeration economies, Glaeser *et al.* included a control variable in their regressions measuring the national employment growth rate of the industry outside the city[47]. This variable was included to account for national demand shifts and to capture general (industry-wide) technological progress (see Blanchard and Katz 1992). In the following chapters we will replicate and subsequently refine the Glaeser *et al.* and Henderson *et al.* research designs for the Netherlands. We will conclude upon the similarities and differences of agglomeration regularities in the light of the framework presented in this chapter.

---

[47] Notice that the variable measuring sectoral national growth rates outside the city would be virtually the same for each observation in the Henderson *et al.* (1995) analysis.

Chapter 3

Heterogeneity in Localized Economic Growth

3.1   Introduction

This chapter describes the heterogeneity in localized economic growth patterns in the Netherlands in general and South-Holland in particular. This heterogeneity concerns growth over *industries* and sectors, *spatial* structures of growth and growth over stages in *firm life-cycles*. These aspects are, although little systematically admitted in the literature, fundamentally important in testing hypotheses on endogenous growth empirically. To identify what heterogeneity is important in our study, we use data on employment dynamics that are available on two spatial levels: for the Netherlands at zip code level for a 2-digit industrial classification covering the period 1991-1997 and for the province of South-Holland at individual firm level for the period 1988-1997 (see appendix A). The heterogeneity embedded in spatial urban structures, industry classifications and life-cycle dynamics that comes to the fore in this chapter will be used in empirical research in following chapters of this study; this chapter therefore functions as a setup and reference for that.

We will discuss the potential influence of industry classification on testing sectoral and spatial growth spillovers and externalities in section 3.2. Especially important is the introduction of the concept of location-industries (used in the benchmarking study by Glaeser *et al.* 1992) as opposed to integral industrial classifications; both will be used in empirical analyses in subsequent chapters. The focus on spatial labor demand developments on several spatial levels in the Netherlands is central in sections 3.3 and 3.4. Section 3.3 focuses on spatial structure in econometric modeling in general. The modeling of conjunct-, proximity- or contiguity-based spatial dependence in externalities, that one thinks of most commonly in agglomerative growth theory, is formally introduced (and will appear in explorative spatial analysis in chapter 4). Section 3.4 then introduces spatial classifications on regional (Netherlands) and local (South-Holland) spatial levels in which spatial observation units are *not* necessarily conjunct to each other (but indeed are functionally related). We base these classifications on the literature of urban economic development. Empirically, we translate the spatial classifications into so-called spatial regimes that will be used to test for spatial heterogeneity in the Dutch data in chapters 5 to 7. Descriptive analysis of national zoning and commuting-based connectedness regimes will be presented. Section 3.5

focuses on the life-cycle aspects of economic developments in industries. The individual firm data on South-Holland allow for an analysis of the nature and magnitude of life-cycle decomposition in relation to (spatial) economic growth. Section 3.6 summarizes and concludes.

3.2 Heterogeneity in Industry Classification

In all studies testing for agglomeration economies, the spatial unit of observation *in combination* with the sectoral (and occupational) unit of observation appears crucial in the interpretation of hypotheses. The treatment of them sometimes is subjective and even misleading in character. Conclusions on individual firms or entrepreneurs are projected on industries or regions, and vice versa. Focusing on a specific industry (say ICT-services or knowledge-intensive manufacturing) supposes a priori a different framework in explaining developments than a pure spatial analysis (Combes 2000, Henderson *et al.* 1995)[1]. Little sensitivity analysis has been carried out over the years into whether the industrial composition of economic activity alters conclusions on agglomeration. Most studies analyzing individual firm growth still restrict themselves to single industries or case studies[2]. The obvious critique then would be that these analyses are too dependent on firm behavior characteristics in that particular industry. To generalize it in terms of 'general firm behavior' (as for instance the title of the article by Harrison *et al.* 1997 suggests) actually is a little sweeping. This generalization of specific industry or firm results to the 'representative firm' is a general accepted case of ecological fallacy in (industrial) economics (see especially Hamermesh 1996 for its scientific embedding). It is by now well known that results from one scale of analysis cannot be readily transferred to another (the problem of cross-level inference). An explanatory variable measures different things depending on the unit of analysis. Robinson (1950) and Wrigley (1995) demonstrated the ecological fallacy of transferring areal, higher-level results to individuals' behavior, while the atomistic fallacy of transferring individual-level results to the aggregate level has been identified as well (Alker 1969, Goldstein 1995). Still, these highly relevant issues are much neglected in empirical geographical analysis.

Several studies on individual firm growth include dummy variables for distinguishing industry-effects (e.g. Crihfield 1989, Henderson *et al.* 1995, Van Wissen 2000). Although significant coefficients then indicate that firms embedded

---

[1] The study of Combes (2000) is an example of research in which no general conclusions on sectoral and spatial growth spillover can be reached because of the large number of industries for which relations are separately tested. It does make clear though that not all industrial or service-based industries perform the same on the growth relations hypothesized.

[2] Good examples are Harrison *et. al* (1997) who focus on US metalworking establishments, Saxenian (1994) who studies firms in the ICT-sector in the USA and numerous examples of industry and firm-level case studies stemming from the Californian School of Geography, as in Scott (2000) and Storper (1997). Limitations and possibilities for case-study research at the individual firm or industry level are given by Markusen (1994), Vaessen (1993) and Van Geenhuizen (1993).

in a certain industry show different statistical association to the subject researched (usually firm growth), it remains unclear what causal (spatial) processes explain this differing behavior. Of course, this depends on the question of what type of relation is being tested for. A general growth process requires a different research setup than individual or industry-specific growth patterns. Glaeser *et al.* (1992) introduced in this context the extreme possibility of the *mixture* of both the spatial and industry dimensions: city-industries. These are combinations of a predefined number of largest industries measured in spatial (urban) units. Cities can thus be represented more than once in a dataset, restricted by the number of largest industries distinguished (in their research this was six). The influential Glaeser *et al.* (1992) study came to remarkable and profound urbanization (diversity-based) conclusions concerning economic growth in cities, that have been cited and discussed intensively in the literature. No analysis up to date deals fully with the spatial and sectoral measurement issues originating from that study. It is important to notice that the outcomes of modeled equations concerning economic growth for (1) individual industries, (2) locations with a mixed number of industries (like the city-industries) or (3) individual firms taking into account the industry it belongs to, potentially affect the interpretation of the research question to a large extent (Plewis 1985). The research undertaken in this study applies to two of these industry-specific growth indicators: individual industries and sectors are analyzed especially in chapter 6 and location-industry analyses are dealt with in chapter 5. Interpretation and validity issues will be dealt with when appropriate. Of course, the question which industrial decomposition is needed for a good understanding always remains significant and cannot be answered unanimously coherent. Research by Moomaw (1988, 1998) showed that when the research question's focus is on spatial externalities in general (the question being whether localization or urbanization economies influencing firm performance are affected by industrial decomposition), the sensitivity for either 3- or 2-digit industry decomposition is limited. Labor demand in this context is analyzed using firm-specific but industry-aggregated CES and Cobb Douglas production functions respectively, which under the constant returns to scales assumption yield local differences in industry employment and value added as localization economies, while an exponential function of city size (population) comprises the urbanization economies.

It is *a priori* useful to identify a classification of economic activities as meant by 'method' (1) above, with neither too many separate industries nor too few, taking into account theoretical considerations of plausibility and functionality. Many hypotheses concerning economic growth and innovation intensity are more appropriate for certain sectors than for other. The detailed industrial classification of the employment data used in this study is initially very detailed, enabling us to apply the concept of location-industries as developed by Glaeser *et al.* (1992), as well as industrial branch classifications for broader sectors. Appendix A shows how the originally 49 2-digit industries of the Dutch and South-Holland data have been aggregated into respectively 16 and 4 sectors of economic production. The classification consists of a typology of 16 complementary economic sectors that can be distinguished in modern economies.

For distinguishing the sixteen types of industrial activities, societal linkages between the different industrial branches are as regarded crucial (see appendix A and Louter and Van Oort 1992 for a full explanation of the categorization). The 16 theoretically distinctive categories are initially all used in exploratory spatial dependence analysis in chapter 4. From this analysis, and from previous literature on Dutch employment dynamics (especially Louter 1997), it becomes clear that econometric spatial agglomeration analyses on the national and regional level in the Netherlands (in chapters 5 and 6) should focus on four broad sectors: production activities, distribution activities, producer services and consumer services. Detailed spatial association over growth and innovation differentials appear most profound over these sectors. They form the basic distinction in this study in terms of 'method' (1) that can be aggregated from both the 16 sectors and the original 49 industries.

Data on sectoral and location-industry employment distributions and development for this study were drawn from Dutch municipalities and from postal zip code areas in the Province of South-Holland. The Netherlands is a small country with a population density of 457 persons per km^2. The province of South-Holland is about $1/12^{th}$ of the country. The province is heavily urbanized with a population density of 1200 inhabitants per km^2. The province covers a substantial part of the core economic region of the Netherlands, the Randstad. It includes the country's second and third largest cities (Rotterdam and The Hague) as well as numerous medium-sized cities such as Leiden and Delft. Both the regional (South-Holland) and national (Netherlands) datasets were constructed using LISA and BZH Firm Registers (see appendix A). These data are of particular interest for agglomeration economies analyses for two reasons. First, they are comprehensive in that they include virtually all establishments present in the Netherlands for the period 1991-1997 and for South-Holland for the period 1988-97. These time intervals are the longest over which employment growth can be measured using these detailed data in both the Netherlands and South-Holland[3]. Second, the data are available at a fine spatial and industrial scale. Questionnaire results identify each establishment's 6-digit zip code (a small area containing about 100 different mailing addresses), and 5-digit activity code. The Dutch and South-Holland datasets, however, are not identical. Whereas for the entire Netherlands, only employment totals are available by industry and zip code, the South-Holland data contains information on individual establishments. Thus, in one respect, the South-Holland data resemble the Longitudinal Research Data made available by the US Census Bureau, but contain information on all establishments located there, not just those engaged in manufacturing. However, a disadvantage of the Dutch and South-Holland datasets is that they do not contain measures of outputs, inputs other than labour, or plant characteristics. Consequently, they are not appropriate for

---

[3] Henderson (1997b) finds that effects of agglomeration economies on employment growth peak after about 5 years and die out after 6-7 years. Thus, for both datasets, the time interval over which employment growth was measured appears to be long enough to allow measurable differences to emerge.

estimating establishment-level production functions, as in Beardsell and Henderson (1999).

Spatial and industrial detail is an obvious advantage, it enables us to construct detailed location-industry combinations, relevant spatial regimes as well as spatially lagged and window-averaged variables (to be discussed in the next sections); however, the level of detail in both the Dutch and South-Holland data is actually too great for the purposes of this study. In principle, a study of growth of individual 2-digit industries (similar to Combes 2000) in the Netherlands or the South-Holland region could be carried out, but practical problems would emerge because beginning-of-period and end-of-period employment would be zero for most sectors in most zip codes. Spatial dependency within employment growth and innovation data in the research area is probably best captured by the four broad sectors: industry, distribution, producer services and consumer services[4]. The aspect of zero observations would be an advantage if the aim of the study asked why new firms choose particular (previously interesting or relatively new and unknown) locations (Carlton 1982, Rigby and Essletzbichler 2000). However, the primary focus for this chapter (and study) is on the closely related issue of agglomeration mechanisms thought to be important to employment growth and innovation intensity. This emphasis motivates the decision to look at the sixteen and four largely defined sectors as well as the six largest (of all 49) industries that were present in a zip code area or municipality at the beginning of the sample period[5].

When the data are actually organized into a location-by-activity matrix, most of the cells contain no information. Many of the 6-digit zip code areas, for example, have only residences and individual 5-digit industries are present in only comparatively few 6-digit zip codes. Consequently, the data were first aggregated up to the 4-digit zip code, 2-digit activity code level (roughly the equivalent of 2 digit industries in the US SIC system). In South-Holland, for example, the average size of a 4-digit zip code is about 5.65 km^2, although they tend to be smaller in urban centers where the density of addresses is high and larger in areas that have more open space. In any case, a zip code is quite small, particularly in comparison to US counties or cities. The South Holland data were left at the 4-digit zip code level (see figure A1 in appendix A), whereas the data for the Netherlands were further aggregated into 548 municipalities (69 of which are in the South-Holland research area) in order to conduct analyses similar to those in earlier studies. These municipalities range in size from international cities such as Amsterdam to small villages. Because of their relative size to other municipalities, Amsterdam, Rotterdam, Utrecht, and The Hague were further subdivided into 3-digit-zip code

---

[4] In chapter 4 this proves to be right: more detailed industries do not show significant spatial dependency at the South-Holland and Netherlands spatial level of analysis.

[5] In their study of industry growth in US cities at 2-digit sectoral level, Henderson *et al.* (1995) incorporated all cities even though many of them had relatively few establishments present. Therefore, they faced the additional problem that because of federal disclosure rules, industry employment values were censored in as many as 30% of the cities studied; censoring is not a problem in the South-Holland data.

                    Urban Growth and Innovation

areas, roughly corresponding to economic areas in the core, intermediate zone and periphery, containing 50,000 to 100,000 persons each. This led to a total of 580 geographic units (still referred to as municipalities). Because previous research dealt with cities, the analysis mainly focuses on 234 municipalities that had a minimum number (20,000) of inhabitants (see figure 3.1). 234x6 (largest industries, as in Glaeser *et al.* 1992) gives 1404 largest location-industries[6].

The calculations concerning the South-Holland location-industry dataset are based on location-industries that contain at least 50 employed persons (in total 1797). Table 3.1 shows the ten industries that turned up most often among the six largest in either the 234 Dutch municipalities and the 416 zip code areas in South-Holland, and the number of employees in each. The most well-represented sectors in each of the two samples are building and construction, retail trade, financial institutions and services, health care, education, and wholesale trade. Notice that manufacturing industries appear less often in these samples than do non-manufacturing industries. Combes (2000) for France and O'Donoghue (2000) for the UK also embarked upon the differences in production structure in West-European regions and cities as opposed to results from US databases.

Table 3.1   Ten largest industries represented in the Netherlands and South-Holland data (number and employment)

Sectors	Netherlands (n=1404)			Sectors	South-Holland (n=1797)	
	# 1991	empl. 1991			# 1988	empl. 1988
Health care	206	545,343	1	Building/cons.	289	67,500
Building/cons.	195	244,735	2	Rem..bus.ser.[1]	263	78,610
Retail trade	179	344,665	3	Retail trade	232	70,929
Rem.bus.ser[1]	156	370,842	4	Education	221	45,116
Wholes. Trade	109	239,908	5	Health care	202	99,656
Education	100	154,444	6	Wholes. Trade	181	67,114
Agriculture	90	88,620	7	Agriculture	132	32,406
Governm/Inst.	73	143,011	8	Distrib. Land	105	23,156
Distrib. Land	33	30,848	9	Governm./Inst	99	52,475
Food industry	27	33,419	10	Consum. serv.	71	1,918

[1] Remaining business services: juridical, public relations & consultancy (see appendix A)

---

[6] See Van Soest *et al.* (2002) for a detailed discussion on the exact definition of, and a sensitivity analysis on (the number of) location-industries. Selecting more than six largest industries in each location or city (which number appears rather arbitrarily in the Glaeser *et al.* 1992 study) does not change agglomeration conclusions significantly.

Figure 3.1   Municipalities with more than 20,000 inhabitants (1991)

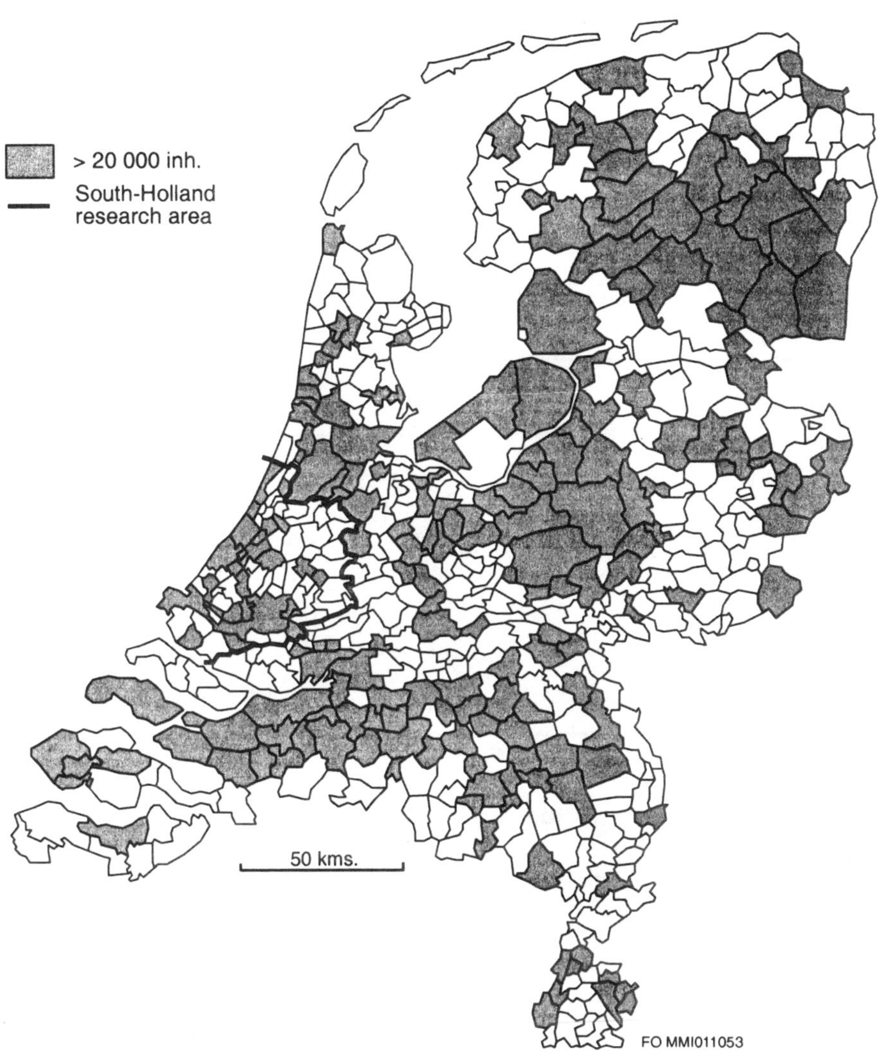

Table 3.2 shows the number of times individual manufacturing industries are among the largest six industries present in Dutch municipalities. The table also shows total employment in the Netherlands dataset for each of these ten industries. In the Dutch municipality data, food and beverages is the most frequently occurring manufacturing sector, but the chemical industry is the largest in terms of employment. Other manufacturing sectors, such as electronics, glass and ceramics, transportation equipment, and medical instruments, also are represented in the province, but in most cases there are too few establishments to permit a meaningful sector-specific analyses.

Table 3.2   Ten largest manufacturing industries in the Dutch (municipal) dataset on location-industries (n=1404)

Industry	Representation (1991)	Employment (1991)
Food- and beverage-processing industry	27	33,419
Furniture industry	25	26,593
Metal products industry	24	12,511
Publishing and reproduction	17	21,177
Chemical industry	17	41,912
Machinery industry	16	16,911
Electrical machinery and instruments	7	16,614
Metal industry (primary)	7	15,089
Glass and ceramics industry	7	8,864

3.3 Modeling Spatial Structure and Heterogeneity

While endogenous growth theory is among the most powerful advances in economics in the past quarter-century, the fact that no clear view has emerged regarding (geographic and agglomeration) situations to which it best applies represents a barrier to its further development and application. In growth models, for example, is it appropriate to treat urban areas as completely and homogeneous specialized as in Black and Henderson (1999b) or to assume that knowledge externalities predominantly function for employees only within the same industry as Glaeser (1999) does? Or, is industrial diversity such a fundamental component of the growth process that it must be captured in models such as those outlined in Fujita, Krugman and Venables (2000)? The lack of agreement on the relative importance of industrial concentration and diversity sends an ambiguous message regarding policy choices to promote or manage growth in urban areas. Besides theoretical considerations, technical solutions in empirical analyses are far from a general accepted framework either. Formal econometric modeling techniques allow for incorporating spatial contiguous and heterogeneity structures, but consistent incorporation of spatial structure in modeling is still far from common practice (Anselin *et al.* 2000). In this section an overview is presented on how spatial structure can be incorporated in econometric modeling. Spatial (inter)dependencies are incorporated in several ways that frequently interact: (1) in the measurement unit; (2) in the spatial structure of the explained variable (and hence the entire model) or in the spatial definition of explaining variables, both measuring contiguous spatial dependency, and (3) in the significance of spatial regime modeling complementary to contiguous (proximity) dependency.

Measurement Units

First, the measurement unit in empirical analyses determines much of the spatial structure incorporated in models. Sectoral and spatial variations in economic growth and innovation intensity can be expressed on several scales: regional or local, in refined industrial structures or in broad ones. This brings along potential aggregation and scale problems (Feige and Watts 1972, Openshaw and Taylor 1979, Wrigley 1995). It is important to realize that the *modifiable areal unit problem* plays an important role along all modeling empirics: when the measurement unit concerns cities, research questions cannot be tested for spatial heterogeneity *within* cities. And when the measurement unit concerns regions, no answers can be formulated concerning growth in cities. In general, cities are (reasonably) well-defined economic areas that form some sort of coherent economic units that suit the purpose of the externalities discussion. From an industrial organization perspective the most suitable unit of observation for growth and innovation is the firm, where, theoretically, space can be induced in models by means of two ways. Either a multilevel approach is taken in which endogenously determined spatial regimes are applied, allowing different slopes to be assigned to different regime-equations (Goldstein 1995), or OLS and FGLS models incorporate predefined higher level (spatial) control variables (Harrison *et al.* 1997, Van Wissen 2000, Wallsten 2001). Concerning industrial composition, the emphasis of research on growth in *industrial* sectors in itself already contains a large amount of heterogeneity (Carree and Thurik 1999), let alone the heterogeneity in the relatively neglected producer and consumer service activities (Audretsch *et al.* 1999). Focusing on either one of the broad sectors (industry or services) neglects possible growth interactions between them. In Glaeser *et al.* (1992) so-called city-industries were introduced as unit of analysis, which meant that individual locations (cities) are allowed to be present in the dataset more than once. The advantage of this measurement unit is the possibility to model inter- as well as intra-industry growth differentials. In our study we use this measurement unit on the level of individual zip codes in the South-Holland research area and cities in the Netherlands (measured on the municipal level). Sectoral analyses over zip codes and municipalities are presented for the four broad sectors distinguished in the previous section[7]. The initial low spatial level of observation has advantages for hypotheses of externalities: they can be tested for on spatially build-up data, aggregated into relevant observation units (like cities, zones within cities and locations outside cities).

Spatial Lag and Error Modeling

A second important conceptual element in spatial econometric modeling concerns the choice of a spatial weight matrix used to test the spatial dependency in the model by focusing on the explained variable (in our case: employment growth and innovation intensity). This method, commonly called spatial lag or spatial error model specification, focuses on a theoretical extension of analyses prevailing in the existing literature on knowledge externalities as measured by spatial employment growth. The concepts of spatial lag and error analysis are especially meaningful for the empirical testing of *contiguous* growth patterns on small spatial scales. In this section we will discuss the usefulness of spatial lag modeling starting from, and hence extending the methodology of Glaeser *et al.* (1992) who analyzed employment growth rates of city-industries. They specified employment growth in a city-industry as a function of the extent of local specialization in that industry, local competition, and local industrial diversity, as well as control variables including the national employment growth rate of the industry outside the city. Data were drawn from the six largest industries in US cities for the period 1956-87. Results generally support the importance of Jacobs-type externalities and have been extensively discussed in the previous chapter. However, attention is drawn here to the treatment and interpretation of national industry growth to motivate the spatial econometric (spatial lag and error) modeling applied later on. Glaeser *et al.* (1992) included national employment growth in industries to account for national demand shifts (compare Blanchard and Katz 1992). This variable was measured as the log of the ratio of national end-of-period employment to beginning-of-period employment. Estimates of the coefficient of the national industry growth rate were significantly larger than unity, suggesting that the industries studied grew faster in cities than in rural areas[8]. Use of this variable, however, has an unusual and perhaps unintended interpretation regarding the way in which growth is transmitted between cities. Consider equation (3.1):

$$y = \rho W y^{*} + X\beta + \varepsilon \qquad\qquad\qquad (3.1)$$

---

[7] In sectoral analyses the (interacting) variation over industries is naturally excluded, inducing all spatial units of observations (zip codes or municipalities) to be present in the dataset only once.

[8] It is interesting to note that had Glaeser *et al.* (1992) constrained coefficients of the national industry growth rate to unity, resulting estimates would be interpreted as an explanation of the differential shift term in shift-share analysis (see Perloff *et al.* 1960). The differential shift term measures the extent to which an industry in a region (or city) grows faster or slower than it does on average in a broader geographic area. In an earlier day, there was considerable debate among regional scientists as to what determines the value of the differential shift term (see Houston 1967). The Glaeser *et al.* (1992) results suggest that Jacobs-type externalities are important in this regard.

in which y denotes an Nx1 vector of city-industry or spatially measured sectoral growth rates, ρ is a scalar, W denotes an NxN^* ($N{\leq}N^*$) weighting matrix, y^* denotes an N^*x1 vector of industry growth rates at *all* locations in the country (which would exceed the number of the locations in the sample), X denotes a matrix of observations on a set of either sectoral predefined or city-industry spatial explanatory variables, β is the coefficient vector and ε denotes a vector of disturbances. In the Glaeser *et al.* (1992) analysis, each row of W was implicitly constructed to create an explanatory variable that measures the national growth-rate of the industry outside the city in question. That is, in a given row of W, each element either would be a national employment share or zero depending on whether it multiplies an own-industry value in y^*. Thus, equation (6.1) in the original city-industry context implies that a change in or of the X variables (a measure of agglomeration economies, for example) for a particular city has both a local effect and a non-local effect that arises via a 'within-industry' growth transmission mechanism. Additionally, this mechanism has the peculiar feature that it functions independently of distance between cities because the weight assigned to the growth rate of an industry in one city would be approximately the same when estimating the growth rate of that industry in any other city in the dataset[9]. One way to account for the role of proximity would be to reformulate equation (6.1) as a spatial lag model (Anselin 1988). In this case, $N=N^*$, $y=y^*$, elements of W would reflect distances between locations (not national employment shares of industries), and the spatial coefficient ρ would index the strength of employment growth linkages over space. Additionally, the spatial lag formulation has at least three attractive features in the context of this study. First, theories (MAR, Porter and Jacobs) regarding the spatial-economic setting in which knowledge spillovers most effectively promote growth at a particular location can be tested using estimates of β. Second, an alternative specification to the spatial lag model is the spatial error specification shown in equation (3.2):

$$y = X\beta + \mu; \qquad \mu = \lambda W \mu + \varepsilon \tag{3.2}$$

In equation (3.2), u is interpreted as the outcome of a spatial autoregressive process involving a weight matrix (W) and a spatial autoregressive coefficient (λ). The distinction between the spatial lag and spatial error specifications is important because in the former case, growth in one location is linked to growth in other locations, whereas in the latter case, linkages between locations occur via the error generation process. Third, estimates of how far growth travels over space can be computed using:

---

[9] Again, notice that the own-city growth rate was excluded in this calculation, an aspect that probably makes little difference except in cases where its share of beginning-of-period employment was large.

$$y = AX\beta + A\varepsilon \tag{3.3}$$

in which elements of the matrix $A=(I-\rho W)^{-1}$ show how a change in X in one location affects employment growth rates in other locations after taking all such spatial linkages into account. Column sums of A have the interpretation of spatial multipliers. Of course, A depends on an estimate of ρ and the specification of W, issues considered more fully in following sections. Yet, it is enough at this point to see that the approach taken here allows different types of agglomeration economies to affect growth in the area where they were generated as well as at other locations. Moreover, this approach is more general than simply including measures of agglomeration economies at other locations as explanatory variables in a regression equation. Whereas this procedure, used by Anselin, Varga, and Acs (1997), shows the partial effect of an agglomeration economy measure in one location on a variable of interest in another location, equation (3.2) allows computation of both the partial *and* total effects of agglomeration economies over space.

A related technical tool that can be used to capture spatial structure of the phenomena studied is the definition of the independent variables in spatially lagged form. Definitions spatial externality explanatory variables are multiple, and careful selection and testing of these variables on their spatial 'reach' is time-consuming but worthwhile. When measurement units are small, as is the case in the analyses in our study, definition of variables as window averages or spatial lags are potentially appropriate, depending on the theoretical spatial hypotheses concerned (Anselin 1995a, 1988). As explained, a spatially lagged variable[10] or a spatial lag is a weighted average of the values of the variable in locations neighboring each observation. For the construction of these kind of (explaining) variables, a spatial weight matrix is necessary, indicating connections or distances between locations. Applying the procedure to location-industry observations as discussed above, inter- and intra-industry matrices of 'functional connections' can be made, useful for testing spatial and inter- and intra-industry hypotheses of growth. By convention, the diagonal elements of a spatial weights matrix are set to zero. As a result, the value for each observation itself is not included in the computation of a spatial lag. This may be achieved by means of a window average spatial transformation in which the value for each observation is incorporated in the computation of a spatially smoothed variable[11]. In the empirical analyses presented in chapters 5 to 7, both spatially lagged variables and window averaged spatial variables are used for testing hypotheses of agglomeration economies. As will be outlined in chapter 4, this study uses full distance weight matrices (of order one, two and three). In location-industry analyses, (possibly up to six) industries in the same location are assumed to be distributed evenly over the surface of the location in question. In

---

[10] Following Anselin 1995a we assign a spatially lagged variable by the *W_variable* notation.

[11] Assigned by *WA_variable* notation. See for a clear empirical application Buettner (1999). Window-averaged variables are only meaningful if the weight matrix used is in unstandardized form (Anselin 1995a, p.18-2).

general, spatial dependency diminishes when using higher order weight matrices. Research by Van Wissen (2000) reveals that distance decay functions differ over industries in the Netherlands. In sectoral and location-industry analyses in our analyses it will always be indicated which distance weight matrix is used for estimation.

Spatial Regime Modeling

A fourth distinction in spatial modeling that influences the interpretation of spatial externalities concerns the focus on spatial heterogeneity as form of spatial dependency, as opposed to spatially autocorrelated, proximity or contiguous dependency[12]. Spatial heterogeneity stresses the lack of uniformity of the effects of space (Anselin 1988). Several theorized and empirical factors, such as central place hierarchies, the existence of leading and lagging locations and regions and vintage effects in urban growth, argue for modeling strategies that take into account these particular features of spatial units different than (contiguous) proximity. This is to accommodate the observed heterogeneity in terms of degree of urbanism, functional connectedness, spatial labor market influences and physical accessibility as emerging from the literature. In spatial econometric work, this can be carried out by explicitly considering varying parameters, random coefficients or forms of structural change such as switching regressions (Goldstein 1995). A lack of structural stability of various phenomena over space causes the spatial units of observation themselves to be far from homogeneous. To the extent that aspects of heterogeneity are reflected in measurement errors (missing variables or functional mis-specification) they may result in heteroskedasticity. The particular contribution of spatial econometrics to the heterogeneity problem consists of applying insights from regional science theory on spatial structures and spatial interaction as the basis for various constraints and re-parameterizations. It is clear that spatial heterogeneity in the economic growth process and in innovation diffusion forms an important ingredient for its understanding and explanation, especially focusing on urban-hierarchical relationships. Spatial heterogeneity can be introduced in econometric modeling by either spatial regimes or spatial (variable) expansion methods. The former concerns an effective and at the same time simple model of structural instability in the situation where the regression parameters take on distinct values in subsets of the sample. In applied regional science this could easily be the case, for example when data are used for recent and older settlement areas, for urban and rural locations, for functionally connected locations and unconnected ones or for central cities and suburban locations[13]. For both the South-Holland research area and the Netherlands, several spatial regimes were identified in order

---

[12] Obviously, contiguous and heterogeneity specifications of spatial structure can be jointly applied in models in order to capture significant spatial dependence.

[13] See for examples Anselin *et al.* 2000, Barkley *et al.* 1996, Boarnet 1994, Coffey *et al.* 1996, Florax and Folmer 1992, Y. Kim *et al.* 2000, Steinnes 1977 and Thurston and Yezer 1994.

to capture hypothesized spatial heterogeneity. These will be discussed in the next section.

3.4   Identifying Spatial Heterogeneity in Regimes

Earlier Studies: the Netherlands an Urban Field?

History, as well as earlier research, sheds light on long-term developments of employment in cities and urban systems in the Netherlands. This section briefly discusses this literature and concludes on important spatial configuration for growth that come to the fore in it. The next sections will then analyze the data for the Netherlands (1991-1997) and South-Holland (1988-1997), in order to combine and interpret the patterns found with the existing literature and distinguish potentially relevant spatial regimes that will be used in later modeling.

By history, the Netherlands is covered by many, but rather small or medium-sized cities (Brakman *et al.* 2001, Burke, 1956). Since the Dutch Golden Age (seventeenth century) the system in Holland of cities (Amsterdam, Haarlem, Leiden, The Hague, Delft, Rotterdam, Gouda and Dordrecht) complementing and competing each other in terms of economic growth never lost its primacy to other cities in the country. During the Golden Age they were relative large cities in a European context (De Vries 1984). The nineteenth and early twentieth centuries though did not bring a large extension of the (urban) growth process. In the 19th century the economic position of the Netherlands was poor when compared to other European regions, and industrialization and emphasis of core industries as typical for that time did not develop or only relatively late (Van der Knaap 1978). Internationally, Holland lost its favorable growth rank to especially London and Paris. Nationally, medium-sized cities in the Dutch periphery grew faster and became relatively more important in the urban hierarchy (Kooij 1988). But still, in absolute terms the cities in Holland (united in the term Randstad Holland) remained the most important in the country: this region still is the economic core region of the country.

After the Second World War the processes of industrialization and urbanization kept in pace with developments elsewhere in Europe. The Netherlands never became a real industry-based country though, business and consumer services and distribution activities are still the most important economic sectors. As in all European countries, over the last 20 years a tendency towards a larger scale of urban functioning is found (Van der Laan 1998). Cities develop into urban regions and agglomerations. Daily urban systems grow larger in reach and suburbanization of population and (as is lately observed) following employment spread economic activity over larger areas (Bruinsma *et al.* 2002). As in other countries, these processes of suburbanization are selective, both for population (only the well to do can pay real estate in suburban locations and transport) and economic activities (firms requiring space and accessibility tend to move out of cities first). Because the urban system in the Netherlands consists of many medium-sized urban agglomerations within close proximity of each other, especially in the Randstad region[14], visually cities grow together, complement each other and seem to form the perfect example of an urban network of economic activities (Hall 1977, Batten 1995, Lambooy 1998b, Atzema and Lambooy 1999). Much of the present discussions on firm externalities caused by information-dense environments in combination with productivity and economic (employment) growth seems to be embedded in a theoretical, visionary environment as depicted in the Randstad urban region. Empirical testing for it only occurred fragmentally.

Some research has been undertaken though, that shows that (local) spatial growth processes are not as negligible as suggested. In an important study, Van der Vegt and Manshanden (1996) find that for the past 25 years, the urban cores of cities grew in terms of employment and production, albeit less than their environments. Also found is that the number of jobs in central cities in the period 1983-1995 do not tend to decline any further. The qualitative structure of employment does change rapidly though, stressing producer and consumer services more. Van der Vegt and Manshanden only briefly indicate which agglomerative forces might be responsible for this, it is not tested for empirically. Differences in labor productivity rates are not found to differ significantly within and between urban agglomerations (in 1995). Another striking outcome of this research is the relatively stable proportions of employment and population concentrations over urban cores, urban environment and autonomous locations over time (1975-1995). In sum, these results do not unambiguously clarify the relation between agglomeration and economic growth. Hoekveld (1999) and Louter (1999) combine localized economic growth in the Netherlands (measured by employment growth) and spatial processes of change in conceptual models. In terms of Louter (1999), the spatial trends distinguished are fourfold. The first concerns urban hierarchical growth patterns. Complementary cities are supposed to have an (unmeasured) network facilitated by urban size, especially concerning office accommodation and growth of consumer and producer services, as well as retail facilities (Pred 1973, 1977, Hepworth 1989). Economic specialization of locations determines which activities are most profitably in urban central locations and which are not. Notably, even retail and office activities are not glued as firmly to specialized urban cores as the description of this trend suggests, many of these activities seem to suburbanize as much as other activities (compare Lang 2000). Therefore, the second spatial diffusion trend noticed is that of concentric diffusive growth. Economic growth requires growth of businesses to be accommodated and therefore space to become available nearby (or not too far away from) the present location to fulfil the needs of firms and their employees. From economic concentrations outwards, the spatial growth process diffuses simultaneously over different spatial scales. The two most observed patterns concern suburbanization out of individual cities (within the relevant agglomerations) and de-concentration from the Randstad core region towards regions that are contiguous neighbors to it (the so-called Intermediate

---

[14] The distance between the city-centres of Amsterdam, Haarlem, Leiden, The Hague, Delft, Rotterdam, Gouda and Utrecht is on average 20 kilometres.

Zone). The third spatial growth tendency marked, concerns developments in and alongside corridors of important (inter-)national transport links between economic foci. Not all growth patterns can be placed in these three spatial regimes of growth, and therefore the fourth type of economic growth locations is labeled 'autonomous impulses'. When autonomous developments can take place anywhere in larger functional area with the same degree of possibility, Hoekveld (1999) argues we can speak of an urban field development (as introduced, on an incomparable US spatial scale, by Friedmann and Miller 1965). When exactly developments are autonomous and what the functional area(s) in the Netherlands should be remains unclear. Empirical studies do not unambiguously clarify the causal processes behind them, and because of the dense system of medium-seized and smaller cities in the Netherlands, it is also often not clear in which (of the four) diffusion trends local economic growth most suitably fits. From the literature on economic growth in the Netherlands four sources of spatial heterogeneity emerge: (1) the distinction Randstad, Intermediate Zone and Periphery; (2) a distinction to urban hierarchy; (3) a distinction according to positions in agglomerations (urban core, suburban) and (4) locations in accessible transport corridors. When these spatial classifications are related to economic growth and innovation patterns, the urban field is probably not the preferred spatial structure to speak of in the Netherlands. The next sections will translate the suggested heterogeneity in the literature into spatial regimes.

Spatial Regimes in South-Holland

Contiguous spatial units of analysis employed in urban and regional research usually displays considerable internal heterogeneity in terms of economic, social or demographic variables used to describe them (Kephart 1988). Spatial regimes can be designed to capture this, not necessarily contiguous spatial, heterogeneity.

The research area of South-Holland, located in the south-western edge of the Randstad (the core economic region of the Netherlands). Figure 3.2 shows the research area and the population density on the 4-digit zip code level. It comprises the urban agglomerations of the second and third largest city in the Netherlands: Rotterdam and The Hague. The harbor of Rotterdam is regarded a major economic growth pole, containing five of the largest oil refineries in the world, and numerous large and medium-sized firms in physical distribution activities. The economic significance of this industrial complex in the Rotterdam harbor region alone has been estimated on 120,000 employed persons with an added value of 13 billion US dollars (NREB 1999).

Figure 3.2　　　**The research area of South-Holland**

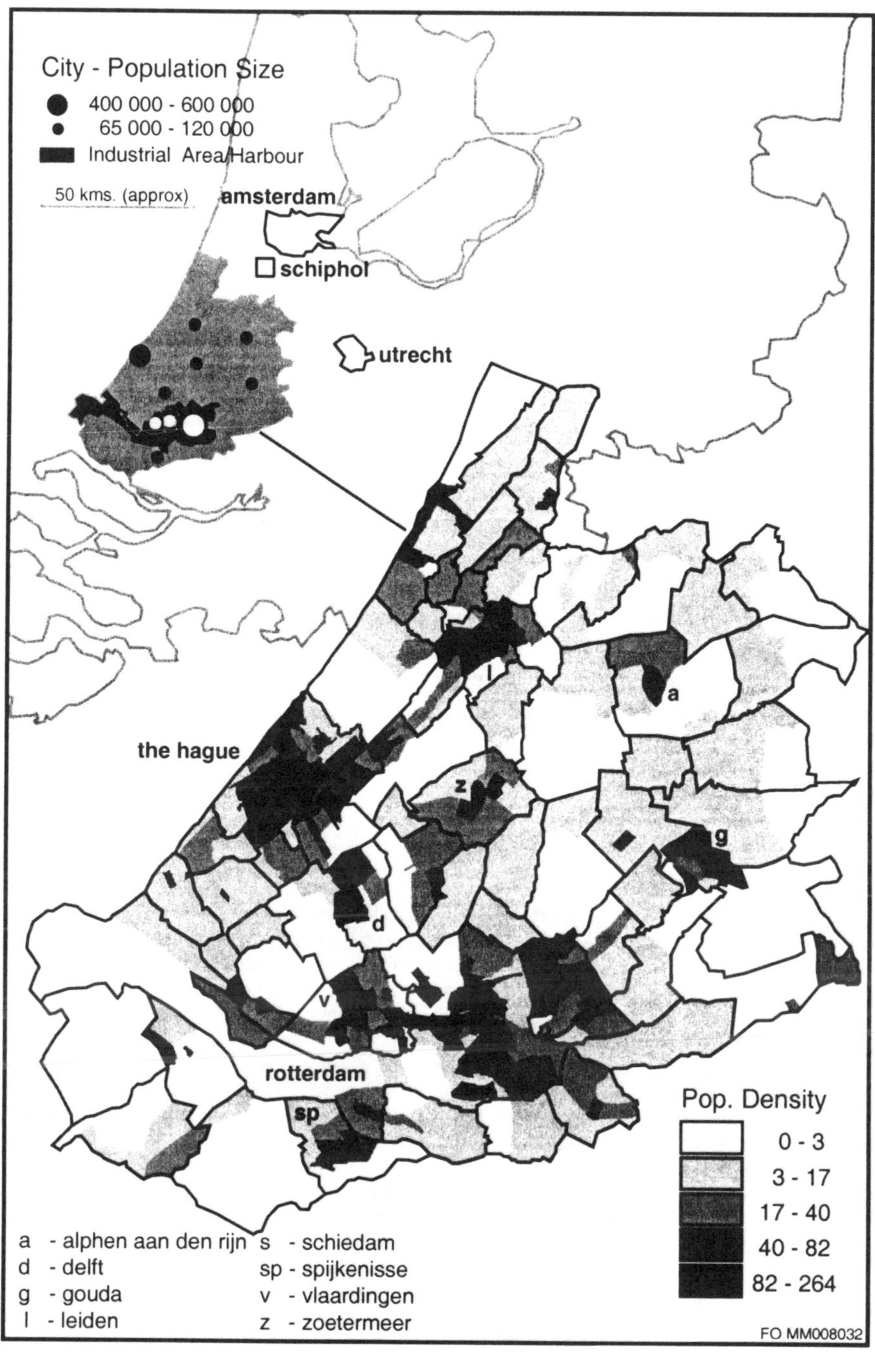

The province of South-Holland is heavily urbanized, and hence all observations are included in the dataset. However, not all areas are urbanized equally, and hence we will include an indicator of the *degree* of urbanization. This indicator will be used to distinguish urban and work-area spatial regimes as discussed in the previous section as well. On the zip code level in the South-Holland research area, *urban areas* can be distinguished from non-urban ones. The distinctions between these areas on the low spatial level are made, based on the density of addresses and urban functions present in locations. Applying these criteria, 62% of the observations for South-Holland are located in urban as opposed to more rural areas (see figures 3.3 and 3.4)[15]. Either by (1) interacting this variable with the spatial knowledge externality indicators, using them as individual explanatory variables or (2) transforming them into spatial regimes, insight is gained in the potential differences in the growth process and innovation intensity in more and less heavily urbanized areas. Within the distinction urban-non urban, locations can be predominantly occupied by living, working or mixed functions (Brouwer *et al.* 2001)[16]. Locations that are purely occupied by *working functions* often (but not necessarily) are industrial sites[17]. More than the South-Holland average of opening up of *industrial sites* in the research period is an important control variable in our modeling, because they attract new firms and economic growth more than other areas tend to do (compare Blackley 1985 and Carlton 1982)[18]. These locations together potentially function as spatial regime in econometric models in the next chapter as well. In a similar manner a spatial regime has been constructed concerning *relative accessible locations* as opposed to inaccessible ones. The average distance to highway entries and exits of all locations in the South-Holland research area is measured. The upper half of the resulting distribution is assigned 'good accessible', the lower half as 'less accessible'[19].

---

[15] The focus and emphasis on urban areas in this and previous studies does not mean that non-urban regions and areas are characterized by a lack of (endogenous) growth potential or spatial clustering of activities (compare Y. Kim *et al* 2000). Several conditions of agglomeration economies are (on theoretical grounds) supposed to function more profound in urban agglomerations though.

[16] An important identification issue emerging from the literature that needs to be addressed here concerns local zoning regulations. Variation across metropolitan areas abstracts from zoning laws, since such laws are typically set *within* metropolitan areas. Given the small units of analyses used in this dissertation, local zoning regulations are likely to be an important factor in determining establishment locations. For example, finding that retail stores tend to concentrate in downtown commercial districts should not necessarily lead to conclude that there are agglomeration externalities, if zoning laws require retail stores to locate in such districts. In the Dutch context however, spatial policy aimed and aims at optimal freedom of location choice of retail and business establishments, especially at the local level. Also, zoning laws that did exist for non-retail industries proved *not* to have functioned as such in the period 1988-1997 (Van Oort 2002a).

[17] Correlation values between the spatial regimes urban, workarea, opening up industrial sites and accessibility are smaller than 0.5 (exact data are available on request).

[18] Source: calculations based on RPD (1998).

[19] Source: calculations based on WMD (1999).

Figure 3.3   **Dominant occupations in urban locations in South-Holland (regimes, 1993)**

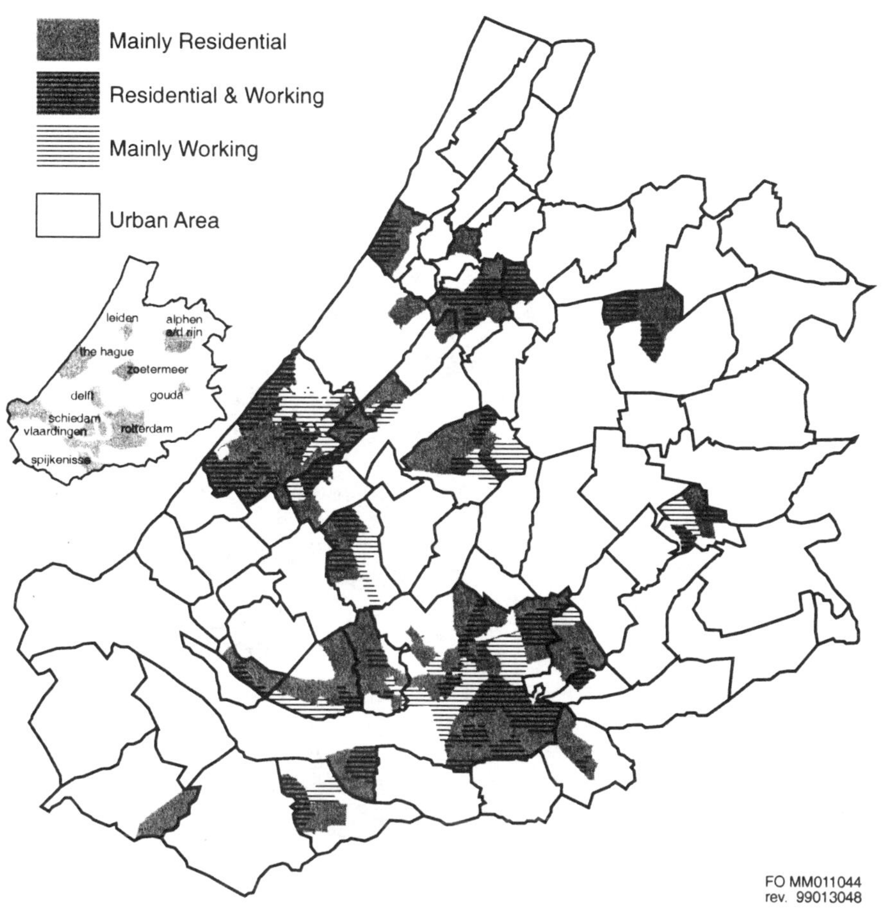

Figure 3.4   **Dominant occupations in non-urban locations in South-Holland (regimes, 1993)**

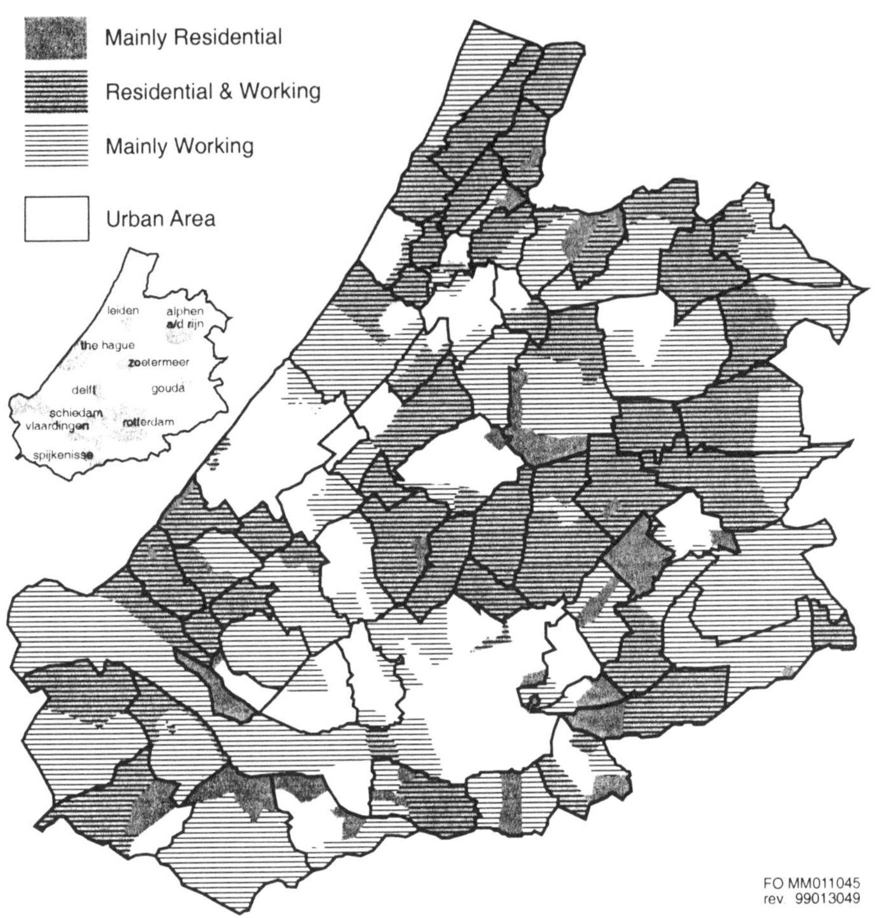

Spatial Regimes in the Netherlands

Spatial heterogeneity on the national level has been captured by several spatial regimes. Two of these are assigned similar to spatial regimes as for the South-Holland research area: degree of *physical accessibility* and the more than average issuing and presence of *industrial sites* over the research period. For both regimes, the Netherlands is reference now (instead of South-Holland) and cities or municipalities are measurement units. A third spatial regime is designed around the *degree of urbanization*. A threefold set of regimes is designed. All 580 municipalities are classified as either being (part of) large cities (the 3-digit zip code observations in Amsterdam, Rotterdam, The Hague and Utrecht), medium-sized cities (larger than 45,000 inhabitants and smaller than 200,000, comparable to Van der Knaap and Louter 1986)[20] and small cities or rural municipalities. Some hypotheses in the literature are postulated in favor of the largest cities and their locational externalities as being important for economic growth (e.g. Ades and Glaeser 1995, Coffey *et al.* 1996). Medium-sized cities in the Netherlands are argued to have favorable production milieus and structures that enhance spatial externalities (and avoid negative ones) for innovation and growth in several studies (e.g. Van Dinteren 1989, Van der Knaap 2002). By tradition, empirical studies have contributed to formulating economic growth and innovation hypotheses for the non-urban locations in the Netherlands as well (see notably Vaessen 1993).

A fourth set of spatial regimes concerns the *macro-zoning of the Netherlands* into the Randstad (core region), an intermediate zone and the national periphery. This is a distinction that is quite commonly used in the Dutch geographical literature, but lacks a common, empirically determined definition. The definition applied in this research is based on a potential model of employment over Dutch municipalities. We explicitly want this notion of agglomerative zoning to be different from concepts as daily urban system and urban agglomeration caused by overrepresentation (specialization) and diversification of economic sectors in urban areas, which are usually seen as expressions of local agglomeration as well as (indirect) spillover indicators. A local score on a national agglomeration indicator should take into account the employment structure present in all other possible localities as well, corrected for distances (Haggett *et al.* 1977, Taylor 1975). The gravity model for (total) employment in the 580 municipalities is distinguished on the national level, making use of the formula:

$$P_i = \sum_{i \neq j} \frac{M_j}{d_{ij}^{\,\alpha}} + \frac{M_i}{d_{ii}^{\,\beta}} \qquad\qquad (3.4)$$

---

[20] Note that medium-sized cities in the American context are much larger. Henderson (1997a, p.586) for instance defines medium-sized cities as having 100,000 to 0.5 million inhabitants, while the smallest metro-area by definition must exceed 50,000 (p.588).

in which P is the gravity value of region i, measured by total employment (M) in the locality itself as well as in all other localities, the latter being corrected for distances (d). We took aggregated employment as a measure, for (as was discussed in the previous section) it is perceived as the most prominent (as well as available) indicator of economic density. By measuring the economic potential value for individual localities in this manner, spatial moving averages are constructed. Individual points (local employment) and lines (distances) have been transformed into surfaces of national agglomeration. Physical distances are extracted from a GIS-database and the intra-regional distance is calculated by means of the formula:

$$d_{ii} = \frac{2}{3} \sqrt{\frac{A_i}{\pi}} \qquad\qquad (3.5)$$

in which the intra-regional distance d is two thirds of the radius of the presumed circular area A (see Bröcker (1989) and Frost and Spence (1995) for the exact derivation and overview of considerations of this). The values of α and β, measuring the magnitude of the intra- and interregional distance decay, is set at one for national gravity values. Rising of α and β from one to three means that distances play a more dominant role and the patterns of zoning would become more local. Figure 3.5 illustrates the resulting pattern of this indicator for α and β set to 1 for total employment presence[21]. Using this map's legend (with an even range distribution of observations) we can distinguish more properly the much acclaimed three-folding macro-economic division in Randstad core region, intermediate zone and national periphery[22]. The six classes of observation are split in three macro-zones of employment gravity. As mentioned in the previous section, the Randstad region then consists of the four largest cities in the Netherlands, as well as numerous medium-sized cities in their surroundings (Haarlem, Delft, Leiden, Zoetermeer, Gouda) as well as their suburban municipalities. The intermediate zone consists of parts of the provinces Noord-Brabant, Gelderland and Utrecht while the national periphery mainly consists of the northern provinces, Limburg and Zeeland. Mapping sectors as distinguished in the previous sections, making use of the same gravity formula, reveals a striking different pattern for the industrial production sector. Industrial activities tend to be far more spread towards the southern part of the country than other activities.

---

[21] The same gravity model ($\alpha=1$) and map made for population reflects a similar pattern, the correlation coefficient with employment is for presence 0.92 (significant at the 0.01 level, n=580).

[22] The relevance of the traditionally anchored division in Ranstad – intermediate zone – national periphery is most strongly expressed and empirically tested for by Atzema and Lambooy (1999), Van der Knaap (1978), Van der Knaap and Louter (1986), Manshanden (1996) and Van Oort (1994).

Figure 3.5   Gravity model (macro-zoning regimes) for employment (α,β=1; 1997)

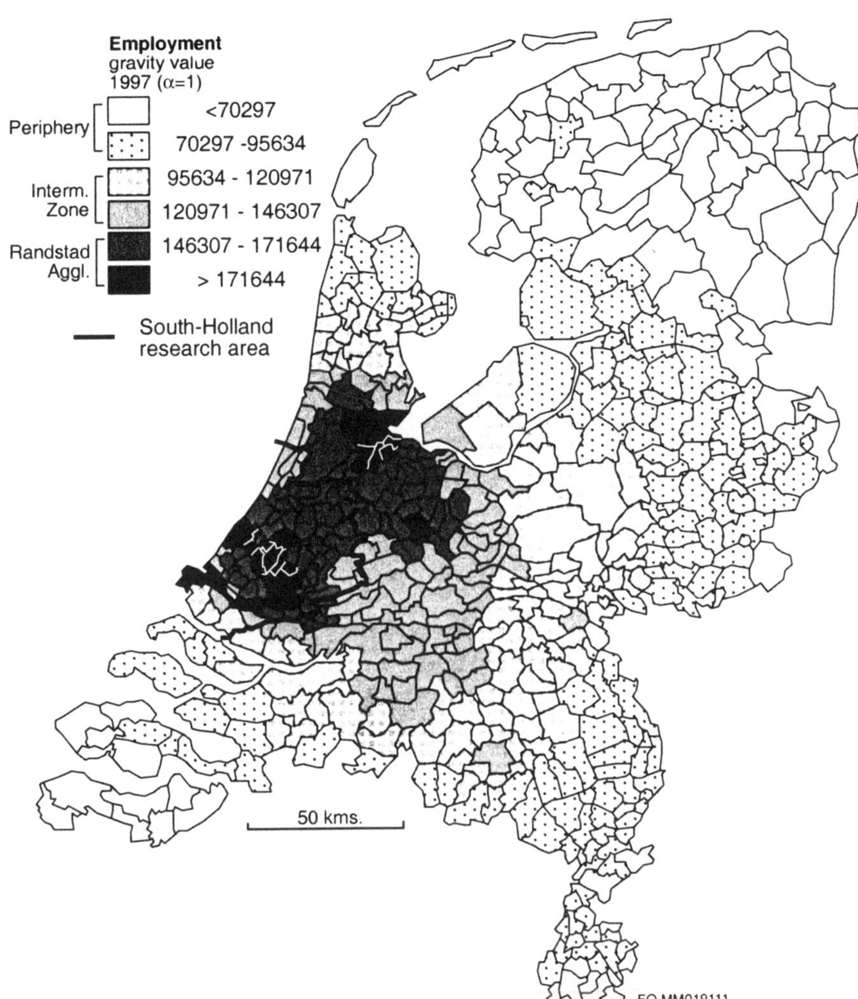

Especially concentrations and complexes of industrial activity in the Geleen/Sittard region (DSM Chemicals and Volvo-car factory), Eindhoven (Philips), Breda, Venlo and Tilburg pull the national spatial gravity of these activities away from the Randstad region towards the southern and eastern regions. Producer and consumer services and distribution activities make up most of the total employment, these activities show spatial patterns very similar to figure 3.5. The patterns of employment gravity can be compared over years, in order to reveal shifts in the national gravity pattern. Figure 3.6 shows the average percentage change in gravity value in the period 1991-1997 for employment. Positive development of the gravity value occurs mainly in the province of Utrecht, in the Intermediate Zone and in the area between the four largest cities in the Randstad region. The largest cities themselves (with the exception of Utrecht) do not show the highest gravity growth. The regions around the largest cities (Amsterdam, Rotterdam and The Hague) show low development values.

Within the Randstad region, an important distinction is often hypothesized (and proven) by the so-called *north-wing* (incorporating Amsterdam and Utrecht) and the *south-wing* (incorporating Rotterdam and The Hague). This in the sense that higher growth rates and more favorable conditions for agglomeration externalities are to be found in the north-wing. This is believed to be due to sectoral composition (more producer service orientation, as opposed to governmental services and industrial activities connected to The Hague and the Rotterdam harbor respectively), better living environments and better international accessibility (Schiphol airport). A threefold set of spatial regimes, containing municipalities in respectively the *north-wing, south-wing* and other locations (n=580), is used to test whether this hypothesis of spatial heterogeneity is structural for which types of economic activities. Figure 3.7 shows the spatial regimes of the north- and south-wing of the Randstad[23]. Figure 3.6 suggests that the distinction north-wing as opposed to south-wing of the Randstad appears (visibly) relevant (see also Van der Knaap and Louter 1986)[24].

---

[23] By defining these spatial regimes we made use of spatial groupings in De Jong (1987), Knol and Manshanden (1990) and Van der Knaap and Louter (1986). The grouping of municipalities is not identical to either one of them, a major difference is the fact that the boundaries of the Green Heart (the open space between the north- and south-wing) were not respected in detail, in order to avoid too much spatial fragmentation.

[24] Of course the gravity models applied, by their nature average out local patterns and developments in favour of an optimum-seeking model (only one location has the highest gravity value). By setting the values of α and β at 3 for instance (measuring the magnitude of the intra- and interregional distance decay) the result will show local pockets of growth instead of the zoning, global pattern of growth. Comparison and testing revealed that values of 3 for α and β in 1991 and 1997 significant correlates to measuring the actual presence and percentage growth of employment in municipalities as measured without distance decay functions (r=0.91 and 0.33 respectively, n=580). The technique of exploratory spatial data analysis (ESDA) applied in chapter 4 shows *both* global and local spatial autocorrelation patterns, combines more information into one analysis and is therefore superior.

Figure 3.6　Percentage change in gravity values for employment ($\alpha,\beta=1$; 1991-1997)

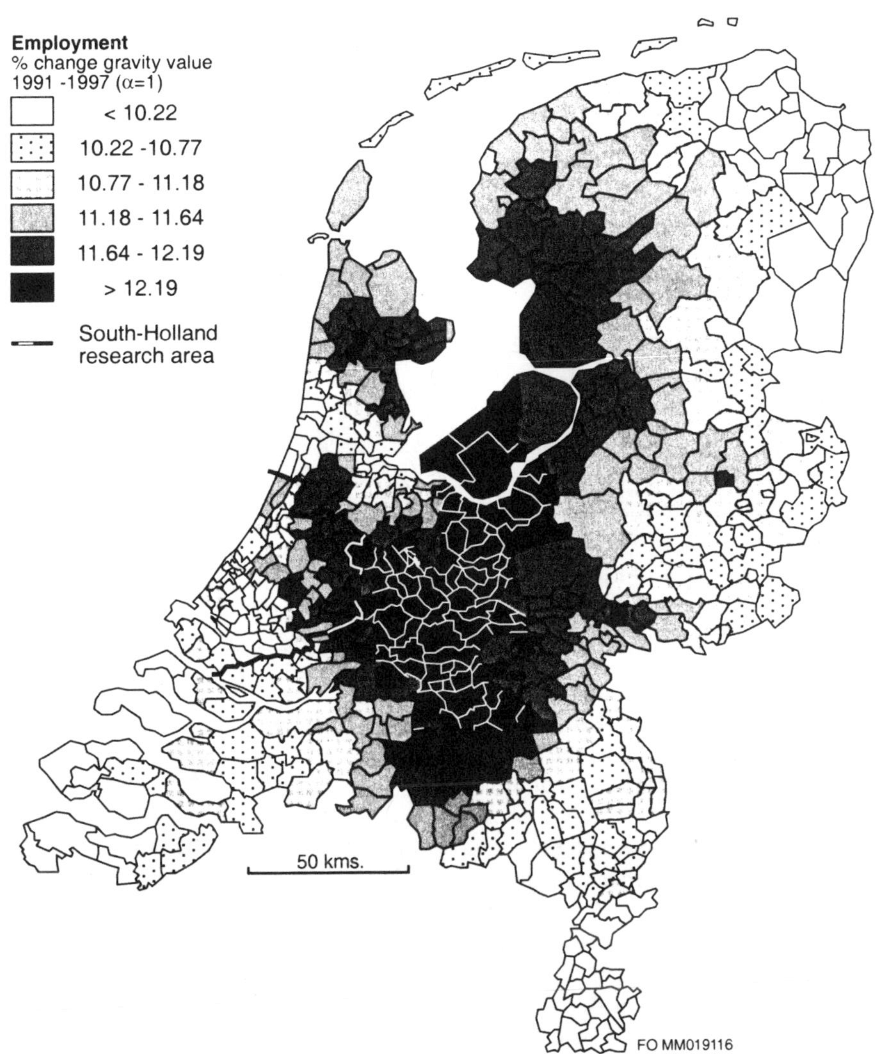

Figure 3.7   North- and south-wing of the Randstad (spatial regimes)

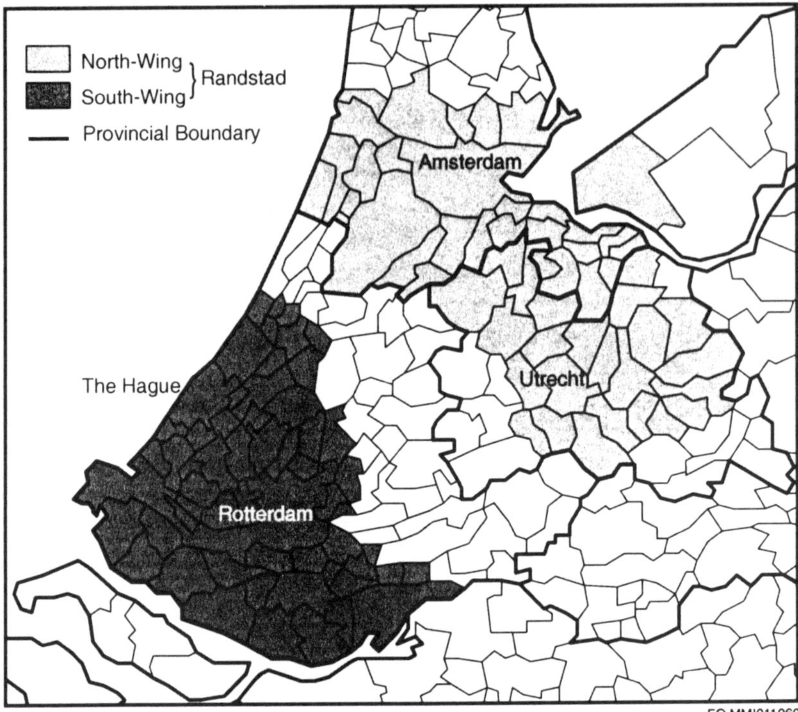

A final classification in regimes is at the level of the daily urban system in the Netherlands. This concerns the so-called *connectedness* of municipalities in terms of functional economic (commuting) linkages as introduced in for instance Brown and Holmes (1971). Anselin *et al.* (2000) in their analyses of knowledge externalities extend the urban definition beyond a hierarchical urban (municipality) regime and find significant differences for knowledge spillovers in connected (central core and suburban) as opposed to unconnected locations. One of the main theories underlying localization economies, since Marshall, postulates that urban labor markets benefit from increased job search efficiency (see chapter 2). The probability of good labor demand and supply matches is an increasing function of the labor market (Helsey and Strange 1990, Van der Knaap *et al.* 1995). By generating better matches and favoring higher specialization, large labor markets result in higher worker productivity. Within the South-Holland research area, all zip codes are within reasonable commuting distances (Van Ham *et al.* 2001), so increased job search efficiency within agglomerations is not an issue in these analyses. On the national level though it definitely is, and therefore the construction of a set of spatial regimes explicitly focuses on connected versus unconnected municipalities. Four types of locations have been distinguished, initially based on municipal data.

Figure 3.8   **The 'connectedness' spatial regime (1990)**

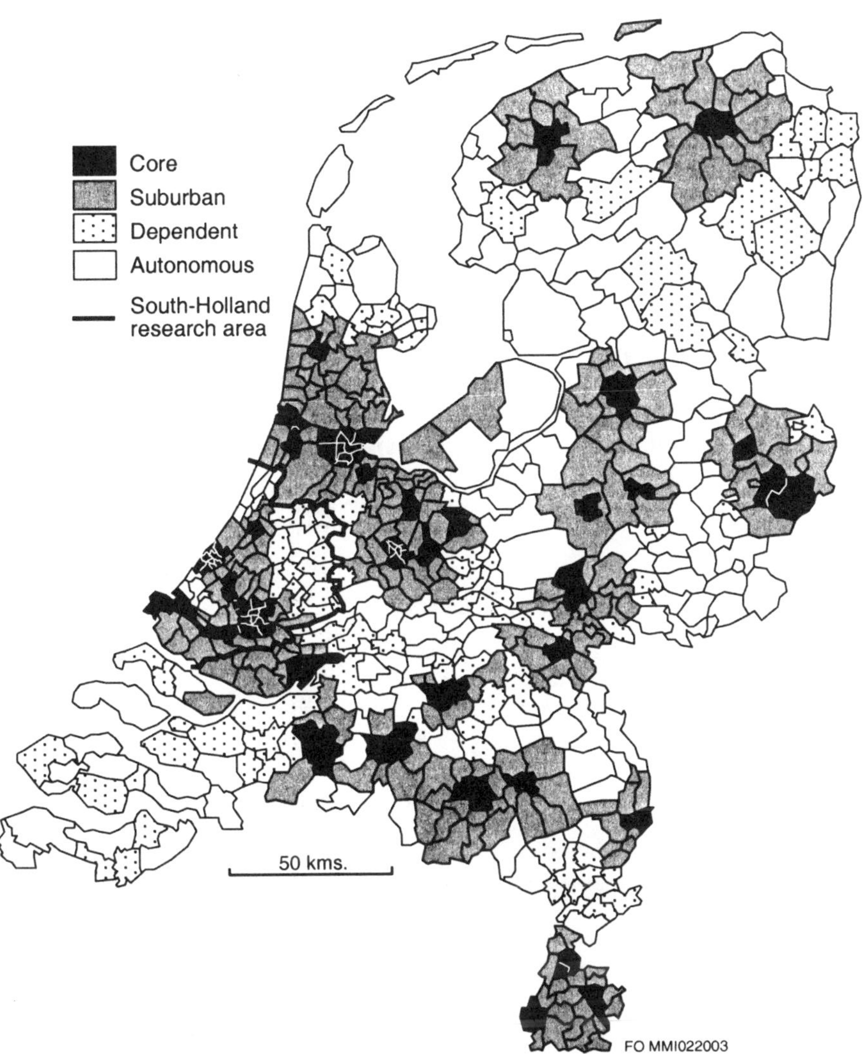

The classification is based on the dependency of a municipality's population upon employment and services proximity and commuting accessibility in 1990 (see figure 3.8). Urban core areas have an important employment function. More than 15,000 persons commute into these municipalities (while living somewhere else) on a daily basis. Five sub-centers of core areas have been distinguished. These areas have more than 15,000 in-commuting persons but between 10 to 20% of the municipality's working population works in a neighboring large(r) city. Suburban municipalities of the sub-core centers are also very much directed towards these larger core areas[25]. Municipalities from which more than 20% of residents commute to central (or sub-central) core locations are labeled suburban[26]. Together the urban core and suburban municipalities make up the urban agglomerations labeled 'connected'. The remaining municipalities (labeled 'unconnected') have been divided into two groups: dependent and autonomous. Autonomous municipalities have a high (>1) score on the location quotient for employment[27].

Table 3.3   Observations in the regimes on national zoning and connectedness (absolute and share)

Connected ↓ *Zoning* →	Randstad	Interme-diate zone	National Periphery	Total
Core Location	40	14	11	65
	6.9%	2.4%	1.9%	11.2%
Suburban	63	102	79	244
	10.9%	17.6%	13.6%	42.1%
Dependent	15	38	48	101
	2.6%	6.6%	8.3%	17.4%
Autonomous	8	48	114	170
	1.4%	8.3%	19.7%	29.3%
Total	126	202	252	580
	21.7%	34.8%	43.4%	100%

---

[25] The five sub-centres are Haarlem (core-area Amsterdam), Zeist (Utrecht), Delft (The Hague), Dordrecht (Rotterdam) and Helmond (Eindhoven).

[26] Incidentally, suburban municipalities themselves attract more than 15,000 in-commuters. This indicates the development of polycentric and edge-city types of urban structures. These municipalities are still designed to be 'suburban'.

[27] The four largest municipalities (all core locations in the Randstad core region) are split into 3-digit zip-code areas in order to make distinctions in harbour, central location and edge-city locations within municipalities possible. This resulted in 36 observations for Amsterdam (10), The Hague (9), Rotterdam (9) and Utrecht (8). In 1998 The Netherlands is build up by 548 municipalities, the four largest are replaced by the 36 3-digit zip code areas (still referred to as municipalities), making in total 580 observations.

In principle, these municipalities can be regarded as self-supporting. All remaining municipalities (that score less than 0.6 on the location quotient for employment) are designed as dependent. Their dependency can be either directed towards autonomous or agglomeration municipalities[28]. As becomes clear from table 3.3 most autonomous areas are located in the National Periphery. Suburban locations are mainly present in the Randstad core region and in the Intermediate Zone. The research area of South-Holland, our main focus of analysis on the lowest possible spatial scale, is within the Randstad core region.

Initially, as in the South-Holland analyses, spatial regimes with (the degree of) predominant work-area functions, as opposed to predominant living and mixed areas, were constructed for the 580 municipalities. Correlation coefficients of a work-area regime with degree of urbanization turn out to be rather high, indicating that the two regimes do capture the same spatial heterogeneity (see table 3.4). Work-area regimes were therefore not individually explored in the spatial econometric models at the national level. All other correlation coefficients in table 3.4 do not show high values (except *within* sets of regimes), indicating they all capture some other aspect of (non-contiguous) spatial heterogeneity at the national level.

Table 3.4   Correlation coefficients of national spatial regimes (n=580)

		(1)	(2)	(3)	(4)	(5)	(6)	(7)	(8)
(1)	industrial site	1.000	-0.18	0.04	0.132	-0.12	-0.03	-0.04	0.04
(2)	Randstad	-	1.00	-0.41	-0.51	0.31	0.34	0.22	0.35
(3)	intermed. zone	-	-	1.00	-0.57	-0.06	0.03	-0.05	0.19
(4)	nat. periphery	-	-	-	1.00	-0.22	-0.34	-0.15	-0.05
(5)	degree urban	-	-	-	-	1.00	0.32	0.60	0.26
(6)	accessible	-	-	-	-	-	1.00	0.29	0.15
(7)	working	-	-	-	-	-	-	1.00	0.34
(8)	connected	-	-	-	-	-	-	-	1.00

Descriptive Analysis of National Spatial Regimes

Because the national zoning regime (Randstad – intermediate zone – national periphery) and the connectedness regime potentially are important spatial sources for heterogeneity in economic growth and innovation, we will simultaneously analyze them in this section. Simultaneous analysis enables us to focus on interaction effects of employment structure and growth effects. Simultaneous regime estimation (in combination with spatial lag or error modeling) cannot be

---

[28] Autonomous municipalities not being urban core areas or commuting flows smaller than 15,000 persons prohibit the dependent municipalities to be labeled suburban.

integrated into econometric modeling in sections to follow because of limitations in computation capacity. Table 3.5 gives employment and population data for the two agglomeration classifications (zoning and connectedness) separate ('total' column and row) and in combination. Data are presented in absolute and percentage (shares of total) terms for 1997, as well as in average yearly growth for the period 1991-1997. Some remarkable patterns come to the fore in the table. Employment growth in all types of locations is larger than population growth. Since we measure growth in jobs, part-time job growth and flexible working hours are related to this. Still, suburban employment and population growth is relatively larger in magnitude. Suburban and autonomous locations show most favorable growth rates, especially in the intermediate zone. Both employment and population are spread evenly over the Randstad, intermediate zone and national periphery (all three have a share of proximately one third of the 15.6 million inhabitants and 6.3 million jobs). Core locations inhabit most employment (41%), while its residential function is relatively smaller (33% of population share). This imbalance is mirrored in suburban locations (relatively high residential share and lower employment share), but the average growth figures show that this is (slowly) changing over time. Autonomous municipalities have on average equal shares of working and residential totals (both approximately 24%). The highest economic growth (in terms of employment change) occurs in the autonomous and suburban municipalities. Core municipalities in the Randstad show lower than average growth figures, both in population and employment. The dependent municipalities score weak in population dynamics, on average they even lose population. In general we can conclude that during the period 1991-1997 average employment change in all locations was positive, including the core municipalities of agglomerations. Core locations in the Randstad though did not catch up completely with the average growth score, while especially core locations in the intermediate zone as well as all types of locations in suburban and autonomous municipalities did. Population tended to grow fastest in locations where employment grew largest. The trend signaled, that employment in central cities (cores) does not decline in proportions as it did 10 to 20 years ago, is confirmed by our data. Although less than average, we signal even positive growth for these locations in general.

This does not indicate anything about the *qualitative* structure of employment in urban centers. Table 3.6 therefore gives for the two spatial regimes the sectoral representation of four types of activities: industry, distribution activities, producer services and consumer services (see previous section 3.2). The table presents the degree of over- or under-representation of these sectors by means of location quotients, as defined by:

$$LQ_i = \frac{E_{i,j} / \sum\limits_{j} E_{i,j}}{\sum\limits_{i} E_{i,j} / \sum\limits_{i,j} E_{i,j}} \tag{3.6}$$

Table 3.5   Employment and population in national spatial regimes (1997: absolute and share; 1991-1997: yearly percentage growth)

connected ↓	*zoning →*	Randstad core region	Intermediate zone	national periphery	total
core location	employment	1,224,518	870,019	528,457	262,2994
		19.34%	13.74%	8.35%	41.42%
		+0.6585%	+1.2579%	+1.0386%	+0.9307%
	population	*2,430,480*	*1,682,790*	*1,021,240*	*5,134,510*
		15.61%	*10.81%*	*6.56%*	*32.98%*
		+0.3788	*+0.8045*	*+0.5454*	*+0.5499*
suburban	employment	729,559	680,820	365,311	1,775,690
		11.52%	10.75%	5.77%	28.04%
		+1.7473%	+2.0550%	+0.8607%	+1.6741%
	population	*1,736,330*	*2,177,780*	*1,292,360*	*5,206,470*
		11.15%	*13.99%*	*8.30%*	*33.44%*
		+1.0309%	*+1.2768%*	*+0.5924%*	*+1.0216%*
dependent	employment	63,991	179,613	157,324	400,928
		1.01%	2.84%	2.48%	6.33%
		+2.4923%	+1.6020%	+0.7845%	+1.4080%
	population	*214,090*	*546,260*	*603,150*	*1,363,500*
		1.38%	*3.51%*	*3.88%*	*8.76%*
		+0.3899%	*-0.3729%*	*-0.3055%*	*-0.2264%*
autonomous	employment	111,486	486,719	934,703	1,532,908
		1.76%	7.69%	14.76%	24.21%
		+2.1895%	+1.7876%	+1.2361%	+1.4760%
	population	*251,580*	*1,220,190*	*2,390,830*	*3,862,600*
		1.62%	*7.84%*	*15.36%*	*24.81%*
		+1.5204%	*+1.2170%*	*+0.5948%*	*+0.8467%*
total	employment	2,129,554	2,217,171	1,985,795	6,332,520
		33.63%	35,01%	31.36%	100%
		+1.1504%	+1.6418%	+1.0774%	+1.2967%
	population	*4,632,480*	*5,627,020*	*5,307,580*	*15567,080*
		29.76%	*36,15%*	*34,09%*	*100%*
		+0.6797%	*+0.9517%*	*+0.4787%*	*+0.7077%*

in which E represents employment level and i and j the location and sector respectively. The location quotient thus calculates the employment share in sectors in a local economy compared to a reference distribution of sectoral shares (here in the Netherlands as a whole)[29]. A value of 1 indicates that the local economic structure equals the national one, higher values indicates a relative over-, lower values an under-representation. It becomes clear that industrial activities are under-

---

[29] In chapters 5 to 7 this location quotient defined for individual and location-industry sectors will be used as an explanatory variable.

represented in urban core locations in the Randstad, as opposed to core locations in the intermediate zone and national periphery. Industrial activities are relatively most present in autonomous locations in the intermediate zone and national periphery, as well as suburban locations in the National Periphery. Producer services, and to a lesser extent consumer services tend to be over-represented in urban core municipalities. Distribution activities are over-represented in suburban locations and autonomous locations in the Randstad. Core locations in general score extremely weakly on the representation of distribution activities: lack of expanding space, road congestion and relatively high prices for real estate and industrial sites make these municipalities less suitable for housing these activities. The overall picture for core locations therefore becomes extreme on all four types of activities: industrial and distribution activities score low in representation, producer and consumer services show the highest concentration ratios. Suburban municipalities score relatively evenly on representation of all four types of economic activities. The specialization patterns further show that the Randstad scores high on producer services, the intermediate zone scores evenly on all sectors (all scores around 1) and municipalities in the national periphery score highly on the presence of industrial employment.

The tables 3.5 and 3.6 underline the observed patterns as present in the literature concerning suburbanization of economic activities out of individual cities (within the relevant agglomerations) and macro-economic deconcentration from the Randstad core region towards regions that are close neighbors to it (the so-called intermediate zone).

3.5   Firm Life-Cycle Heterogeneity

Localized Competition and Firm Life-Cycles

Heterogeneity caused by firm-level life-cycle dynamics is incorporated in our study in two ways: (1) by the construction of localized competition indicators based on age and size structures and turbulence in (new, replacing shake-out) firms, and (2) by distinguishing incumbent populations of firms from new ones. The region of South-Holland, in chapters 4, 5 and 6 subject to a study of localized knowledge and growth externalities on the small spatial scale zip codes, allows us to focus on such components of change structuring employment growth. Not much empirical research is able to capture this dimension of heterogeneity properly in urban growth and innovation analysis (interesting recent contributions to this dimension are by Dumais *et al.* 2002, Rosenthal and Strange 2002 and Davis *et al.* 1996). It appears that the taxonomy of employment change can be wide, according to what is being researched. The geographical labor market literature often focuses on specific processes like job creation and destruction, employment growth and decline, hires and layoffs. These terms are central in the description and explanation of changes in number of jobs, changes in employment and flows of workers, respectively. The terms are interchanged frequently.

Table 3.6   Location quotients of employment in zoning and connectedness regimes (1997)[1]

connected ↓	*zoning* →	Randstad	Intermed. zone	National periphery	total
core location	industry	0.4975	1.1255	1.2179	0.8510
	distribution	0.8448	0.8753	0.7920	0.8443
	producer serv.	1.4967	1.1155	0.9235	1.2548
	consumer serv.	1.1765	1.0671	1.1462	1.1341
Suburban	industry	0.7417	0.9514	1.3874	0.9549
	distribution	1.3871	1.0856	1.0121	1.1943
	producer serv.	1.2868	0.8980	0.4844	0.9726
	consumer serv.	0.8179	0.9993	0.8832	0.9009
dependent	industry	0.9725	1.1496	0.9049	1.0253
	distribution	1.4575	1.2770	1.0469	1.2155
	producer serv.	0.7006	0.6150	0.5869	0.6176
	consumer serv.	0.6446	0.8067	0.8813	0.8101
autonomous	industry	0.8059	1.3068	1.3564	1.3006
	distribution	1.2193	1.0824	0.9063	0.9850
	producer serv.	1.1238	0.7821	0.5997	0.6958
	consumer serv.	0.8323	0.8815	0.9750	0.9350
total	industry	0.6116	1.1138	1.2895	1.0000
	distribution	1.0686	1.0179	0.9065	1.0000
	producer serv.	1.3813	0.9350	0.6637	1.0000
	consumer serv.	1.0197	0.9845	0.9963	1.0000

1   For industry classification: see appendix A.

As Hamermesh (1996, p.357) concludes, these terms seem to have no economic content as such and are certainly not obviously an issue in (mainstream) labor demand research. It is embedded in evolutionary economic and industrial organization studies that components of change approaches on life cycles have become more appreciated in economics recently.

Recently, Porter (1996, 1998), Van der Wiel (1999), Caroll and Hannan (2000) and Van Wissen (2000) remark that the role of competition in the economic processes of starting and ending businesses is a crucial factor related to economic growth. At the same time, they notice that in empirical research the relation between productivity, employment growth and business cycle dynamics of firms is very ambiguous. Our study uses firm-size concentration ratios (large firms are in general less exposed to competition than small ones) and firm-level turbulence (entrants and firm 'victims' of shake-out as indicators of carrying capacity alterations) on a spatial basis as indicators of local competition. Intuitively, it appears logical to 'explain' new firm formation rates and individual firm employment and productivity growth by the level of competition encountered: the market allows for entrants and hence growth if competition is more fierce. But using these volatility and size-concentration indicators as measures of competition (as in Glaeser *et al.* 1992) implies that certain (maybe unintended) theoretical implications should be addressed (compare Henderson 2003). We will shortly discuss four of them. First, one could argue that entrants in business services (the industry most prominent in sectoral growth in the Netherlands) might operate in niche markets, and are in first instance not competing directly against incumbents. Over the years, business service (as well as industrial products) markets may have become more segmented, where entrants probably pursue a strategy of seeking new segments and products, whereas incumbents stick to their regular customers. On the *regional scale* though, firm births and employment growth are in general found to be positively linked (see for instance Ashcroft and Love 1996). On the one hand this means that turbulence indicators are to some degree endogenous on employment growth by construction. On the other hand it means that explanations of endogenous employment growth in terms of agglomeration variables potentially benefit from controlling growth rates explicitly for business entrants and exits. Second, business service and industrial product markets may not yet be in equilibrium. New firms, either viable or incompetent, are attracted to the market. A measurable relation between a price-cost margin, concentration rate and productivity growth might then only become apparent in the long-run (future). Rapidly changing demand opportunities, measurement difficulties, a possible lack of or insufficient competitive pressure because of niche markets, insufficient managerial effort or shift in demand towards new products possibly disguise a clear positive relation between entrants dynamics and economic (productivity) growth. Third, not all large firms by definition are embedded in less competitive market structures than small firms (Harrison 1994). It should be realized that this proposition is highly stylized and general. Fourth, local competition not always has a clear hypothesized influence on employment growth of firms that produce traded goods. Establishments that produce traded goods potentially compete with establishments that produce similar goods everywhere in the world (Dicken 1992, Frenkel 2001), albeit recent empirical research shows that 'performance' of these firms is dependent on localized externalities as well (Chevassus-Lozza and Galliano 2003). It is important to acknowledge that an (urban) localized measure of competition can capture firm- or industry-specific competing conditions but not by definition is the only spatial level that matters. Especially on the small spatial scales of analyses applied in this dissertation, multiple scale aspects have to be incorporated as much as possible. Variable definition (of which competition is one) therefore should comprise composition aspects of neighboring areas, ranging to *at least* the national scale.

Geographical research in the Netherlands has a strong tradition in testing life-cycle-induced hypotheses. Using organizational ecological and evolutionary frameworks, research on life-cycle patterns of firm growth have been applied to (spatial) economic contexts. Regional employment growth in this context can be unraveled in various components: job creation in new and existing firms, job destruction in existing firms or due to closures and spatial movements of firms and jobs. In geographical and social research traditions these foci on components of change exist for a longer time (Birch 1979, De Jong 1987). Still it is difficult to (fine)tune this strand of empirical research with economic theory-induced research as such. The geographical literature states that it is clear that economic outcomes differ in the several life-cycle stages of firms and industries. But whether the economic processes explaining these outcomes are substantially *spatially* different across stages of growth in firms and industries remains largely unclear in the literature. As stylized facts are observed that life cycles of products, translated to small-scale industries, are started up by entrepreneurs within centrally located environments that facilitate the optimal use of urban(ization) economies. Once these core localities exhibit over-representation of new and growing firms, persistent growth of firms appears by processes of cumulative causation in the same localities, or they spill over to those nearby. Although initially developed for different spatial levels of analysis, seedbed and incubation theory, cumulative causation theory and filtering-down theory can be expressed in terms of the theoretical framework of endogenous economic growth (Davelaar 1989, Evans 1987, Combes 2000). From an empirical perspective then it appears important to distinguish incumbent from new firm growth patterns. The new and incumbent stocks of firms should ideally be researched separately under their relevant competitive economic conditions. The South-Holland data by their detailed (individual and longitudinal) structure allows for such an analysis.

Components of Employment Change in South-Holland

From the literature discussed in previous sections, it became clear that entrants and exits of firms as opposed to incumbent ones potentially capture an interesting economic variable, namely the degree of competition. We will apply this principle in chapters 5 and 6, in this section we will introduce the components of change associated with such an analysis for the research area of South-Holland.

After correcting for changing municipal boundaries, establishments without any employees, unknown, missing and mis-specified postal area codes and mis-specifications of activity codes (due to definition changes), in total 1,004,410 observations were present in the South-Holland dataset (see appendix A). By comparing every two successive years of stocks of establishments, we constructed a database containing only the firms established during the period between the two observations (total number of observations 59,490). These new firms are thus really newly founded in that locality, or moved in from another jurisdiction of observation (or from outside the research area) and observed for the first time. Short-distance movements in general count for the majority of firm migrations (Van Dijk and Pellenbarg 2000), and is observed as changes in 6-digit postal zone locations. Table 3.7 presents the resulting distribution over sectors (the average over ten years is taken). In absolute terms, new establishments are on average predominantly present in consumer services, knowledge services and, to a lesser extent, in administrative distribution. Low entry barriers and renewed organizations of production in terms of subcontracting favor especially these industries in terms of firm formation. In relative terms, the highest percentages of the formation of new establishments are within knowledge services and administrative distribution. These are the industries showing the highest dissolution rates as well. On average, the rate of dissolution is smaller in magnitude than the rate of new firm formation.

Table 3.7   Firm formation, dissolution and migration in South-Holland (average 1988-1997)

	All firms		New firms		Dissol. firms		Migrated firms	
	#	%	#	%	#	%	#	%
Labour int. production	2,064	2.1	135	6.5	130	6.3	75	3.6
Capital int. production	1,096	1.1	28	2.6	48	4.4	18	1.6
Process industry	204	0.2	7	3.5	9	4.4	11	5.4
Knowl. int. production	1,321	1.3	84	6.4	59	4.5	41	3.1
Administr. distribution	9,791	9.6	849	8.7	752	7.7	411	4.2
Physical distribution	2,903	2.9	169	5.8	166	5.7	143	4.9
Physical infrastructure	6,349	6.3	362	5.7	319	5.0	266	4.2
Co-ordination act.	1,459	1.5	55	3.8	96	6.6	40	2.7
Knowledge services	16,694	16.5	1,699	10.2	1,186	7.1	826	4.9
Mineral resources	11	0.0	0	0.0	0	0.0	0	0.0
Agriculture	10,792	10.6	245	2.3	332	3.1	143	1.3
Consumer services	27,459	27.2	1,316	4.8	1,322	4.8	500	1.8
Institutions	2,008	2.6	82	4.1	107	5.3	63	3.1
Education	3,198	3.2	138	4.3	152	4.8	83	2.6
Health care	6,130	6.1	315	5.1	232	3.8	176	2.9
Leisure	8,962	8.8	464	5.2	371	4.1	129	1.4
Total (South-Holland)	100441	100	5,949	5.9	5,280	5.2	2,919	2.9
Agriculture	10,803	10.7	245	2.3	332	3.1	143	1.3
Manufacturing	4,685	4.7	254	5.4	246	5.3	145	3.1
Distribution	19,043	18.9	1,380	7.2	1,237	6.5	820	4.3
Producer services	18,153	18.1	1,754	9.7	1,282	7.1	866	4.8
Consumer services	47,757	47.5	2,315	4.8	2,184	4.6	951	2.0

The relative small net growth of new over dissoluted establishments in the database over the ten years of observations is remarkable, because in analysis of Chamber of Commerce and Central Bureau of Statistics data (see appendix A) the general firm formation rate is approximately twice as high as the firm dissolution rate (Van Oort 2002a). Three possible explanations of this difference can be mentioned. The incomparability of the datasets on a national level is largely attributable to definition and measurement differences.

The signaled average growth in jobs hides different components of growth and decline of employment in firms. Figure 3.9 gives an overview of the components of change in South-Holland concerning employment growth. The measurement of

102,940 new jobs being created in the period is only the net outcome of six underlying processes. In total 845,035 new jobs were created in the period, of which 56% were by means of growth in existing firms and 44% by growth in new formed firms (25% of these growing new firms finally still dissolute).

Figure 3.9　　Components of change in South-Holland (employment 1988-1997)

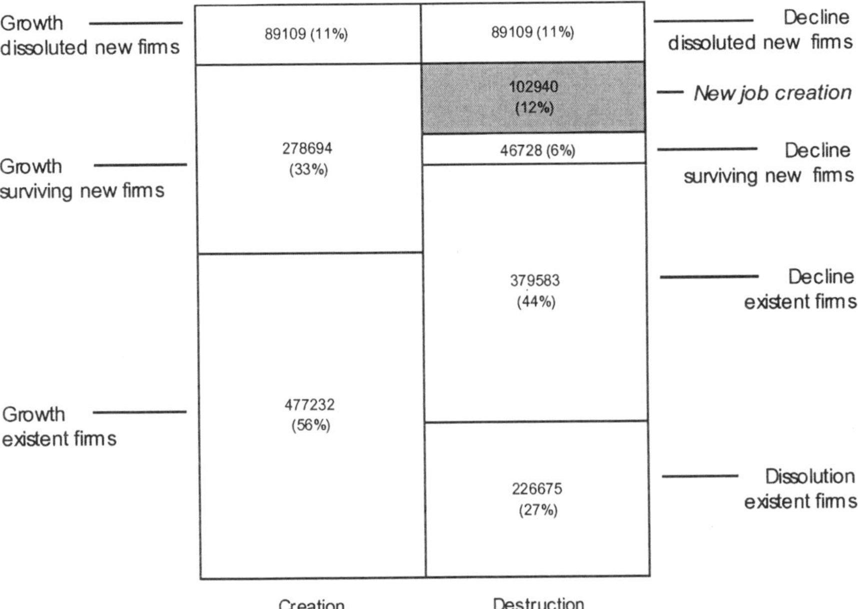

The job destruction categories contain dissolution (bankruptcy or moving out of the registration area) of existing firms (27% of the total) and decline in existent and surviving new formed firms (respectively 44% and 6%). Interesting detail is the role of moved firms in the job creation and destruction process. It turns out that establishments that move on short distance (within the research area of South-Holland) create considerable more net jobs (especially in existing firms) than non-moving firms (for details see Van Oort 2002a). The net job creation percentage of firms that moved (once or several times) in the period 1988-1997 is about 27%. This is 16% higher than the average job creation percentage. It is often assumed that firms move because they grow larger and have too little space for physical expanding. Figure 3.10 sheds some more light on the components of change in the BRZ-firm register in a longitudinal perspective.

Figure 3.10   Components of change in South-Holland compared to base year 1988 (number of firms and employment)

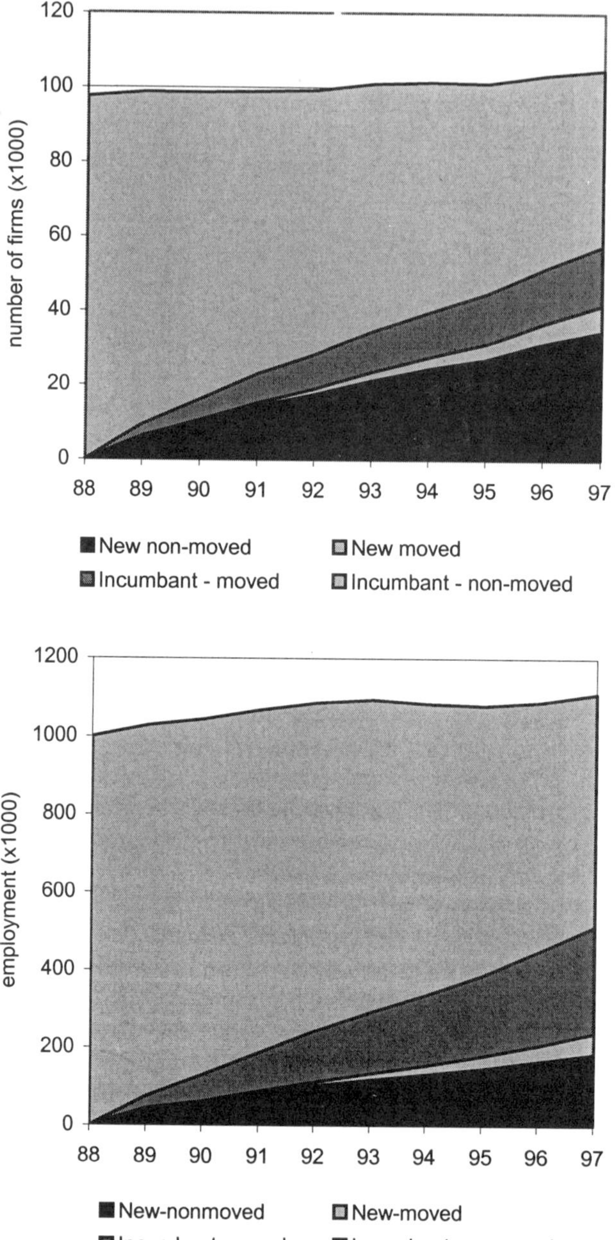

For all activities aggregated, we distinguish employment development in non-moving new firms (started and being present at any year in the period 1988-1997), new firms (same definition) that once relocated in the period, incumbent firms that were present any year and once moved in the period, as well as incumbent firms that did not relocate but were present any year. From figure 3.10 we may conclude that one fifth of total employment in establishments in the South-Holland research area, as well as one third of the number firms is being replaced in nine years time. In terms of employment, the component of relocation (movement) is larger than that of new firm formation, whilst in terms of number of firms this relationship is reverse. We signal a relatively small increase in employment and number of firms in the research area over the nine years[30].

This section has shown that firm dynamics in terms of entrants, relocations, dissolutions and growth of firms constitutes a complex interplay in identifying life-cycle circumstances of firms for explaining localized endogenous growth patterns. Potentially, these indications of business volatility can be helpful in formulating hypotheses on the role of competition in local markets of production and consumption in a better way than is the case in concentration-based indicators, that more probably reflect internal economies of scale or size effects of firms and industries (Combes 2000, Reynolds 1994).

3.6   Summary and Synthesis

In this chapter, heterogeneity stemming from industry classifications, spatial dependency and life-cycle development of firms is explored. Empirically, employment structure and growth in the Netherlands is described on a macro-economic level (zoning), a regional level (connectedness) and a local level (South Holland) respectively. Because this study deals with spatial structures of numbers of jobs, interpretation of growth has to acknowledge differing (heterogeneous) underlying processes.

It is therefore important to use sensible industry-classification schemes when analyzing economic growth and innovation intensity (section 3.2). Research in this study uses three kinds of spatial-sectoral classifications: (1) spatial analyses for industry, distribution, producer service and consumer service sectors separately, (2) location-industries as flexible combinations of spatial and sectoral detailed functional components and (3) dummy variables for certain industries or types of locations. None of these classifications is superior to others, but some are more suitable for the analyses presented in subsequent chapters. It will be clearly mentioned which type of industrial classification is used, since the industry classification used influences the empirical outcomes of analysis.

The recent literature discussed in this chapter, along with own calculations on the South-Holland and Dutch longitudinal data, reveal certain spatial-economic trends (sections 3.3 and 3.4). The first concerns urban (size) hierarchical growth

---

[30] For sector-specific versions of figure 3.10 see Van Oort (2002a).

patterns. Complementary cities are often supposed (but relatively little convincingly found) to have an (unmeasured) network facilitated by urban size, especially concerning office accommodation and growth of consumer and producer services, as well as retail facilities. In general, these growth patterns are difficult to prove or measure. The second is that of concentric diffusive growth, either by spatial patterns of connectedness (functional regions in terms of commuting) or macro-economic zoning. Economic growth requires growth of businesses to be accommodated and therefore space to become available nearby (or not too far away from) the present location to fulfil the needs of firms and their employees. From economic concentrations outwards, the spatial growth process diffuses simultaneously over different spatial scales. The two most observed patterns concern suburbanization out of individual cities (within the relevant agglomerations) and de-concentration from the Randstad core region towards regions that are contiguous neighbors to it (the so-called intermediate zone). A third spatial growth tendency marked in the literature concerns developments in and alongside corridors of important (inter-)national transport links between economic foci. Physical accessibility of firms is the central focus in this. The fourth type of economic growth locations distinguished in the literature is labeled 'autonomous impulses'. When autonomous developments can take place anywhere in larger functional area with the same degree of possibility, Hoekveld (1999) argues we can speak of an urban field development. When exactly developments are autonomous and to what extent (parts of) the Netherlands function as an urban field in which economic *growth* patterns level out is not unambiguously analyzed though. The analyses presented in this chapter and in earlier studies all confirm some of the logic of these spatial growth patterns, but they do not reveal systematically the causal (economic) processes of agglomeration externalities feeding them. Because of the dense system of medium-sized and smaller cities in the Netherlands, it is also often not clear in which (of the four) diffusion trend local growth most suitably fits. As outlined in chapter 1, the focus of our study is to systematically analyze both contiguous spatial growth patterns and spatial heterogeneous growth patterns. The following chapters will build up a modeling framework that incorporates the spatial hypotheses posted in the scattered literature. Contiguous growth is incorporated by spatial lag modeling on city (municipality) and local (zip code) scale. Spatial heterogeneity will be introduced most importantly by means of spatial regimes concerning connectedness (commuting induced functional areas), physical accessibility, macro-economic zoning (in Randstad, intermediate zone and national periphery regimes) and urban size.

From the analyses presented in section 3.5 it can be concluded that many processes of growth occur on lower levels of analysis than the macro- and meso-economic developments described. To test this proposition (in the literature made by Wallsten 2001, Olsen 2002 and Rosenthal and Strange 2001) the study focuses in detail on one region in the Netherlands, the province of South-Holland. Detailed data availability in a longitudinal dataset comprising all individual firms present in the research area in the period 1988-1997 make analyses on a lower spatial scale possible. The province makes up most of the South-wing of the Randstad region, the core economic region in the Netherlands. The last section of this chapter has shown that firm dynamics in terms of entrants, relocations, dissolution and growth of firms constitute a complex interplay in identifying life-cycle circumstances of firms and industries for explaining localized endogenous growth patterns in this region. Potentially, indications of business volatility embedded in localities can be helpful in formulating hypotheses on the role of competition in local markets of production and consumption, complementary to general (macro-economic) concentration-based indicators, that more probably reflect internal economies of scale or size effects of firms and industries (Rosenthal and Strange 2002). From the descriptive analyses in this chapter it became clear that econometric modeling of firm and industry growth would benefit when controlled for firm and industry life-cycle phases. From an empirical perspective it is thus important to distinguish incumbent from new firm growth patterns. The total, new and incumbent stocks of firms should thus ideally be researched separately, under their relevant competitive economic conditions comprising agglomeration economies. Externality indicators explicitly need to be conditioned on neighboring values as well (reaching as far as at least regional or even national scales), since it is not to be expected that zip code internal agglomeration conditions sufficiently capture the spatial extent of externalities influencing firm growth and innovation intensity. The three types of industry classifications, the identification of spatial heterogeneity and spatial autocorrelated growth patterns and the firm life-cycle heterogeneity distinguished, all form input for models to develop in subsequent chapters.

Chapter 4

Exploratory Spatial Data Analysis

4.1 Introduction

This chapter focuses on the description of spatial distribution patterns in employment density, employment function, innovation intensity and employment growths. The employment growth and innovation intensity indicators are central (explained) variables in this dissertation, and a thorough insight in their spatial configuration is essential for their modeling in chapters 5 to 7. The technique used for the spatial descriptions in this chapter is exploratory spatial data analysis (ESDA). This is a set of techniques aimed at describing and visualizing spatial distributions, at identifying atypical localizations or spatial outliers, at detecting patterns of spatial association, clusters or hot spots, and at suggesting spatial regimes or other forms of spatial heterogeneity (Haining 1990, Bailey and Gatrell 1995, Anselin 1988, Le Gallo and Ertur 2003). These methods provide both measures of global and local spatial autocorrelation, which will be technically discussed in this introduction. The following sections in this chapter are arranged as follows. In section 4.2, exploratory spatial data analysis (ESDA) using global and local indicators of spatial association are applied to the South-Holland data on the firm and employment structure and distribution over the zip codes. Section 4.3 then focuses on spatial data analyses of the *growth* of number of firms and employment in the South-Holland research area. In section 4.4 spatial autocorrelated patterns of new and dissolute firms in South-Holland are the main focus. Section 4.5 gives similar spatial data analyses on the national (municipal) scale, focusing on employment and structures and growth respectively. Because chapter 3 already put some descriptive light on these national structures and growth by use of gravity models, results in section 4.5 will be discussed more briefly. Emphasized are similarities and differences with the South-Holland analyses. In sections 4.2 to 4.5 the classification of 16 sectors (between 49 industries and 4 large sectors) is tested for being appropriate for econometric analysis to follow in the next chapters. Section 4.6 concentrates on ESDA analyses for innovation intensity using the Senter database (described in appendix B). Section 4.7 summarizes and evaluates.

Global Spatial Autocorrelation

Spatial autocorrelation can be defined as the coincidence of value similarity with locational similarity. Positive spatial autocorrelation occurs when high or low values of a random variable tend to cluster (agglomerate) in space; negative spatial autocorrelation occurs when geographical areas tend to be surrounded by neighbors with very dissimilar values. The measurement of global spatial autocorrelation in this chapter is based on Moran's I statistic, which is the most widely known measure of spatial clustering (Cliff and Ord 1973, 1981, Goodchild 1986, Haining 1990)[1]. For each year or period (of change) of observation, this statistic is given by:

$$I_t = \frac{n}{S_0} \frac{\sum_i \sum_j w_{ij}\,(x_{it} - \mu_t)(x_{jt} - \mu_t)}{\sum_i (x_{it} - \mu_t)^2} \tag{4.1}$$

where x_{it} is the observation in region i and year (period) t, μ_t is the mean of the observations across regions in year (period) t, n is the number of regions and w_{ij} is the interregional element of the spatial weight matrix W. This matrix contains the information about the relative spatial dependence between the n regions i and j. The elements on the w_{ii} diagonal are set to zero whereas the elements w_{ij} indicate the way region i is spatially connected to region j (compare the treatment of inter- and intra-regional dependency in the gravity formula in chapter 3). S_0 finally is a scaling factor equal to the sum of all elements of W. For row-standardized spatial weight matrices, which are the preferred way to implement the Moran's I test statistic, the normalizing factor S_0 equals n, since each row then sums to 1 (see Anselin 1995a, p.22-1 and further)[2]. The statistic of equation 4.1 then simplifies to the ratio of a spatial cross products to variance. This makes Moran's I similar but not equivalent to a correlation coefficient; it is not centered around 0. The theoretical mean of Moran's I is $-1/N$-1. The expected value is thus negative and is only a function of sample size (N). This means it will tend to zero as the sample size increases. The theoretical variance of Moran's I depends on the stochastic assumptions made. Either the assumption of a normal distribution of variables in question (normality assumption), the assumption that each value observed could equally likely have occurred at all locations (randomization assumption) or a randomization approach using a reference distribution for I that is generated empirically (permutation assumption) can be tested for[3]. Albeit all three variance assumptions were tested for on employment and population structure and development indicators, in this chapter only the results for the randomization

---

[1] Other well-known measures are Geary's c- statistic and Getis and Ord's G-statistic, see Anselin (1995a, p.22-1 and p.23-1).

[2] In this chapter only row-standardized weight matrices are used.

[3] The software used for testing is SpaceStat (Anselin 1995a).

assumption will be presented[4]. Inference is based on a standardized z-value of I that is computed by subtracting the theoretical mean and dividing the result by the theoretical standard deviation. A positive and significant z-value for Moran's I (as can be judged from accompanying low probability values) indicates positive spatial autocorrelation. Similar values of the variable, either high or low, are more spatially clustered than could be caused purely by chance. In contrast, a negative and significant z-value for Moran's I indicates negative spatial autocorrelation, the opposite of spatial clustering[5]. The results for Moran's I are to a large extent determined by the choice of the spatial weight matrix. Interpretations of contiguity-based physical distance measures (see Kuiper 1985, Paci and Usai 2000) differ from both functional distance measures (see Esparza and Krmenec 1996, 2000, Brown and Holmes 1971) and full physical distance measures as applied in the models in this dissertation. In general, a pattern of decreasing autocorrelation with increasing orders of contiguity is typical of many spatial autoregressive processes[6].

Local Spatial Autocorrelation

Moran's I statistic is a global statistic: it does not enable us to take into account the regional and local structure of spatial autocorrelation. However, which regions or locations contribute most to the global spatial atocorrelation, if there are specific local or regional clusters of high or low values and to what point the global evaluation of spatial autocorrelation masks atypical localizations or 'pockets of nonstationarity' (deviations from the global pattern) are interesting questions. Analysis of local spatial autocorrelation can be carried out using two tools. The first is the Moran scatterplot (Anselin 1996), which can be used to visualize local spatial instability. The spatial lag Wz_I is plotted against the original values zi, resulting in four different quadrants of the scatterplot that correspond to four types of local spatial association between a location and its neighbors. The HH quadrant comprise locations with a high value surrounded by locations with high values. LH locations have low values surrounded by locations with high values, LL locations have low values surrounded by locations with low values and HL locations have high values surrounded by locations with low values. HH and LL refer to positive spatial autocorrelation, indicating spatial clustering of similar values, whereas LH and HL represent negative spatial autocorrelation indicating spatial clustering of dissimilar values. The locations in each quadrant can be mapped. The Moran scatterplot may thus be used to visualize atypical localizations and the use of standardized variables allows Moran scatterplots to be comparable across time.

---

[4] The three approaches implicate the use of different models. Inference results from the normal distribution- and (10000-) permutation approach (see Anselin 1995a, p.22-2) are because of economizing reasons not presented in this chapter. Results of the three models of inference specification are very similar in terms of significance though; all directions and magnitudes of spatial association are confirmed.

[5] The concept of negative spatial autocorrelation is harder to grasp; it reflects a lack of clustering, more so than would be the case in a random pattern. Perfect negative spatial autocorrelation is represented by a checkerboard pattern.

[6] In this chapter first, second as well as third order distance weight matrices are used for spatial autoregressive modeling, while in following chapters emphasis will be on first order weight matrices only.

The global spatial autocorrelation may also be visualized in the graph since Moran's I is formally equivalent to the slope coefficient of a linear regression of Wz_i on z_i using a row-standardized weight matrix. This regression can therefore be assessed with diagnostics for model fit.

The Moran scatterplot does not give any indications of significance of spatial clustering, and therefore it cannot be considered as a Local Indicator of Spatial Association (LISA, see Anselin 1995b). This second tool for local statistics can be used to test the hypothesis of random distribution by comparing values of each specific localization with the values in the neighboring locations. Anselin defines a local indicator of spatial association as any statistics satisfying two criteria. First, the LISA for each observation gives an indication of significant spatial clustering of similar values around that observation; second, the sum of the LISA for all observations is proportional to a global indicator of spatial association. The local version of Moran's I statistic for each region i and year (period) t can then be written as:

$$I_{it} = \frac{(x_{it} - \mu_t)}{m_0} \sum_j w_{ij}(x_{jt} - \mu_t) \qquad with \quad m_0 = \sum_i (x_{it} - \mu_t)^2 / n \tag{4.2}$$

where the summation over j is such that neighboring values (contiguous analysis) or values within a predefined distance (full distance analysis with or without cut-off) of j are included. The sum of local Moran's statistics is then:

$$\sum_i I_{it} = \frac{1}{m_0} \sum_i (x_{jt} - \mu_t) \sum_j w_{ij}(x_{jt} - \mu_t) = \frac{1}{m_0} \sum_i \sum_j w_{ij}(x_{it} - \mu_t)(x_{jt} - \mu_t) \tag{4.3}$$

From equation (4.1) it follows that the global Moran's I statistic (for a row-standardized weight matrix, so $S_0 = n$) is indeed proportional to the mean of the local Moran's statistics:

$$I_t = \frac{\sum_i I_{it}}{n} \tag{4.4}$$

Positive values for I_{it} indicate clustering of similar values (high or low), whereas a negative value indicates clustering of dissimilar values[7]. Anselin (1995b) gives two interpretations for local Moran's statistics. They can be either used as indicators of local spatial clusters (called hot spots), which can be identified as locations or sets of neighboring locations for which the LISA are significant or as diagnostics for

---

[7] For a technical discussion on inference and significance levels see Anselin (1995a) and Le Gallo and Ertur (2003).

local instability, i.e. for significant outliers with respect to the measure of global spatial autocorrelation. This second interpretation of the LISA statistics is similar to the use of a Moran scatterplot. In this interpretation we will apply the two tools of local spatial autocorrelation in following sections.

4.2   South-Holland Firm and Employment Density and Function

Employment and Firm Density

Employment and firm density measurement is at the heart of exploratory spatial data analysis concerning economic development. When interested in the economic functioning of urban locations, high-density concentration of economic activities is in this respect by nature most served by (log) absolute measurement or (log) measurement per square kilometer (Henderson *et al.* 1995, Combes 2000). Average zip code areas are smaller in urban locations and smaller denominators induce potential higher autoregressive values of spatial concentration. A disadvantage of this measurement is that urbanization is the only measured phenomenon. In this section, employment and firm density have been calculated per square kilometer in 1997 comparable to Dutch policy-induced research as presented in NREB (1999). It should be remarked that because of the denominator-dependency of the outcomes, this calculation and presentation is not the preferred one. Population or total employment denominators are scientifically more interesting because of equal over-representation in smaller urban areas (compare Henderson *et al.* 1995). Relative specialization of economic activities in locations will then come more to the front, naturally correcting for urban size dependency.

Table 4.1 gives an overview of the Moran's *I* statistics for employment density and density of number of firms, both for the economic sectors as distinguished in chapter 3 and appendix A. Not surprisingly, in terms of density most economic sectors are clustered in space. Figure 4.1 shows the Moran scatterplot for employment in all economic activities. The positive global Moran's *I* (z-value 34.7), represented by the thick line, is on a local level confirmed by the shape and direction of the scatterplot. 73% of all (416) observations are in either quadrants HH (37%) or LL (36%), indicating that there are relatively little 'atypical' locations, i.e. deviating from the global pattern of positive spatial autocorrelation. Figure 4.2 presents the accompanying map of the South-Holland research area showing the four quadrants of figure 4.1. The urban central areas of The Hague and Rotterdam show the largest number of contiguous HH-scores, while LL-scores are to be found in the eastern (Green Heart, rural) part of the province and south of Rotterdam. Local spots of higher values surrounded by lower ones (HL) comprise the medium-seized cities of Leiden, Alphen, Gouda and Zoetermeer. The LH-localities, showing low values in proximity of high values, can in general be observed between and around the conurbation of Rotterdam and The Hague.

Table 4.1   Moran's *I* statistics for employment and firm density (South-Holland 1997, w_1, randomization assumption)[1]

		Moran's *I* w_1 [2]	standard. dev. w_1	standard. value w_1	standard. value w_2	standard. value w_3
Labour int. product.	emp	0.03570617	0.003869	9.851	6.779	5.081
	firms	0.08553586	0.003870	22.722	15.130	11.023
Capital int. product.	emp	0.01296095	0.003871	3.971	3.929	3.501
	firms	0.05105592	0.003871	13.811	10.114	7.715
Process industry	emp	-0.00418813	0.003851	-0.462*	-0.010*	0.371*
	firms	-0.00262533	0.003850	-0.056*	0.526*	0.916*
Knowledge int. prod.	emp	0.03287458	0.003870	9.118	6.566	5.193
	firms	0.07112432	0.003871	18.995	13.044	9.881
Admin. distribution	emp	0.07111530	0.003864	19.027	13.265	9.953
	firms	0.11222660	0.003865	29.657	19.414	14.177
Physical distribution	emp	0.05543077	0.003866	14.960	8.984	6.089
	firms	0.14070570	0.003869	36.987	20.498	13.532
Physical infrastruct.	emp	0.05746770	0.003861	15.509	10.039	7.243
	firms	0.09240374	0.003864	24.538	16.123	11.847
Co-ordination act.	emp	0.05626628	0.003868	15.168	10.597	7.859
	firms	0.08451513	0.003870	22.463	14.495	10.442
Knowledge services	emp	0.10549780	0.003836	27.931	18.721	13.871
	firms	0.11573130	0.003864	30.571	20.474	15.116
Consumer services	emp	0.09766963	0.003862	25.917	17.520	12.961
	firms	0.11952990	0.003865	31.548	20.656	15.034
Institutions	emp	0.08977064	0.003871	23.816	15.120	11.019
	firms	0.14701710	0.003870	38.613	23.317	16.387
Education	emp	0.07354743	0.003867	19.644	13.278	9.836
	firms	0.09381211	0.003870	24.862	16.855	12.598
Health care	emp	0.09181840	0.003867	24.366	15.848	11.512
	firms	0.11864750	0.003870	31.285	20.154	14.640
Leisure	emp	0.12361770	0.003865	32.611	21.271	15.502
	firms	0.15145730	0.003867	39.788	25.429	18.250
Total South-Holland	emp	0.1316172	0.003865	34.681	22.287	16.253
	firms	0.1394602	0.003866	36.697	23.421	16.919
Manufacturing	emp	0.0403315	0.003869	10.767	8.453	6.816
	firms	0.1016588	0.003869	26.879	18.304	13.640
Distribution	emp	0.0801451	0.003864	21.364	14.022	10.204
	firms	0.1244291	0.003867	32.803	20.899	15.088
Producer services	emp	0.1119770	0.003866	29.589	19.945	14.815
	firms	0.1239072	0.003866	32.670	21.887	16.253
Consumer services	emp	0.1287489	0.003865	33.934	21.949	15.998
	firms	0.1366058	0.003867	35.048	23.167	16.802

1   Agriculture and mining activities are not presented because of an insufficient number of observations. w_1, w_2 and w_3 express row standardized higher order weight matrices (weights divided by distances d_{ij} raised to integer powers 1, 2 and 3).

2   The expected value for Moran's *I* statistic is constant over each sector, both for employment and number of firms: $E(I)$=-0.002. All statistics except for 'knowledge intensive process industry' (marked *) are significant at p=0.01.

Figure 4.1   Moran scatterplot employment density South-Holland (1997, n=416, w_1)

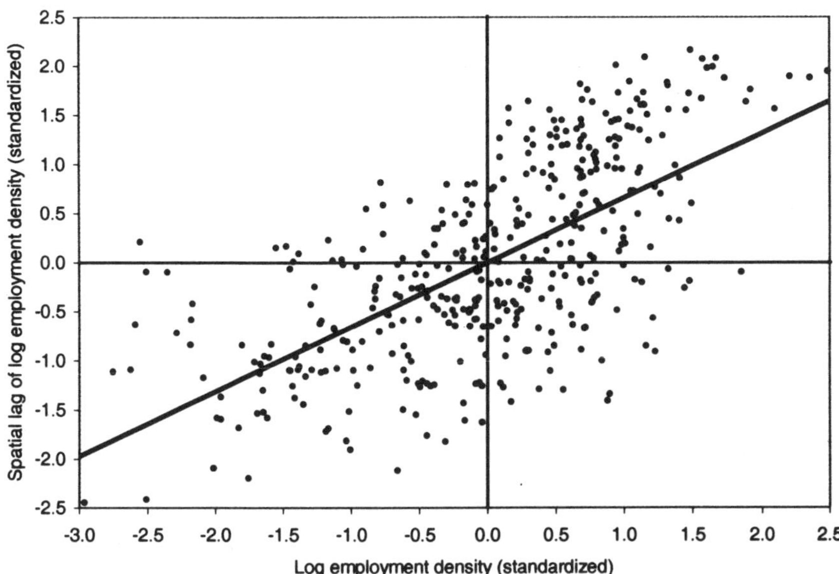

Outliers, defined as points further than 2 units away from the origin, are not clearly present, except for three zip code areas without any presence of firms and employment. In terms of sectors, consumer and producer service activities show the highest spatial autocorrelation pattern[8]. This is to be expected, since urban areas comprise potentially many urbanization as well as localization economies for producer services, and a population carrying capacity for consumer services. Manufacturing activities show the lowest degree of spatial autocorrelation. Especially knowledge-intensive process industry shows no significant patterns of spatial autocorrelation. Only a few large factories, like the oil refineries in the Rotterdam harbour region and the AKZO-coating factory in Sassenheim build up this industry (compare Cortright and Mayer 2001). Other industrial sectors show significant values of Moran's *I* coefficient, albeit less than other sectors. The number of firms as indicator of economic density shows overall higher values of spatial autocorrelation than employment, especially in industrial and distribution sectors. These sectors are characterized more than other ones by average large firm sizes.

---

[8] Because of the large 'common' influence of the areal denominator, *sectoral* visualizations of Moran scatterplots (available on request) resemble that of total activities as presented in figure 4.1.

Figure 4.2   Moran scatterplot map employment density South-Holland (1997, w_1)[9]

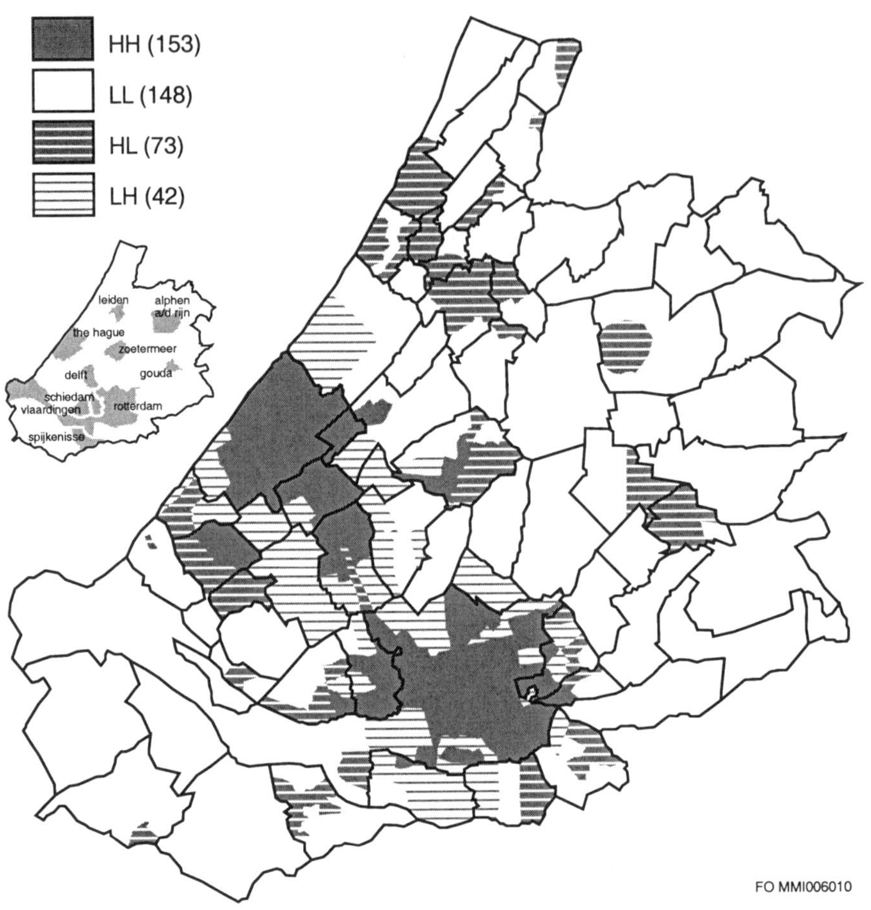

---

[9] The reported LISA-statistics reveal that not all observations plotted in the map are significant at the 0.05 level; indications for outliers are limited though.

The typical pattern of decreasing autocorrelation with increasing orders of contiguity becomes clear in the spatial autoregressive processes described in table 4.1. Further, producer and consumer services are the most spatially autocorrelated sectors over time, as is confirmed by table 4.2 that shows the longitudinal development in the period 1988-1997 of the standardized values for the employment density function. The relative increase in clustering of total activities (in terms of employment) is mainly due to increasing spatial employment clustering of consumer services. Since this category makes up most of the production structure in the research area, it is the main component in the (change in) value of all activities. Notice that when measuring in number of firms, this dominance of this sector is much less profound[10].

Table 4.2   **Standardized values Moran's *I* statistics for employment and firm density (South-Holland 1997, randomization assumption, w_1)[1,2]**

		Total activities	Basic activities	Industrial activities	Distribut. activities	Producer services	Consum. activities
1988	empl	31.601	26.605	12.777	25.084	30.633	32.657
1989		31.795	26.599	12.563	25.192	30.997	32.137
1990		32.263	27.088	11.587	25.035	31.303	32.897
1991		32.787	27.316	11.566	25.310	30.867	31.951
1992		32.861	27.401	11.748	24.933	31.716	32.437
1993		33.638	27.273	11.031	24.321	31.306	32.992
1994		35.356	27.136	10.367	23.872	31.256	34.082
1995		35.406	27.084	10.318	24.041	30.896	33.755
1996		35.035	26.465	10.518	23.035	30.056	33.801
1997		34.681	25.574	10.767	21.364	29.589	33.934
1988	firms	35.663	34.775	30.561	36.716	35.524	36.347
1989		36.024	35.595	30.746	37.976	36.003	36.054
1990		36.464	36.173	30.201	38.027	36.830	36.205
1991		37.013	36.640	30.056	38.172	36.706	36.221
1992		37.992	37.795	29.660	38.441	37.618	36.816
1993		38.906	38.048	29.710	37.979	38.491	37.358
1994		39.321	37.226	28.779	37.339	36.991	37.220
1995		38.596	35.820	28.341	36.303	35.924	36.818
1996		37.435	33.613	26.791	33.695	33.529	36.544
1997		36.697	33.082	26.897	32.803	32.670	35.949

1   Agriculture and mining activities are not presented because of an insufficient number of observations.
2   The expected value for Moran's *I* statistic is constant over each sector, both for employment and number of firms: $E(I)=-0.002$. All statistics are significant at $p=0.01$.

---

[10] Some consumer-service sectors contain very large establishments, like governmental institutions (ministries), education (universities and high schools) and health care (hospitals).

All basic (non-population dependent) sectors show a stabilization or relative decline in their standardized value of Moran's *I*, in terms of employment as well as (less profound) in number of firms. Producer services (the largest 'component' within the basic sectors) as well as distribution and industrial activities are thus becoming less spatially autocorrelated over time, meaning their location becomes relatively less clustered. Total activities are spatially autocorrelated over time to a much lesser extent when measured in number of firms (due to the smaller dominance of the consumer service sector). The degree of spatial clustering of establishments in consumer services then remains relative stable over time. For all non-industrial activities a split in development of firm density over time occurs before and after 1992/1993: a relative increase in standardized value proceeds, and a decrease following these years. This coincides with a general economic upheaval that started in 1992, after a less favorable growth period in the years 1990/1991.

Employment Function and Firm Representation

As remarked in the previous section, the denominator of total area of zip codes emphasizes urban locations naturally, which are more densely built up and populated by economic activities then non-urban areas. To correct for physical size dependency, applying another denominator to employment and firm representation is preferable. Total employment, total stock of firms and total population are potential better measurements of relative specialization of locations, corrected for density of activities in general. It is interesting to find out to what degree locations then remain sectoral and spatially autocorrelated in terms of number of firms and employment. Residential areas comprising little economic activities are usually mixed with industrial sites (usually without population) and mixed environments (Brouwer *et al.* 2001). Urban density is then not the main focus of analysis anymore, relative economic specialization of locations is. Next we present Moran's *I* coefficients when the denominator is total local population, representing what will be called the employment *function* and firm representation of locations (relative to population)[11]. Table 4.3 presents Moran's *I* statistics for the employment function and relative firm representation in 1997 (again only presenting the results using the randomization assumption for inference). The correction for size results in overall smaller standardized values of significance for the employment and firm representation functions when compared to the density measurement. Not surprisingly, for consumer-based services (dependent upon (urban) population density) the largest decline in significance appears. But also industrial and distribution activities show considerably smaller significance levels. Figure 4.3 presents the accompanying scatterplot for the employment function. Albeit the overall direction of autocorrelation is still positive, the degree of association is much less profound than in figure 4.1.

---

[11] The exact sector-specific specification is $\log[(emp_i/pop_i) \times 1000]$ and $\log[(firms_i/pop_i) \times 1000]$ for individual sectors of employment.

Table 4.3   Moran's *I* statistics for employment function and firm representation (South-Holland 1997, randomization assumption)[1]

		Moran's *I* w_1 [2]	Standard dev. w_1	standard. value w_1	standard. value w_2	standard. value w_3
Labor int. production	emp	0.01361383	0.003855	4.156	2.691	2.070
	firms	0.02425651	0.003838	6.947	4.766	3.737
Capital int. prod.	emp	0.00788572	0.003845	2.677	2.163	1.967
	firms	0.00462085	0.003836	1.832*	1.259*	0.723*
Process industry	emp	0.00349513	0.003813	1.549*	0.805*	0.380*
	firms	0.00513439	0.003841	1.964*	1.171*	1.065*
knowledge int. prod.	emp	0.01248678	0.003853	3.867	2.927	2.464
	firms	0.01211255	0.003837	3.785	2.920	2.328
Admin. distribution	emp	0.02993515	0.003857	8.386	5.601	4.186
	firms	0.04409805	0.003836	12.125	7.302	5.257
Physical distribution	emp	0.02269944	0.003858	6.508	3.877	2.917
	firms	0.06075799	0.003838	16.459	8.450	5.610
Physical infrastr.	emp	0.01253736	0.003855	3.877	2.985	2.429
	firms	0.02101038	0.003833	6.109	5.137	4.238
Co-ordination act.	emp	0.01859474	0.003855	5.448	4.913	3.877
	firms	0.00565159	0.003847	2.095	1.606*	1.174*
Knowledge services	emp	0.02986669	0.003857	8.368	6.320	4.887
	firms	0.02454125	0.003838	7.022	5.223	3.844
Consumer services	emp	0.00714499	0.003845	2.485	1.414*	0.613*
	firms	0.02020240	0.003839	5.889	3.839	2.569
Institutions	emp	0.02934632	0.003866	8.214	5.375	3.704
	firms	0.02006955	0.003848	5.842	4.449	3.378
Education	emp	0.01599100	0.003855	4.773	3.477	2.472
	firms	0.00978401	0.003806	3.204	2.420	1.633*
Health care	emp	0.03540529	0.003866	9.7811	6.424	3.467
	firms	0.04990808	0.003854	13.575	9.182	6.812
Leisure	emp	0.02312096	0.003853	6.626	4.802	3.729
	firms	0.03998242	0.003851	11.009	7.937	5.692
Total (S-Holland)	emp	0.01333627	0.003844	4.096	3.317	2.671
	firms	0.01331820	0.003833	4.103	3.509	2.892
Manufacturing	emp	0.01833395	0.003859	5.375	3.959	3.309
	firms	0.02649326	0.003841	7.525	5.448	4.356
Distribution	emp	0.02096385	0.003855	6.032	4.329	3.499
	firms	0.03682102	0.003828	10.250	6.613	5.146
Producer services	emp	0.03083023	0.003857	8.617	6.590	5.081
	firms	0.02429481	0.003838	6.957	5.233	3.900
Consumer services	emp	0.02851874	0.003849	8.036	5.215	3.729
	firms	0.02219886	0.003838	6.411	4.239	2.792

1   Agriculture and mining activities are not presented because of an insufficient number of observations. w_1, w_2 and w_3 express row standardized higher order weight matrices (weights divided by distances d_{ij} raised to integer powers 1, 2 and 3).

2   The expected value for Moran's *I* statistic is constant over each sector, both for employment and number of firms: $E(I) = -0.002$. All statistics except those marked * are significant at $p=0.05$.

Figure 4.3   Moran scatterplot employment function South-Holland (1997, n=416, w_1)

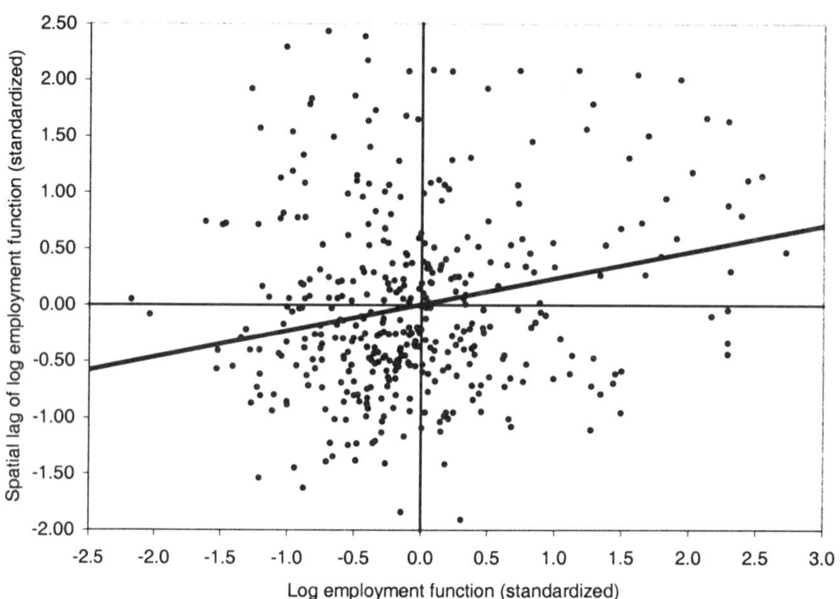

Figure 4.4 shows the spatial distribution of the employment function in the research area of South-Holland. 58% of all 416 observations are in the HH or LL quadrants of positive spatial autocorrelation (compared to 73% in figure 4.2). Compared to the visualization of employment density (figure 4.2), the spatial pattern of positive autocorrelation is much more diffused. Within the urban areas of Rotterdam and The Hague, other than HH concentrations are present. Relative higher degrees of spatial autocorrelation are present in the Westland region, in the area north of Leiden and in the triangle between The Hague, Rotterdam and Leiden. Corrected for size, sectoral patterns of spatial autocorrelation deviate from the general pattern as well. In Van Oort (2002a) scatterplot maps are presented for employment functions of industrial activities, distribution activities, producer services and consumer services[12]. Especially industrial and distribution activities appear not to be central-urban specialized (as could be suggested by examining density functions of sectoral employment). Instead, spatial autocorrelated patterns of distribution activities are to be found in the north-eastern part of the province (positive) and in the inner-city urban locations (negative).

---

[12] The reported LISA-statistics reveal that on a sectoral basis, outliers are more numerous and larger in magnitude than is the case for the distribution of all activities aggregated. The figures in Van Oort (2002a) are corrected for absence of population (zero denominator) and extreme observations.

Figure 4.4   Moran scatterplot map employment function South-Holland (1997, w_1)[13]

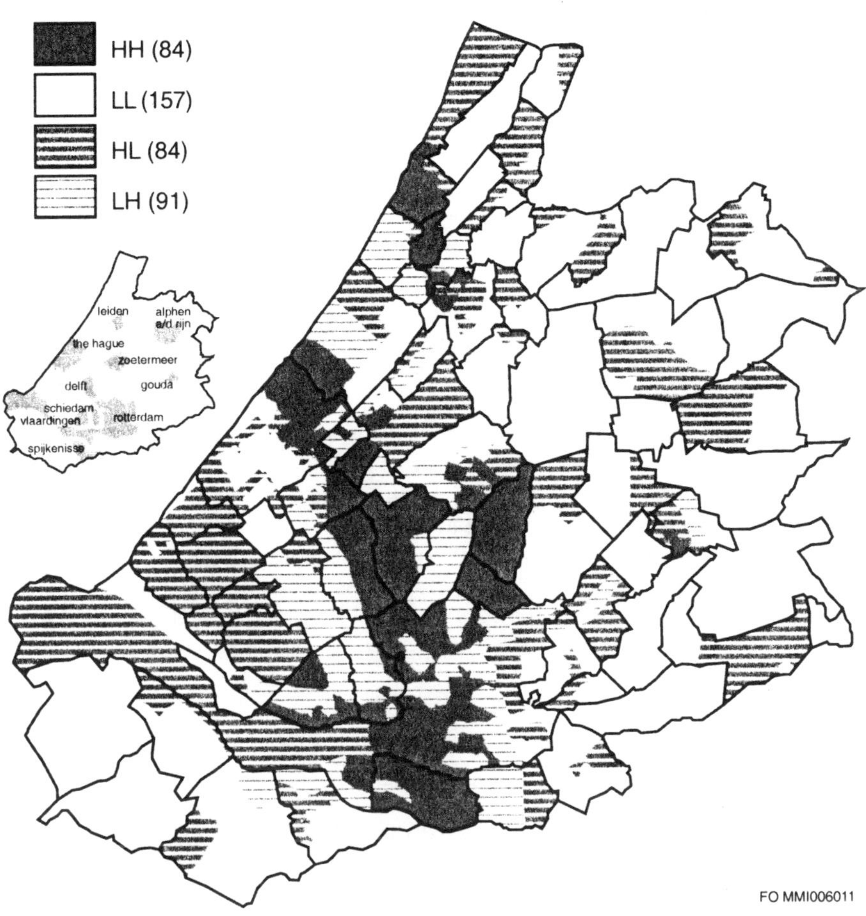

---

[13] The reported LISA-statistics reveal that not all 416 observations plotted in the map are significant at the 0.05 level. Specific outliers occurred because of the absence or extremely small numbers of population in certain zip code areas. When the area inhabits a lot of firms and subsequent employment though, corrections were made. This especially concerned zip codes 2909, 3165, 3196, 3197,3198 and 3199 which are located in the Rotterdam harbour region. Table 4.3 and figures 4.3 and 4.4 were (re-)constructed after these corrections.

Industrial activities show relative specialization around the Rotterdam urban region and in the north-eastern area of the province as well, combined with low inner-urban values of autocorrelation. Producer and consumer services on the other hand tend to be relatively agglomerated in urban locations. The dominance of these two economic sectors in the range of all other activities restricts most analyses and policy to focus on urbanization as main characteristic of all economic activity in the region (NREB 1999). Again, looking carefully at table 4.3, it should be noticed that Moran's *I* coefficients for spatial autocorrelation differ considerably for employment as compared to number of firms. Most notable are the only slightly and even non-significant values for firm agglomeration for co-ordination activities (part of the sector of producer services). Again, the pattern of decreasing autocorrelation with increasing orders of contiguity shows clearly in spatial autoregressive processes described in table 4.3.

4.3 South-Holland Firm and Employment Growth

The employment and firm density as well as function patterns presented in the previous section are not the prime aim of analysis in this research. The main focus is on employment *growth* as a measure for economic performance over time and space[14]. Population growth patterns over space are, simultaneously with employment growth modeling, subject to analysis in this chapter as a reference as well. Following Henderson *et al.* (1995) and Combes (2000) in their growth definition, this section presents analyses of spatial autocorrelation, using the notion:

$$G_i = \log\left[\frac{X_{i,t}}{Xi_{,t-10}}\right] \tag{4.5}$$

In which *X* represents employment, number of firms (both aggregated and per sector) or population for regions *i* for years 1988 (*t-10*) and 1997 (*t*). Table 4.4 presents Moran's *I* statistics for employment, number of firms and population growth (1988-1997, randomization assumption) using this definition. The computation of Moran's *I* statistics on the growth rate of employment and number of firms reveals a global positive spatial autocorrelation. It means that the locations with relative high (respectively low) growth rates are localized close to the locations with relatively high (low) growth rates, more than if this localization was purely random.

---

[14] As in Glaeser *et al.* (1992), Henderson *et al.* (1995) and Combes (2000), this study uses employment data for empirically testing endogenous employment growth and the agglomeration circumstances in which this growth most favourable is embedded. Because of lack of data on sectoral output and capital stock at the level of locations (as defined by zip codes and municipalities) an appropriate measure of total productivity (growth) cannot be constructed.

Table 4.4 **Moran's *I* statistics for employment and firm growth (South-Holland, 1988-1997, randomization assumption)[1]**

		Moran's *I* w_1 [2]	Standard dev. w_1	Standard . value w_1	Standard . value w_2	Standard . Value w_3
Labor int. prod.	emp	0.00137674	0.003843	0.985*	0.796*	0.684*
	firms	0.02980270	0.003854	8.359	4.913	3.226
Capital int. prod.	emp	0.00042139	0.003832	0.739*	1.285*	1.286*
	firms	0.00087018	0.003853	0.851*	1.073*	0.813*
Process industry	emp	-0.00054202	0.003832	-0.500*	1.171*	1.562*
	firms	-0.00158910	0.003801	0.216*	0.832*	1.039*
Knowl. int. prod.	emp	0.00334548	0.003840	1.498*	1.175*	1.021*
	firms	0.01402685	0.003861	4.258	1.497*	0.465*
Administr. istribution	emp	0.02399841	0.003840	6.877	4.993	4.197
	firms	0.04058514	0.003813	11.277	6.920	5.255
Physical distribution	emp	0.00686644	0.003847	2.411	1.557*	1.164*
	firms	0.01991490	0.003860	5.784	2.967	1.906*
Physical infrastructr.	emp	0.01455770	0.003841	4.418	2.077	0.994*
	firms	0.04732793	0.003851	12.917	7.990	5.652
Co-ordination act.	emp	0.00189672	0.003836	1.123*	0.536*	0.349*
	firms	-0.00128157	0.003858	-0.292*	-0.241*	-0.301*
Knowledge services	emp	0.00470298	0.003817	1.863*	0.936*	0.462*
	firms	0.03467084	0.003808	9.737	5.129	3.335
Consumer services	emp	0.00388335	0.003778	1.665*	0.868*	0.495*
	firms	0.01962485	0.003810	5.784	4.174	3.395
Institutions	emp	0.00041016	0.003848	0.637*	0.521*	0.083*
	firms	0.01298690	0.003860	3.989	2.742	2.193
Education	emp	-0.00418403	0.003790	-0.468*	-0.476*	-0.621*
	firms	0.00618397	0.003844	2.236	1.565*	1.455*
Health care	emp	0.00396504	0.003849	1.656*	1.602*	1.234*
	firms	0.01654211	0.003842	4.932	4.495	3.639
Leisure	emp	0.01094526	0.003841	3.477	2.773	2.154
	firms	0.01763864	0.003840	5.221	3.396	2.545
Total (S-Holland)	emp	0.01719049	0.003645	5.377	3.882	2.760
	firms	0.02506017	0.003696	7.433	4.997	3.629
Manufacturing	emp	0.00402447	0.003849	1.671*	1.129*	0.914*
	firms	0.03908257	0.003859	10.754	5.732	3.275
Distribution	emp	0.03004956	0.003806	8.528	5.638	4.228
	firms	0.05542841	0.003808	15.189	8.978	6.301
Producer services	emp	0.00597481	0.003811	2.200	1.116*	0.581*
	firms	0.03112461	0.003801	8.823	5.091	3.631
Consumer services	emp	0.01415147	0.003831	4.324	3.722	3.044
	firms	0.0165112	0.003783	5.001	3.667	2.998
Population		0.00909073	0.003682	3.124	2.278	1.631*

1 Agriculture and mining activities are not presented because of an insufficient number of observations. w_1, w_2 and w_3 express row standardized higher order weight matrices (weights divided by distances d_{ij} raised to integer powers 1, 2 and 3).

2 The expected value for Moran's *I* statistic is constant over each sector, both for employment and number of firms: $E(I)$=-0.002. All statistics except those marked * are significant at p=0.05.

**Figure 4.5   Moran scatterplot employment growth South-Holland
                (1988-1997, n=416, w_1)**

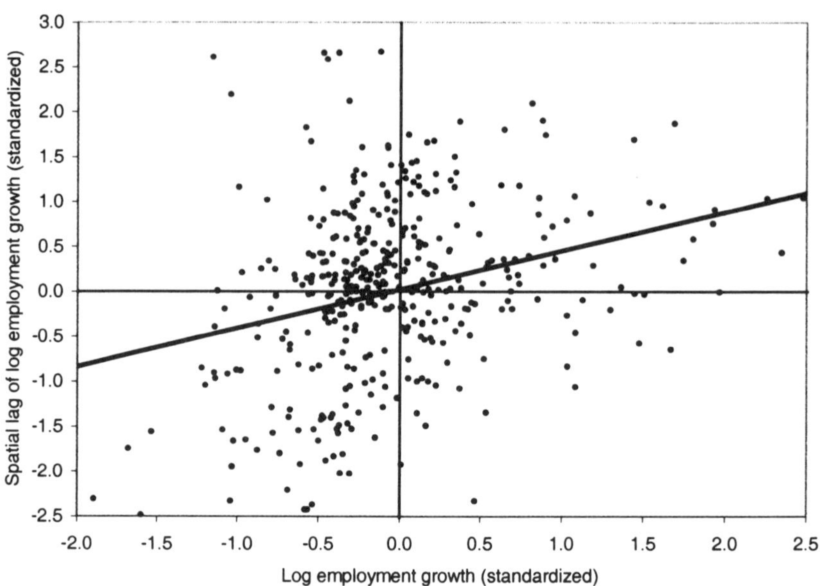

Spatial autocorrelation of growth in number of firms again shows clearer patterns, as do sectoral aggregates (the division in industry, distribution, producer and consumer services) as opposed to individual sectors[15]. The Moran scatterplot for total employment growth rates is displayed in figure 4.5 and the Moran scatterplot map in figure 4.6. Compared to the employment density and function scatterplots (figures 4.1 and 4.3) there is much more instability. Only 55.6% of the South-Holland locations show association of similar values (24.8% in quadrant I (HH) and 30.8% in quadrant III (LL)), while 44.4% of the locations are negatively associated (30.5% in quadrant II (LH) and 13.9% in quadrant IV (HL)).

---

[15] Combes (2000) in a study of employment growth in French regions on 94 individual sectoral levels in the period 1984-1993, did not test for the extent of spatial autocorrelation in the data used. Table 4.4 suggests that many individual growth rates are initially not spatially agglomerated to a degree that conclusions on agglomeration economies can properly be made in the sectoral endogenous growth framework as applied in Combes (2000) and Henderson *et al.* (1995).

**Figure 4.6   Moran scatterplot map employment growth South-Holland
(1988-1997, w_1)**

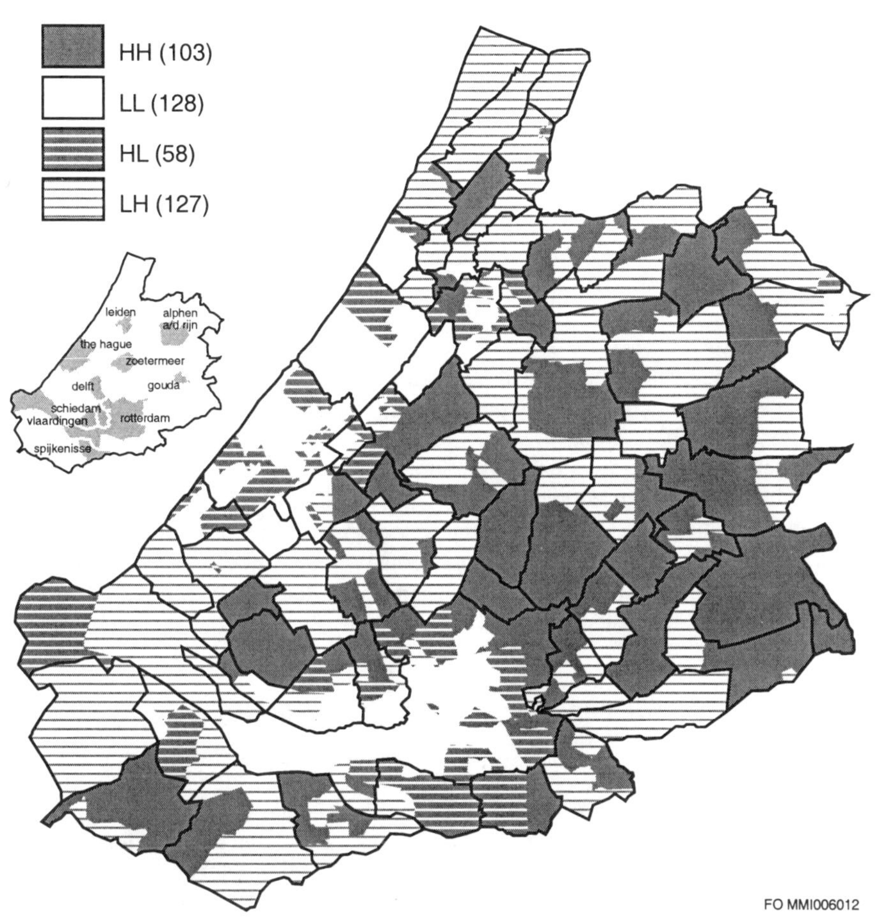

From figure 4.6 it becomes clear that the LL-classification of spatial autocorrelation of employment growth[16] is concentrated in the urban core locations of The Hague and Rotterdam. The agglomerated growth locations are to be found on the edges of the main urban municipalities and in the region north-east of Rijnmond[17]. This confirms the local and regional growth patterns as outlined in previous research as discussed in chapter 3. Sectoral scatterplot maps of employment growth for industrial and distribution activities, as well as producer and consumer services, can be found in Van Oort (2002a). The four sectors show specific local growth concentrations, especially industrial activities shows from the general pattern differing localizations of spatial autocorrelation. Growth in producer services shows specific LL-concentrations of spatial autocorrelation in the Westland region and larger cities and HH-concentrations in non-urban areas and medium-sized cities like Gouda, Alphen aan den Rijn and Zoetermeer. Overall growth patterns do not differ much on global sight though. Variations in growth only come to the front when studying the maps on a very detailed level. In order to capture relevant local differences in agglomeration circumstances explaining sectoral (endogenous) employment growth, formulation and construction of relevant variables in the next chapters should therefore be done on the lowest spatial level possible. Table 4.4 also reveals that the most significant spatial autocorrelation in the growth data is captured when using the w_1 weight matrix, which will therefore be used most in the following chapters. From table 4.4 it also becomes clear that the degree of spatial autocorrelation of population growth is significant but not very high. For simultaneously determined causal relationships between employment and population dynamics in the South-Holland data see Bruinsma *et al.* (2002).

4.4   New Firm Formation and Exit in South-Holland

An important question to be answered in endogenous growth models in an economic agglomeration context is the identification of spatial growth determinants among establishments that have remained at one location for a period of years. Previously, studies have used aggregated regional or locational employment growth as the focus of analysis. This inhabits two separate elements: employment growth may arise both in existing establishments and changes in sectoral employment might be due to new establishments settling in the region or dissoluting firm leaving the region. Indeed, Henderson *et al.* (1995) attribute part of the differences between their results and those of Glaeser *et al.* (1992) to

---

[16] The Moran scatterplot map for growth of total *number of firms* (available on request) shows broadly a spatial pattern similar to figure 4.6 of employment growth.

[17] The reported LISA-statistics reveal that not all observations plotted in figure 4.6 are significant at the 0.05 level. Outliers occurred because of the opening of new, and more than average expansion of existing business sites in zip code areas in the period 1988-97, inducing employment to grow disproportionally. See for outlier-corrections Van Oort (2002a). In the models in chapters 5 and 6 a controlling variable or spatial regimes for the opening and disproportional expansion of business sites will be used to capture these supply-induced outlier values.

whether one is analyzing young industries that are still expanding in terms of number of establishments, or more mature industries. Due to the availability of establishment-level data for the province of South-Holland, it is possible to identify growth in existing and new, dissoluting or moving firms. In this section Moran's *I* statistics are discussed for new firm formation, firm exit and their relation with employment creation and destruction rates. This is important for identifying whether aggregated locational or location-industry results apply to establishments present in the base year of analyses, or whether they merely reflect a tendency for new establishments to start up (or exit) in areas where their sector is under- (or over-)represented. Sectoral new firm formation and exit rates and accompanying employment creation and destruction are calculated as a percentage of the total stock of firms or employment in a certain location. Table 4.5 shows standardized Moran's *I* values for each year in the period 1988-1997 for industrial and distribution activities, for producer and consumer services as well as for all activities aggregated (total)[18].

Striking is the instability of significance levels in both employment and number of firms over the years. New and dissoluting firms show particularly high patterns of spatial autocorrelation in 1992, and low values in 1996. Remember from chapter 3 that the largest absolute changes in number of firms are in producer and consumer services (retail). In general, less clustered new firm formation rates and rates of exit (both in firms and employment) occur after 1992 in all economic sectors, the period of relative economic upheaval. Figures 4.7 and 4.8 show the Moran scatterplot maps for average employment creation in new firms and employment destruction in firm exits (over the period 1988-1997) respectively. High spatial autocorrelated (HH) values of both new and dissoluted firms are present in both urban central locations as well in suburban locations and medium-sized cities. This confirms the extended incubation theory of large urban agglomerations as formulated by Leone and Struyck (1976), Davelaar (1989) and Brouwer *et al.* (1999). Albeit some locations, especially inside and north-east of Rotterdam, show high HH-values of spatial autocorrelation on both employment creation by new as well as employment destruction in exiting firms, the spatial configuration of figure 4.7 differs substantially from that in figure 4.8[19]. Especially the locations in The Hague, as well as some between Rotterdam and The Hague show different autocorrelation values (in general LL for new firm employment and HH/HL for employment destruction by exits). Average job creation (by new firms) does thus have a significant different spatial autocorrelated pattern when compared to job destruction (by exiting firms). Pearson's correlation coefficients comprising total employment growth (figure 4.6) with new firm employment creation and destruction are respectively 0.309** and –0.151**. With population growth these

---

[18] Comparison of stocks of firms reveals new and dissoluted firms, present in one year and absent in the former/later. Therefore, only 9 years of comparison are available.

[19] The Pearson's correlation coefficient for (log) new firm and (log) firm exits employment is 0.394 (n=416). For individual sectors the correlation coefficients are: 0.503 (industry), 0.357 (distribution), 0.485 (producer services) and 0.280 (consumer services).

coefficients are respectively 0.141** and 0.049[20]. Employment creation by new firm formation and exits is thus significantly correlated with total employment growth, confirming the hypothesis that explanations of *endogenous* growth of employment in a spatial context potentially gain from correcting for dynamics caused by new and dissoluting firms.

Table 4.5   Standardized values of Moran's *I* statistic for new firm formation, exit and employment creation (South-Holland, 1997, randomization assumption, w_1)[1,2]

	1988	1989	1990	1991	1992	1993	1994	1995	1996
New firms									
Firms									
Industry	6.69	12.29	5.97	10.82	9.11	1.52*	2.28	12.81	6.49
Distribution	22.16	19.03	24.17	20.70	24.82	7.22	21.12	14.25	15.34
Prod. Services	17.32	20.49	17.33	20.59	17.80	12.30	10.08	16.95	4.52
Cons. services	8.35	11.72	8.60	13.24	29.07	13.46	2.29	9.30	6.50
Total	21.22	25.70	20.48	27.75	41.01	15.30	10.26	26.07	13.61
Employment									
Industry	5.67	9.53	5.18	8.22	7.51	1.07*	1.53*	9.57	7.37
Distribution	12.94	13.17	14.93	15.10	15.81	3.66	9.40	7.42	12.36
Prod. Services	12.21	13.32	12.48	13.58	10.16	8.39	4.11	10.27	2.63
Cons. services	5.12	5.53	5.42	6.45	16.71	4.89	1.99	5.17	5.37
Total	9.08	9.70	9.89	10.39	21.35	5.68	3.14	11.05	7.09
Exit firms									
Firms									
Industry	5.38	4.25	4.54	4.27	10.29	4.13	3.38	2.09	0.02*
Distribution	5.73	9.17	5.53	13.86	23.98	20.57	7.59	6.69	4.25
Prod. Services	5.52	6.08	6.24	7.63	16.61	5.47	5.30	5.03	2.18
Cons. services	10.21	11.38	5.74	7.22	20.66	10.54	6.53	9.23	2.53
Total	13.23	15.24	10.52	14.35	30.23	21.39	11.33	7.63	5.50
Employment									
Industry	6.28	3.41	3.56	3.86	6.79	3.42	3.58	3.02	0.50*
Distribution	2.81	7.13	4.53	8.60	14.25	19.65	6.38	4.67	3.46
Prod. Services	4.31	5.29	4.24	6.73	6.75	3.81	4.92	4.44	0.81*
Cons. services	8.18	8.77	3.48	3.71	11.82	3.50	4.57	9.27	2.40
Total	6.87	5.75	3.21	3.46	13.70	8.66	5.04	3.19	2.21

1   Agriculture and mining activities are not presented because of an insufficient number of observations.
2   The expected value for Moran's *I* statistic is constant over each sector, both for new and exiting employment and number of firms: $E(I)=-0.002$. All statistics except those marked (*) are significant at $p=0.05$.

---

[20] Coefficients marked by ** are significant at the 0.01 level. The Pearson's correlation coefficient (n=416) of total employment growth (figure 4.6) with population growth is 0.228**.

Figure 4.7　Moran scatterplot map new firm employment South-Holland (average % 1988-1997, w_1)

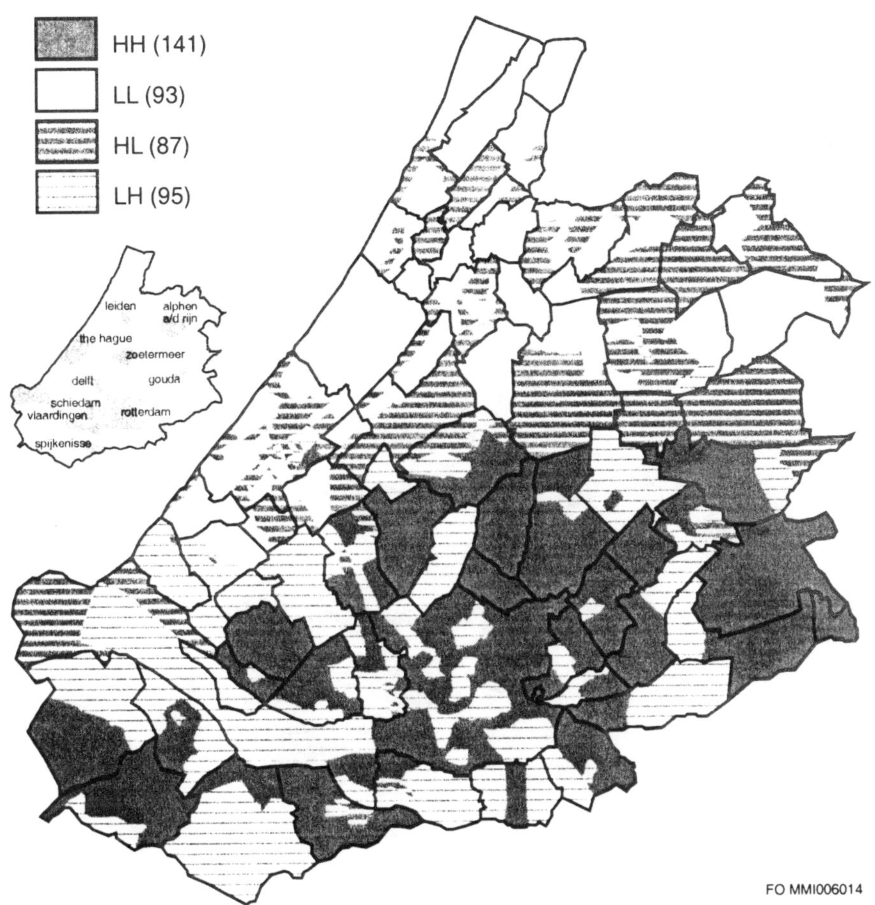

 Urban Growth and Innovation

Figure 4.8   Moran scatterplot map firm-exit employment South-Holland (average % 1988-1997, w_1)

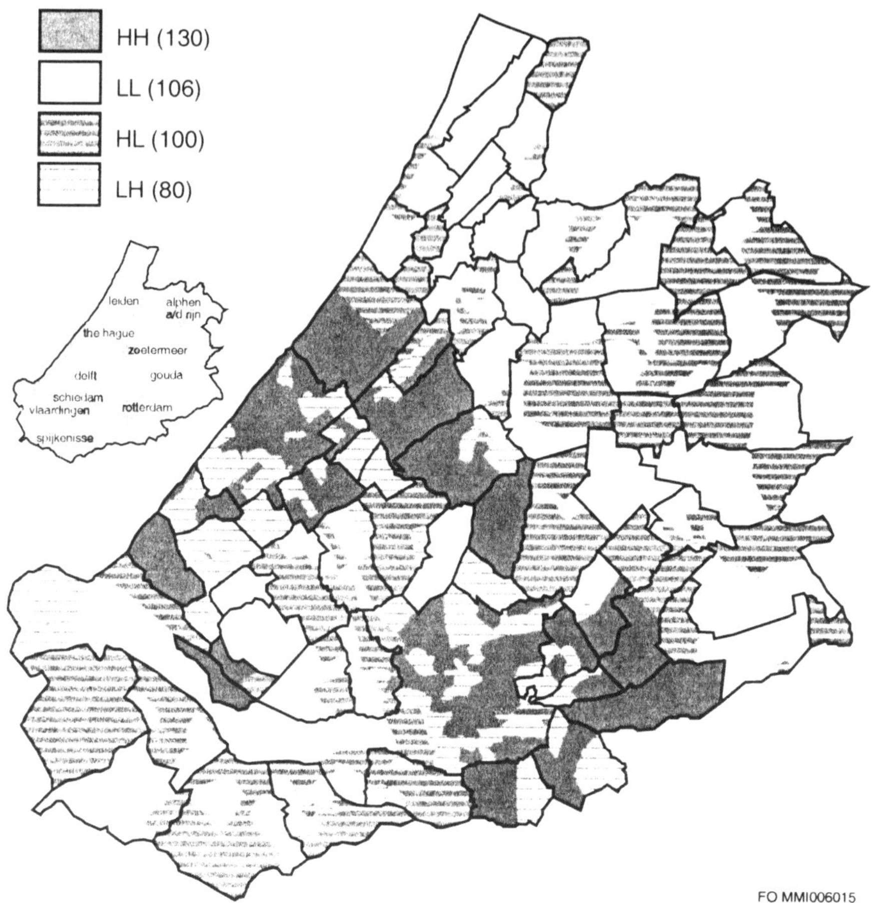

4.5 Employment Density, Function and Growth in the Netherlands

In chapter 3 potential models for employment growth in municipalities for the period 1991-1997 were analyzed to visualize relative spatial changes in macro-economic regimes. On a national scale it is interesting to analyze spatial dependency in structure and growth of employment using ESDA, similar to analyses in previous sections for the South-Holland research area.

Table 4.6 presents the standardized values of Moran's *I* statistics for the employment density and function for sectors as presented in the previous section for the region of South-Holland. Although the different spatial scales of analysis (zip code areas in South-Holland versus municipalities in the Netherlands) prohibits close comparison, the global sectoral (growth) statistics show quite similar development patterns. On the national scale, patterns of spatial autocorrelation are more profound, both for employment density and functions, as well as for employment growth. Especially for manufacturing more significant spatial agglomerated patterns evolve over the period 1991-1997. Figure 4.9 shows the Moran scatterplot map for the employment *function* (employment relative to total population) for all activities aggregated (total). For individual sectors, the scatterplot maps are presented in Van Oort (2002a). From these figures, spatial autocorrelation patterns become clear. Figure 4.9 in fact combines the pattern of figure 3.5 (gravity model for $\alpha=1$) and with that of a more localized spatial weight matrix (e.g. $\alpha=3$) in one figure, which therefore is superior. The suggestive maps resulting from gravity models level out local pockets of representation or growth compared to their environment and therefore preferable are not to be used for other purposes than global description. Figure 4.9 shows that the overall high agglomeration scores of the Randstad regions are determined by the scores in the larger urban agglomerations. Locations in the Green Heart region (in between the cities) typically show LH-scores of spatial autocorrelation (low own value, higher neighborhood values). Relative specialization of locations in industrial activities shows typically a non-Randstad pattern (Van Oort 2002a). Noord-Brabant, Gelderland and Twente show relative high HH-values of spatial autocorrelation. Distribution activities though are significantly spatially autocorrelated in the Randstad region (both in the urban areas as in the Green Heart region) and in the western parts of Noord-Brabant. Producer services finally are typically focused on the urban dimension of the locational segmentation. These activities on a national scale became relatively less agglomerated. This development comes more to the fore than in the South-Holland analysis, where especially consumer activities (which make up a large part of all activities) showed a stabilizing or even agglomerating tendency over the period 1988-1997.

As was the case in the South-Holland analyses, population and employment developments (as defined by equation 4.5) show different degrees of spatial autocorrelation (see table 4.6). Population growth, as well as growth of employment in industrial activities, is only significant (at the $p=0.05$ level) in terms of spatial autocorrelation when analyzing at the w_1 level of spatial interaction (weight matrices).

Table 4.6   **Standardized values of Moran's *I* statistic for employment function and firm representation (Netherlands, 1997, randomization assumption)[1,2]**

		manu-facturing	distribution	producer services	consum. services	total
employment density 1997	W_1	19.439	52.405	54.238	41.366	48.078
	W_2	11.401	29.069	31.676	26.031	28.725
	W_3	7.568	19.282	21.554	18.033	19.513
employment density 1991	W_1	18.287	51.033	47.006	37.540	45.583
	W_2	10.687	28.840	28.376	24.242	27.785
	W_3	6.890	19.210	19.565	17.004	19.057
firm density 1997	W_1	43.209	64.215	61.273	49.859	58.589
	W_2	25.990	35.774	35.545	30.328	34.977
	W_3	17.886	23.849	24.242	20.663	23.996
employm. function 1997	W_1	10.402	16.388	35.559	9.035	7.934
	W_2	6.823	9.659	20.960	7.701	5.084
	W_3	4.932	6.508	14.391	6.018	3.158
firm representation 1997	W_1	21.850	41.681	61.088	29.809	26.030
	W_2	16.100	26.116	37.828	20.639	17.691
	W_3	11.964	17.763	26.269	15.337	12.589
employm. growth 91-97	W_1	1.982	4.969	8.912	6.036	7.020
	W_2	1.758*	4.643	7.249	4.069	5.604
	W_3	1.540*	3.710	5.983	2.766	4.860
popul. growth 1991-97	W_1	-	-	-	-	2.052
	W_2	-	-	-	-	1.419*
	W_3	-	-	-	-	1.191*

1   Agriculture and mining activities are not presented because of an insufficient number of observations. w_1, w_2 and w_3 express row standardized higher order weight matrices (weights divided by distances d_{ij} raised to integer powers 1, 2 and 3).

2   The expected value for Moran's *I* statistic is constant over each sector, both for employment and number of firms: $E(I)=-0.002$. All statistics except those marked * are significant at $p=0.05$.

Employment growth patterns show considerable spatial (contiguous) dependency Figure 4.10 reveals that for employment development, 61% of all (580) observations show positive spatial autocorrelation (196 HH-values and 160 LL-values). The pattern of positive spatial autocorrelation in employment growth shows relative more HH-scores in the Randstad region and in the northern part of North-Holland and Friesland. Employment dynamics on small spatial scales is influenced by zoning policy-based spatial planning (e.g. by the opening up of new industrial sites). It is important to correct for these outliers that (un)naturally cause large growth rates. Still, changing spatial scales for (sectoral decomposed) employment patterns and developments require careful interpretations of analyses.

Figure 4.9   Moran scatterplot map employment function Netherlands (1997, w_1)

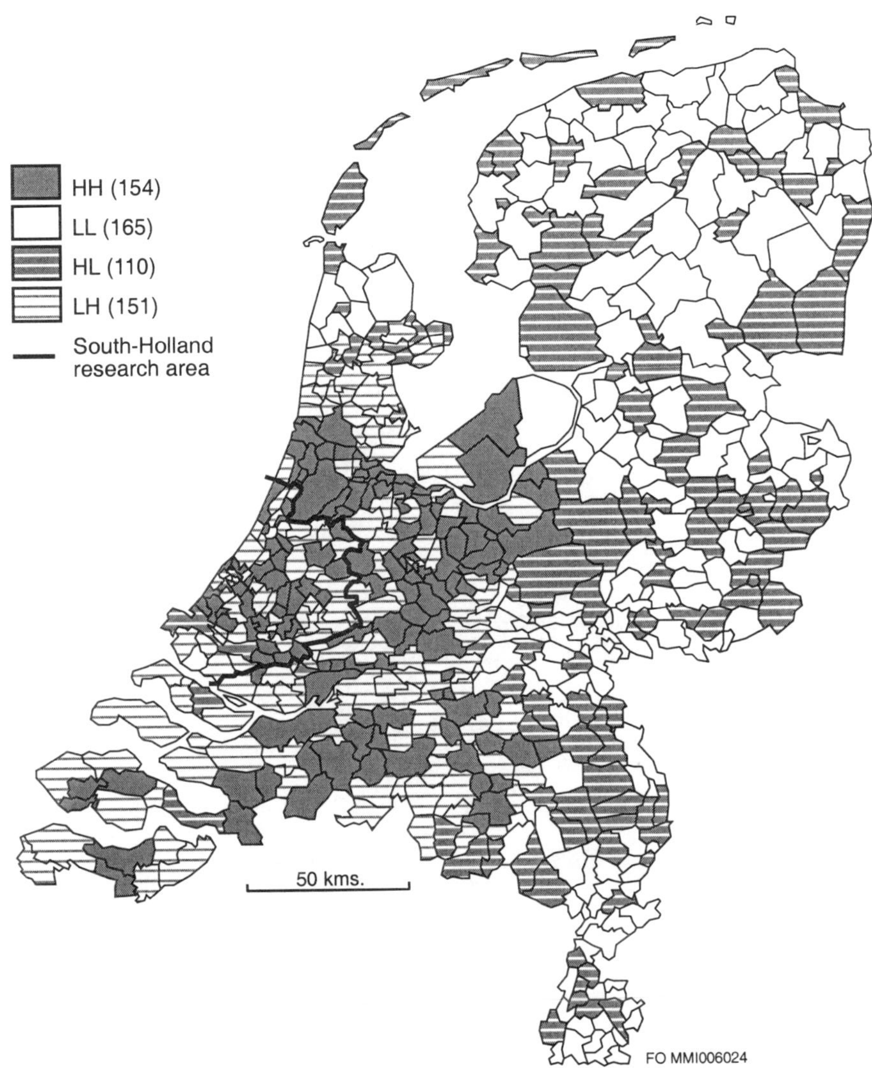

Figure 4.10   **Moran scatterplot map employment growth Netherlands (1991-1997, w_1)**

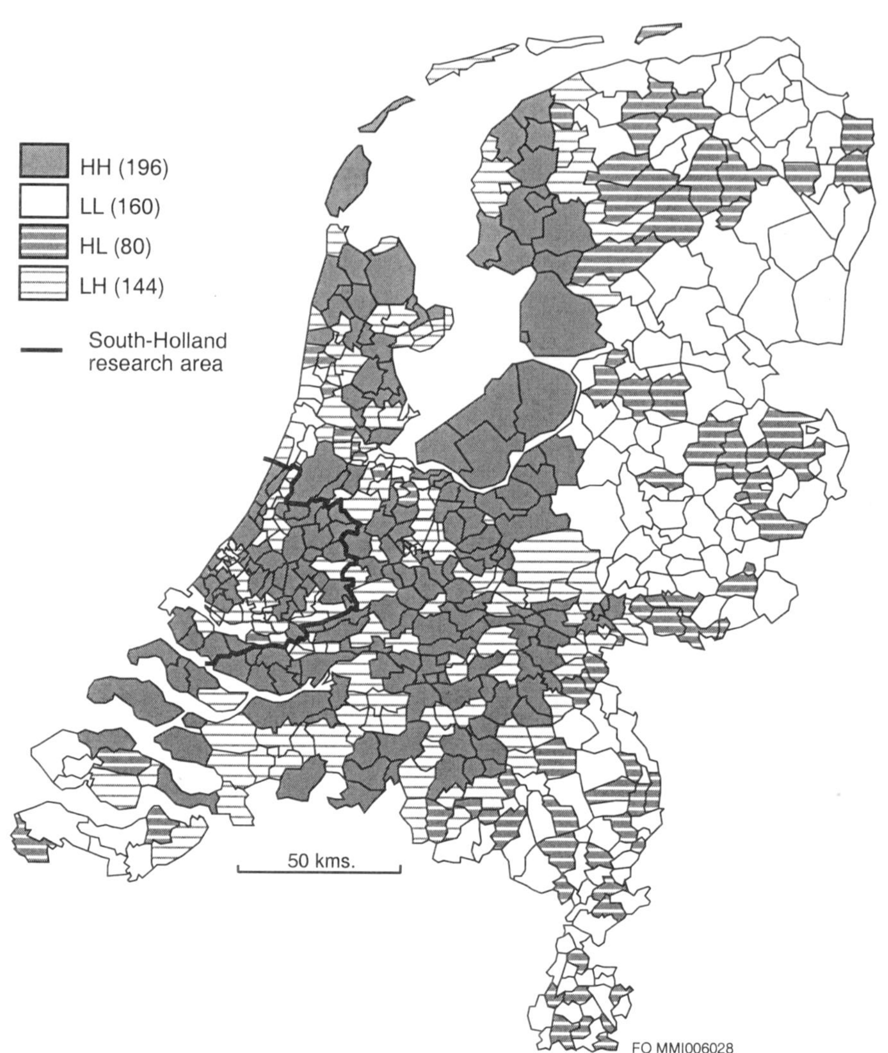

4.6   Innovation Intensity in the Netherlands

In this section, the technique of explanatory spatial data analysis is applied to the degrees of innovation intensity in Dutch municipalities (for a technical description of the data see appendix B). Innovation intensity is defined as the total sum of wage costs divided by the persons employed in firms. As in the employment dynamics analysis, 580 observations are present[21]. Table 4.7 gives Moran's *I* statistics measured over industries and technology groups.

Table 4.7   Moran's *I* statistics for innovation intensity (Netherlands 1999, w_1, randomization assumption)[1]

	Moran's *I* w_1 [2]	standard dev. w_1	standard. value w_1	standard. value w_2	standard. value w_3
sectors (sbi):					
labour intensive production	0.0219576	0.002872	8.246	4.926	3.043
capital intensive production	0.0111597	0.002873	4.486	4.177	3.422
knowledge int. process ind.	0.0082968	0.002873	3.489	3.327	2.974
knowledge intens. production	0.0060746	0.002869	2.719	2.636	2.500
manufacturing	*0.0123010*	*0.002851*	*4.919*	*4.292*	*3.553*
distribution	0.0064673	0.002873	2.852	2.567	2.192
producer services	0.0169813	0.002874	6.510	5.204	4.134
consumer services	0.0001396	0.002869	0.651*	0.117*	-0.126*
Agriculture	0.0191952	0.002873	7.284	5.588	4.402
non-manufacturing	*0.0242352*	*0.002872*	*9.041*	*7.241*	*5.893*
total	0.0176075	0.002858	6.765	5.670	4.509
activity-code (bsi):					
chemical technology	0.0008784	0.002873	0.907*	0.498*	0.187*
commun. & computer techn.	0.0132539	0.002873	5.215	4.880	4.340
production technology	0.0027438	0.002867	10.174	7.917	6.016
agriculture and food techn.	0.0156237	0.002872	6.041	6.803	6.080
scientific technology	0.0107463	0.002873	4.342	4.191	3.893

1   w_1, w_2 and w_3 express row standardized higher order weight matrices (weights divided by distances d_{ij} raised to integer powers 1, 2 and 3).

2   The expected value for Moran's *I* statistic is constant over each sector and activity code: $E(I)=-0.002$. All statistics except for 'consumer services' and 'chemical technology' (marked*) are significant at $p=0.01$.

---

[21] On the municipal level only a few zero locational observations per industry or technology group remain present, indicating that the municipal level from a spatial-econometric point of view is a good level to work on. It should be remarked that the spatial econometric software used (SPACESTAT) is unable to handle truncated or count data correctly.

Because the R&D innovation data mainly concern manufacturing activities, the manufacturing sector has been divided in four separate sectors (see chapter 3). Within manufacturing activities, labor-intensive production firms show the highest degree of spatial autocorrelation in terms of innovation intensity. R&D expenditures concerning consumer services do not show any spatially autocorrelated pattern. From table 4.7 it also becomes clear that besides consumer services, non-industrial R&D expenditures are more spatially autocorrelated than industrial. Figure 4.11 shows the scatterplot map of total innovation intensity in the Netherlands. Since innovation intensity is defined as the R&D wage sum denominated by employment, the figure shows the *difference* in spatially autocorrelated values of R&D expenditures relative to employment density (as discussed in the previous section). The figure makes clear that positively spatially autocorrelated values (HH and LL) are to be found outside the Randstad core region. HH values of autocorrelation are clustered in Southeast Noord-Brabant (around Eindhoven), Twente (around Enschede), Nijmegen, Geleen/Sittard and the Veluwe region. In general, large complexes of industrial firms (Philips, AKZO-Nobel, DSM Chemicals) or technical university complexes (Enschede, Eindhoven, Wageningen) are present in these regions. Clearly, this spatial pattern of innovative activity is different from the employment and population density functions applied in this chapter. Concentration of LL scores is to be found in the northern and southern provinces of the country. The Randstad region shows local pockets of high innovation intensity (HL) mixed with low scores (LH). Urban regions tend to score either HH or HL, indicating that urbanization or urban induced functional (connectedness) spatial regimes might be appropriate for modeling explanatory models for this R&D pattern. From table 4.7 it becomes clear that the distinction manufacturing- and non-manufacturing-induced R&D expenditures is important[22]. Figures 4.12 and 4.13 show the spatially autocorrelated patterns for industrial and non-industrial R&D expenditure patterns respectively. Both industrial and non-industrial innovation intensities are spatially autocorrelated, but two elements are important to notice. First, non-industrial innovation shows a higher degree of autocorrelation than industrial. Second, except for the difference in magnitude of correlation, the clustering of especially HH values of autocorrelation takes place in different regions as well. From figure 4.12 it becomes clear that the intermediate zone on a macro scale, Twente and the north-wing of the Randstad (Amsterdam-Utrecht) are clusters or hot spots of *industrial* innovation intensity. Figure 4.13 shows that for *non-industrial* innovation intensity, the main density of HH values shifts towards the (south-wing) of the Randstad.

---

[22] For all industries and technology fields listed in table 4.7 and appendix B Moran scatterplots and Moran scatterplot maps were made. Because of lack of space, not all are presented. Instead, they are available on request. The variation in spatially autocorrelated patterns across individual industries is limited, knowledge-intensive process industries being the exception. This industry is concentrated in a few (extreme) large industries in the Rotterdam harbour, Terneuzen, Geleen/Sittard, Arnhem and Moerdijk. Schmitz and Heijs (2001, figures 4.6 and 4.7) clearly show the sensitivity of spatial innovation intensity indicators for these 'outliers' in this industry. Still, the patterns presented in this chapter of our study show larger degrees of spatial aiutocorrelation than these single establishments justify, indicating the presence of agglomerated structures stretching over contiguous (proximate) municipalities.

Figure 4.11 Moran scatterplot map innovation intensity (1999, w_1)

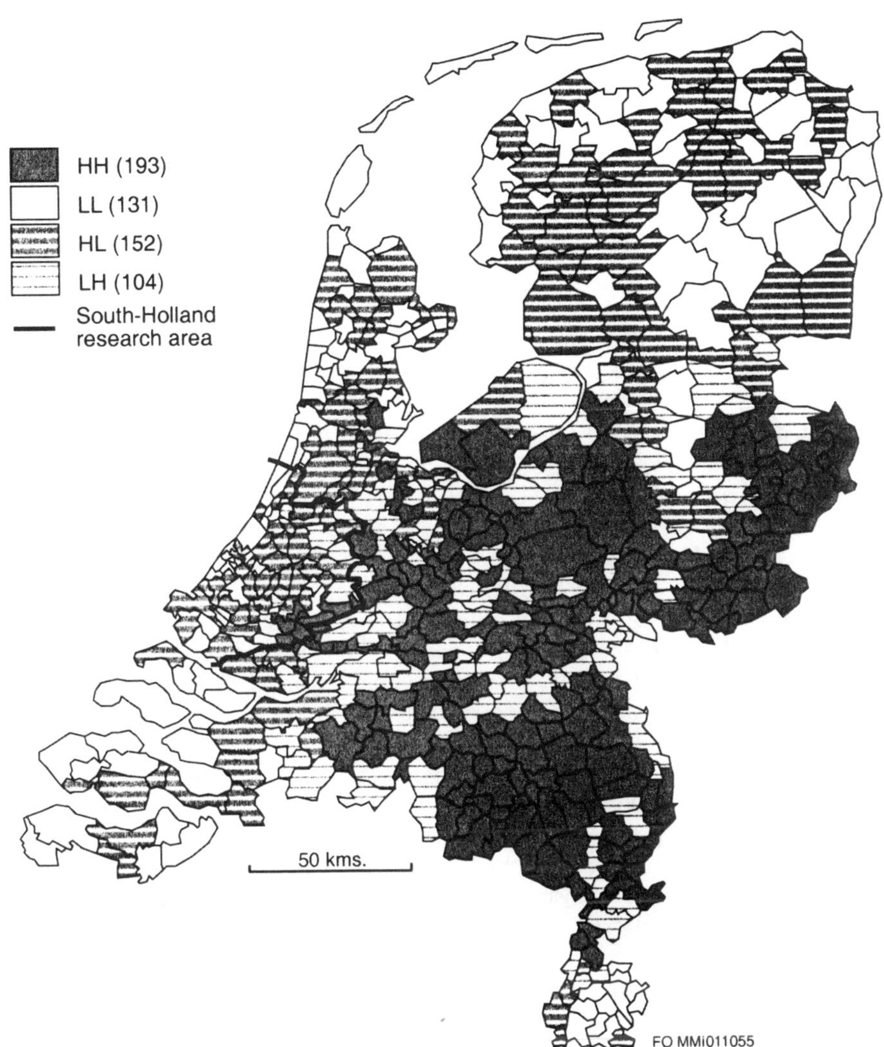

Spatial patterns of non-industrial innovation intensity resemble employment and population density more, while industrial innovation intensity differs substantially from that pattern[23]. The Eindhoven region and the Veluwe region show clusters of HH values in both industrial and non-industrial innovation intensity. This highlights their more diversified innovation structure. Remarkable is the cluster of LL values of non-industrial innovation intensity scores in and around Tilburg, a region known for its 'industrial innovative character'. The lower part of table 4.7 shows Moran *I* statistics for technology fields of R&D projects (see appendix B for their definition). Besides chemical technology, all BSI-clusters show considerable spatial autocorrelated patterns. Because of the comparability with sectoral segmented data on employment patterns and employment growth, the dissertation will concentrate on sectoral modeling.

4.7 Synthesis and Conclusions

The study of the spatial distribution of local employment and innovation concentration as well as employment growth in the research area of South-Holland (1988-1997) and the Netherlands (1991-1997) using Exploratory Spatial Data Analysis (ESDA) highlights the importance of spatial interactions and dependence on geographical locations in local growth issues. In this chapter, ESDA appears to be a useful tool to finely reveal the characteristics of economic and population growth of each location in relation to its geographical environment. ESDA reveals positive global spatial autocorrelation, which is to a large degree persistent over time[24], for employment density, firm density, employment function, relative firm representation and employment and population growth in the research area of South-Holland as well as for the Netherlands. On the latter spatial scale, innovation intensity is spatially autocorrelated to significant degrees as well. Employment *density* expresses the number of working persons per square kilometer, an often-used indicator for economic density used in the Dutch empirical and policy-oriented literature. As is argued in this chapter this indicator stresses, by the nature of its denominator, urban density. Average zip code areas and municipalities are smaller in urban locations, and smaller denominators induce potential higher autoregressive values of spatial concentration. A disadvantage of this measurement is that urbanization is the only measured phenomenon. An alternative measure applied to spatial autocorrelation indicators concerns the employment *function* and relative firm representation. The denominator of employment data applied is total population present in a location.

---

[23] Because industrial innovation (3,138 million guilders) exceeds non-industrial innovation (1,040 million guilders) by far, the overall (weighted) innovation pattern resembles the industrial pattern most.
[24] Some indications were found that the general economic situation matters for proximity-based agglomeration patterns over time. In times of relative economic upheaval, both growth patterns and business-cycle-related new firm formation and exit rates occur less agglomerated. Because of the relative short time series of the data and the fact that the 1991/1992 economic stagnation was a relative short break in general growth it is rather speculative to draw conclusions out of these observations. For a more robust statement on this, a longer time series of data is requested.

Figure 4.12　**Moran scatterplot map industrial innovation intensity (1999, w_1)**

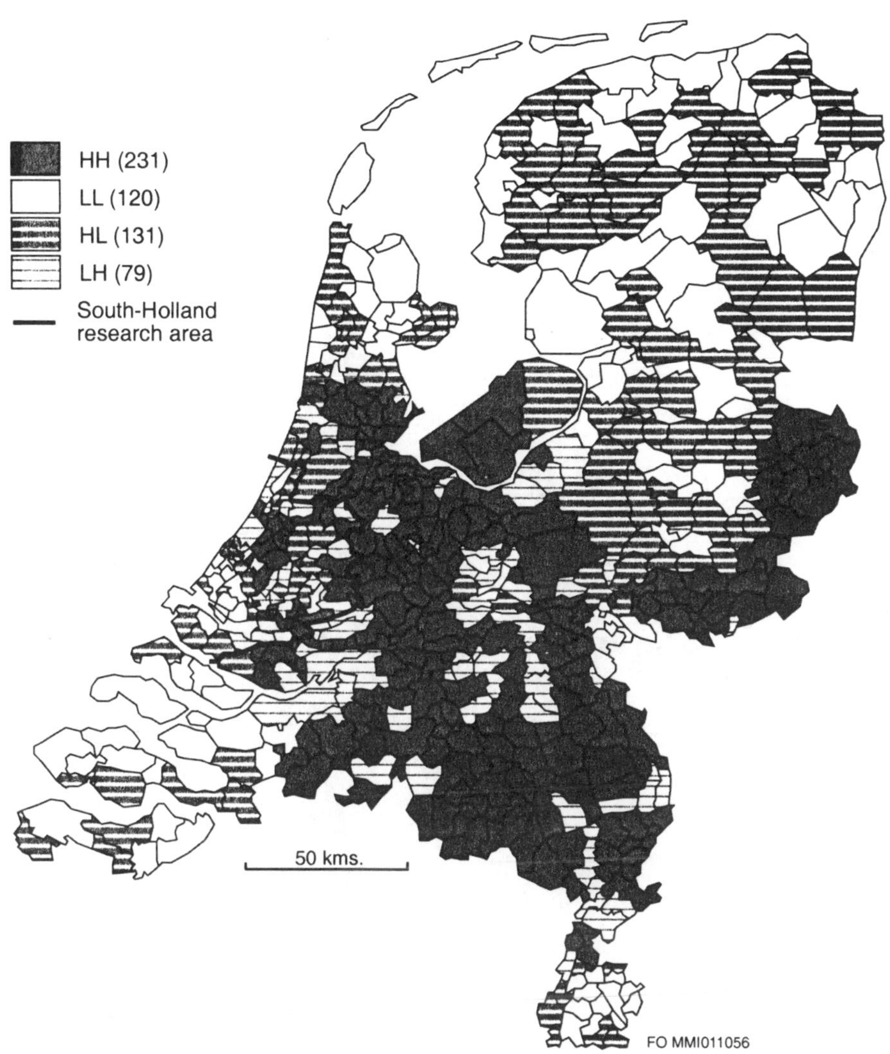

Figure 4.13   Moran scatterplot map non-industrial innovation intensity (1999, w_1)

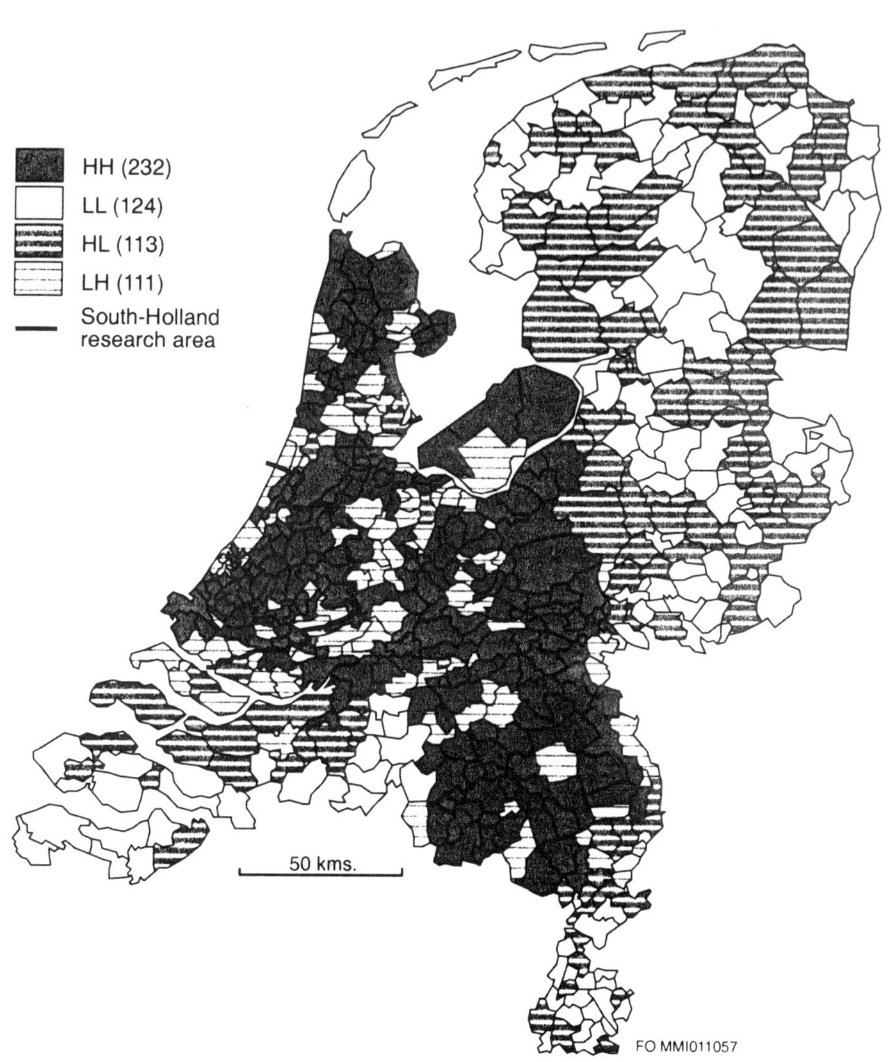

This measures relative specialization, corrected for the size of locations: population tends to be over-represented in urban locations as well. Statistics of spatial autocorrelation become considerably less (but remain) significant using this measurement. Moran scatterplot maps reveal that the largest urban agglomerations of the South-Holland research area as well as for the Dutch case are characterized by HH-scores of local spatial autocorrelation: urban locations show significant higher degrees of density *and* specialization values of economic activity. Rural regions score low (LL) on a national scale. Comparison of standardized values of Moran's *I* statistic over time (1988-1997 for the South-Holland research area and 1991-1997 for the Netherlands) reveal that economic activities in general become relatively less agglomerated over time. Consumer services show different 'behavior' in this respect. On the spatial level of zip codes in the South-Holland research area, stabilization or even a tendency to further agglomeration occurs for this broad sector. Since this type of activity is closely related to the distribution of population, it is no surprise that proximity-based agglomeration indicators in South-Holland (n=416) for both population and consumer service growth show considerable less spatial variability than that of other economic sectors. On the national level though (n=580), all types of economic activities (as distinguished by their sectoral composition) show a development towards less agglomeration.

The technique of explanatory spatial data analysis has been further applied to the degrees of innovation intensity in Dutch municipalities. Innovation intensity is defined as the total sum of wage costs divided by the persons employed in firms. Moran's *I* statistics were presented for industries and technology groups. The definition of innovation intensity by its nature shows the *difference* in spatially autocorrelated values of R&D expenditures relative to employment density. Positively spatially autocorrelated values of overall innovation intensity are to be found *outside* the Randstad core region. Clearly, this spatial pattern of innovative intensity is different from the employment and population density functions applied in this chapter. Scores of urban regions indicate that urbanization or urban-induced functional (connectedness) spatial regimes (as presented in chapter 3) might be appropriate for modeling explanatory models for R&D patterns. Albeit both industrial and non-industrial innovation intensities are spatially autocorrelated, two striking differences appear. First, non-industrial innovation shows a higher degree of autocorrelation than industrial. Second, except for the difference in magnitude of correlation, the clustering of high values of positive spatial autocorrelation takes place in different regions. The intermediate zone on a macro scale, Twente and the north-wing of the Randstad (Amsterdam-Utrecht) are clusters or hot spots of *industrial* innovation intensity. For *non-industrial* innovation intensity, the main density of positive values shifts towards the south-wing of the Randstad. Spatial patterns of non-industrial innovation intensity resemble employment density more, while industrial innovation intensity differs substantially from that pattern. The Eindhoven and Veluwe regions show clusters of positive values in *both* industrial and non-industrial innovation intensity, highlighting their more diversified innovation structure.

The central focus of this dissertation is on economic (employment) *growth* though. It appears that employment and population growth patterns are not distributed spatially randomly either. Cross-section and dynamic specifications reveal a significant tendency for (economic) growth to cluster in space. Local indicators of spatial autocorrelation of employment growth show contradicting patterns when compared to those of employment density and function. Urban areas are characterized by LL-spatial autocorrelation (as opposed to HH-values for representation). Non-urban areas, still close to the Randstad region and urban areas in general, show relatively most local spatial autocorrelation characterized as HH. Most significantly and robust, this appears from Moran's I test statistics when broad economic sectors (industry, distribution, producer services and consumer services) are analyzed, using (row-standardized) first-order distance weight matrices. Population growth in the regional (South-Holland) as well as national setting shows (albeit significant at the specified conditions) considerable less degrees of spatial autocorrelation than employment growth. Housing supply by local institutions appears influential in this respect.

The spatial contiguity-based, proximate spatial dependency of employment (growth) and innovation concentrations reaches over zip code- as well as municipal (city) boundaries. This is suggested both in global terms (from the Randstad region towards and into the intermediate zone and national periphery) as in local terms (from urban centers towards connected suburban locations and medium-sized cities throughout the region and country) by the analyses in this chapter. This confirms the literature and analyses discussed in chapter 3. Exploratory Spatial Data Analysis in itself does not yet reveal whether proximity-based (spatial lag/error), spatial heterogeneity (spatial regimes/expansion) or combined econometric specifications are best to capture the spatial structures explored. Additional relevant (causal) segmentation further appears to be that based on life stages and positions in the business cycle of firms. New firm formation and exit rates of firms, as well as their hypothesized job creating and destruction capacities, show significant degrees of spatial autocorrelation in the research area of South-Holland. High spatial autocorrelated (HH) values of both new and dissoluted firms are present in both central urban locations as well in suburban locations and medium-sized cities. This suggests the relevance of the extended incubation theory as formulated in the literature (see also Van Oort and Atzema 2003). Since employment creation by new firm formation and firm exits is significantly spatially correlated with total employment growth, the hypothesis that explanations of endogenous employment growth in spatial contexts potentially gain from correcting for these dynamics gains in importance. Finally we conclude that the division in 16 sectors appears relatively little fruitful for spatial analysis, while from the ESDA analysis growth and innovation patterns in four broad industries appears spatially significant. The next chapters will take into account these findings.

Chapter 5

Location-Industry Employment Dynamics

5.1 Introduction

This chapter takes three steps toward a better understanding of the relationship between knowledge externalities and economic growth using location-industry data for the South-Holland research area and the Netherlands. First, insight is provided into potential explanations for differences in results of two highly influential papers, Glaeser *et al.* (1992) and Henderson *et al.* (1995), using data from outside the United States. Like Combes (2000), who analyzed data from France, we draw attention to the importance of differences in the sectoral composition of the two datasets analyzed, and also focus on the differences in methodologies used. Second, we address several of the long-standing issues using data at the municipality (city) level from the entire country, as well as data from individual postal zip codes in South-Holland. This province, which is about the size of the Dallas-Ft. Worth metropolitan area, covers a substantial part of the country's core economic area, the Randstad. Because zip codes average less than 6 km^2 in size, we can analyze employment growth in very small areas within an already small heavily urbanized region. As explained more fully below, this affords better controls for spatial aggregation and unobserved location attributes (heterogeneity) than can be found in prior studies. Third, we are able to identify growth determinants among establishments that have remained at one location for a period of years and develop an alternative measure of local competition. Previous studies on agglomeration economies have not been able to distinguish between employment growth in existing establishments and employment growth attributable to establishment births, deaths, and relocations.

This chapter presents econometric models that aim at capturing several by now generally accepted geographically induced characteristics of agglomeration and knowledge externalities (see chapter 2): local specialization, local diversity and indicators of the local degree of competition. For the latter we are able to develop (in the South-Holland context) an alternative and to our opinion complementary indicator when compared to existing ones. The measurement unit in this chapter concerns location-industries, while chapter 6 focuses on spatial econometric modeling of growth in industrial, distribution, producer and consumer service sectors separately. The OLS models presented in this chapter (sections 5.3 and 5.4) try to shed an initial light on the spatial circumstances that foster or retard employment growth in location-industries in the research area of South-Holland and the Netherlands. These analyses will function as a starting point of analysis (null-model) for more for more sophisticated spatial econometric models presented in following sections and chapters. The null-model analyses presented in this chapter are most closely reminiscent to the influential (OLS) analyses presented by Glaeser *et al.* (1992) that have set an analytical standard for agglomeration externalities on the urban level. The Netherlands-analyses focus on the urban growth level as well, while the South-Holland analyses focus on spatial heterogeneity and contiguous dependency in intra-urban spatial settings of growth. Intra- as well as inter-industry linkages are more adequately captured by spatial weight matrix definitions that suit location-industry analyses, while only inter-industry linkages are served by separate industry-specific analyses in chapters 6 (on employment dynamics) and 7 (on innovation intensity). Separate industry-specific analyses *a priori* seem most fruitful for testing spatial heterogeneity hypotheses[1].

A theoretical and empirical aspect on which emphasis is put in this chapter is how readily knowledge (through either the growth process and the intensity and adoption of innovation) is transmitted through space. Using data on innovations and patents, several papers find that knowledge appears to be geographically bounded (Acs 2002, Audretsch and Feldman 1996 and Jaffe *et al.* 1993). However, if knowledge creation affects local growth, its impact still could travel over space through (direct or indirect) economic linkages present in the growth process (compare Hornstein and Praschnik 1997). The relative importance of various types of externalities in fostering both localized economic growth and growth among more geographically dispersed areas has broad implications ranging from the formulation and interpretation of endogenous growth models to practical conclusions that might be drawn by policy makers regarding city planning and development.

This chapter is further built up as follows. Section 5.2 introduces the variables that are used in the location-industry analysis applied in this chapter. Section 5.3 then examines geographical determinants of employment growth in 234 Dutch municipalities, while section 5.4 looks at employment growth in 416 zip (postal) code areas in South Holland. Comparable to the Henderson *et al.* (1995) study, OLS regressions are applied on individual industries concerning employment *levels*. Then, comparable to the Glaeser *et al.* (1992) study, OLS regression results are presented for location-industries concerning employment *growth* on two spatial scales. For the South-Holland analyses the alternative local-competition indicator is introduced and applied. In section 5.5 spatial lag and error specifications that capture contiguous spatial dependence are introduced in the South-Holland analysis[2]. Special attention is given to effects generated by applying intra- and inter-industry spatial weight matrices in the analysis, and conclusions are drawn concerning the magnitude of spatial multipliers. These latter indicate how readily knowledge is transmitted through space. Broadly, results presented show that local industrial diversity and local competition foster employment growth within a location. Using a reduced form

---

[1] Compare Alperovich and Deutsch (2002) and Arbia (2001). The analytical 'benchmark'-study by Gleaser *et al.* (1992) does not use spatial weight matrices for inter- and intra-industry linkages, inter-urban zoning and spatial heterogeneity for individual industries, nor does it provide an adequate treatment of locations outside cities.

[2] Comparable contiguous spatial dependence modeling on the national level are discussed in Van Soest, Gerking and Van Oort (2002).

spatial multiplier definition, it is also shown that employment growth is potentially transmitted contiguously across zip codes, but that this effect appears to fade quickly with distance. Section 5.6 summarizes and discusses the significance of extending the OLS null-models of location-industry specifications into contiguously defined spatial econometric ones. In chapters 6 and 7 spatial heterogeneity will be introduced in sectoral analyses.

5.2   Construction of Variables

The Dutch municipality and South-Holland (location-industry as well as individual sectoral) datasets were used to construct indicators for various types of agglomeration economies that are similar or as close as possible reminiscent to those used in prior studies[3]. These indicators and other (controlling) variables are constructed using data from the base year (1991 respectively 1988) to reduce simultaneity problems. The variable definitions and sample means of the Netherlands and South-Holland datasets are summarized in table 5.1. Also, the base-year approach, unlike the inverse input demand function framework as adopted by Feser (2001), facilitates testing whether effects of different types of agglomeration economies on growth persist over time. *CONCENTRATION* is defined as a location quotient showing the percentage of employment accounted for by an industry in a municipality (or zip code) *i,j* relative to the percentage of employment accounted for by that industry in the Netherlands (or South-Holland):

$$CONC_i = \frac{E_{i,j} / \sum_j E_{i,j}}{\sum_i E_{i,j} / \sum_{i,j} E_{i,j}} \tag{5.1}$$

This indicator comprises localization economies[4]. *COMPETITION* is measured as establishments per worker in a municipality (or zip code) industry divided by establishments per worker in that industry in the Netherlands (or South-Holland), see equation 5.2. It indicates whether establishments in industries (*j*) tend to be larger or smaller in a municipality or zip code (*i*) compared to the country (province) as a whole.

$$COMP_{i,j} = \frac{firms_{i,j} / employment_{i,j}}{\sum_i firms_{i,j} / \sum_i employment_{i,j}} \tag{5.2}$$

---

[3] To economize notation, the same names are used for certain variables that appear in both the Dutch municipality and South-Holland analyses. For each dataset, these variables are defined differently as the remainder of this chapter emphasises.

[4] It should be emphasized that different measurements of concentration and diversity indices largely contribute to different modeling outcomes, see Champernowne (1974), Encaouda and Jacquemin (1980), Y. Kim *et al.* (2000) and Maurel and Sédillot (1999) for overviews.

Table 5.1   Definition of location-industry variables and average values for South-Holland (n=1797) and the Netherlands (n=1404) [5]

	Definition	South-Holland average	Nether-lands average
EMPLOYMENT GROWTH	Change in the natural log of employment	-0.263	-0.170
CONCEN-TRATION	Share of the sector's employment in total employment in the zip code or municipality, divided by the sector's employment share in total employment in South-Holland or the Netherlands	4.823	4.959
COMPETITION	Number of establishments per worker in a zip code or municipality divided by the South-Holland or Netherlands establishments/worker ratio	1.129	0.788
TURNOVER	Zip code- or municipality-specific sum of establishment births, relocations and deaths over the estimation period divided by the initial stock of establishments	1.105	---
SHARE	Employment share of the 5 largest sectors in total regional employment	0.590	0.484
GINI or LACK OF DIVERSITY	Gini coefficient for the distribution of employment over 49 sectors in the zip code or municipality under observation	0.477	0.292
HHI	Hirschman-Herfindahl coefficient for the distribution of employment over sectors in the zip code or municipality under observation	---	0.076
URBAN AREA	Dummy indicating whether the zip code is of an urban area (see figure 3.3)	0.620	---
GROWTH	Change in the natural log of total (South-Holland or Dutch) employment excluding the zipcode/municipality under consideration	0.082	0.004
INITIAL WAGE	Natural log of (regional) sectoral wage rates	3.881	3.818
ΔWAGE	Change in natural log of (regional) sectoral wage rates	0.278	0.301
INITIAL EMPLOYMENT	Natural log of initial zip code or municipality employment	5.448	6.820

---

[5] For location-industry analyses *COMPETITION* and *CONCENTRATION* indices are measured per location-industry (instead of locations).

Table 5.1   (continued)

WORKAREA	Dummy variable indicating whether the zip code's or municipality's function is predominantly work-oriented as opposed to residential (see figures 3.3 and 3.4)	0.263	8.850
INDUSTRIAL SITES	Dummy variable indicating more than South-Holland or Netherlands average of opened up industrial sites (IS) in the zip code or municipality over the estimation period relative to stock of IS	0.151	0.459
DISTANCE ROTTERDAM	Distance from the zip code's center to Rotterdam harbor	21465.5	---
LACK OF ACCESSIBILITY	Distance from zip code's or municipality's center to nearest highway exits/entries	6.597	0.639
POPULATION GROWTH	Change in natural log of the zip code's or municipality's population size	0.094	0.066
RANDSTAD	Dummy indicating location within the country's core economic region, the Randstad (see figure 3.5)	---	0.317
INTERM. ZONE	Dummy indicating location in area between core and periphery in the Netherlands (see figure 3.5)	---	0.379

This spatial indicator of relative firm size fits in a tradition of identifying the most common competition and market structure indicators. In Lever and Nieuwenhuijsen (1999) an overview of (non-spatial) economic competition indicators measuring market shares is given. They mention: degree of profitability, the presence or absence of more than five (or any number) direct competitors (competitor concentration measured by for instance a Herfendahl index), a firm's import share, a firm's export share and relative firm size (relative to the total market). Combes (2000) and Rosenthal and Strange (2002) do not agree that the COMPETITION or ESTABLISHMENT SIZE variable as constructed by Glaeser *et al.* (1992) is a proper measure of the degree of competition an industry faces. However, given that this variable measures the impact of relative firm size on employment growth, Combes argues that it can be used as a test for the importance of internal economies of scale. His alternative proposal is to measure competition by the inverse of a local Herfindahl index of productive concentration. As the main issue to capture in an indicator of local competition concerns market share in relation to growth and innovation potential, some interesting, relatively new concepts of competition emerged recently in the industrial organization literature. Theoretical models that incorporate endogenously determined externalities do so by including market expansions, causing firms to enter and the accessibility and variety of products to be thereby enlarged. This creates additional consumer surplus that is not fully captured by the entrants (Anas *et al.* 1998, p.1449). In this vein, local competitive factors are incorporated into frameworks of carrying capacity (growth potential) in organizational ecology induced research, notably in Hannan and Freeman (1989, p.131-141) and Van Wissen (2000). As long as market niches remain to be filled, new firms enter the market until carrying capacity is maximized and room for market expansion reduced to zero (Agerwal and Audretch 1999, Bradburd and Ross 1989). Entrants and new firms that are not able to adjust to market conditions and produce a viable product are confronted by a lower likelihood of survival, especially in highly innovative environments. The entry of new firms thus is important in a static framework of analyses because they provide an equilibrium function in the market. In the presence of market power, the additional output provided by the new entrants restores the levels of profits and prices to their long-run competitive equilibrium. Recent literature analyzing the dynamics of firms and industries suggests that the contribution of small and new firms to the dynamics of competition is significantly greater than found in static analyses (Geroski 1991, Davis *et al.* 1996). These theoretical considerations lead Lever and Nieuwenhuijsen (1999, p.115) and Carree and Thurik (1999, p.95) to argue that market contestability, measured by the sum of entry and exit rates (turbulence), captures the degree of potential competition in the economic sense of reasoning. Competitive selection proceeds through entry, exit and mobility of firms[6]. It is expected that a high degree of turbulence (competition) has a positive impact on productivity growth. Although intuitively appealing, this approach also has some drawbacks. First, a turbulence or firm turnover indicator stresses the emergence and survival of new firms, but it is well documented that firm age and size in general are positively correlated (Van Wissen 2000). This might lead to unanticipated interrelationship with relative firm size indicators (the measure of *CONCENTRATION* defined above). Second, as an explanatory variable for *productivity growth*, a measure of turbulence is relevant. For localized firm (employment) growth though, its construction appears endogenous in nature: high numbers of new entrants induce or coincide with local employment growth as was concluded at the end of section 4.4. There it was argued that explanations of endogenous employment growth in a spatial context potentially gain from *correcting* for employment dynamics caused by new and dissoluting firms. Third, firm size and age as such are theoretically interesting as firm-specific, industrial organization regimes. Separate analyses for new, incumbent and all firms, as well as small and large firms proved significantly different in several studies (e.g. Lever 1996, Broersma and Gautier 1997, Rigby and Essltzbichler 2000). Concluding, we notice that from a theoretical point of view, size and age are not (right-hand) explanatory variables in a strict sense. Because of its theoretical and empirical ('correcting') significance though, an alternative measure of local competition (of firm-size) is developed for use in the South Holland analysis as the sum of new, dissoluting and moving firms. This indicator is more fully discussed in section 5.4.

Two variables are used as a measure of industrial diversity to indicate how evenly employment in a municipality is spread across economic sectors. *GINI*, the

---

[6] Lever and Nieuwenhuijsen (1999, p.115) also remark that this variable unfortunately is not available in the database they use for their analyses.

Gini-coefficient for the distribution of employment by sector in a municipality (or zip code) measures the absence of diversity:

$$GINI_g = \frac{1}{2n} \sum_{i=1}^{n} \sum_{j=1}^{n} \left| s_{i.g} - s_{j.g} \right| \tag{5.3}$$

in which $s_{i(j)}$ represent location's $i(j)$ shares of employment in sector g. Most commonly *GINI* is measured over space to represent the total or (within-) sectoral (g) degree of diversification (Y. Kim *et al.* 2000). Summation over sectors (g) instead of locations and calculating absolute differences of sectoral employment shares in locations with those in a global reference region (the Netherlands or the research area of South-Holland as a whole) results in location specific values of *GINI* (compare Paci and Usai 1999). The locational Gini-coefficient has a value of zero if employment shares among industries are distributed identically to that of total employment in the reference region (in our case across 49 sectors in the Netherlands and the South-Holland research area). A value of 0.5 results if employment is concentrated in only one sector. Lower values of *GINI* thus implicate higher degrees of diversity. *GINI* resembles the Hirschman-Herfindahl index (*HHI*) used by Henderson *et al.* (1995) and Henderson (1997b):

$$HHI_{i,k} = \sum_{j \in k} s_{i,j}^{2} \tag{5.4}$$

where s_{ij} is the share in location i of the (49) industries j in local all other sectoral employment (thus 2-digit industry squared employment shares in a location, excluding own industry). Both *GINI* and *HHI* are location specific in character; the latter is also industry specific in character. As Glaeser *et al.* (1992) focus on changes in employment among the six largest sectors in each city, the employment share of the other five largest sectors in total employment in a municipality or zip code can be used as an alternative measure of (the lack of) diversity: *SHARE*. This variable represents higher degrees of diversity with lower values as well. Whereas *GINI* as defined above varies only across municipalities or zip codes, the *SHARE* index varies across both locations and industries at a particular location as well. All diversity indices are treated as indicators of urbanization economies. A positive coefficient of *CONCENTRATION* and a negative coefficient of *COMPETITION* support the MAR hypothesis. A positive coefficient of *CONCENTRATION* and a positive coefficient of *COMPETITION* support the Porter hypothesis. Both hypotheses put more emphasis on localization economies. A negative coefficient of *GINI* or *SHARE* and a positive coefficient of *COMPETITION* support the Jacobs hypothesis of the relevance of urbanization economies.

5.3 OLS Analysis for the Netherlands

The Dutch municipality data in this section are used to compare results from the city-industry (here, municipality-industry) approach applied by Glaeser *et al.* (1992) and the individual-industry approach applied by Henderson *et al.* (1995). The aim here is not to attempt an exact reconciliation of their results. Rather, this starting point is adopted because it is useful to have an idea of how results from the Netherlands compare to those from the US The analyses in this section and in section 5.4 are as close as possible to the highly appreciated Glaeser *et al.* (1992) framework of agglomeration economies in an OLS setting.

First, an individual-industry (cross-section, n=239) approach was implemented by running the seven regressions presented in table 5.2 in which the dependent variable was the natural logarithm of 1997 employment (*EMPLOYMENT 1997*)[7]. Industries selected represent both traditional manufacturing as well as industries that are more technologically oriented. This distinction appeared convincingly significant in the work of Anselin *et al.* (1997), Harrison *et al.* (1997), Henderson *et al.* (1995) and Cortright and Mayer (2001). It is hypothesized that especially high-technology firms and industries are most 'affected' by the advantages of agglomeration economies for their employment growth (see also chapter 2). Three of the explanatory variables (*COMPETITION, CONCENTRATION,* and *GINI*) already have been discussed. Control variables measuring initial employment in a municipality-industry, and regions of the country also were included. *RANDSTAD* indicates a location in the core economic region of the country and *INTERM.ZONE* indicates a location in the intermediate zone between the country's core economic region and its periphery[8]. The specification shown in table 5.2 is not as full as that used by Henderson *et al.* (1995) because no reliable data on local labor market conditions, such as wage payments or educational attainment, are available for the low spatial levels used. However, we have also included *COMPETITION* as an explanatory variable to achieve consistency with Glaeser *et al.* (1992)[9]. Because of the truncated character of observations in the municipality dataset (the selected industries are not present in all 239 locations) Tobit is used as an estimation method for all seven equations[10]. Estimates converged in eight or fewer iterations.

Similar to findings by Henderson *et al.* (1995), coefficients of *(INITIAL EMPLOYMENT)*, included to capture persistence of industry employment levels, are positive and highly significant in all seven regressions. In most respects, however, similarities stop there.

---

[7] A related analysis also was performed using the 580 municipalities dataset (i.e., after including the smallest municipalities) with similar results to those presented in table 5.2.

[8] According to analysis of urbanization in the Netherlands (summarized and presented in chapter 3), economic activity spreads from the Randstad region towards this so-called Intermediate zone, especially comprising the provinces of Gelderland and Noord-Brabant. Recall that the zoning of Randstad, intermidate zone and national periphery were also discussed as spatial regime factors).

[9] Correlation analysis revealed that the variables included in the equations do not show significant (>0.4) statistical association, indicating the absence of multicollineartiy among the variables.

[10] This method is equivalent to least squares in the primary metals/metal products sector in which observations on the dependent variable are always positive (Greene 1997, p.965).

Table 5.2   Explanation of 1997 employment levels in 7 selected industries (t-values in parenthesis)

	primary metal and metal products	machinery industry	electrical machinery and instruments	Transport equipment	computers	audio, video and telecom equipment	medical instruments
CONSTANT	0.596 (1.622)	0.838 (1.804)	-0.196 (-0.283)	1.646 (4.004)	-1.739 (-1.243)	-1.319 (-1.191)	1.774 (3.939)
INITIAL EMPLOYMENT	0.937 (20.456)	0.920 (15.124)	0.874 (9.953)	0.762 (15.514)	0.795 (3.525)	0.810 (5.891)	0.652 (9.574)
COMPETITION (ESTABL. SIZE)	-0.005 (-0.194)	0.009 (0.499)	-0.001 (-0.196)	0.002 (0.310)	0.001 (0.005)	0.013 (1.631)	0.002 (0.114)
CONCENTRATION	-0.059 (-3.168)	-0.092 (-1.663)	-0.158 (-1.840)	0.026 (1.002)	-0.255 (-1.569)	0.025 (0.222)	0.068 (1.144)
GINI	-0.672 (-1.120)	-0.642 (-0.695)	-0.179 (-0.093)	-3.100 (-2.744)	-5.165 (-1.252)	-4.684 (-1.478)	-2.40 (-2.164)
RANDSTAD	-0.189 (-2.003)	-0.542 (-3.532)	0.423 (1.289)	-0.031 (-0.168)	1.695 (2.580)	0.559 (1.083)	0.327 (1.649)
INTERM. ZONE	-0.033 (-0.361)	-0.077 (-0.518)	0.526 (1.680)	0.091 (0.500)	0.506 (0.808)	0.390 (0.814)	-0.166 (-0.886)
Log likelihood	-190.430	-298.283	-412.078	-336.139	-264.570	-325.118	-351.006
No. of iterations	1	4	5	4	8	7	3
No. of observations	234	234	234	234	234	234	234
No. zero employment	0	7	48	23	154	122	10

Findings of Henderson *et al.* (1995) strongly support the idea that the degree of past concentration of an industry positively affects later employment levels (the MAR view) in both traditional capital goods and newer high-tech manufacturing sectors. Furthermore, they report that historical industrial diversity in an area positively affects later employment levels only in high-technology manufacturing. In the results presented in table 5.2, however, *CONCENTRATION* has either a negative effect or no significant effect on *EMPLOYMENT 1997* in the seven sectors considered. *GINI* has a negative and significant coefficient with a t-statistic exceeding 2.0 in absolute value in just two sectors, one of which is a newer, technology-oriented manufacturing sector (medical instruments). Coefficients of *COMPETITION*, a variable not used by Henderson *et al.* (1995), have relatively small t-statistics[11].

Additionally, coefficients of dummy variables for location perform unevenly, showing that in some modern industries persistence of employment levels appear to be larger inside the Randstad, while others (mainly mature industries) show little persistent development levels in that region. In any case, results presented in table 5.2 provide no consistent support for MAR, Porter, or the Jacobs hypotheses. Reasons why results in table 5.2 differ from corresponding estimates for the US are not obvious. It is possible to speculate, however, that possible explanations rest on the short time interval (1991-97) for the Dutch municipality data, censoring of the US data, and the role of unmeasured establishment and/or municipality characteristics. The issue of unmeasured characteristics is discussed more fully in the next section.

Next, an analysis of municipality-industries *growth* (similar to Glaeser *et al.* 1992) was performed using data from the 234 Dutch municipalities. Results from two regressions are presented in Table 5.3. Column (1) shows the outcome of using data on the six industries with largest employment in each municipality and column (2) shows the outcome from using data on just the manufacturing sectors among the six largest sectors in each municipality. In all regressions the dependent variable is the change in the natural logarithm in municipality-industry employment over the period 1991-97. Explanatory variables included *CONCENTRATION* and *COMPETITION* (defined above) but used two alternative indicators for industrial diversity. For consistency, *SHARE* is used as an indicator in the regression using all sectors (the first column in table 5.3), but the Gini coefficient yields the same qualitative results. Because *GINI* was found to perform best in the manufacturing regression, results are presented using that indicator in the second column. Six control variables also were included in each of the regressions. *INITIAL EMPLOYMENT* measures the number of employees in a municipality-industry at the beginning of the sample period. *GROWTH* is the change in the natural logarithm of employment in an industry outside the municipality (for an economic embedding of this variable see Wozniak and Babula 1992). *WAGE* measures the difference in wages between industries at the national level (in the Netherlands) in 1991 and *ΔWAGE* measures the change in the natural

---

[11] These results differ from those obtained by Combes (2000) in his analysis of (regional) employment growth in France. For manufacturing industries, he finds that diversity slows down employment competition.

logarithm of wages for each industry at the national level over the sample period[12]. *RANDSTAD* and *INTERM.ZONE* were defined before. In table 5.3, both equations are estimated by least squares. Values of R^2 are 0.177 for the all sectors regression and 0.195 for the manufacturing regression. Thus, the explanatory power of both equations is rather low. The small size of many of the municipality-industries may be partly responsible for this outcome. In situations where employment is comparatively low in the base year, relatively small absolute employment changes over the sample period can produce relatively large changes in growth rates. Correspondingly, with a small number of establishments operating in some municipalities, there is more likelihood for growth rates to be affected by firm-specific factors (discussed momentarily) that are not controlled in the analyses presented in this section.

Table 5.3 Determinants of employment growth per municipality-industry (OLS, n=1404)

(t-values in parenthesis)	Employment growth (all sectors)		Employment growth (manufacturing sectors)	
CONSTANT	-0.103	(-0.520)	-1.925	(-2.197)
CONCENTRATION	-0.020	(-10.425)	-0.016	(-4.677)
COMPETITION (ESTABL. SIZE)	0.154	(5.609)	0.369	(4.005)
GINI	-0.172[1]	(-0.934)	-1.323[2]	(-2.236)
GROWTH	0.820	(5.532)	0.269	(0.609)
INITIAL WAGE	-0.001	(-0.726)	0.013	(1.249)
INITIAL EMPLOYMENT	0.009	(1.209)	-0.006	(-0.018)
ΔWAGE	0.196	(0.547)	4.377	(1.905)
RANDSTAD	-0.020	(-0.578)	-0.032	(-0.313)
INTERM. ZONE	0.055	(1.612)	0.053	(0.555)
N		1404		370
R^2		0.177		0.195

[1] The *SHARE* indicator yields similar results.
[2] The *SHARE* indicator turns out to be insignificant.

Results for the agglomeration indicators *CONCENTRATION, COMPETITION,* and *GINI* are at least broadly consistent with those obtained in the study by Glaeser *et al.* (1992). In both regressions, the coefficient of *CONCENTRATION* is negative and significantly different from zero at conventional levels; results that do not support the MAR and Porter hypotheses. The coefficient of *COMPETITION* also goes against MAR as more

---

[12] Notice that the two wage variables could not be used in the individual industry analysis as they have little variation within a sector. In Western Europe in general and the Netherlands especially, wage setting *within* industries is highly institutionalized and regulated.

competition is found to increase growth in both manufacturing and non-manufacturing industries. The various measures of sectoral diversity do not appear to play a role in explaining employment growth for *all* sectors presented in the first column of table 5.3. However, there is evidence that industrial diversity matters in determining growth in manufacturing sectors as the coefficient of the *GINI* index is negative and significant. This outcome stands in contrast to the individual-industry analysis presented earlier and supports the notion that the Jacobs hypothesis has greater applicability to sectors in which employment has already reached some minimum threshold size. But if *SHARE* is substituted for *GINI,* its coefficient is not significantly different from zero at conventional levels, thus weakening the conclusion about the role of industrial diversity. Coefficients of control variables performed unevenly. For example, the coefficient of *GROWTH* is positive and highly significant in the column (1) regression, but is not significant at conventional levels in the column (2) regression. The distinctions RANDSTAD and INTERM.ZONE appear little or not significant for overall employment growth rates as analyzed by city-industries in this section.

5.4   OLS Analysis for South-Holland

Results presented in the previous section are of interest because they highlight the role of agglomeration economies in the Netherlands in analyses similar to those conducted for the US; yet, they can be questioned from at least six (interrelated) perspectives. First, do the Dutch data (that most closely represent cities as in Glaeser *et al.* 1992) offer adequate controls for unmeasured intra-urban and/or establishment specific effects? Second, does *COMPETITION* measure the degree to which establishments in a sector actually are confronted with competition, or does it just measure the relative size of establishments in a sector? Third, do the municipality-industry results apply to establishments present in the base year, or do they merely reflect a tendency for new establishments to start up or move into areas where their sector is under-represented (Fritsch 1997)? Fourth, are the Dutch municipality-industry results misleading because of biases arising from spatial aggregation and at what costs in terms of the modifiable areal unit problem can this be tested for? Fifth, to what extent does sectoral heterogeneity influence the model? And sixth, to what extent is spatial lag (proximity) and heterogeneity (regimes) specification fruitful for a better fit of the model? The first four questions, which equally apply to prior empirical studies on the role of knowledge spillovers and agglomeration economies in urban growth, can be addressed more easily with the South-Holland data and are taken up in turn below. The latter two questions will be addressed in econometric models in section 5.5 and in chapter 6.

Variables used in the analyses of this section differ somewhat from those used in the previous section. South-Holland's small size and high degree of economic integration offers an important natural control for location-specific attributes. Between locations in South-Holland, there are few differences in resource endowments, political institutions, taxes, culture, environmental amenities (including climate), and environmental regulations. Additionally, the province is small enough that the labor market is tightly integrated. Workers can live in one zip code and commute to work in any other using either public or private transport modes (Lambooy 1998b). Thus, wage rates *within* a sector show little variation between locations and there is no obvious need to control for labor force characteristics such as level of education, percent of workers with particular skills, or percent of workers who are union members. Also, the role of history in determining the spatial economic layout of the province can be at least partially controlled[13]. This is done by using variables measuring distance of a zip code from major highway entries and exits (*LACK OF ACCESSIBILITY*), the harbor at Rotterdam (*DISTANCE ROTTERDAM*), and whether the zip code is in an heavily urbanized area (*URBAN*). Controls for land use patterns are partially obtained by using variables showing whether a zip code is classified as predominately a work area (*WORKAREA*) and whether the municipality has issued more than average new industrial sites (*INDUSTRIAL ZONES*). Additional control variables included *INITIAL WAGE* and *ΔWAGE*, defined in the previous section and zip code *POPULATION GROWTH* [14]. Variable definitions and their sample means are presented in table 5.1.

Unmeasured establishment-specific effects are difficult to control using the South-Holland dataset. Because establishments are aggregated into zip code-industries, some of these effects will average out. Other sources of these effects, e.g. clustering of high quality entrepreneurial talent, clustering of older and/or newer plants, and clustering of firms using particular specialized inputs, may remain (see for instance Variyam and Kraybill 1992, Schutjens and Wever, 2000). This problem can be treated using establishment-level data in a fixed effects (multilevel) framework. However, this approach involves sacrificing information by restricting the sample to establishments that appear in the South-Holland Firm Register in consecutive years. In fact, in their attempt to develop a panel of plants, Black and Henderson (1999a) ended up with sample sizes averaging only 8% of plants in an industry. The same effect occurred in the studies by Harrison *et al.* (1997) and Kelley and Helper (1999), using questionnaire data on innovation adoption. Using the South-Holland data, estimation of establishment-specific effects *in a purely economic* framework is not a realistic option in any case because employment is the only establishment-specific variable on inputs or outputs available. In consequence, the South-Holland data are aggregated into zip code totals and analyzed as a cross-section for 1988-1997.

On the other hand, an advantage of the establishment-level South-Holland data is that they can be used to develop an alternative measure of competition that may be complementary to those used in prior studies. More specifically, the relative establishment size-variable (*COMPETITION*) used in the previous section and by Glaeser *et al.* (1992) may not be appropriate for two reasons. First, as is also noted by Combes (2000) and Rosenthal and Strange (2000), it is not clear whether this variable measures the extent of competition, internal diseconomies of scale, or

---

[13] Although not applied as such in this section, the variables discussed will be used for spatial regime analyses (covering spatial heterogeneity) in subsequent sections.

[14] See for an overview of the interacting agglomeration forces of employment and population development Bruinsma *et al.* (2002).

broader aspects of industrial organization. Second, this indicator may be inappropriate in cases where competition is faced from outside the local area and is particularly questionable when the 'local area' is as small as a South-Holland zip code. Thus, for South-Holland the individual establishment data are used to develop an alternative measure of competition, *TURNOVER*, defined for each sector in each zip code as the sum of establishment births plus relocations plus deaths over the period 1988-97 divided by the number of establishments in the base year. *TURNOVER* may be a complementary and more useful measure than *COMPETITION* because it is based on establishment dynamics in a zip code (see the discussion in section 5.2).

Additionally, spatial aggregation and varying scale in the Dutch municipality (and US city) data is a potentially serious (modifiable areal unit) problem. Imagine an urban area that can be divided into a number of zones, each of which has the same number of employees and is completely specialized in the output of goods produced by a single (different) industry. Thus, each zone would have a high concentration index and no industrial diversity. From the standpoint of the urban area as a whole, however, concentration in production by a particular industry may or may not exceed its counterpart on a broader geographic scale and a Gini index will reflect maximum possible industrial diversity. Of course, an urban area is unlikely to develop as described in this stylized example. Yet, it is important to realize that an entirely different view of the contribution of knowledge externalities to growth could emerge from analyzing parts of cities (and their embeddedness in spatial structures) as compared with analyzing cities as a whole. In any case, as mentioned previously, the South Holland data permit the province to be divided into very small spatial units, so possible spatial aggregation and scale error can be better controlled.

A limitation of the South Holland data, however, is that they are not well suited to individual-industry analyses along the lines of those presented by Henderson *et al.* (1995). Most industries are present only in a small number of zip codes; in consequence, both beginning-of-period and end-of-period employment would be zero for most observations. This aspect would not be a problem if the aim of the study were to ask why particular industries chose to locate in particular zip codes. However, the primary focus here is on the closely related issue of mechanisms thought to be important to the growth process. This emphasis motivates the decision to look only at employment growth in firms that were present at the beginning of the sample period.

Results from the South-Holland zip code-industry regressions, using the 1988-1997 change in natural logarithms of employment (*EMPLOYMENT GROWTH*) as dependent variable, are shown in table 5.4. Explanatory variables again are constructed using data from the base year (1988 in this case) to minimize simultaneity problems. Similar to the municipality-industry analysis reported in the previous section, attention is restricted to the six largest sectors in each zip code. Because the province contains 416 4-digit zip code areas, a total of 2408 observations are possible. However, in some zip code areas, fewer than six sectors are present and in other zip code areas some of the largest six sectors have little base year employment making growth rate calculations problematic. In consequence, zip code-industries with fewer than 50 employees in 1988 were excluded yielding a dataset with 1797 observations.

Table 5.4 **South-Holland regression results per zip code-industry (OLS, n=1797)**

(*t*-values are presented in parenthesis)	Employment growth (all establishments)		Employment growth (all establishments)		Employment growth (old establishments)		Employment growth (old establishments)	
CONSTANT	0.675	(2.246)	0.844	(3.060)	0.546	(1.747)	0.724	(2.307)
URBAN AREA	-0.260	(-1.109)	-0.188	(-0.781)	-0.332	(-1.239)	-0.261	(-0.950)
CONCENTRATION	-0.009	(-2.354)	-0.008	(-2.434)	-0.009	(-2.076)	-0.009	(-2.075)
COMPETITION (ESTABL. SIZE)	0.089	(1.972)	---		0.095	(1.829)	0.080	(1.537)
TURNOVER	---		0.059	(1.452)	---		-0.110	(-2.409)
SHARE	-0.576	(-1.896)	-0.541	(-1.761)	-0.848	(-2.446)	-0.846	(-2.458)
URBAN CONCENTRATION	-0.009	(-2.250)	-0.011	(-2.707)	-0.008	(-1.782)	-0.009	(-2.000)
URBAN COMPETITION	0.147	(2.690)	---		0.123	(1.961)	0.143	(2.285)
URBAN TURNOVER	---		0.009	(0.175)	---		-0.079	(-1.301)
URBAN SHARE	-0.012	(-0.033)	0.111	(0.298)	0.122	(0.290)	0.158	(0.378)
GROWTH	1.063	(6.848)	1.027	(6.390)	0.762	(4.306)	0.943	(5.232)
INITIAL WAGE	-0.010	(-2.784)	-0.011	(-3.094)	-0.012	(-2.910)	-0.011	(-2.739)
INITIAL EMPLOYMENT	-0.0012	(-0.244)	-0.00079	(-1.633)	0.00038	(0.069)	0.00086	(0.016)
ΔWAGE	-1.478	(-3.358)	-1.604	(-3.571)	-1.108	(-2.207)	-1.446	(-2.739)
WORKAREA	0.166	(2.440)	0.140	(2.025)	0.173	(2.223)	0.208	(2.687)
INDUSTRIAL ZONES	0.118	(1.908)	0.046	(0.743)	0.090	(1.283)	0.102	(1.459)
DISTANCE ROTTERDAM	0.0039	(1.712)	0.0039	(1.677)	0.0052	(1.970)	0.0048	(1.817)
LACK OF ACCESSIBILITY	0.009	(2.011)	0.010	(2.227)	0.011	(2.331)	0.011	(2.257)
POPULATION GROWTH	0.132	(2.275)	0.112	(1.911)	0.084	(1.267)	0.087	(1.319)
N	1797		1797		1797		1797	
R^2	0.165		0.143		0.121		0.134	

To gain insight in the potential differences in the growth process in more and less heavily urbanized areas we have interacted key variables of interest with *URBAN* to create *URBAN COMPETITION, URBAN CONCENTRATION,* and *URBAN SHARE*[15].

Column (1) presents results from a regression analysis, specified similarly to those used in the analysis of the Dutch municipality-industries[16]. The value of $R^2=0.166$ is, due to the large number of observations, once again rather low, however most of the coefficients estimated have significant (at 5% under a one-tail test) with plausible signs. Additionally, coefficient estimates obtained are broadly consistent with results presented by Glaeser *et al.* (1992) and support the Jacobs hypothesis. *CONCENTRATION* and *SHARE* enter with negative and significant coefficients. The effect of *CONCENTRATION* is stronger in more heavily urbanized areas as indicated by the outcome for the variable *URBAN CONCENTRATION.* Furthermore, *COMPETITION* is found to be positively correlated with employment growth at least in urban areas. Thus, these results give additional support for the previous section's conclusion (based on municipality data for the entire country) that Jacobs externalities are the dominant type of knowledge externalities. The fact that the Jacobs hypothesis is supported in this study of very small areas within an urbanized region strengthens the interpretation of our results, suggesting that they are not driven merely by spatial aggregation.

Regarding control variables, the coefficient of *GROWTH* suggests that a 10% increase in the growth rate of an industry in South Holland is associated with an increase in the growth rate of that industry in a zip code by 10.8%. This outcome indicates a tendency for industries to grow at about the same rate in zip codes where they are among the largest employers. Also, results from column (1) indicate that industries with comparatively favorable wage levels and wage increases tend to grow more slowly than other industries. Furthermore, employment growth is faster (i) if over the estimation period industrial zones expanded by more than the South-Holland average (*INDUSTRIAL ZONES*), (ii) if the area is a work area rather than a residential area (*WORKAREA*), (iii) the faster the zip code's population growth (*POPULATION GROWTH*)[17]. Coefficients of *URBAN AREA, DISTANCE ROTTERDAM* (which also measures *proximity* to Amsterdam and Utrecht, which, in turn, represents the country's hinterland), *LACK OF ACCESSIBILITY* and *INITIAL EMPLOYMENT* in a zip code-industry are not found to be significant at conventional levels.

The specification shown in column (2) of table 5.4 is the same as for the regression in column (1) except that *TURNOVER* is substituted for *COMPETITION.* The positive coefficients of *TURNOVER* and *URBAN TURNOVER* do not differ significantly from zero at the 5% level under a one-tail test. Thus, the alternative measure of competition indicates that greater numbers of establishment births, deaths, and relocations in a zip code-industry do not lead to higher growth rates.

---

[15] This way of handling the urban dimension paves the way for urban spatial regime modeling in chapters 6 and 7. The interacting technique is only limited reminiscent to the spatial regime technique, since the latter involves different slopes estimation following an urban regime variable and the former does not.

[16] Correlation analyses showed no clear (> 0.4) interdependencies for all models presented in table 5.4, meaning multicollinearity is not a potential problem.

[17] For a 2SLS simultaneous analysis of employment and population dynamics in the South-Holland research area see Bruinsma *et al.* (2002).

This outcome weakens support for the Jacobs hypothesis found in the column (1) regression. Other coefficient estimates in the column (2) regression are similar to those presented in column (1). Also, as previously described, an advantage of the South-Holland data is the ability to distinguish establishments present at the beginning of the sample period from others that either moved in or started up after that time. Consequently, a regression was estimated (see column (3) in table 5.4) to look at the growth of zip code-industry employment only by the original (old) establishments present in 1988. In 1997, these establishments accounted for 64% of all South-Holland establishments (in location-industries) as well as 83% of total South-Holland employment. Results from this regression again support the Jacobs hypothesis. Coefficients of *COMPETITION* and *SHARE* are significantly different from zero and effects are equally strong in more heavily urbanized areas. *COMPETITION* is found to be positively correlated with employment growth only in more heavily urbanized areas. This outcome is important because it suggests that the results focusing exclusively on existing firms reflect more than just a tendency for new firms to move into an area where their line of business is under-represented. With respect to the other explanatory variables, two differences are worth mentioning. When analyzing growth in existing firms, proximity to Amsterdam and the region's hinterland (as measured by the (reciprocal) distance to Rotterdam) is positively related to employment growth in zip codes, whereas the coefficient on local population growth is no longer significant. Thus, local population growth may be a factor attracting new establishments, but not a factor in the growth of old ones. Third, the larger the distance to highway entries and exits, the faster is employment growth. Thus, a mildly surprising result is that congestion appears to hamper growth in existing firms in the province of South-Holland, of course given the extreme small spatial scales on which this is analyzed.

Because *COMPETITION* and *TURNOVER* may not measure the same phenomenon, a regression using employment growth in old establishments as the dependent variable with both indicators included as explanatory variables was applied. Results are presented in the fourth column of table 5.4. The coefficient of *TURNOVER* is lower (actually, it is negative and significant) than that reported in column (2) of table 5.4. This outcome would be expected because in the all-establishments regression, establishment births and relocations contribute to both *TURNOVER* and employment growth, whereas in the old establishments regression, births and relocations contribute only to *TURNOVER*. In contrast, *COMPETITION* and *URBAN COMPETITION* have positive coefficients, although only the coefficient for *URBAN COMPETITION* is significantly different from zero. Hence, if Combes' (2000) and Rosenthal and Strange's (2002) interpretation of this variable is accepted (that is, the variable measures internal diseconomies of scale or broader aspects of industrial organization), the conclusions concerning the dominant type of externalities are substantially altered. Whereas regional diversity and lack of specialization still foster employment growth (as hypothesized by Jacobs), regional competition (as appropriately measured by *TURNOVER*) is found to hamper rather than to foster growth in *existing* firms. In other words, although Jacobs' ideas concerning the regional composition is found to be supported by the South-Holland data, the fact that *lack* of competition is found to foster growth gives partial support to the views of

MAR and Porter. The negative and significant coefficient of *TURNOVER* also emerges when *COMPETITION* and *URBAN COMPETITION* are dropped from the model.

5.5   Spatial Econometric Models for South-Holland

OLS Null-Model

In the previous section, OLS-models were presented for employment growth and agglomeration economies in the province of South-Holland. This section (5.5) concentrates on (maximum likelihood estimated) spatial lag models for South-Holland employment growth in location-industries. First, OLS models are presented in which the differences with the models in 5.4 are first the exclusion of the variables *URBAN AREA, INDUSTRIAL ZONES, ΔPOPULATION* and *LACK OF ACCESIBILITY,* mainly because of non-significance in fully specified models[18]. A second difference is that the main agglomeration variables are not interacted with the urban/non-urban dummy variable. This is because the models to follow as well as conclusions and interpretations drawn, are based on spatially weighted observations (spatial lag and error models) explicitly.

Table 5.5   OLS analysis of change in employment in location-industries in South-Holland (n=1797)

explanatory variables	(1) all establishments		(2) old establishments		(3) old manufacturing establishments	
CONSTANT	0.778	(3.328)	0.914	(3.451)	1.333	(1.603)
CONCENTRATION	-0.015	(-8.454)	-0.016	(-7.626)	-0.013	(-4.675)
LACK OF DIVERSITY	-0.783	(-4.047)	-0.956	(-4.366)	-2.060	(-3.624)
TURNOVER	0.073	(2.640)	-0.144	(-4.621)	-0.221	(-2.702)
ESTABLISHMENT SIZE	0.191	(6.846)	0.174	(5.513)	0.336	(3.867)
GROWTH	0.758	(4.890)	0.719	(4.093)	0.320	(0.759)
EMPLOYMENT88	-0.0057	(-1.191)	-0.0054	(-0.929)	-0.0023	(-1.347)
WAGE88	-0.014	(-3.760)	-0.014	(-3.429)	-0.017	(-1.255)
ΔWAGE	-1.504	(-3.307)	-1.570	(-3.105)	-1.941	(-1.941)
WORKAREA	0.237	(4.028)	0.215	(3.230)	0.648	(4.314)
ROTTERDAM	0.0005	(2.542)	0.0006	(2.451)	0.0114	(1.793)

summary statistics:						
N		1797		1797		457
R^2		0.142		0.108		0.175

z-values are presented in parenthesis.

---

[18] This insignificance has theoretical implications in itself, but these are not the main research subject in this dissertation. They are therefore only briefly discussed.

The OLS regression results are only briefly discussed and presented in table 5.5. In column (1), the dependent variable is the growth rate of all employment in a zip code. This is regardless of whether it arises from growth of old establishments present in 1988, from the birth of new establishments, or from the arrival or departure of establishments that have relocated either from within or from outside South-Holland. Column (2) presents results focusing only on growth of employment in old establishments present in 1988. In 1997, old establishments represented 64% of all establishments and employment in old establishments represented 83% of employment in all establishments. Thus, new and relocating establishments are relatively small compared to old establishments. The regression presented in column (3) further restricts consideration to employment growth in old manufacturing establishments. Values of R^2 range from 0.108 to 0.175; thus, explanatory power of these equations is rather low. The small size of the zip code areas and the relatively large number of observations may be partly responsible here.

Coefficient estimates in column (1) are similar in many respects to those found by Glaeser *et al.* (1992). The regression shows that concentration of industries retards growth, while industrial diversity and competition (either measured by *TURNOVER* or by *ESTABLISHMENT SIZE*) foster growth. Thus, the results here support the idea that Jacobs-type externalities foster growth and MAR-type externalities tend to slow it down. Coefficients of most other explanatory variables are different from zero at conventional significance levels and have expected signs. The coefficient of *GROWTH* is 0.76, suggesting that a 10% increase in industry growth outside the zip code is associated with a 7.6% increase in growth in that industry in the zip code. As indicated previously, Glaeser *et al.* (1992) interpret this variable as a measure of demand shifts, but as shown in chapter 3, redefining it invokes the spatial econometric analysis reported in sections to come. The fact that the coefficient of initial employment (*EMPLOYMENT88*) was not found to be significant suggests that there is no tendency for employment levels to converge between zip codes. Coefficients of both the initial wage (*WAGE88*) and the change in wages (*ΔWAGE*) turn out to be negative and significant, as might be expected. *WORKAREA* indicates that sectors located in areas that historically have been specialized in commercial activity (such as industrial sites) grow faster than those located in residential areas. The coefficient of *ROTTERDAM* indicates that employment growth is higher the further away establishments are located from Rotterdam harbor.

Except for the coefficient of *TURNOVER*, results presented in columns (2) and (3) are broadly similar to those presented in column (1). Focusing first on the similarities, results for both old and old manufacturing establishments again suggest that growth is highest for small establishments located where industrial diversity is high and industrial concentration is low, so the industrial diversity aspect of the Jacobs-hypothesis is again supported. This finding is important because it suggests that results reported in the all-establishment regression in column (1) reflect persistence of agglomeration economies on growth rather than just a tendency for new retail and service establishments to move into an area where their line of business is under-represented. In fact, industrial diversity and small establishment size tend to foster faster growth among old manufacturing establishments than other types of establishments. Implications for growth from greater competition, however, differ between old establishments and all establishments. As expected, the coefficient of TURNOVER is lower (and in fact negative) in columns (2) and (3), whereas it was positive in column (1). When all establishments are considered, births and relocations contribute both to TURNOVER and to employment growth, whereas when only old establishments are considered, births and relocations contribute only to TURNOVER. To the extent that TURNOVER indexes local competition faced by old establishments during the sample period, a negative coefficient of this variable suggests that an aspect of the MAR theory may well be correct despite findings to the contrary in prior empirical work. Growth is faster when knowledge externalities are more easily internalized, especially by large firms. Moreover, this interpretation is strengthened if both knowledge and the effects of knowledge on growth are geographically bounded. If lower levels of local competition promote employment growth, then this effect would be reinforced if the transmission of knowledge does not directly or indirectly create more competition from elsewhere. Several previous papers find that spatial transmission of knowledge is limited. The extent to which growth can be transmitted through spatial economic linkages is the subject of next sections.

Intra- and Inter-Industry Specifications

This section reports results on estimating determinants of employment growth using spatial econometric models. Procedures used involve specifying equation (3.1) and equation (3.2) (see chapter 3) so that the weight matrix W reflects the location of zip codes in relation to each other. Several alternative specifications of W are plausible and it is not possible to say definitely which one is 'best' (Griffith and Lagona 1998). For example, W could be specified as a contiguity matrix with elements of ones and zeros indicating whether zip code borders touch each other or are located within some number of kilometers of each other. This alternative, however, was not pursued in order to focus on specifications of W that posit different mechanisms by which growth might be transmitted across space and allow for effects of growth to decay with distance. Two alternative specifications of W were applied in this section. The first, W_D, allows for spatial linkages that depend on distance, and do not distinguish between industries. Elements of this matrix are reciprocals of distance (in kilometers) between pairs of zip code centers. For a given pair of zip codes, all pairs of industries get the same distance weight. Industries in the same zip code are assumed to be less than one kilometer apart. In the second specification though, W_I allows for links only between a given (2-digit) industry in one location and that same industry in other locations. Thus, because of both the spatial and sectoral detail, as well as the relative specialization of locations, most elements of W_I are zero. Non-zero elements are reciprocals of kilometers of distance between zip code centers. This formulation is similar to the one used by Glaeser *et al.* (1992) except that elements are distance weights, rather than employment shares. Prior to estimation, elements of W_D and W_I are standardized so that each row sums to unity.

Table 5.6   Spatial lag analysis of change in employment in location-industries in South-Holland: spatial linkages across all industries (n=1797)

explanatory variables	(1) Spatial lag (W_D) all establishments		(2) Spatial lag (W_D) old establishments		(3) Spatial lag (W_D) old manufacturing establishments	
CONSTANT	1.366	(6.410)	1.705	(6.979)	2.317	(3.063)
CONCENTRATION	-0.017	(-9.268)	-0.017	(-8.335)	-0.013	(-4.765)
LACK OF DIVERSITY	-0.695	(-3.617)	-0.865	(-3.984)	-2.122	(-3.855)
TURNOVER	0.102	(3.795)	-0.115	(-3.797)	-0.228	(-2.846)
ESTABLISHMENT SIZE	0.199	(7.150)	0.182	(5.786)	0.340	(3.973)
EMPLOYMENT88	-0.00133	(-0.283)	-0.0005	(-0.098)	-0.0003	(-1.361)
WAGE88	-0.017	(-4.939)	-0.018	(-4.395)	-0.025	(-1.899)
ΔWAGE	-1.825	(-4.123)	-1.875	(-3.750)	-1.948	(-1.940)
WORKAREA	0.185	(3.206)	0.167	(2.560)	0.620	(4.193)
SPATIAL COEFFICIENT (ρ_D)	0.803	(6.464)	0.809	(6.718)	0.428	(1.332)
Summary statistics:						
N	1797		1797		457	
R^2/log likelihood	0.136/-1548.36		0.106/-1271.71		0.170/-831.92	
LR(ρ)	14.902		15.726		2.148	
LM ρ (λ)	4.490		3.899		1.564	
LM(BP)	0.319		3.526		0.001	

Estimates of R^2 using maximum likelihood estimation are not reliable. Values of log-likelihood are uncomparable over populations of all, old and old manufacturing establishments. LR(ρ) tests for the significance of the spatial dependence coefficient. LM (ρ) and LM (λ) statistics for the presence of a spatial lag in the dependent variable and in the residual respectively, following Anselin *et al.* (1996) with a critical value of 3.84 at 5% level of significance, were significant but non-conclusive on either specification. LM (BP) tests for homoskedasticity of regression errors using the Breusch-Pagan Lagrange multiplier test for normal distributed errors. For homoskedasticity purposes, the variance matrices have been made dependent on the instruments POPULATION88 and WORKAREA. The spatial weight matrix used is W_1 (row standardized), z-values are presented in parenthesis. All variables are log transformed unless stated otherwise and corrected for extreme values. Significance levels of summary statistics are discussed in the main text.

Spatial lag estimates of determinants of zip code industry employment growth are presented in tables 5.6 and 5.7[19]. Each table is similar to table 5.4 in that results for all establishments, old establishments, and old manufacturing establishments are presented.

---

[19] OLS and spatial lag estimation applying spatial regimes (on urban and non-urban locations) and/or window average estimation of the agglomeration variables did not turn out make significant and useful interpretable contributions to the location-industry analyses in this section. Considering the small spatial scale of analyses in this study as well as the hypothesized influence of the agglomeration variables, especially the latter is remarkable. For several individual sector estimations, spatial regimes on the urban/non-urban and work/other area distinction turned out relevant though (see chapter 6).

The table 5.6 estimates use W_D and the table 5.7 estimates use W_I.[20] Estimation is by maximum likelihood. Coefficients of determination, presented only to give a crude indication of goodness-of-fit, are somewhat higher in table 5.7 than in table 5.6, but are always less than or equal to 0.20. Results presented correct for heteroskedasticity by making the variance matrices dependent on *POPULATION88* or *WORKAREA*, depending on the specification. Spatial Breusch-Pagan Lagrange multiplier test statistics LM(BP), suggest that heteroskedasticity remains an issue in the table 5.7, column 2 regression; in all other regressions the null hypothesis of homoskedasticity cannot be rejected at the 5% level. Coefficient estimates turn out to change little whether or not correction for heteroskedasticity is made. In both tables 5.6 and 5.7, the first column shows regression results for all establishments, and the second and third columns show results for old and old manufacturing establishments, respectively. Likelihood ratio test statistics (LR(ρ) in tables 5.6 and 5.7) indicate strong evidence of spatial autocorrelation in the dependent variable in five of the six regressions, an outcome that supports use of the spatial lag specification. The spatial lag specification appears unwarranted only for the old manufacturing establishments' regression in table 5.6. Also, Lagrange multiplier test statistics on remaining spatial dependence (LM ρ (λ)) suggest that an additional spatial error specification might be appropriate in the table 5.7 regressions. Spatial error models were run for all six specifications presented in tables 5.6 and 5.7. These estimates are not presented here (they are available from the author on request) because coefficient estimates and their significance levels are quite similar to those for the spatial lag models[21]. In tables 5.6 and 5.7, coefficients of *CONCENTRATION, TURNOVER, LACK OF DIVERSITY* and *ESTABLISHMENT SIZE* are quite similar to each other and to those presented in table 5.5. Thus, these estimates are not greatly affected by estimation method or by choice of weight matrix and conclusions reached in the previous sections appear to carry over to both sets of spatial lag estimates[22]. The regressions using all establishments provide greatest support for the Jacobs hypothesis, while the old establishments and old manufacturing establishments regressions support the ideas that industrial diversity and lack of competition foster more rapid growth rates. Also, coefficients of control variables appear to change little when looking at the results across the three tables. The coefficient of *ROTTERDAM* is an exception in this regard as it turned out to be consistently insignificant in the spatial econometric estimates.

---

[20] Common specifications of weight matrices are cells containing simply the inverse of the distance between two zip codes (W_1), or the squared inverse distance (W_2, see chapter 4). The latter specification awards a relatively larger weight to nearby zip codes as compared to the former. We have performed the analysis for W_D and W_I using both the simple inverse-distance and the squared inverse-distance specifications. Whereas spatial autocorrelation is somewhat weaker using the squared inverse-distance specification (as chapter 4 showed), the main conclusions remain unchanged. The results presented in tables 5.6 and 5.7 are based on the simple inverse-distance specification (W_1).

[21] Combined spatial lag-spatial error models were not estimated because of computational burdens involved (see Anselin 1988, 1995a).

[22] The robustness of general spatial interaction patterns (concerning the dependent variable) in econometric models, indicating little sensibility of the model for specifications of the weight matrix W, is also found in Buettner (1999) and Anselin *et al.* (2000).

Table 5.7   Spatial lag analysis of change in employment in location-industries in South-Holland: spatial linkages only within industries (n=1797)

explanatory variables	(1) Spatial lag (W_l) all establishments		(2) Spatial lag (W_l) old establishments		(3) Spatial lag (W_l) old manufacturing establishments	
CONSTANT	0.571	(2.696)	0.682	(2.927)	1.223	1.726)
CONCENTRATION	-0.013	(-7.570)	-0.013	(-6.896)	-0.013	(-4.712)
LACK OF DIVERSITY	-0.657	(-3.523)	-0.806	(-3.875)	-2.083	(-3.903)
TURNOVER	0.087	(3.290)	-0.096	(-3.308)	-0.233	(-2.999)
ESTABLISHMENT SIZE	0.169	(6.163)	0.154	(5.097)	0.262	(3.119)
EMPLOYMENT88	-0.0033	(-1.377)	-0.0033	(-1.044)	-0.001	(-2.191)
WAGE88	-0.007	(-1.958)	-0.005	(-1.261)	-0.004	(-0.327)
ΔWAGE	-0.968	(-2.218)	-0.964	(-2.006)	-1.078	(-1.092)
WORKAREA	0.231	(4.124)	0.226	(3.615)	0.595	(4.142)
SPATIAL COEFFICIENT (ρ_l)	0.442	(9.320)	0.517	(11.805)	0.396	(4.839)

Summary statistics:			
N	1797	1797	457
R²/log likelihood	0.171/-1521.36	0.159/-1213.66	0.200/-827.22
LR(ρ)	107.559	154.575	24.963
LM ρ (λ)	5.234	5.144	6.973
LM(BP)	1.895	12.794	0.274

See notes below table 5.5.

As a consequence, this variable was excluded from the regressions presented here partly for this reason and partly because it reproduces information about distance already contained in the weight matrices. One reason why coefficient estimates are highly stable across both weight matrices and estimation methods is that Pearson correlations between explanatory variables are quite low. In fact, the largest of these pair-wise correlations (in absolute value), the one between *WAGE88* and *ΔWAGE*, is about 0.5. This means that multicollinearity as a destabilizing factor is not present in both weight matrix specifications. Estimates of the spatial lag coefficients range from 0.43 to 0.82 in table 5.6 and range from 0.40 to 0.52 in table 5.7. Values of these coefficients are lowest for the old manufacturing establishment regressions. Coefficients are highly significant in five out of the six regressions (see above discussion regarding the likelihood ratio tests); the coefficient does not differ significantly from zero in the old manufacturing establishment regression in table 5.6 (confirming expectations from the exploratory spatial data analysis on manufacturing industries in chapter 4). Thus, employment growth in a zip code area has a positive net effect on employment growth in other (neighboring) zip code areas, but this effect is weaker when the analysis is limited to manufacturing. A possible explanation for this outcome is that an analysis of one sector such as manufacturing ignores linkages with other sectors. Additionally, employment growth in one zip code area may harm competitor establishments in other zip code areas. This factor is likely to be more important in analyses of single sectors because competitor establishments represent a larger fraction of the total number of establishments in the sample. The next section will focus on such analyses.

Spatial Multipliers

The spatial lag and error results can be further analyzed to show to what extent employment growth in one location is found to create growth externalities for other locations. As explained in chapter 3, column sums of $A_i=(I-\rho W_i)^{-1}$, with $i=D,I$ have the interpretation of spatial multipliers. Let x_{jk} be the value of the kth explanatory variable for the jth zip code-industry. Then, $\beta_k=\partial y_j/\partial x_{kj}$ denotes the local effect on the log of employment growth of a one-unit change in x_{jk} on y_j, ignoring indirect effects arising from linkages between the jth zip code-industry and all other zipcode-industries. The total (local plus non-local) effect on the log of employment growth of a one-unit change in x_{jk} on growth rates in all areas is given by β_k times the sum of the elements in the jth column of A (i.e., $\beta_k\Sigma_i a_{ij}=dy_j/dx_{kj}$). Column sums of A, of course, will differ, but if W is standardized so that each of its row sums equal unity, the average of the column sums equals $1/(1-\rho)$ (see C. Kim *et al.* 2000). For example, if $\rho=0.80$, as was approximately the case in the all establishments regression in table 5.6, the average value of the associated spatial multipliers would be 5.0. This result suggests that, on average, about 20% of any change in an explanatory variable such as *CONCENTRATION, TURNOVER,* or *LACK OF DIVERSITY* would be felt in the zip code-industry where it occurred. About 80% of the effect of this change would be felt either in other industries in the same zip code area or in other zip code areas[23]. In the corresponding regression reported in table 5.7, which ignores linkages between industries in the construction of W, the estimate of ρ is lower (0.44) as would be expected. In this case, the average column sum is about 1.78 implying that about 56% of the effect of a change in an explanatory variable is felt locally as compared to that experienced in the same industry elsewhere. Also, in both cases, the largest share of the non-local effect is felt in neighboring zip code areas in light of the distance weights used to construct W. Table 5.8 presents all spatial multipliers calculated for location-industry models in section 5.5. In general, employment growth in a zip code area has a positive net effect on employment growth in other (neighboring) zip code areas, but this effect is rather weak. The results presented in this section add perspective to conclusions of Jaffe *et al.* (1993) and Anselin *et al.* (1997) that knowledge appears to be geographically bounded within the region where it was generated. This perspective is obtained using implications from an analysis of growth, rather than a study of patent citations or the geographic distribution of innovations and innovative behavior.

---

[23] Interindustry spillovers within a zip code area turn out to be very small in comparison to spillovers between zip code areas.

Table 5.8   Spatial multipliers in employment growth models in South-Holland

		N	$1/1$-ρ	Spatial multiplier	
				Intra-local	Inter-Local
Inter-industry (W_D)	all establishments	1797	5.076	0.197	0.803
	old establishments	1797	5.236	0.191	0.809
	old manuf. establ.	457	1.748	0.572	0.428
Intra-industry (W_I)	all establishments	1797	1.792	0.558	0.442
	old establishments	1797	2.070	0.483	0.517
	old manuf. establ.	457	1.656	0.604	0.396

5.6   Synthesis and Conclusions

The theory of endogenous growth emphasizes the importance of knowledge and knowledge externalities in the growth and innovation process. Considering the alternative hypotheses concerning the circumstances under which knowledge externalities are most likely to foster growth, the question arises whether knowledge spills over primarily between firms in the same sector, or whether growth is determined predominantly by knowledge externalities between industries. In other words, is knowledge sector-specific or can ideas conceived in one sector be fruitfully applied in other sectors as well? And what exactly is the role of the economic theorem of competition in this?

This chapter addresses these questions by location-industry modeling, initially in relative space-neutral formulations (in OLS-equations spatial observations are not related to each other or weighted by spatial composition and magnitude), providing empirical evidence on the basis of Dutch datasets. As null-models, analyses in this chapter are kept as close as possible to Glaeser *et al.*'s (1992) analytical (OLS) framework on employment growth in cities and agglomeration externalities. The regression results using data on Dutch municipalities give general support for Jane Jacobs's (1969) hypothesis that knowledge spills over between sectors and that competition fosters growth because of the necessity to innovate and survive. In this respect, the results are similar to the Glaeser *et al.* analysis of employment growth in US cities, and are in conflict with Henderson *et al.*'s (1995) findings that industrial concentration is more important than industrial diversity. However, the dataset for the province of South-Holland, which covers a substantial part of the core economic region of the country, enables us to correct several flaws in the Netherlands municipality regression. The most important is that it allows for a sources-of-growth analysis in the sense that changes in regional sectoral employment can be decomposed into business cycle changes (firm births and deaths) and employment growth occurring in existing firms. It also enables us to construct an alternative, complementary indicator of local competition: by means of the components of change of employment dynamics as outlined in chapter 3. As the theory of knowledge externalities and growth focuses on dynamic externalities rather than at location choice, the appropriate dependent variable in the analysis is employment changes in existing firms. The results are markedly different from the results mentioned above. The results for regional composition still give support to Jacobs' theory that knowledge is not necessarily sector-specific and that ideas conceived in one sector can fruitfully be applied in others. However, the fact that lack of regional competition is found to foster growth in *existing* firms gives support to the ideas of Marshall, Arrow, Romer and Porter that knowledge creation is stimulated by the possibility of rent capture. Hence, this outcome does not give full support to any of the existing hypotheses concerning the spatial-economic circumstances that foster growth.

Section 5.5 brought together two strands of literature on the relationship between knowledge externalities and employment growth. The first strand tests for evidence of endogenous growth linked to agglomeration economies between economic agents *within* cities and the second tests whether knowledge spills over between economic agents *in different locations, not necessarily being located in the same city.* The link between these two topics is made by extending the work of Glaeser *et al.* (1992) by developing spatial econometric models that allow employment growth in one location to affect growth in other locations. Several modeling techniques are explored, the central questions being whether urban economic growth models improve over the 'null-model' (as presented in sections 5.3, 5.4 and 5.5), when additive and finally simultaneously four spatial extensions are introduced. A key finding is that local industrial diversity, rather than industrial concentration tends to promote growth, but this general conclusion is heavily conditioned on the research design.

First, estimation improvements occur when explicitly *proximity-based spatial research designs* are applied by spatial lag and error specifications on the intra-urban (zip code) level. Results in this chapter on location-industry analyses suggest that knowledge externalities (spillovers) between locations can occur *indirectly* through the growth process (spatial contiguous design of the *dependent* variable). In other words, increased spillovers (externalities) can lead to increased growth in one location that can lead to increased growth elsewhere. Empirical estimates suggest that between 20% and 60% of the growth induced by agglomeration economies occurs locally, depending on whether the model allows for inter-industry linkages over space, or just intra-industry linkages over space (the sectoral models by their definition and construction only focus on intra-industry linkages). These findings are particularly significant in light of the small size of the regions studied and suggests that areas with a relatively high knowledge generating capacity may be expected to grow faster than others, while 'proximate leakage effects' turn out to be limited.

Second, *sectoral interrelations* captured in location-industry spatial weight matrices that allow for inter- as well as intra-sectoral growth interchanges add additional light on spatial externality structures. The outcome that local industrial diversity, rather than industrial concentration tends to promote growth, holds for inter- as well as intra-industry specifications of the weight matrices in the spatial lag models for location industries. The fact that no substantial change in performance of agglomeration variables occurred when changing from an inter- to an intra-industry specification, and the dominance of industrial diversity over industrial concentration in the models suggest that urbanization economies are more important attributes for the growth process than localization economies. However, the choice of the dependent variable is found to be of crucial importance when determining the impact of competition on growth. If the dependent variable measures all employment growth, as is the case in for example Glaeser *et al.* (1992), competition is found to foster growth in the location-industry analyses. If, on the other hand, only growth in (1988) existing establishments is analyzed, we find that competition is found to retard growth in location-industry analyses. This remarkable research results sets our research apart from previous studies. The findings in this chapter stress the fact that analyses are sensitive to explicit spatial contiguous specifications to a larger degree than suggested by the OLS-based location-industry results.

Chapter 6

Sectoral Employment Dynamics

6.1 Introduction

According to endogenous growth theory, knowledge and knowledge spillovers give rise to external economies of scale in production. As we saw in the previous chapters, competing theories have been proposed regarding the geographic circumstances under which knowledge is most easily transmitted within and between industries. Prior empirical research has predominantly considered possibilities for knowledge transmission between economic agents in cities. In chapter 5, cross-section models were presented that on the city-industry scale (municipalities) as well as on the intra-urban location-industry scale confirmed the empirical strength of the agglomeration externalities framework developed in Glaeser *et al.* (1992). In this chapter we will use these agglomeration and externality indicators again, as well as the spatial regimes presented in chapter 3. Because the literature is ambiguous about the spatial and sectoral treatment of economic observation, explicit and detailed focus will be on determinants of *sectoral* employment growth at the municipal and zip code level and accompanying, proximate locations (contiguous spatial lag modeling), or locations unified in theoretical relevant spatial regimes. A major flaw in the present literature that was also dealt with in the previous chapter, concerns the exact definition of spatial circumstances under which knowledge spills over most easily between economic agents. Whereas some research (as mentioned in chapter 5) finds that local employment growth and technology adoption is enhanced by diversity of activity across a broad range of sectors, others find faster growth when more activity is concentrated in a single sector.

The central question asked in this chapter is whether urban economic growth models improve over the (OLS, location-industry) null-model, when three alterations of the original model are implemented. First, we explicitly apply proximity-based spatial research designs for both explained and explaining variables, either by spatial lag or window average specifications. Second, we explore separate sectoral models for industrial, distribution, producer and consumer service activities (as were judged relevant in chapter 4). And third, spatial heterogeneity modeled by spatial regimes is introduced. Incorporating these aspects of spatial modeling makes optimal use of the spatially disaggregaed character of the data. The theoretical hypotheses in chapters 2 and 3 indicated the importance of both contiguous and heterogeneity based spatial relations for knowledge externalities and economic growth. Similar to studies previously cited, knowledge spillovers are not directly measured, and instead the focus is on identifying economic settings that most effectively enhance links between knowledge externalities and growth. The centerpiece of the chapter comprises a series of sectoral cross-sectional spatial econometric analysis on employment dynamics in the Netherlands and in the heavily urbanized province of South-Holland. The models show how various types of knowledge externalities not only affect growth at the location where they are present, but at other locations as well. South-Holland's small size reduces the problem of unmeasured heterogeneity that has become an important issue in evaluating related studies of US metropolitan areas. One way to minimize this problem is to focus on a small enough area so that locations are relatively alike in terms of natural resources, climate, and cultural and economic history. Still, spatial heterogeneity might remain present in terms of degree of urbanization and dominant occupation, physical accessibility and the status of a newly opened industrial site. This *intra-urban heterogeneity* will be introduced in the models when empirically found relevant.

The remainder of the chapter is divided into three sections. The key aspects of previous studies in relation to the conceptual framework for our empirical chapter, as well as descriptive analyses of data, variables and spatial regimes were already presented in chapters 2 and 5. Section 6.2 therefore only broadly discusses estimation elements that are altered when compared to these previous sections, and then focuses on spatial econometric models of the four sectors in South-Holland. Spatial lag and error modeling tests for contiguity growth hypotheses while, complementarily, growth patterns are tested for spatial regimes that stress non-contiguous parameter shifts within the urbanized area. It is found that spatial lag specifications of the agglomeration variables on specialization, diversity and competition are significant, often in contradicting directions of the original specification. Also, spatial regime specifications (especially concerning the level of urbanization) appear highly significant for capturing spatial variability in the employment growth data. These significant extensions of the OLS-oriented city-scale analyses are important contributions for understanding the complexity of inter- and intra-urban economic growth processes. Prior empirical research discussed in the literature has predominantly considered possibilities for knowledge transmission between economic agents and growth in *cities* and section 6.3 therefore focuses explicitly on the urban (municipal) scale in the Netherlands, in a similar manner as section 6.2 focuses on zip codes. Again, models are presented for industrial, distribution, producer service and consumer service growth respectively. For the municipal analyses central in section 6.3, the regimes for macro-economic zoning (Randstad, intermediate zone and national periphery), zoning within the Randstad (north-wing, south-wing, all other municipalities), urban size (large, medium-sized and small cities) and physical accessibility appeared significant. It should be noted that, because of lack of space, only parsimonious models containing *significant* spatial regimes and significant spatially lagged explained and agglomeration variables are presented in this chapter[1]. Focusing on the three questions stated above, section 6.5 summarizes. General conclusions concerning the agglomeration hypotheses tested and the aggregation levels of are drawn.

---

[1] OLS estimates testing on the potential significance of spatial regimes for employment growth in the four broad sectors for zip codes and municipalities are available on request.

6.2   Sectoral Models for South-Holland

Introduction

In the previous chapter, inter- and intra-industry spatial spillover conditions were modeled by means of industry-specific weight matrices. Occurrence of a specific 4-digit industry in a location then was related to occurrence of that industry in other locations[2]. In this section though, this could not be accomplished, since all four (broad) sectors are represented in almost all locations by at least one establishment and hence, industry-specific weight matrices would be almost identical to a unit vector. Instead, agglomeration variables of specialization and competition (*TURNOVER* and *ESTABLISHMENT SIZE*) are calculated separately for the four sectors. The variable of diversity (*GINI*) is location-specific, calculated over 49 individual 2-digit industries. Industry differences in employment growth in location-industry models in the previous section analyses were controlled by the variables *GROWTH, WAGE,* and *ΔWAGE.* The *GROWTH* variable, measured as the change in the natural logarithm of employment in an industry in South-Holland outside the zip code area under observation, cannot be calculated for the four sectoral analyses in this section with the same interpretation. The broad aggregation level of the four sectors results in very little variation over locations for this variable. Therefore, to correct for aggregate industry effects, the dependent variable is calculated as the difference between the employment growth of a broad sector in a location between 1988 and 1997 and the regional South-Holland growth of this sector during the same period (compare Combes 2000, p.336)[3]. Further, most of the variables used in the empirical analyses in this chapter are similar in construction of those used in the previous sections. An additional data transformation applied to the sectoral analyses is that of all four agglomeration variables (*CONCENTRATION, LACK OF DIVERSITY, TURNOVER* and *ESTABLISHMENT SIZE*) window-averaged transformations of the variables were tried in estimations in sector-specific models (Anselin 1995a p.18-2). Because of the small spatial scale of analysis used in our study, this transformation might be useful, either in a theoretical way or technically for bypassing multicollinearity problems. Another additional alteration, suggested by Combes (2000, p.338) that a better variable for employment levels at begin of period would be employment *density* (employment divided by area), is not included in the analyses. Although experiments with that variable have been made with the Dutch and South-Holland data, the explicit spatial character of this variable causes problems of multicollinearity, unanticipated heterogeneity and heteroskedasticity in spatial lag modeling (see also chapter 4 on

---

[2] The focus on location-industries (inclusion of the largest six of 49 industries in each location) in the previous sections allowed for composing the weight matrix as indicated. By designing alternative spatial weight matrices, for instance by including more (than six possible) relations between larger/denser cities or locations in principle offers further possibilities for testing hierarchical interaction patterns. Physical distances as such are then not the most appropriate denominator in the spatial models though. In this section, spatial functional heterogeneity is introduced via spatial regimes focusing on theoretical relevant spatial distinctions.

[3] In order to rule out year-specific outliers, observations of 1988 and 1989 (referred to as 1988) as well as 1996 and 1997 (referred to as 1997) are averaged in this section's analyses.

the discussion on employment density functions). The focus of this section will be on modeling spatial heterogeneity and spatial contiguous dependence in relation to the spatial agglomeration variables introduced in earlier sections. Window-averaged and spatial lagged versions of these agglomeration variables were all tried, specifying (mixtures of) different spatial weight matrices (w_1, w_2 and w_3). Additionally to the *GINI, CONCENTRATION, TURNOVER* and *SIZE* variables, several variables are used to capture historical factors affecting the spatial organization of economic activity in South-Holland, most important being *EMPLOYMENT88* that measures employment in a location (-industry) in 1988 in number of workers. All variables are corrected for outliers and measured in log transformation and normalized to the South-Holland average (compare Combes, p.336), unless stated different. Correlation analyses over all variables revealed multicollinearity problems concerning several variables. By experiments using window-averaged variables of some of the variables concerned, this problem was tackled. Window-averaged variables have a slightly differing interpretation though, and in the description of model outcomes we will pay explicit attention to that[4].

Industrial Employment Growth

From chapter 4 it became clear that both spatial contiguous dependency and spatial heterogeneity are initially limited in the South-Holland data on industrial employment growth. The first column of table 6.1 does indeed indicate that a spatial lag or error specification is not appropriate to capture the spatial structure of all establishments' growth. For incumbent ('old') establishments neither spatial contiguous dependence nor significance of spatial regimes is apparent. OLS estimates on all establishments in column (1) of table 6.1 show some remarkable deviations from regression results presented on location-industry growth in South-Holland in chapter 5. It should be remarked beforehand that within the location-industry dataset of South-Holland (n=1797), industrial activities are rather under-represented. The coefficient for *CONCENTRATION* shows a significant negative significant sign indicating that industrial concentration as such hampers industrial employment growth. *LACK OF DIVERSITY* does not show to be significant. The variables *TURNOVER* and *ESTABLISHMENT SIZE* (after a window-averaged transformation), measuring the degree of sector-internal competition in the tightness of the industrial organization of the industrial sector, both appear

---

[4] Some technical remarks apply to all models presented:
values of log-likelihood are not comparable over populations of all and old establishments. LM (ρ) and LM (λ) are statistics for the presence of a spatial lag in the dependent variable and in the residual respectively, following Anselin *et al.* (1996) with a critical value of 3.84 at 5% level of significance (marked +). LR(ρ) tests for the significance of the spatial dependence coefficient. LM (BP) tests for homoskedasticity of regression errors using the Breusch-Pagan Lagrange multiplier test for normal distributed errors. The spatial weight matrix used is w_1 (row-standardised), only probability levels (p-values) are presented in the tables. Significant results (95% confidence interval) of the spatial Chow-Wald in general and on individual coefficients (rejection of H_0 of joint equality of coefficients over regimes) are marked (*). All variables are log transformed and corrected for extreme values (found in ESDA analyses in chapter 4). For the exact definition of the sectoral activities see appendix A. For the definition of spatial regimes see chapter 3.

significant[5]. The level of employment in the base year appears not significant, as was the case in most of the location-industry analyses discussed before. The wage structure and change variables are not significant either. The LM(λ) and LM(δ) statistics do not reveal significant spatial dependence in the regression. This indicates that spatial error or spatial lag formulations are not appropriate modifications to the model. The explained variance is again rather low (0.106) and the LM(BP) test statistic indicates that heteroskedasticity is a potential problem. Column (2) in table 6.1 shows the optimal equation when spatial lags (using w_1)[6] of the spatial externality indicators are introduced to the model.

Some remarkable results can be noticed from this addition. The degree of industrial concentration in a zip code remains negatively significant related to industrial employment growth, but the spatial lag of the concentration variable (*W_CONC*) is positively related to growth. Being surrounded by industrial concentrated spatial structures fosters employment growth, where own representation of industrial activities retards it. For the *GINI* variable an opposite structure is found: the spatial lagged (lack of) diversity variable fosters growth, while the location internal diversity variable remains insignificant. The spatial lagged competition variables of *TURNOVER* and *ESTABLISHMENT SIZE* did not comprise significant signs; the *ESTABLISHMENT SIZE* variable is not significant in this model. Model fit improved (R^2=0.156) but heteroskedasticity remains a potential problem. Still no indications of spatial lag or error dependency are present in the summary statistics of the column (2) equation.

Column (5) in table 6.1 presents a spatial error version of the model for all establishments, using a heteroskedastic error model (FGLS), (see Anselin 1995a, p.30-6). The estimates on all establishments are made for two spatial regimes: work-area as opposed to non-work-area locations. The fit of the model is substantially better compared to the specification without spatial regime according to the increase in R^2 (0.206). The significance of the heteroskedastic instrument variables (*SIGMA*) indicate that the work-area regime captures the heteroskedasticity present in the model. The Chow-Wald statistic of spatial heterogeneity indicates that the distinction in work-area regimes is significant (while the other regimes tried were not). On an individual basis, it turns out that the variables *LACK OF DIVERSITY* and *W_LACK DIV,* the *CONSTANT* and the *WAGE* variables perform significantly different over the two regimes. For working areas, industry-level diversity hampers industrial employment growth, whereas for non-working areas diversity in surrounding areas fosters growth. The signs and significance of the *CONCENTRATION* and *W_CONCENTRATION* variables do not differ over the two regimes.

---

[5] Combes (2000) finds in growth models on employment in France for industrial activities that specialization and the inverse of establishment size (measured as our CONCENTRATION and SIZE variables) hamper growth significantly. Diversity fosters growth also in the models presented by Combes. Models presented by Combes are not exactly comparable to ours though: divisions are made in order to categorize all activities as industry or services, while we instead use four categories of industry clusters.

[6] Experiments with w_2 and w_3 spatial weight matrices in this respect did not result in significant contibutions to the model.

Table 6.1 OLS **and spatial lag models for employment growth in manufacturing activities in South-Holland (n=416, w_1)**

eplanatory variables	(1) OLS all establ.	(2) OLS all establ.	(3) OLS old establ.	(4) OLS old establ.	(5) FGLS all establ. spatial regimes	
					work areas	non-work
CONSTANT	0.049	-0.382	-0.708	-0.493	5.635	-3.024
	(0.028)	(-0.223)	(-0.377)	(-0.267)	(2.172)*	(-1.397)*
CONC.	-0.123	-0.137	0.013	0.031	-0.121	-0.153)
	(-5.108)	(-5.760)	(0.491)	(1.184)	(-3.623)	(-4.821)
W_CONC.	-	2.487	-	-2.480	3.044	2.260
		(4.680)		(-4.334)	(3.148)	(3.687)
LACK OF DIV.	0.263	0.265	-0.309	-0.304	0.573	-0.007
	(1.768)	(1.832)	(-1.942)	(-1.952)	(2.419)*	(-0.036)*
W_LACK DIV.	-	-1.880	-	1.079	-1.109	-2.364
		(-3.065)		(1.628)	(-0.996)	(-3.349)
TURNOVER	0.148	0.120	-0.222	-0.196	0.082	0.155
	(3.267)	(2.708)	(-4.588)	(-4.097)	(1.182)	(2.806)
WA_EST. SIZE	0.018	-0.0124	-0.009	0.023	-0.030	-0.0012
	(2.548)	(-1.247)	(-1.296)	(2.164)	(-1.704)	(-1.005)
WA_EMPL88	-0.003	0.035	0.020	0.041	-0.004	-0.029
	(-0.175)	(-2.019)	(1.299)	(2.174)	(-1.348)	(-1.409)
WAGE88	0.119	0.241	0.047	-0.022	-1.135	0.815
	(0.280)	(0.578)	(0.104)	(-0.049)	(-1.81)*	(1.534)*
$\Delta WAGE$	-0.244	-0.402	0.530	0.754	-1.947	0.406
	(-0.664)	(-1.102)	(1.347)	(1.920)	(-3.44)*	(0.882)*
SIGMA	-	-	-	-	0.325	0.434
					(7.906)	(12.062)
sum. statistics:						
N	416	416	416	416	416	
R^2	0.106	0.156	0.108	0.147	0.206	
LM (BP)	14.5 (0.00)	13.89 (0.00)	6.28 (0.04)	6.65 (0.036)	-	
LM (ρ)	0.351 (0.55)	0.04 (0.84)	0.92 (0.34)	2.34 (0.126)	0.888 (0.346)	
LM (λ)	0.723 (0.39)	0.19 (0.65)	0.26 (0.61)	0.40 (0.527)	0.403 (0.525)	
Sp. Chow-Wald	-	-	-	-	28.776 (0.001)	

SIGMA reports FGLS-hetreoscedastic variance coefficients. Z-values (upper part of the table) and probability levels (lower part of the table) are presented in parenthesis. The spatial Chow-Wald test is distributed as an F variate and tests for structural instability of the regression coefficients over regimes (Anselin 1995a, p.32-2). W_ and WA_ indicate (row standardized) spatial lag and (row unstandardized) spatial average transformation of variables (w_1 unless stated differently, see Anselin 1995a p.18-2). Because of multicollinearity problems, the models were in their final form estimated using window-averaged transformations of the variables *ESTABLISHMENT SIZE* and *EMPLOYMENT88* using row-unstandardized weight-matrix W_2.

For incumbent ('old') establishments no explicit spatial design of the models appeared significant, hence none is inserted. The OLS models in columns (3) and (4) appear homoskedastic according to the LM(BP) test. As in previous models for incumbent (industrial) firms the competition variable *TURNOVER* is negatively related to employment growth. *CONCENTRATION, LACK OF DIVERSITY* and *WA_EST.SIZE* appear not significant in equation (3). *W_CONC* is negatively significant in equation (4), as was the case in the all-establishments equation (2).

Competition, concentration and diversity appear key variables for spatial heterogeneity in industrial employment growth over the work-area regime. It should be noticed that the distinction work-area/non-work-area is different from the distinction urban/non-urban. Predominant working areas are to be found outside urban areas as well. The introduction of spatial lag transformations of the agglomeration variables and the spatial regime of work-areas revealed some interesting additional insight in the spatial structure of industrial employment growth data in the research area. Spatial (contiguous) dependency appears not significant for both all- and old establishments estimations. Incorporation of spatially lagged and window-averaged explanatory variables, spatial heterogeneity and auto-correlation does alter general conclusions on the spatial externalities hypotheses. The estimated results presented in this section leave some of the general conclusion drawn from location-industry analyses unchanged. Jacobs' externalities focusing on diversity and industrial concentration retarding industrial growth, as well as the degree of competition fostering growth for the all-establishments and retarding growth for the incumbent establishments samples appear again important. Additional insight gained in this section concerns the fact that surrounding industrial specialization is significantly related to industrial growth. Diversity indicators also are significant when analyzed for the surrounding area (spatial lag) definition. Although it should be remarked that industrial activities for the South-Holland research area analyses are of relatively little importance, for understanding the region's spatial endogenous growth conditions the spatial specifications presented improve the model fit and makes the externality discussion more balanced on the intra-urban level of analysis. We clearly find evidence for both MAR and Jacobs-related spatial externalities in the own *and* neighboring locations to be related to employment growth in manufacturing.

Employment Growth in Distribution Activities

Distribution activities, either concerning physical distribution or wholesale, are often hypothesized to grow just outside or on good accessible fringes of urban agglomerations because of their space consuming character (negative agglomeration externality) on the one hand and proximity to customers on the other hand (positive agglomeration externality). Especially in a distribution-dense region as South-Holland, containing numerous large cargo firms in the Rotterdam harbor and truck transport firms that spin off from this, this process of growth appears important. Table 6.2 presents spatial designs that optimally capture the spatial heterogeneity and spatial autocorrelation patterns present in the data on employment growth in distribution activities. For both the all-establishments and the old establishments specifications, the model incorporates spatial heterogeneity by means of an urban/non-urban regime.

Table 6.2 OLS and FGLS models for employment growth in distribution activities in South-Holland (n=416, w_1)

eplanatory variables	(1) OLS all establish-ments	(2) OLS old establish-ments	(3) FGLS est. all establ. urban spatial regimes		(4) FGLS old establ. urban spatial regimes	
			urban	non-urban	Urban	non-urban
CONSTANT	1.150	-4.183	1.145	2.855	-5.950	-3.589
	(0.818)	(-2.142)	(0.614)	(1.441)	(-2.495)	(-1.200)
CONCENTR.	-0.105	-0.112	-0.012	-0.163	-0.087	-0.137
	(-3.099)	(-2.518)	(-0.229)*	(-3.90)*	(-1.268)	(-2.181)
W_CONC.	0.881	-0.666	1.157	0.358	-0.914	0.194
	(4.076)	(-2.218)	(4.144)	(0.950)	(-2.558)	(0.341)
LACK	-0.198	-0.294	-0.323	-0.153	-0.153	-0.468
DIVERS.	(-2.020)	(-2.156)	(-1.930)	(-1.132)	(-0.712)	(-2.665)
TURNOVER	0.263	-0.405	0.364	0.151	-0.746	-0.155
	(4.689)	(-5.192)	(3.924)	(2.135)	(-6.27)*	(-1.453)*
ESTABL. SIZE	0.049	-0.063	0.164	-0.053	-0.101	-0.062
	(1.338)	(-1.233)	(3.320)*	(-0.98)*	(-1.600)	(-0.762)
WA_EMPL88	-0.026	0.023	-0.041	0.023	0.030	-0.029
	(-3.693)	(2.346)	(-4.496)*	(0.069)*	(2.599)*	(-1.534)*
WAGE	-0.142	0.937	-0.048	-0.625	1.247	0.768
	(-0.389)	(1.846)	(-0.100)	(-1.211)	(2.034)	(0.987)
ΔWAGE	0.865	-1.256	1.017	0.458	-2.074	0.454
	(2.309)	(-2.416)	(2.244)	(0.778)	(-3.57)*	(0.511)*
SIGMA	-	-	0.197	0.186	0.322	0.423
			(10.606)	(9.772)	(10.606)	(9.772)
Summ. Statistics:						
N	416	416	416		416	
R^2	0.210	0.223	0.277		0.291	
LM (BP)	11.281 (0.003)	8.941 (0.011)	-		-	
LM (ρ)	3.145 (0.0768)	0.519 (0.471)	2.773 (0.144)		3.258 (0.071)	
LM (λ)	2.334 (0.1266)	0.222 (0.637)	1.666 (0.255)		2.867 (0.090)	
Spat. Chow-Wald	-	-	39.148 (0.000)		38.392 (0.000)	

See the notes below table 6.1 for explanation. Because of multicollinearity problems, the models were in their final form estimated using window-averaged transformations of the variable *EMPLOYMENT88* using row-unstandardized weight-matrix W_2.

The specialization and competition variables perform according to the general South-Holland spatial design of location industries. Some differences in the estimates occur though, either by incorporating spatial lag transformations and spatial regimes. The variables *W_CONC* (positive significant in all-establishments and negative significant in old establishments analyses) and *WA_EMPL88* (negative in the all-establishments and positive in the incumbent specification) show patterns differing from the location-industry analyses. The LM(λ) and LM(δ) statistics do not reveal significant spatial dependence in the regression, indicating that spatial error or spatial lag formulation are not appropriate modifications to the model. The explained variance is higher than in the manufacturing estimates (0.210 and 0.223 respectively for all- and old establishment models); the LM(BP) test statistic indicates that heteroskedasticity is a potential problem. Therefore, as a potential useful modification, FGLS heteroskedastic error models using an urban regime (significantly indicated in the previous section) have been estimated. For the all-establishment specification (column 3), the variables of *CONCENTRATION, W_CONC, ESTABL.SIZE* and *WA_EMPL88* show different slopes over the spatial regimes. Most relations found in the OLS specification (1) are to be found in urban areas, as opposed to non-urban ones. The exception is the *CONCENTRATION* variable, being especially significant in the non-urban regime. For the incumbent specification (column 4), besides the specialization indicator the diversity indicator shows significance in the non-urban regime as opposed to the urban. These two spatially lagged variables both reinforce the own-location direction of significance. In general, in the regimes and heteroskedasticity models the explained variance is improved and the spatial Chow-Wald test and the heteroskedastic instrumental variables (*SIGMA*) are all highly significant. From the individual variables statistics of the spatial Chow-Wald test it becomes clear that for both models (all- and incumbent firm specifications) non-urban locations comprise higher employment growth rates for distribution activities. In this section, we predominantly find evidence for Jacobs-related spatial externalities in the own *and* neighboring locations concerning local employment growth in distribution activities. Only the neighboring variable of specialization forms an exception on the Jacobs externalities.

Employment Growth in Producer Services

From the literature[7] it becomes clear that especially spatial producer services growth is embedded in two, non-exclusive hypotheses: that of proximate, urban growth caused by knowledge spillovers and that of urban-hierarchical growth because of headquarter and decision making linkages. It should be clear that for some of the hypotheses made in the literature the research area of South-Holland is too small (e.g. the headquarter information flow hypothesis) and that for other hypotheses the area decomposition in zip codes is just about most suitable for testing (e.g. spatial auto-correlation hypothesis). Table 6.3 presents the spatial econometric results that most suitably fit the spatial variation in producer service growth in South-Holland. All models initially show low explained variance levels, as do virtually all models discussed in this chapter. Our focus is on spatial heterogeneity, spatial autocorrelation and the signs of the individual agglomeration-coefficients, not on an excellent model fit. Column (1) shows OLS estimates for all-establishment variation. Except for the diversity variable, all coefficients of the agglomeration variables conform to the location-industry growth analyses presented in chapter 5. The LM(ρ) and LM(λ) statistics show insignificance of spatial dependency in spatial lag and error specification.

---

[7] See especially Bennet and Smith (2002), Daniels (1991), Manshanden (1996) and Marshall and Wood (1995), also discussed in chapter 2.

Table 6.3   OLS and spatial lag models for employment growth in producer services in South-Holland (n=416, w_1)

eplanatory variables	(1) OLS all establ.	(2) OLS all establ.	(3) OLS old establ.	(4) OLS old establ.	(5) FGLS all establishments spatial regimes urban	non-urban
CONSTANT	4.732	5.560	-2.394	-2.329	6.800	3.350
	(2.694)	(3.149)	(-0.989)	(-0.947)	(2.763)	(1.396)
CONC.	-0.122	-0.142	0.098	0.100	-0.213	-0.062
	(-2.845)	(-3.294)	(1.654)	(1.679)	(-3.328)	(-1.122)
W_CONC	-	1.912	-	-2.337	2.200	1.126
		(3.635)		(-3.225)	(3.392)	(1.418)
LACK DIV.	0.108	0.041	-0.088	-0.013	0.047	0.149
	(0.878)	(0.326)	(-0.516)	(-0.074)	(0.261)	(0.941)
W_LACK DIV.	-	-0.483	-	2.164	-0.683	-0.012
		(-2.009)		(2.698)	(-2.608)*	(-0.002)*
TURNOVER	0.102	0.104	-0.239	-0.242	0.470	-0.015
	(2.000)	(2.049)	(-3.378)	(-3.454)	(4.085)*	(-0.262)*
ESTABL. SIZE	0.111	0.099	0.008	0.016	0.090	0.158
	(2.867)	(2.590)	(0.149)	(0.298)	(1.768)	(2.829)
WA_EMPL88	-0.007	-0.030	0.011	0.083	-0.037	-0.014
	(-1.225)	(-3.556)	(1.328)	(3.806)	(-2.633)	(-0.745)
WAGE	-1.106	-1.333	0.485	0.491	-1.294	-0.903
	(-2.499)	(-2.989)	(0.795)	(0.791)	(-2.083)	(-1.492)
Δ WAGE	-0.762	-0.818	0.421	0.292	-2.821	0.879
	(-1.681)	(-1.824)	(0.673)	(0.469)	(-4.789)*	(1.412)*
SIGMA	-	-	-	-	0.239	0.265
					(10.606)	(9.772)
sum. statistics:						
N	416	416	416	416	416	
R^2	0.158	0.185	0.065	0.098	0.261	
LM (BP)	3.89(0.014)	2.64 (0.026)	3.47 (0.18)	3.49 (0.17)	-	
LM (ρ)	0.14 (0.71)	0.17 (0.68)	0.78 (0.38)	0.48 (0.49)	0.291 (0.589)	
LM (λ)	0.42 (0.51)	0.11 (0.74)	0.39 (0.53)	1.06 (0.30)	0.112 (0.738)	
Sp. Ch-Wald	-	-	-	-	42.777 (0.000)	

See the notes below table 6.1 for explanation. Because of multicollinearity problems, the models were in their final form estimated using window-averaged transformations of the variable *EMPLOYMENT88* using row-unstandardized weight-matrix W_2.

The LM(BP) test reveals that heteroskedasticity is a potential problem. Column (2) reveals that the diversity indicator in neighboring locations (*W_LACKDIV*) has the positive effect on own employment growth. Another additional feature that is not remarked in the original OLS equation is the *positive* relation of neighboring producer service specialization on own employment growth. In column (5) it is revealed that the relationships thus revealed are most prominently present in urban areas. The FGLS analyses with the urban spatial regimes is highly significant (according to the spatial Chow-Wald test and the z-values of the heteroskedasticity instruments *SIGMA*) and model fit improves considerable over the models evolving from column (1) over column (2) to column (5). For the all-establishment specification, the Jacobs-induced hypotheses concerning specialization, competition and diversity indicators perform profoundly as in the location-industry analyses of previous sections, the performance of spatially lagged variables of specialization and diversity being additional elements. Column (3) and (4) show OLS estimates for incumbent establishments. Remarkable is the insignificance of the agglomeration variable measuring diversity and the significant retarding effect concerning diversity in neighboring locations. The *TURNOVER* variable changing sign for the incumbent establishment specification is consistent with the overall South-Holland location-industry analyses. The negative relation of producer service specialization with employment growth in that sector comes to the fore in the neighboring specification (*W_CONC*). It is remarkable that neighboring diversity *retards* employment growth of incumbent firms in own locations. For the incumbent establishments population, no spatial regime specifications are significant. The LM(BP) test reveals no problems on heteroskedasticity. The model fit improves from the column (3) specification to the column (4) specification.

As was observed in Combes (2000) for France, urbanization economies are observed in global regressions for producer and consumer services much more profound than for industrial and distribution activities. Especially the agglomeration variables of economic diversity and local competition make the difference in the urban regime specification for all firms in a positive sense. Firms having their business in producer services consequently benefit from facing a great variety of sectors located in the same or neighboring locations, because of both supply and demand linkages (Combes 2000, p.348). This section shows a general conclusion that confirms this (broad) set of hypothesis, but remarkable are four empirical observations, namely that: (1) a relative small establishment structure (the variable *SIZE*) fosters employment growth for the all-establishment specification in especially non-urban locations, (2) diversity predominantly matters for the all-establishment specification when present in neighboring locations, (3) neighboring specialization in producer services fosters employment growth in this sector in the all-establishment specification, (4) neighboring diversity retards producer service employment growth in the incumbent establishments specification. Producer service growth in South-Holland is distinguished as a process taking place in urban locations that are characterized by a large degree of own and surrounding economic diversity and local competition. The general conclusion should be conditioned on three interdependent elements: on the definition of competition, on the distinction in own and surrounding relationships (especially relevant on the spatial scale of zip codes central in this chapter) and on the distinction in all and incumbent populations of firms.

Table 6.4   OLS and spatial lag models for employment growth in consumer services in South-Holland (n=416, w_1[8])

eplanatory variables	(1) OLS all establishments	(2) OLS old establishments	(3) spatial lag all establishments
CONCENTRATION	-0.036	0.028	-0.036
	(-2.498)	(0.872)	(-2.543)
LACK OF DIVERSITY	-0.775	-0.059	-0.770
	(-2.009)	(-0.579)	(-2.018)
TURNOVER	-0.047	0.153	-0.042
	(-1.104)	(2.676)	(-0.994)
ESTABLISHMENT SIZE	-0.005	-0.004	0.002
	(-0.322)	(-0.177)	(0.070)
EMPLOYMENT88	-0.048	0.039	-0.046
	(-4.255)	(2.518)	(-4.153)
WAGE88	0.041	-0.081	0.029
	(1.295)	(-1.889)	(0.916)
DWAGE	0.810	-1.004	0.798
	(2.808)	(-2.587)	(2.808)
SPATIAL COEFFICIENT (ρ)	-	-	0.692
			(3.533)

Summary statistics:

	(1)	(2)	(3)
N	416	416	416
R^2/*log likelihood*	*0.097/-114.87*	0.076	*-112.794*
LM (BP)	12.21 (0.003)	7.765 (0.021)	13.715 (0.110)
LM (ρ)	5.221 (0.022)	1.102 (0.294)	-
LM (λ)	4.257 (0.039)	0.496 (0.481)	-
LR (ρ)	-	-	4.158 (0.041))
LM ρ (λ)	-	-	4.100 (0.052)

See the notes below table 6.1 for explanation. For homoskedasticity, the variance matrices in spatial lag analysis have been made dependent on the instruments *POPULATION88* and *WORKAREA*. The models were estimated without intercept.

Employment Growth in Consumer Services

Chapter 5 showed that consumer service activities make up a growing part of the economic build-up of the research area of South-Holland. From a theoretical point of view, consumer service activities as a non-basic sector is of little importance. Table 6.4 shows the optimal spatial estimation design for employment growth in this sector. Spatial regime specifications appeared little fruitful. Weighted-average and spatial lag specifications of individual variables were not significant in the specifications tried (and therefore resemble the location-industry analyses in the

---

[8] Based on empirical research by Van Wissen (2000), who uses a dataset to a large extent comparable to those used in this dissertation for calculating industry-specific distance decay functions, the distance weight matrix used for consumer services initially was w_2. Calculations using w_1 did not alter the outcomes substantially though, so for comparability with previous analyses in this chapter the matrix W_1 is used.

previous sections in that respect). For the all establishment population a spatial lag or error model appeared relevant from the LM(ρ) and LM(λ) test statistics. Column (1) and (2) in table 6.4 show that the OLS-estimates are similar to the South-Holland location-industry estimates of chapter 5. for several individual coefficients: *LACK OF DIVERSITY* and *CONCENTRATION*. The *TURNOVER* variable appears significant in the old establishment specification. The *ESTABLISHMENT SIZE* variable lacks significance in any of the specifications. The spatial lag model in column (3) confirms the presence of spatial (contiguous) dependency in the data. The LR(ρ) test confirms the spatial lag significance. Heteroscedasticity problems remain present even after the variance matrixs was made dependent on appropriate instrumental variables.

6.3 Sectoral Models for the Netherlands

Industrial Employment Growth

Table 6.5 presents OLS and FGLS models for industrial employment growth on the municipal level (n=580) in the Netherlands for the period 1991-1997. Column (1) shows the most parsimonious OLS specification. Compared to the initial municipality-industry specifications in chapter 5, several remarkable model results come to the fore. The negative significant municipal coefficient for *CONCENTRATION* is in line with the analyses of chapter 5, but the spatial lag of this variable (*W_CONC*) is positively significant in the model. Industrial specialization in regions surrounding municipalities thus has a strong positive relation with own industrial employment growth. The same pattern for the all-establishment population was observed in the zip-code level analyses of industrial growth in South-Holland. Diversity (measured by *GINI*) and the degree of local competition (measured by *ESTABLISHMENT SIZE*) show no significant relation with industrial employment growth. Initial employment level and the initial wage structure (*EMPL91* and *WAGE91*) are negatively related to employment growth in the industrial sector. Summary statistics of column (1) reveal potential problems concerning heteroskedasticity and initially no spatial lag or error dependence.

In order to capture relevant spatial heterogeneity and to ensure homoskedasticity in modeling, FGLS specifications with urban and Randstad spatial regimes are presented in columns (2) and (3)[9]. Both spatial regimes appear highly significant (according to significance levels of *SIGMA* and the spatial Chow-Wald test). The results show, in addition to equation (1), that the negative relation of industrial concentration with industrial employment growth is significantly relevant in the small city regime (municipalities with less than 45,000 inhabitants).

---

[9] Only the most parsimonious model specifications are presented because of lack of space. This means for instance that specifications including W_GINI and W_ESTABL.SIZE did not significantly improve the model fit or individual coefficient estimation.

Table 6.5   OLS and FGLS models for industrial employment growth in the Netherlands (n=580, w_1)

explanatory variables	(1) OLS	(2) FGLS estimation urban spatial regimes			(3) FGLS estimation Randstad spatial regimes		
		large	medium	small	n-wing	s-wing	other
CONST.	0.065	-0.243	1.387	0.201	0.874	0.349	0.248
	(1.054)	(-0.229)	(2.144)	(0.805)	(1.332)	(0.670)	(1.002)
CONC.	-0.191	0.065	0.052	-0.228	-0.294	-0.079	-0.198
	(-5.907)	(0.392)*	(0.562)*	(-5.575)*	(-2.374)	(-0.979)	(-5.217)
W_CONC.	0.663	2.520	-0.126	0.264	2.323	0.122	0.172
	(4.504)	(2.580)*	(-0.458)*	(2.051)*	(2.233)	(-0.356)	(1.157)
GINI	-0.203	3.304	-2.434	-0.313	-1.199	0.395	-0.210
	(-1.150)	(2.625)*	(-3.779)*	(-1.31)*	(-1.449)	(0.757)	(-0.837)
ESTABL.	0.027	0.372	0.092	-0.017	0.062	-0.048	-0.018
SIZE	(0.786)	(1.816)	(0.797)	(-0.399)	(0.376)	(-0.413)	(-0.698)
EMPL. 91	-0.679	-0.048	-0.094	-0.011	-0.040	-0.081	-0.015
	(-2.181)	(-0.463)	(-1.364)	(-0.405)	(-0.550)	(-1.393)	(-0.608)
WAGE 91	-1.767	-10.284	2.979	-1.551	-1.099	-4.944	-0.894
	(-2.528)	(-1.631)*	(2.092)*	(-2.11)*	(-0.405)	(-2.386)	(-1.248)
ΔWAGE	-1.066	-7.288	0.742	-0.882	-0.383	-1.257	-0.485
	(-1.331)	(-0.901)	(0.361)	(-1.031)	(-0.119)	(-0.446)	(-0.609)
SIGMA	-	0.230	0.057	0.140	0.274	0.129	0.117
		(4.243)	(5.522)	(15.540)	(5.958)	(6.042)	(14.764)

sum. statistics:			
N	580	580	580
R^2	0.178	0.248	0.246
LM (BP)	8.929 (0.012)	-	-
LM (ρ)	0.119 (0.729)	0.635 (0.426)	0.218 (0.640)
LM (λ)	1.382 (0.239)	1.779 (0.182)	0.149 (0.698)
Chow-Wald	-	53.121 (0.000)	37.873 (0.001)

See notes below table 6.1 for explanation. SIGMA reports FGLS-hetreoskedastic variance coefficients.

The distinction in municipalities in the north-wing of the Randstad and municipalities outside the Randstad as opposed to municipalities in the south-wing of the Randstad also is a relevant change-in-slope distinction (the latter shows an insignificant coefficient). This negative relation of concentration with employment growth fits in Jacobs' hypotheses of spatial externalities in urban growth. More MAR-oriented agglomeration externalities are reflected in the positive contribution of the spatially lagged concentration variable to local industrial employment growth. Diversity turns out to be a significant (Jacobs-related) variable for the medium-sized urban regime, while it tends to hamper industrial employment growth in municipalities in the large city urban regime (MAR-related hypothesis). The competition and initial employment variables do not show significant structural changes over the regimes specified (recall that the OLS specification of initial employment in column (1) shows significant negative in relation to industrial employment growth). The wage structure works out positively on employment growth in medium-sized cities and negatively in small cities and rural municipalities.

The results confirming Jacobs-induced hypotheses on agglomeration externalities in cities found on an OLS-basis in the municipality-industry models presented in chapter 5 only to a limited degree survive in the spatial econometric models on employment growth specified in this section. The positive relation of industrial diversity (measured over 49 industries) with industrial employment growth is only found for the spatial regime of medium-sized cities. Concentration variables, as in the analyses on zip code level in South-Holland, besides a negative 'own-location' (local) relation to growth, show a positive 'spatially lagged' (regional) relation to local growth. Local competition (measured by relative establishment size) does not have a significant relation to employment growth in any of the specifications. The addition in this section of spatially lagged (regional) and spatial heterogeneity model specifications on sectoral (industrial) level (the three model additions appointed central in the previous section) reveal that the patterns of industrial employment growth move away from the relative clear-cut Jacobs-confirming hypotheses found in earlier models.

Employment Growth in Distribution Activities

From table 6.6 it becomes clear that spatial models for employment growth in distribution activities in the Netherlands are complex in form. All spatially lagged (regional) agglomeration variables are significant, as is the spatial lag variable of the dependent variable. The spatial regimes of national zoning and physical accessibility appear significant indicators of spatial heterogeneity. From the OLS equation in column (1) it is learned that concentration of distribution activities, the initial stock of employment (measured as window-average variable for multicollinearity reasons), sectoral diversity and the degree of regional competition (measured by relative firm size in neighboring locations corrected for distance) hamper distribution employment growth. Regional diversity and regional concentration foster local growth, however. The spatial externality variables thus show support for both Jacobs-hypotheses and MAR-hypotheses of urban growth: no clear-cut picture arises. The regression results of equation (1) appear to be homoskedastic, and both test statistics on spatial lag and spatial error dependence are significant. From equation (2), introducing spatial heterogeneity by means of the national zoning regimes (Randstad, intermediate zone, national periphery) it becomes clear that the equation concerning the Randstad municipalities in general differs substantially from the intermediate zone and national periphery equations. The spatial Chow-Wald test concludes positive upon the significance of the spatial regimes. The Randstad region, containing the harbour of Rotterdam and Schiphol airport, historically grew into the major distribution focus of the Netherlands.

Table 6.6 **OLS and spatial lag models for employment growth in distribution activities in the Netherlands (n=580, w_1)**

explanatory variables	(1) OLS	(2) OLS estimation national zoning spatial regimes			(3) spatial lag-estimation access. spatial regimes	
		randstad	iz	periphery	access	non-access
CONSTANT	-0.075	-0.382	-0.011	0.038	-0.151	-0.016
	(-1.847)	(-3.447)	(-0.152)	(0.579)	(-2.993)	(-0.248)
CONC.	-0.154	-0.012	-0.240	-0.169	-0.099	-0.240
	(-4.754)	(-0.218)*	(-3.943)*	(-3.146)*	(-2.545)*	(-4.575)*
W_CONC.	0.769	1.429	-0.236	0.629	0.187	0.393
	(4.946)	(5.554)*	(-0.653)*	(1.810)*	(4.194)	(1.479)
GINI	0.235	1.157	0.063	-0.060	0.391	0.122
	(2.044)	(5.367)*	(0.261)*	(-0.322)*	(2.692)	(0.682)
W_GINI	-0.408	0.781	0.496	-0.502	-0.389	-0.169
	(-1.970)	(1.618)	(0.771)	(-1.294)	(-1.418)	(-0.547)
ESTABL. SIZE	0.035	0.122	0.001	0.048	0.080	-0.031
	(1.213)	(2.434)	(0.012)	(1.018)	(2.128)	(-0.694)
W_ESIZE	-0.312	-0.553	-0.716	-0.489	-0.568	0.098
	(-2.345)	(-2.014)	(-1.825)	(-1.800)	(-3.448)*	(0.466)*
WA_EMPL91	-0.011	-0.032	0.015	-0.007	0.019	0.005
	(-4.265)	(-5.822)*	(1.826)*	(-0.991)*	(-5.724)*	(1.129)*
WAGE 91	0.411	0.566	1.758	0.268	0.516	0.664
	(0.892)	(0.710)	(1.660)	(0.386)	(0.895)	(0.898)
ΔWAGE	-0.093	1.467	0.629	0.124	0.516	-0.094
	(-0.152)	(1.449)	(0.492)	(0.127)	(0.690)	(-0.093)
SPATIAL COEFFIC. ρ	-	-			0.701 (3.688)	
Sum. Statistics:						
N	580	580			580	
R^2/ML	0.109/-30.91	0.185			-13.084	
LM (BP)	1.365 (0.502)	0.241 (0.886)			3.675 (0.055)	
LM (ρ)	6.107 (0.013)	0.143 (0.704)			-	
LM (λ)	8.367 (0.030)	1.107 (0.292)			-	
LR (ρ)	-	-			4.420 (0.035)	
LM λ (ρ)	-	-			11.234 (0.803)	
Chow-Wald	-	2.843 (0.000)			31.764 (0.000)	

See notes below table 6.1 for explanation.

Concentration of distribution activities in the Randstad municipalities appears to have no direct significant relation to employment growth, but *regional* concentration of distribution activities fosters growth. Local sectoral diversity hampers growth predominantly in the Randstad regime. Relative small firm sizes of distribution firms restricts *municipal* growth in the Randstad equation, while simultaneously *regional* (surrounding) competition conditions tend to induce employment growth. Equation (3) in table 6.6 presents results when using the (non-)accessibility regime in a spatial lag modeling framework. Again, the spatial Chow-Wald test concludes upon the significance of this regime in the distribution growth context. As for the Randstad spatial regime, most significant relations on the agglomeration externality indicators concern accessible locations. Relative less accessible locations show a different (less significant) outcome of coefficient slopes. The spatial coefficient (indicating contiguous spatial dependency using weight matrix W_1) appears significant, confirmed by the test statistics. A complex set of spatial research designs is found relevant in the data on distribution employment growth, stressing the unique spatial structure of the Randstad region as well as physical accessible locations concerning growth of distribution employment. No clear evidence in favor of MAR, Porter or Jacobs-induced spatial externality circumstances appears from the analyses. City (municipality) border crossing, regional fertilizing effects of the agglomeration indicators specialization, diversity and competition are also important differentiating modeling aspects. On the spatial analyses concerning zip codes in South-Holland (completely located within the Randstad region), a similar complex pattern for agglomeration externality indicators was found. Recall that the non-urban spatial regime in particular appeared important for employment growth in distribution on the zip code scale (n=416).

Employment Growth in Producer Services

Table 6.7 presents the spatial econometric models estimated for employment growth in producer service activities in the Netherlands. Spatially lagged transformations of the agglomeration variables on concentration, diversity and competition (relative establishment size) appear relevant, as do the spatial regimes on urban size, national zoning and the north/south segmentation within the Randstad region. Column (1) starts with the OLS estimation. As in the zip code equations in chapter 5, diversity of economic activities in 'own' municipalities restricts producer service growth, while neighboring diversity fosters growth. Concentration of producer service employment is positively related to growth on the municipal scale of analysis. The relative small establishment size of producer service activities (degree of local competition) is significant to a large degree in growth data on this sector. The *regional* competitive market structure (using spatially lagged variables with weight matrix W_1), though, shows a negative relation with employment growth in producer services. The summary statistics of equation (1) show that heteroskedasticity is a potential problem in the regression results. In addition, the LM-statistics on contiguous spatial dependence in the data reveal the significance of both spatial lag and spatial error dependence in the explained variable.

The equation presented in column (2) therefore estimates a spatial lag model using the urban spatial regime. Remarkably, medium sized cities do not show profound estimation results concerning the agglomeration variables and employment growth, although the literature assigns a large influential role to them (Van der Knaap 2002, Van Dinteren 1989).

Table 6.7 OLS, spatial lag and FGLS models for employment growth in producer services in the Netherlands (n=580, w_1)

explanatory variables	(1) OLS	(2) spatial lag estimation urban spatial regimes			(3) FGLS estimation nat. zoning spatial regimes			(4) FGLS estimation Randstad spatial regimes		
		large	medium	small	Randstad	iz	periphery	n-wing	s-wing	other
CONSTANT	-0.197	-1.326	-0.248	-0.283	-0.240	-0.228	-0.022	0.063	-0.103	-0.099
	(-3.544)	(-2.534)	(-1.243)	(-4.099)	(-1.625)	(-2.438)	(-0.271)	(0.243)	(-0.570)	(-1.685)
CONC.	0.037	0.189	-0.002	0.015	0.073	-0.018	-0.051	0.125	0.015	-0.003
	(2.079)	(3.270)*	(-0.018)*	(0.843)*	(2.228)*	(-0.659)*	(1.658)*	(2.577)*	(0.373)*	(-0.133)*
W_CONC.	-0.302	1.619	-0.385	-0.146	0.308	0.271	-0.836	3.764	0.127	-0.415
	(-1.714)	(1.162)	(-0.549)	(-0.795)	(0.678)*	(0.800)*	(-2.980)*	(3.247)*	(0.241)*	(-2.302)*
GINI	0.526	2.915	0.490	0.489	1.500	0.513	0.087	2.362	1.174	0.267
	(3.270)	(3.318)*	(0.605)*	(2.762)*	(4.665)*	(1.697)*	(0.381)*	(4.469)*	(3.057)*	(1.502)
W_GINI	-0.824	1.534	-0.683	-0.479	0.284	0.676	-0.085	3.116	-0.081	-0.340
	(-2.858)	(0.546)	(-0.681)	(-1.604)	(0.301)	(0.871)	(-0.229)	(1.597)	(-0.076)	(-1.160)
ESTABL.	0.226	0.209	0.128	0.232	0.228	0.247	0.201	0.340	0.181	0.214
SIZE	(8.622)	(2.081)	(1.254)	(7.695)	(4.661)	(5.127)	(5.131)	(4.455)	(2.657)	(7.194)
W_ESIZE	-1.095	-0.893	-0.483	-0.999	-1.480	-1.171	-0.703	-0.739	-2.181	-0.929
	(-6.773)	(-0.938)	(-0.894)	(-5.863)	(-3.335)	(-3.443)	(-2.921)	(-1.057)	(-1.176)	(-5.576)
WA_EMPL91	-0.005	0.032	-0.007	0.015	-0.025	0.005	-0.001	-0.004	-0.030	-0.001
	(-1.709)	(1.229)	(-0.597)	(0.043)	(-2.934)*	(0.663)*	(-0.218)*	(-0.307)	(-1.597)	(-0.427)
WAGE 1991	1.166	5.281	1.403	0.620	2.651	-0.730	1.480	3.408	2.379	0.792
	(1.198)	(1.448)	(0.490)	(0.580)	(1.567)	(-0.372)	(1.069)	(0.980)	(1.269)	(0.734)
ΔWAGE	-1.394	1.290	-1.318	-1.532	-1.621	-2.370	-0.022	-0.818	0.359	-1.462
	(-2.584)	(0.626)	(-0.543)	(-2.757)	(-1.416)	(-2.701)	(-0.029)	(-0.419)	(0.240)	(-2.642)
SPATIAL COEFF. ρ	-	0.717 (3.995)			-			-		

Table 6.7 (continued)

explanatory variables	(1) OLS	(2) spatial lag estimation urban spatial regimes			(3) FGLS estimation national zoning. spatial regimes			(4) FGLS estimation Randstad spatial regimes		
		large	medium	small	Randstad	iz	periphery	n-wing	s-wing	other
SIGMA	-	-	-	-	0.143 (8.916)	0.091 (9.591)	0.090 (10.886)	0.160 (5.958)	0.088 (6.042)	0.094 (14.765)
sum.statistics										
N	580		580			580			580	
R^2/ML	0.205/-200.5		-180.85			0.285			0.307	
LM (BP)	7.534 (0.023)		19.068 (0.007)			-			-	
LM (ρ)	11.43 (0.008)		-			0.487 (0.485)			0.994 (0.318)	
LM (λ)	7.302 (0.066)		-			0.102 (0.749)			0.105 (0.746)	
LR (ρ)	-		5.032 (0.024)			-				
LM λ (ρ)	-		0.751 (0.386)			-				
Chow-Wald	-		30.251 (0.045)			58.098 (0.000)			67.104 (0.000)	

SIGMA reports FGLS-hetreoskedastic variance coefficients. W_ and WA_ indicate spatial lag and spatial average transformation of variables (using W_1 weight matrix, see Anselin 1995a p.18-2).

This might be due to the limited time horizon of the temporal lag in the analyses (1991-97), for this implies that growth patterns of firms are monitored only between those years. The facilitating role of medium-sized cities in the Netherlands concerning growth of producer services tends to come to the fore over longer observation periods (compare Van der Knaap and Louter 1986). The equation concerning the large cities regime shows significant values for concentration of producer service firms, the lack of diversity and a relative small local establishment structure, and therefore suggests a significant relation to employment dynamics. The indicator of establishment size is most profoundly significant, however, in the small cities and rural municipalities regimes. The regionalized version of the diversity indicator (W_GINI) is not significantly related to employment growth in any of the three urban regimes. The negative effect of the regional competition variable on local growth comes to the fore only in the small cities regime. The spatial coefficient (measuring contiguous spatial dependency of the explained variable) significantly differs from zero, as is confirmed by the summary statistics. The spatial Chow-Wald test reveals that the urban regimes are significantly different in slopes of coefficient estimation, while at the same time it is indicated that heteroskedasticity remains a potential problem. In order to capture this degree of heteroskedasticity, equation (3) presents FGLS estimation results using the national zoning regimes. The competition variables on establishment size show the same pattern on the municipal and regional level: small establishment sizes favor local employment growth, while on a regional scale relative small establishment sizes restrict growth. The Randstad regime differs from the intermediate zone and national periphery regimes in the significance of the specialization variable (*CONCENTRATION*). The concentration of producer service firms in the Randstad is positively related to the employment growth in that sector. A negative regionalized relation of concentration with local producer service growth is present in the national periphery regime. Equation (4) sheds more light on the spatial structure of the positive effect of concentration on employment growth in the Randstad: this relation is profoundly present in the north-wing of the area. Local diversity of the production structure impeding growth is a relation found in both the north- and the south-wing of the Randstad. Local competition (measured by relative small firm size) favors growth in all regimes of equation (4), while regionalized competition hampers growth in locations other than the north- and south-wing of the Randstad. The summary statistics of equations (3) and (4) show that the results are homoskedastic and that the spatial regimes are significantly different from each other.

To summarize, employment growth in producer service activities is characterized by a different blend of explanatory agglomeration variables than industrial and distribution activities. Local (municipal) concentration of producer service employment fosters growth, a result not encountered in other sector equations nor in the zip code analyses of producer service growth in South-Holland. Regional concentration patterns of producer services (outside the 'own' municipality) are negatively related to growth. Local diversity of the production structure is negatively related to employment growth in producer services, while regional diversity is positively linked to growth. Local competition facilitates growth, while regional competition retards growth. Spatial heterogeneity specifications reveal that medium-sized cities show no profound model fit concerning these variables, while especially the north-wing of the Randstad does. All these findings indicate that Jacobs- and MAR-induced hypotheses of agglomeration economies and growth simultaneously play a role on *both* local and regional levels of analyses, while at the same time the non-contiguous spatial heterogeneity of urban size plays an important role in the producer service growth pattern. The OLS-induced city-industry analyses presented earlier only form part of the agglomeration story.

Employment Growth in Consumer Services

Table 6.8 presents regression estimates concerning employment growth in consumer service activities in the Netherlands. Since consumer service activities make up a large and growing part of the Dutch economy, it is no surprise that the relations of the individual agglomeration variables for concentration, diversity and local competition with employment growth in this sector resemble a great deal the OLS relations presented in chapter 5. Consumer services are to a large degree dependent on local (urban) population density, hence the fact that the spatially lagged variables of agglomeration are found insignificant and are not included in the parsimonious equations presented in table 6.8. Column (1) gives the OLS estimates for consumer service growth. Concentration of consumer services (window-averaged using W_2 for multicollinearity reasons), *lack of* diversity and competition (average small establishment size) all positively contribute to the model fit, as in the city-industry models presented in chapter 5 and the zip code analyses presented in section 6.2. The initial employment level contributes positively to the employment growth. Summary statistics below equation (1) reveal that error terms are homoskedastic and that spatial contiguity dependence is present. Equation (2) therefore additionally estimates a spatial lag model, leaving the structure of the equation (1) model identical. The spatial coefficient appears significant and the model fit improves slightly. The spatial coefficient captures some of the spatial content of the window-averaged concentration and employment variables as defined in column (1). That in turn becomes insignificant. Equation (3) estimates an OLS model using the urban size spatial regimes. The spatial Chow-Wald test indicates the significance of this regime. It becomes clear that the relations found in equation (1) hold especially well for the *smallest* cities and rural municipalities. It appears that analyzing agglomeration economies in a consumer service framework points at a highly localized, small-scale process. Regional linkages (captured in spatially lagged variables) appear insignificant, only some degree of general (explained variable induced) spatial contiguous dependency emerges from the analyses. The spatial regime models estimated confirm the relevance of the Jacobs-based externality economies on the spatial scale of the smallest category of municipalities (having less than 45,000 inhabitants).

Table 6.8 OLS **and spatial lag models for employment growth in consumer services in the Netherlands (n=580, w_2)**

explanatory variables	(1) OLS	(2) spatial lag estimation	(3) OLS estimation urban size spatial regimes		
			Large	medium	small
CONSTANT	-0.131	-0.149	0.262	-0.069	-0.166
	(-4.225)	(-4.844)	(0.946)	(-0.601)	(-4.536)
WA_CONC.	-0.046	-0.032	0.021	-0.009	-0.047
	(-2.403)	(-1.638)	(1.984)*	(-1.619)*	(-2.245)*
GINI	-0.432	-0.432	-0.151	0.343	-0.538
	(-4.812)	(-4.866)	(-0.302)*	(0.715)*	(-5.245)*
ESTABL. SIZE	0.062	0.065	0.077	0.103	0.064
	(2.962)	(3.100)	(0.904)	(0.863)	(2.787)
WA_EMPL91	0.0035	0.0023	-0.0021	-0.0002	0.0077
	(2.170)	(1.393)	(-1.579)*	(-0.206)*	(3.728)*
WAGE 1991	0.553	0.552	1.543	0.878	0.650
	(2.382)	(2.402)	(1.328)	(0.719)	(2.561)
ΔWAGE	-0.186	-0.156	3.807	0.724	-0.454
	(-0.333)	(-0.283)	(1.569)	(0.307)	(-0.760)
SPATIAL COEFFICIENT ρ	-	0.708 (3.791)	-		
Sum. Statistics:					
N	580	580	580		
R^2/ML	0.079/-125.83	-123.51	0.119		
LM (BP)	4.171 (0.124)	15.489 (0.004)	4.744 (0.093)		
LM (ρ)	5.907 (0.015)	-	3.804 (0.051)		
LM (λ)	4.968 (0.025)	-	3.403 (0.065)		
LR (ρ)	-	4.647 (0.311)	-		
LM λ (ρ)	-	3.033 (0.082)	-		
Chow-Wald	-	-	1.826 (0.032)		

See notes below table 6.1 for explanation.

6.4 Synthesis and Conclusions

The central question asked in this section is whether individual sectoral models of employment growth are characterized by conceptualizations and indicators for agglomeration economies as developed in the spatial-economic literature. Controlling for other important (statistical) attributes of localized growth patterns, the focus is on the spatial role of concentration, diversity and competition as posited by MAR, Jacobs' and Porter's theories of localized endogenous growth. To distinguish models and model extensions from those presented in previous sections, this chapter asks whether urban economic growth models improve over (so-called) null-models of location-industry OLS estimation, relative space-neutral, city-industry composition when additionally and simultaneously: (1) explicitly proximity-based spatial research designs are applied on the regional (South-Holland) and national scale, either by spatial lag and window-average specifications of explained and explaining variables; (2) separate sectoral models for industrial, distribution, producer- and consumer service activities are explored; (3) spatial heterogeneity modeled by spatial regimes on the national scale is introduced. We conclude that all three questions should be answered in the affirmative. The introduction of spatially lagged agglomeration variables capturing regional externality circumstances are significant contributions to improved model fit in the national spatial analyses of industrial, distribution and producer services employment growth (the 'basic' economic activities). Regional localization and urbanization economies frequently interfere with local growth patterns, indicating the importance of multilevel-based analyses as introduced in this section (as well as in the previous chapter). Often, regionalized (spatially lagged) agglomeration indicators show *inverse* relations to employment growth compared to 'own' city relations. Regional concentration of manufacturing or distribution activities has a positive effect on local manufacturing and distribution employment growth, while local concentration tends to hamper growth. On the other hand, local concentration of producer services enhances growth while regional concentration impedes it. Local diversity is positively related to manufacturing employment growth and negatively to distribution and consumer service growth. For the latter two, though, regional diversity patterns stimulate growth. A relative small average establishment size (an indicator of local competition) is positively related to distribution and producer service growth, while both sectoral models show a negative relation with the regionalized version of this competition indicator. Employment growth in consumer service activities shows the largest similarity to the OLS models on municipality-industries presented in chapter 5 in terms of the 'performance' of the agglomeration variables. Regionalized agglomeration variables appear insignificant for consumer service growth. For the South-Holland research area, the question asked whether separate sectoral models for industrial, distribution, producer and consumer service activities add value to location-industry mixed models should be answered in the affirmative as well. As these models, besides common Jacobs-favoring results, show considerable variation over sign, significance and magnitude of individual coefficients and spatial regime design, it is clear that the aggregation of the data into the four broad sectors is relevant from an empirical and theoretical point of view. Consumer activities show less clear overall *individual* agglomeration externalities and spatial design significance than the three basic sector models.

Regional and national spatial growth models also are conditioned by spatial heterogeneity (non-contiguous spatial dependence) patterns to a large degree The role of spatial heterogeneity in the South-Holland analyses when introduced by spatial regimes is substantial. An advantage of looking at the region of South-Holland is that it is small enough that location-specific factors, such as those related to cost, demand, and resource endowments, do not differ greatly between locations. In consequence, the choice of an area to study ameliorates an important objection to previous empirical analyses of the role of agglomeration economies in urban growth. Furthermore, the availability of establishment level data for this province enable us to better define two crucial variables, the dependent variable (employment growth in establishments that already existed in the base year, rather than growth in all establishments including new establishments) and the measure of competition. South-Holland's small size potentially reduces the problem of unmeasured heterogeneity that has become an important issue in evaluating related studies of US metropolitan areas. Still, spatial regimes turned out to be highly relevant modeling attributes for the sectoral models though. Employment growth in manufacturing is fostered by the agglomeration variables predominantly in locations characterized as working areas. These areas are not all urban in character and indicate that a scattered spatial structure is underlying the spatial growth process of this sector in the research area. For distribution activities the non-urban regime (as opposed to urban) contributes significantly to embed the spatial externalities model and represent the data most adequately. Producer services growth on the contrary, captured in an urban regime, is closely related to intra-local development trajectories in the models presented. For young firms this aspect is more important than for old, incumbent firms. In the national municipality-analyses, growth of manufacturing activities is conditioned by small urban (concentration and regionalized concentration), medium-sized urban (diversity), large urban (regionalized concentration) and the south-wing of the Randstad (negatively) spatial regime respectively. Growth of distribution activities is conditioned by non-Randstad (concentration), Randstad and accessible (regionalized concentration, diversity, competition and regionalized competition) spatial regimes. Growth in producer services is conditioned by (north-wing) Randstad (concentration, diversity), large urban (concentration, diversity, regionalized competition), and small urban (regionalized competition, diversity) spatial regimes. Growth in consumer services is particularly conditioned by the small urban spatial regimes.

The initial OLS models (conceptual design-copies of Glaeser *et al.* (1992) on location-industries presented in the South-Holland research area and the Netherlands almost unanimously favor Jacobs-related agglomeration externality hypotheses. The introduction of spatially lagged explained and explaining variables, individual sector estimation and the inclusion of spatial heterogeneity regimes (not encountered this explicitly and systematically in previous empirical research) change the picture to a considerable extent. It is clear that a universally accepted theory on urban economic growth, capturing all the empirical aspects envisaged in this dissertation, cannot be concluded. Instead, an eclectic theoretical approach is more appropriate. Spatial, sectoral and life cycle heterogeneity of firm growth make an integral theory on 'the representative firm', commonly introduced in the economic literature, unsuitable for a thorough understanding of spatial-economic dynamics. This chapter indicates that the individual city[10] (municipality) level of analysis of agglomeration externalities might even be too small in itself to capture regionalized growth linkages for certain sectors. Urban hierarchical linkages and national zoning regimes appear highly significant in relation to producer service growth, for instance. Other model results point at physical accessibility and small-scale urbanization (outside the largest cities) as significant conditions for distribution activity growth. Consumer service growth is to a large

---

[10] It should be remarked that cities in American studies usually comprise much larger areas than the (municipal) definitions applied in this dissertation.

degree spatially determined in small-scale urban and rural areas. For growth in manufacturing activities, work-area zoning and medium-sized urban regimes appear significant distinctions. This means that growth diffusion patterns are found to be not always concentric and contiguous in character, as was already suggested in the literature discussed in chapter 2. The research results suggest the potential appropriateness of conceptual frameworks not explicitly envisioned in the contiguity-based agglomeration and dynamic externality literature, like spatial network and urban linkage structures. Another important conceptual lesson concerns the fact that, simultaneously, agglomeration indicators on different spatial scales are related to localized growth patterns. This lesson points at the need for consistent multilevel modeling, something not envisioned explicitly in the current literature.

Chapter 7

Innovation Intensity

7.1 Introduction

In academic and economic policy circles an increased interest in knowledge and innovation creation and distribution has emerged from discussions about competitive advantage in industrial countries of the West. Research and development, innovation and knowledge availability are said by some commentators to be good for economic growth. As we discussed before, the embedding of knowledge externalities in endogenous growth theory leads to several important contributions that stress the spatial character of (urban) knowledge transmission. As indicated in chapter 2, the knowledge creation and transfer discussion in empirical research does not focus solely on innovation. Knowledge is also supposed to be locked in human and social capital, in learning and trust relations, in post-Fordist production structures, in tacit knowledge based transactions and in institutional embedding (Oinas 2000, Howells 2002). We notice that many theoretical concepts, like industrial districts, regional innovation systems and learning regions link geographically concentrated networks of firms to the innovativeness and growth potential of those firms[1]. And although economic theory and some scarce empirical studies stress the importance of proximity, 'the relevance of proximity is one of the most controversially discussed topics in the context of innovative linkages and networks' (Sternberg 1999, p.533).

The hypothesis that agglomeration and proximity are important for the promotion of innovation, knowledge transfer and growth is central in our study. This chapter does not focus on (employment) growth patterns resulting from hypothesized knowledge and agglomeration externalities, but on research and development (R&D) clustering as indicator of economic agglomeration[2]. The data used stem from labor costs estimates related to R&D in Dutch firms as collected by Senter (see appendix B for a description of the data and a comparison to other data sources in the Netherlands). The main advantages of this dataset are its integral character and spatial detail. The level of analysis will again be that of 580 municipalities. Similar spatial-econometric frameworks as in previous chapters on employment growth will be applied in order to determine the significance of

---

[1] See for a critical survey on territorial innovation models (TIM) Moulaert and Sekia (2003). They conclude that 'the use of the concept of economies of agglomeration for defining TIM leaves a tremendous ambiguity regarding their spatial character' (p.296).

[2] The heterogeneous character of the concept of 'spillovers' leads to recommendations of careful conceptualisation and thoughtful application, as in Breschi and Lissoni (2001). We therefore prefer to use the more neutral term 'externalities'.

agglomeration and spatial composition hypotheses postulated by Marshall, Arrow and Romer (MAR), Porter and Jacobs. Recent, Anglo-Saxon-based research generally finds very limited extent of spatial spillovers and a large degree of local clustering. Similarly, a body of literature on the Dutch spatial configuration of innovation and high-technology firms predominantly stresses the supposed 'urban field' character of the Dutch case: location and agglomeration aspects do not seem to have a systematic impact on the distribution of innovative activities over space. It is argued that production structure and milieu factors are spread homogenously over the country[3]. As argued in this chapter, many of these stylized conclusions depend heavily on the definition of R&D, innovation, research population, hypothesized functional relations over space and spillovers. The central question in this chapter is whether the testable hypotheses from the theoretical agglomeration frameworks of MAR, Porter and Jacobs, together with systematic spatial econometric modeling techniques, contribute to understanding the relation between proximity, agglomeration and innovation intensity in the Dutch case.

An important aspect of this research should be noted at the outset. The data used indicate inputs to innovation: R&D investments not necessarily lead to innovation or productivity growth. Since input and output indicators of innovation are usually highly correlated over time and space, this should not be regarded as a too serious problem concerning the spatial analyses in this research[4]. This aspect should however be kept in mind when interpreting results. Recall that the same conceptual drawback is attached to employment growth analyses in the previous chapters: employment growth as one of the production factor inputs does not necessarily lead to firm-economic growth in terms of output and profits (Hamermash 1996).

Research and development (R&D) is often considered as one of the main determinants of economic growth. R&D aimed at new or better products and production technologies boosts productivity in the sector undertaking R&D but potentially also in other sectors. These spillovers must be taken into account when assessing the impact of R&D on sectoral or firm productivity, and is the basic notion underlying the attention in the recent literature on R&D spillovers, productivity and economic growth. This economic discussion in first instance was *not* spatial in character, but it is useful to summarize this influential strand of literature for putting the research difficulties into perspective when introducing the spatial dimension. A central element of economic theories of innovation therefore is the concept of knowledge spillovers. Griliches (1985, 1992) distinguishes two kinds of spillovers: rent spillovers and (pure) knowledge spillovers. Rent spillovers arise

---

[3] See for instance Kleinknecht and Poot (1992) and Wever and Stam (1999).

[4] For discussions concerning knowledge and innovation production functions, relating input (R&D expenditures) to output indicators (patents, productivity growth) of innovation, see Griliches (1990, 1992), Acs *et al.* 1994, Dosi (1988) and Ke and Luger (1996). As becomes clear from Griliches (1985), input and output indicators of innovation, as well as productivity measures *over time and space*, are highly correlated. As Griliches (1985, p.94) puts it: '(...) most of the variables of interest tend to move together over time and space, making it hard to entangle their separate effects. Moreover, it is not easy to establish causality. Research and development investments are themselves affected by the level of output and by past profits and productivity, forcing one to formulate simultaneous equations models and to turn to much more complex estimation techniques'.

when quality improvements by a supplier are not fully translated into higher prices for the buyer(s). Productivity gains are recorded in a different firm or industry than the one that generated the productivity gains in first instance. Rent spillovers occur in input-output relations (Hornstein and Praschnik 1997). Pure knowledge spillovers refer to the impact of discovered ideas or compounds on the productivity of the research endeavors of others. Pure knowledge spillovers are benefits of innovative activities of one firm that accrue to another following market transactions. R&D enhances the productivity in another sector. Knowledge spillovers can arise in many different ways (learning, copying, job mobility, joint ventures) and are not necessarily a by-product of intermediate deliveries (Cooper 2001). The degree to which R&D in a sector is relevant for other sectors is usually postulated on the basis of a so-called technology flow matrix[5]. These approaches all seem to be arbitrary in assigning the label 'spillovers' to interaction patterns based on indirect (input-output, stock and patent data) measurement and evidence. For that reason, in this chapter we refer to the relation of agglomeration variables with R&D intensities as agglomeration and R&D externalities. Remarkably, very little research in the (mainstream) strand of literature is concerned with spatial circumstances of R&D externalities (spillovers). The following sections concentrate on *regional and local* circumstances found relevant for R&D externalities in the economic-geographical literature.

This chapter is further built up as follows. In section 7.2, descriptive analyses of R&D intensity over industries and locations in connected and national zoning spatial regimes (introduced in chapter 3) are presented. Shift and share analyses indicate whether localized innovation intensity depends on municipal industry composition (e.g. chemical industries tend to be more innovative than furniture industries) and which types of locations come to the fore as being R&D-intensive, once data are 'corrected' for this. Descriptive analyses using exploratory spatial data analyses (ESDA) on the municipal level were already presented in chapter 4. Section 7.3 presents spatial econometric models on the municipal level of the Netherlands regarding innovation (R&D) intensity in 1999 for industrial and non-industrial activities. As R&D intensity predominantly concerns industrial economic activities, a four-fold division of industrial sectors is used for modeling. Labor and capital intensive industries are distinguished from knowledge- and process-intensive industries. The models make use of the agglomeration variables as defined in chapter 5. Section 7.4 provides a summary and conclusions.

---

[5] See Wolff (1997) for a flow matrix constructed from input-output data, Verspagen (1997) for a sectoral flow matrix constructed on patent data and Verspagen and Los (2000) for a matrix based on R&D stocks.

7.2   Descriptive Analysis

Connected and National Zoning Regimes

In this chapter innovation density of firms in municipalities is the central element of analysis. As explained in chapter 4 and appendix B, innovation intensity is defined as R&D wage expenditures per employee. It represents a *relative* indicator of innovation efforts made by firms rather than an absolute measure. It corrects for average firm size (as measured by employment) and it enables the analysis of spatial innovation patterns *in contrast to* spatial employment patterns. Table 7.1 presents total (absolute) R&D wage expenditures and innovation intensity (innovation per employee) for the urban agglomeration (connectedness regime) and national zoning spatial regimes. In total 4.179 billion guilders is involved in fiscal tax deductions concerning R&D wages in the Netherlands. Approximately half of this sum of money is transferred to firms in urban core locations, and another quarter to suburban metropolitan municipalities. The connectedness spatial regime therefore turns out quite important for the spatial distribution of R&D expenditures, indicating that innovation is predominantly an urban subject. Innovation expenditures are distributed equally over the Randstad, intermediate zone and national periphery zoning regimes (all have approximately a share of one third), as is the case with employment and population numbers (see chapter 3). In relative terms though, the index of R&D intensity (per employee) shows that especially core locations in the intermediate zone and the national periphery have higher shares than expected from employment data. Autonomous municipalities in the intermediate zone also show an intensity score higher than 1, indicating that innovation per employee exceeds the national average. In general terms core municipalities (119.34) and municipalities in the intermediate zone (113.35) clearly score higher than average on the innovation intensity index. Dependent municipalities score lowest in both share and index intensity terms[6].

Table 7.2 focuses on the spatial distribution over zoning and connectedness regimes of *industrial* innovation expenditures only. Industrial R&D expenditures make up 75% of all R&D expenditures[7]. From the location quotients (expressed in relation to total expenditures) presented in each second row of table 7.2 we see the *relative spatial specialization* patterns of industrial innovation reflected. Core locations in the intermediate zone and national periphery, but also in suburban and autonomous municipalities, come to the fore. Remarkably, the Randstad municipalities score very low on this specialization index on all (combinations of) spatial regimes. This corresponds with low concentration and specialization values of industrial employment in the Randstad region.

---

[6] As the relative small number of observations in this category and the similarities with autonomous municipalities these two categories (they both are part of the non-connected spatial regime) are merged in some of the following analysis (still referred to as autonomous municipalities).
[7] Industrial and non-industrial activities were distinguished using the industrial classification scheme presented in appendix A.

Table 7.1 Innovation intensity in connected and national zoning regimes (absolute[a], share, intensity[a] and index intensity)

Connected ↓	*Zoning* →	Randstad Core Region	Intermediate Zone	National Periphery	Total
Core	Absolute	830,737,664	706,824,640	526,383,168	2,063,945,728
location	Share	19.88%	16,91%	12,60%	49,39%
	Intensity	597	928	1128	787
	Index int.	90.40	140.62	170.98	119.34
Suburban	Absolute	541,645,888	359,511,264	191,874,528	1,093,031,808
	Share	12,96%	8,60%	4,59%	26,15%
	Intensity	630	587	635	615
	Index int.	95.38	88.88	96.16	93.27
Dependent	Absolute	27,877,084	46,955,852	70,048,416	144,881,360
	Share	0.67%	1,12%	1,68%	3,47%
	Intensity	387	269	454	361
	Index int.	56.69	40.72	68.81	54.76
Autonom.	Absolute	90,402,992	377,437,920	409,527,200	877,368,000
	Share	2,16%	9,03%	9.80%	20,99%
	Intensity	471	851	455	571
	index int.	71.34	128.96	68.96	86.59
Total	Absolute	1,490,663,936	1,490,729,344	1,197,833,216	4,179,227,648
	Share	35,67%	35,67%	28,66%	100%
	Intensity	592	748	657	660
	Index int.	89.74	113.35	99.57	100.00

[a] in guilders 1999

Autonomous municipalities in the Randstad region and core locations in the intermediate zone being the main exceptions, the figure shows that the other classifications of municipalities are in quadrants 1 (top-left) and 4 (bottom-right), indicating a negative correlation between spatial concentration and intensity. Being spatially specialized in industrial innovation activities does not automatically induce high intensity indicators. On the contrary, this spatial relationship appears the inverse of that. When expressed as *index per employee* (in relation to total expenditures) though, the Randstad locations show relative high values. The industrial innovation intensity per employee is therefore much larger in Randstad locations, although this region does not have the largest shares in industrial production and innovation in general. Industrial activities in the Randstad are underrepresented, but those that are present are more innovative in character than comparable firms elsewhere. The index of innovation intensity lowers consequently when moving away from the Randstad region to the intermediate zone and the national periphery, and from core locations to suburban and autonomous locations.

Table 7.2 Industrial innovation intensity in connected and national zoning regimes (absolute[a], location quotient[b], intensity[a] and index intensity[b])

Connected ↓	*Zoning* →	Randstad Core Region	Intermediate Zone	National Periphery	Total
Core	Absolute	478,494,912	611,187,264	471,812,384	1,561,494,91
Location	Loc. quotient	76.70	115.14	119.36	2
	Intensity	4700	5952	5737	100.75
	Index int.	141.70	115.36	91.44	5446
					124.37
Suburban	Absolute	359,557,792	279,800,704	168,974,336	808,332,544
	Loc. quotient	88.40	103.64	117.27	98.48
	Intensity	4461	3245	2709	3526
	Index int.	127.46	99.51	76.77	103.05
Dependent	Absolute	18,568,104	36,744,176	32,926,742	88,239,008
	loc. quotient	88.70	104.21	62.60	81.10
	Intensity	2061	1282	1625	1523
	Index int.	95.70	85.81	64.38	75.82
Autonom.	Absolute	50,923,264	304,815,200	324,554,880	680,293,440
	Loc. quotient	75.01	107.54	105.54	103.25
	Intensity	2506	3372	1901	2417
	Index int.	95.71	71.27	75.12	76.08
Total	Absolute	907,544,192	1,232,547,328	998,268,352	3,138358784
	Loc. quotient	81.07	110.10	110.98	100.00
	Intensity	4286	4003	2974	3669
	Index int.	130.16	96.23	81.41	100.00

[a] in guilders 1999

[b] expressed as index in relation to indicator-values for total innovation (table 7.1), which are set to 100.

Table 7.2 suggests a negative relationship between the relative specialization (share) of industrial innovation and the innovation intensity (per employee), a relationship confirmed by figure 7.1. Table 7.3 presents *non-industrial* versions of the indicators of the spatial distribution of R&D wage expenditures, similar to table 7.2 on industrial ones. Non-industrial R&D expenditures only account for one quarter of all wage expenditures in the Senter database. From table 7.3 it becomes clear that for non-industrial innovation intensity the relation of presence (specialization, measured by the location quotient) with intensity (index) is almost linear. Concentration of innovation in municipalities coincides with high average intensity per employee. Concentration and intensity are highest in all types of municipalities in the Randstad core region. Concentration and intensity ratios outside the Randstad are considerably smaller than the average.

Figure 7.1 Location quotients and index intensity of industrial innovation in connected and national zoning regimes [a,b]

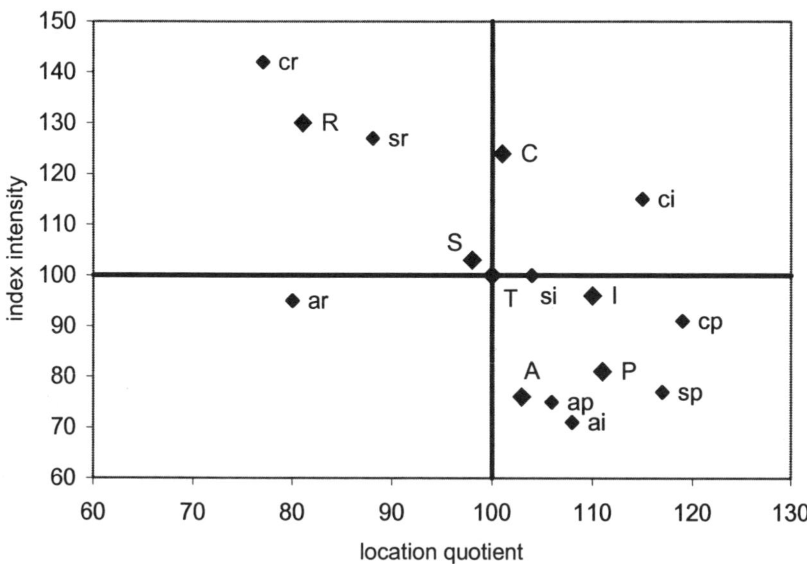

[a] Abbreviations of regimes:
cr = core location/Randstad ar = autonomous location/Randstad
ci = core location/intermediate zone ai = autonom. loc./intermediate zone
cp = core location/national periphery ap = autonom. loc./national periphery
C = core location A = autonomous location
sr = suburban location/Randstad R = Randstad
si = suburban location/intermediate zone I = intermediate zone
sp = suburban location/national periphery P = national periphery
S = suburban location T = total
[b] Autonomous and dependent locations are aggregated (still referred to as autonomous).

Chapter 4 indeed revealed that positive (HH) values of spatial autocorrelation (using a w_1 distance weight matrix) of non-industrial innovation intensity are concentrated in the Randstad region to a much larger extent than industrial or general innovation intensities.

Table 7.3   **Non-industrial innovation intensity in connected and national zoning regimes (absolute[a], location quotient[b], intensity[a] and index intensity[b])**

connected ↓	*zoning* →	Randstad Core Region	Intermediate Zone	National Periphery	Total
Core	Absolute	352,242,848	95,637,288	54,570,772	502,450,848
Location	Loc. quotient	170.25	54.33	41.63	97.75
	Intensity	273	145	142	215
	Index int.	158.87	54.31	43.71	94.93
Suburban	Absolute	182,088,176	79,710,488	22,900,212	284,698,752
	Loc. quotient	134.98	89.02	47.92	104.58
	Intensity	233	151	95	184
	Index int.	128.82	89.61	52.22	103.86
Dependent	Absolute	9,308,980	10,211,680	37,121,680	56,642,344
	Loc. quotient	134.08	87.32	212.78	156.97
	Intensity	148	70	277	165
	Index int.	132.56	90.34	211.87	158.70
Aautonom.	Absolute	39,479,712	72,622,720	84,972,312	197,074,768
	Loc. quotient	175.34	77.26	83.31	90.19
	Intensity	230	206	117	157
	Index int.	169.62	83.93	88.93	95.52
Total	Absolute	583,119,680	158,182,112	199,564,928	1,040867264
	Loc. quotient	157.06	69.54	66.89	100.00
	Intensity	253	153	134	190
	Index intensity	148.33	71.14	70.92	100.00

[a] in guilders 1999
[b] expressed as index in relation to indicator-values for total innovation (table 7.1), which are set to 100.

Summarizing we conclude that the distinction industrial[8] versus non-industrial economic activities and the national zoning and connected spatial regimes are potentially relevant segmentations for exploring spatial dependency in R&D intensity data over municipalities in the Netherlands. Industrial innovation concentration is, in general, concentrated outside the Randstad core region, while high values of industrial innovation intensity (per employee) are concentrated both inside and outside the Randstad region. Both non-industrial innovation concentration *and* intensity are found in the Randstad region. Industrial innovation concentration ratios do not vary much over the connectedness regimes, while

---

[8] As industrial activities make up such a large part of the innovation expenditure data, a segmentation into four types of industrial sectors will be applied in subsequent modeling. Distinguished are labour-, capital-knowledge- and process industries. See appendix A.

industrial innovation *intensity* is predominantly found to be high in core municipalities and to a lesser extent in suburban locations, especially in the Randstad region.

Sectoral and Spatial Components of Innovation Intensity

The previous section concluded with the notion that industrial composition to a large extent determines the spatial geography of R&D wage expenditure in the Netherlands. An interesting extension of the descriptive spatial analyses is therefore the distinction between structural industry composition and pure spatial composition effects (labeled sector and spatial effect in this section). In order to picture this, an industry-structural and spatial intensity indicator is constructed reminiscent to structural and differential effects in shift and share analyses. The sectoral component depicts the influence of industry composition on spatial R&D intensity. It is calculated by multiplying the relative share of industries in a regional employment structure by national R&D intensities per industry:

$$\mathit{sector\ effect} = \sum_{industry} \left[\frac{empl._{industry,location}}{empl._{location}} \times \left(r\ \&\ d\ \text{intensity}_{industry,national} \right) \right]$$

The spatial effects depict the degree to which innovation intensity in industries in a region (location) differs from that of the same industries in other locations. It is calculated as the R&D intensity per industry in a location compared to the national intensity for that industry multiplied by national sectoral employment:

$$\text{spatial effect} = \sum_{industry} \left[\frac{r\ \&\ d\ \text{int}_{industry,location}}{r\ \&\ d\ \text{int.}_{industry,national}} \times \left(empl._{industry,national} \right) \right]$$

The effects are measured over 49 sectors (see appendix A). In figure 7.2 the two effects are shown for 580 municipalities in the Netherlands. On the horizontal axis the sector effect is presented, on the vertical axis the spatial effect. The effects are expressed in guilders in difference from the national R&D wage per employee (which is 641 guilders per employee). The figure shows a scattered picture, but in general high sector effects coincide with low spatial effects (quadrant 4, bottom-right), while low sector effects seem to be more correlated to relative high spatial effects (quadrant 1, top-left). Since the observations in the other two quadrants might as well be important in quantitative terms, a spatial aggregation of the 580 municipalities into provinces (12) and connectedness and national zoning types might be useful for interpretation.

Figure 7.2   Sectoral and spatial effects in the distribution of innovation intensity (n=580)

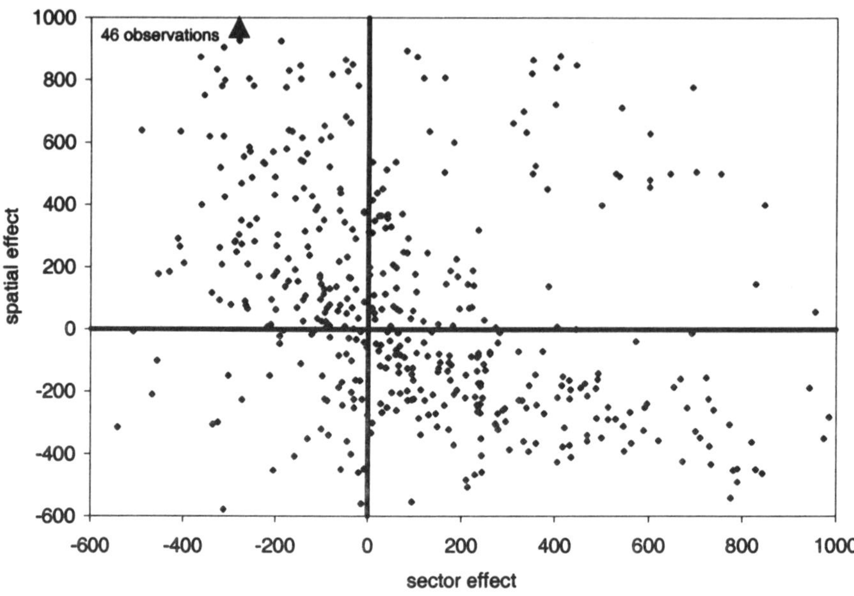

Figure 7.3 shows that especially municipalities in the provinces Utrecht, North-Holland and South-Holland (together making up the Randstad core region) are characterized as having a negative sector effect combined with a positive spatial effect. This means that the actual R&D intensity of firms in these provinces is higher than should be expected from industry structure. Involvement in R&D in firms in the Randstad region is higher when compared to similar firms (in the same industry) outside the Randstad. Favorable scores on both the sector and spatial components of innovation intensity characterize firms in the provinces of North-Brabant and Overijssel. Corrected for the excellent innovation-sensitive, industry-specific specialization and embedding, firms in these provinces (making up a large part of the intermediate zone) perform better in terms of actual innovation intensity than should be expected from this favorable structure. The provinces of Limburg, Drenthe and Zeeland are all characterized by a favorable sectoral structure concerning innovation intensity, but their spatial effect turn out to be negative. Corrected for their advantageous industry structure, they perform relatively poorly. The industrial base in these provinces is characterized as dependent on a few very large-scale, R&D intensive firms (e.g. DSM Chemicals in Limburg and Dow-Chemical in Zeeland). This is relatively unfavorable for their regional score on innovation intensity. Figure 7.4 shows region and sector effects for the (combinations of) connected and national zoning spatial regimes, as discussed before.

Figure 7.3   Provincial, sectoral and spatial effects in the distribution of innovation intensity (n=12) [a]

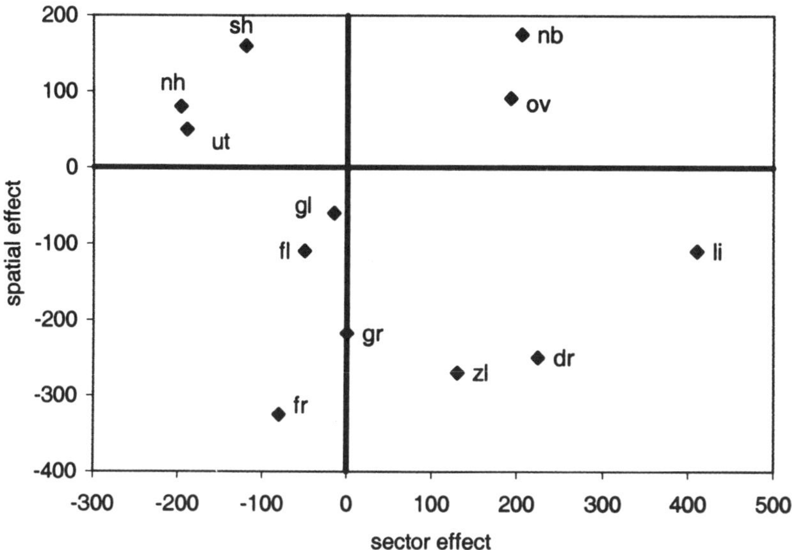

[a] Abbreviations:

gr = Groningen	ov = Overijssel	nh = North holland	nb = North-brabant
fr = Friesland	gl = Gelderland	sh = South-holland	li = Limburg
dr = Drenthe	ut = Utrecht	zl = Zeeland	fl = Flevoland

Core and Randstad municipalities show large positive spatial effects combined with negative sector effects. Core locations within the Randstad are particularly characterized by this pattern. Despite the negative sectoral composition of central urban locations, innovation intensity is relatively high. Suburban and autonomous types of municipalities in the Randstad region are characterized by positive spatial effects combined with negative sector effects, but to a lesser degree. Municipalities in the intermediate zone of the Netherlands show positive sector and spatial effects to a limited extent. Municipal typologies concerning the national periphery and autonomous locations in general show a combination of positive sector and negative spatial effects. No typologies are in the quadrant of both negative spatial and sector effects.

To summarize, urban core and suburban locations in general show positive spatial effects when decomposing innovation intensity data into spatial and sector effects. This metropolitan relationship is particularly strong in the Randstad region. Albeit the sectoral structure of metropolitan (connected) municipalities is initially unfavorable for enhanced chances of spatial innovation intensity, the *actual* innovation intensity indicates that spatial effects are on average positive.

Figure 7.4 Sectoral and spatial effects in the distribution of innovation intensity in connected and national zoning regimes (n=16)[a]

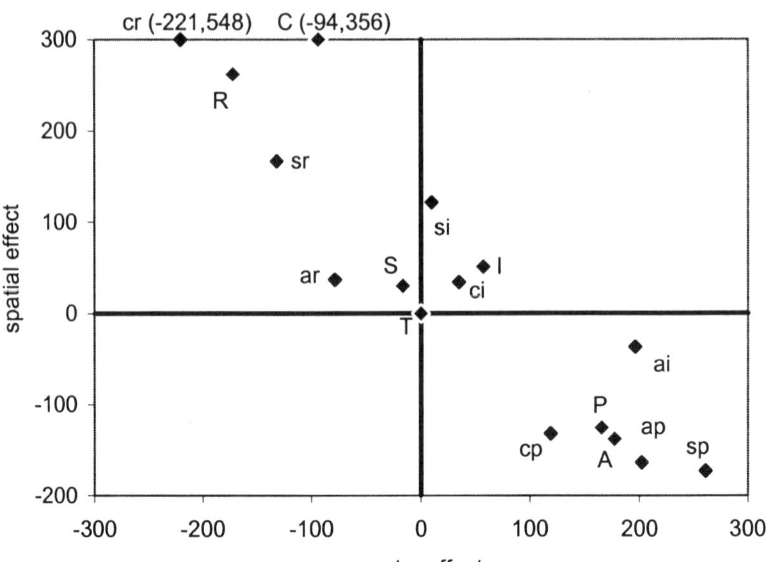

[a] See figure 7.1 for explanation of abbreviations of regimes

Peripheral locations do not confirm to this general notion: urban core and suburban typologies of locations scores show negative spatial effects on innovation intensity indicators despite their usually favorable sectoral composition. This strengthens the conclusion drawn on urban and national zoning spatial regimes in the previous section.

7.3   Spatial Econometric Models

Spatial Models for Industrial Innovation

This section concentrates on spatial-econometric models of (log) *industrial* innovation intensity in 1999. The next section discusses spatial models concerning (log) *non-industrial* innovation intensity. These models are designed to 'explain' spatial patterns of *relative* innovation expenditures per employee (an innovation input indicator) from agglomeration variables and modeled (contiguous and heterogeneous) spatial structures. As in the analyses on employment growth presented previously, several general technical aspects apply to all models presented in this chapter. Concerning the variables presented in earlier chapters, the following should be noted (see also chapter 5). The agglomeration and externality variables of *CONCENTRATION*, *DIVERSITY* (the *GINI* coefficient based on 49 localized industries) and *ESTABLISHMENT SIZE* (a measure for local competition) were left untouched. Spatial lags of these variables on the municipal level (using the w_1 spatial weight matrix) created regional variables for the agglomeration externalities indicators outside the own location. The *INITIAL EMPLOYMENT* (a control for 'sector effect' innovation intensity, see previous section), *WAGE91* and *ΔWAGE* variables were also left unaltered. Employment change during the period 1991-97 (*ΔEMPIND9197*) is introduced as a control for general industrial growth previous to the measurement of industrial innovation intensity. Work-area, industrial site, proximity to Amsterdam, Rotterdam and Utrecht and physical accessibility are transformed into spatial regime indicators and in that form initially tested for significance in all models. *ΔPOPULATION* is left out of the analyses because of density endogeneity problems (see Bruinsma *et al.* 2002). Further references for explanation of diagnostic statistics are below the tables presenting the model results. All variables are log transformed and standardized unless otherwise stated. In order to avoid multicollinearity problems, some agglomeration variables are window averaged (using unstandardized spatial weight matrix w_2). No correlation higher than 0.5 between explanatory variables exists. Only the most parsimonious model results are presented. Non-inclusion of variables indicates that they were not significant in the final versions of models.

Table 7.4 in column (1) presents the parsimonious OLS model for industrial innovation intensity. One remarkable difference with the municipal employment growth models presented in chapter 6 comes to the fore: the spatially lagged agglomeration variables are *not* found significant in any of the specifications. This indicates that municipal innovation structures do not depend on *regionalized* agglomeration externalities like industrial specialization, industry diversity or competition (establishment size). Significant spatial lag and error model specifications concerning the *dependent variable* (innovation intensity) exists according to the LM(λ) and LM(ρ) test statistics, however. The indicator on industrial concentration appears insignificant. The degree of sectoral diversity appears significant. Remarkably, the average firm size (the indicator of local competition) indicates that *large* average firm size fosters innovation intensity in municipalities, and confirmed in other studies (Schmitz and Heijs 2001 and E. Brouwer *et al.* 1999). R&D externalities do differ fundamentally from employment growth externalities in this respect. Large firms internalizing rents stemming from market conditions (market power) is a central element in Porter's and MAR's hypotheses on agglomeration externalities. Heteroskedasticity does not appear to be a problem in the equation presented in column (1).

The previous sections of this chapter stressed the potential relevance of national zoning (Randstad, intermediate zone and national periphery) and connectedness (functional labour market, metropolitan areas) spatial regimes. These indeed proved to be significant contributions to modeling spatial heterogeneity in the industrial innovation intensity models (see columns (2) and (3) in table 7.4).

Table 7.4   OLS and spatial lag models for industrial innovation intensity in the Netherlands (n=580)

explanatory variables	(1) OLS	(2) OLS estimation national zoning spatial regimes			(3) Spatial lag-estimation connected spatial regimes	
		Randstad	iz	periphery	connected	unconnected
CONSTANT	8.337	8.553	8.354	7.879	3.544	2.648
	(9.915)	(6.159)	(6.863)	(7.668)	(2.473)	(1.827)
CONCENTR.	-0.220	-0.678	0.236	0.439	-0.470	-0.630
	(-1.595)	(-2.304)*	(0.944)*	(1.779)*	(-2.690)*	(2.870)*
LACK OF DIVERSITY	-2.710	-2.998	-2.796	-3.021	-2.595	-2.272
	(-3.405)	(-2.045)	(-1.807)	(-2.444)	(-2.622)	(-1.903)
ESTABL. SIZE	-0.969	-0.858	-0.748	-0.504	-1.059	-0.405
	(-6.362)	(-2.879)	(-2.689)	(-1.903)	(-5.583)*	(-1.607)*
WA_EMP91	0.312	0.300	-0.067	0.006	0.329	-0.019
	(0.761)	(0.711)	(-0.081)	(0.031)	(0.812)	(-0.042)
ΔEMPL. IND. 1991-97	0.126	-0.330	0.804	0.511	0.017	0.591
	(0.679)	(-1.277)*	(2.162)*	(1.513)*	(0.073)	(2.080)
WAGE 1991	-4.737	-4.118	-5.554	11.690	-5.207	13.585
	(-1.500)	(-0.690)*	(-1.004)*	(2.278)*	(-1.229)*	(3.012)*
ΔWAGE	-1.475	2.310	-2.323	-8.211	-2.562	-6.030
	(-0.408)	(0.283)	(-0.412)	(-1.367)	(-0.533)	(-1.187)
SPATIAL COEFF. ρ	-		-		0.689	
					(3.508)	
Sum. Statistics:						
N	580		580		580	
R^2/*ML*	0.131/*-1147*		0.185		*-1123.36*	
LM (BP)	5.812 (0.121)		2.165 (0.338)		0.033 (0.857)	
LM (ρ)	13.295 (0.000)		1.735 (0.188)		-	
LM (λ)	10.158 (0.002)		0.345 (0.557)		-	
LR (ρ)	-		-		4.464 (0.034)	
LM λ (ρ)	-		-		0.853 (0.356)	
Chow-Wald	-		2.617 (0.001)		42.401 (0.000)	

See chapters 5 and 6 for technical explanation. For the exact definition of industrial activities see appendix A.

The Randstad and connected spatial regimes most profoundly depict the agglomeration indicator performance as basically introduced in column (1). Notably, the *CONCENTRATION* variable becomes negatively significant in the Randstad observations. The change in pre-period employment levels ($\Delta EMPIND9197$) is positively significant in the intermediate zone observations, while in the national periphery the wage structure is positively related to industrial innovation intensity. The effect of large average establishment sizes in relation to innovation intensity is *not* heterogeneously distributed over the national zoning regimes. This is indeed the case when comparing slopes of regression analyses concerning connected versus unconnected municipalities: the relation of large firm dominance and industrial innovation intensity is significant in the connected observations only. The diversity variable is also relevant in the connected observations as opposed to the unconnected ones. Concentration of industrial employment fosters innovation intensity in the unconnected spatial regime while the wage structure is found positively related to innovation intensity of unconnected observations. In the equation presented in column (3) the estimation results indicate the presence of both spatial heterogeneity between the two (conectedness) spatial regimes as well as a spatial lag model. Although there is a strong indication of positive spatial lag autocorrelation in the innovation intensity variable (as already envisaged in section 4.6), its incorporation in the model (*SPATIALCOEFFICIENTρ*) does not alter the evidence on regional heterogeneity nor individual agglomeration variables. There is little change between the interpretation of the model with and without spatial autocorrelation of the dependent variable. The main effect of the spatial lag autocorrelation is usually on the precision of the estimates, but in this case this effect is insufficient to alter any of the indications of significance of the regimes (see the summary statistics concerning the spatial Chow-Wald test) or the individual explanatory variables.

As industrial activities are comprised of many individual sub-sectors, models were constructed for four types of industrial activities. These were already summarized in terms of global spatial autocorrelation in chapter 4. Tables 7.5 and 7.6 present parsimonious models for each of the types of industry. Column (1) and (2) in table 7.5 concentrates on OLS and spatial lag models on municipal innovation intensity of labor intensive production. For this broad sector no spatial regimes appeared relevant and agglomeration and spatial lag indicators performed as in the general industrial model estimation of table 8.4. Column (3) of table 8.5 presents an OLS model for capital intensive industrial activities. Since neither spatial lag and error test statistics, heteroskedasticity statistics nor spatial regimes appeared relevant in this model, no further model extensions proved relevant for capturing the variety in innovation intensity over municipalities. The agglomeration variables were similar in sign and magnitude to the general industrial model estimation in table 8.4. Equations (4) and (5) in table 8.5 concentrate on knowledge-intensive process industries. Because of potential heteroskedasticity problems a FGLS model was estimated, incorporating the urban regimes of large medium-sized and small municipalities. The spatial Chow-Wald test indicates the significance of incorporating this regime for model improvement.

Table 7.5   OLS, spatial lag and FGLS models for industrial innovation intensity in the Netherlands (n=580)

explanatory variables	(1) OLS industry I	(2) Spatial lag industry I	(3) OLS industry II	(4) OLS industry III	(5) FGLS estimation ind. III urban spatial regimes large	medium	small
CONSTANT	6.907	2.878	8.775	0.754	3.745	5.083	0.509
	(4.197)	(3.314)	(7.481)	(0.965)	(0.869)	(1.557)	(0.616)
CONCENTR.	-0.232	-0.228	-0.210	-0.258	0.298	0.629	-0.068
	(-1.084)	(-1.082)	(-1.030)	(-1.896)	(0.372)	(1.107)	(-0.445)
LACK OF	-3.462	-3.656	-8.346	-3.242	-5.747	-3.308	-2.408
DIVERSITY	(-2.490)	(-2.669)	(-5.955)	(-2.021)	(-0.594)	(-0.464)	(-1.426)
ESTABL.	-1.118	-1.072	-1.086	-0.117	2.201	0.227	-0.096
SIZE	(-4.504)	(-4.383)	(-4.353)	(-0.276)	(2.196)*	(0.404)*	(-0.69)*
WA_EMPL.	0.008	0.005	-0.010	1.028	0.743	0.493	0.961
1991	(2.893)	(1.963)	(2.957)	(9.073)	(2.132)	(1.394)	(10.026)
ΔEMPL.IND	0.232	0.192	-0.070	0.684	1.096	0.872	0.786
1991-97	(0.768)	(0.643)	(-0.224)	(2.073)	(0.834)	(0.532)	(2.207)
WAGE 1991	7.996	8.227	12.850	12.113	2.178	-1.776	7.561
	(2.120)	(2.214)	(0.634)	(2.758)	(0.583)	(-0.119)	(1.655)
ΔWAGE	12.468	12.253	-15.469	3.591	3.030	-0.063	4.054
	(3.338)	(3.331)	(-1.469)	(1.046)	(1.106)	(-0.006)	(1.160)
SIGMA	-	-	-	-	19.776	7.098	7.793
					(4.242)	(5.523)	(15.540)
SPATIAL	-	0.773	-	-	-	-	-
COEFF. ρ		(5.161)					
Sum. Statist.							
N	580	580	580	580	580		
R^2/ML	0.121/-1465	-1460	0.148	0.347	0.390		
LM (BP)	21.8	14.5	7.79	16.7	-		
	(0.00)	(0.01)	(0.51)	(0.00)			
LM (ρ)	11.1	-	0.83	3.35	1.159		
	(0.00)		(0.36)	(0.07)	(0.282)		
LM (λ)	9.3	-	2.27	3.39	0.584		
	(0.02)		(0.13)	(0.06)	(0.444)		
LR (ρ)	-	7.2	-	-	-		
		(0.007)					
LM λ (ρ)	-	3.2 (0.07)	-	-	-		
Chow-Wald	-	-	-	-	26.449		
					(0.040)		

See chapter 5 and 6 for technical explanation. SIGMA reports FGLS-heteroskedastic variance coefficients. For the exact definition of industrial activities see appendix A (industry I = labor-intensive industry, industry II = capital-intensive industry, industry III = knowledge-intensive process industry).

Table 7.6 OLS, spatial lag and FGLS models for industrial and non-industrial innovation intensity in the Netherlands (n=580)

explanatory variables	(1) OLS industry IV	(2) FGLS estimation industry IV national zoning spatial regimes			(3) OLS non-industry	(4) spatial lag non-ind. connected spatial regimes	
		Randstad	IZ	Periph.		connect	unconn.
CONSTANT	9.928	9.882	10.916	9.274	3.008	0.317	0.024
	(7.179)	(7.727)	(8.784)	(6.644)	(6.183)	(0.407)	(0.029)
CONCENTR.	-0.266	0.242	-0.339	-0.163	1.382	0.874	2.163
	(-1.970)	(0.716)	(-1.522)	(-0.837)	(2.472)	(1.202)	(2.486)
LACK OF	-8.402	-8.221	-11.315	-7.744	-1.579	-2.600	-1.406
DIVERSITY	(-6.001)	(-3.317)	(-4.667)	(-3.420)	(-1.748)	(-2.269)	(-0.971)
ESTABL.	-0.653	0.406	-0.616	-1.087	-0.941	-1.376	-0.301
SIZE	(-3.859)	(0.989)*	(-2.245)*	(-4.428)*	(-4.390)	(-5.19)*	(-0.765)*
WA_EMPL.	0.009	-0.012	0.002	0.004	-	-	-
1991	(0.282)	(-1.933)	(0.629)	(0.629)			
INDUSTR.	-	-	-	-	0.193	0.171	0.220
INNOV.					(4.217)	(2.734)	(3.436)
ΔEMPL. 1991-	-0.064	-0.617	0.569	0.184	1.299	1.254	1.193
97	(-0.210)	(-1.414)	(1.035)	(0.309)	(3.195)	(2.384)	(1.948)
WAGE 1991	-9.258	7.634	-10.891	-31.078	0.820	-3.526	7.332
	(-1.738)	(0.766)	(-1.230)	(-3.320)	(0.363)	(-1.19)*	(2.173)*
ΔWAGE	-6.914	2.462	-9.083	-22.187	8.669	1.898	14.295
	(-1.082)	(1.755)*	(-0.982)*	(-2.031)*	(1.554)	(0.255)	(1.780)
SIGMA	-	8.768	7.810	9.809	-	-	-
		(8.916)	(9.592)	(10.886)			
SPATIAL	-	-	-	-	-	0.819	
COEFF. ρ						(6.855)	
Sum. Statist.							
N	580	580			580	580	
R²/LM	0.082	0.140			0.142/-1195	-1182.63	
LM (BP)	26.5	-			21.7	0.147	
	(0.00)				(0.00)	(0.700)	
LM (ρ)	1.9	0.028			14.8	-	
	(0.167)	(0.866)			(0.000)		
LM (λ)	2.5	0.334			15.5	-	
	(0.112)	(0.563)			(0.000)		
LR (ρ)	-	-			-	10.175	
						(0.001)	
LM λ (ρ)	-	-			-	9.132	
						(0.251)	
Chow-Wald	-	38.053			-	15.948	
		(0.001)				(0.043)	

See chapters 5 and 6 for technical explanation. SIGMA reports FGLS-heteroskedastic variance coefficients. For the exact definition of industrial activities (industry IV = knowledge-intensive process industry) see appendix A. ΔEMPL1991-97 measures *industrial* employment change in column (1) and (2) and *non-industrial* employment change in column (3) and (4).

Large cities show significant relations of large establishment sizes, as well as initial employment on the innovation intensity in the knowledge-intensive process industry. This observation is mainly due to the location of a few headquarters (containing R&D departments) of chemical industrial firms (e.g. Akzo Nobel in Arnhem and Shell Research in Amsterdam). Large average establishment sizes (indicating little local competition) also appear significant in the small urban regime observations. In the latter regime, employment growth in the recent past (*ΔEMPIND9197*) also contributes to the innovation intensity of this category of industrial activities.

In table 7.6, column (1) and (2) focus on the municipal structure of knowledge-intensive industrial R&D intensity of firms. An FGLS model is estimated following the OLS model in column (1) because of heteroskedasticity problems. The national zoning spatial regimes of the intermediate zone and the national periphery appear significant in this model. The large firm dependence of innovation intensity is found particularly significant in the intermediate zone and national periphery observations and not in the Randstad observations. Again, certain 'hot spots' of highly localized concentration of innovative intensive firms in this industrial sector causes these model outcomes[9]. Model outcomes, apart from this observation, resemble the general industrial innovation intensity model (table 7.4) a great deal, indicating the robustness of the agglomeration variables and spatial relations found for industrial innovation patterns in the Netherlands.

Spatial Models for Non-Industrial Innovation

Columns (3) and (4) in table 7.6 present models for *non-industrial* innovation intensity in the Netherlands. The connected spatial regime observations differ significantly from the unconnected ones. The relation of large firm size and local industry diversity with non-industrial innovation intensity is particularly significant in the connected (metropolitan labor area) regime. Notably, a positive relation of (non-industrial employment) concentration with innovation intensity results for the *non*-connected observations. In equation (4) the estimation results indicate the significance of a spatial lag model. Although there is a strong indication of positive spatial lag autocorrelation in the non-industrial innovation intensity variable, its incorporation in the model (*SPATIALCOEFFICIENTρ*) does not alter the evidence on regional heterogeneity (connected regime) nor individual agglomeration variables. As in *industrial* innovation intensity models with spatial lag significance, there is

---

[9] Schmitz and Heijs (2001), using the same database in their analyses, test on the sensitivity of the data on a few very large firms. It turns out that this dependence is quite large (p.47-48) since a substantial change in ordering of largest innovation (corop) regions occurs when leaving out the largest innovative firm or industry in each region. The presence of technical universities and knowledge institutions (subject to study of knowledge spillovers in knowledge production function frameworks, see Acs (2002) for an overview) is also important for total R&D wage expenditures in regions. As knowledge institutions and universities themselves (or in co-operation with innovative firms) apply for R&D wage grants to large extents they are endogenous in the model construction and cannot be separated from left and right hand elements of the estimated equations.

little difference between the interpretation of the model with and without spatial autocorrelation of the dependent variable.

7.4   Synthesis and Conclusions

The hypothesis that agglomeration and proximity is important for the promotion of innovation, knowledge transfer and growth is central in this dissertation. This chapter focuses on spatial research and development (R&D) clustering as indicators of economic agglomeration. The data used stem from labor costs estimates related to R&D expenditures in Dutch firms. Recently, the Anglo-Saxon literature concludes upon a very limited extent of spatial spillovers and a large degree of local clustering (see also chapter 2). At the same time, a body of literature on the Dutch spatial configuration of innovation and high-technology firms predominantly stresses the supposed urban field character of the Dutch case: location and agglomeration aspects do not seem to have a systematic impact on the distribution of innovative activities over space. As argued in this chapter, many of these 'stylized' conclusions depend heavily on definitions of R&D, innovation, research population, hypothesized functional relations over space and spillovers. The central question in this chapter is whether the testable hypotheses from the theoretical agglomeration frameworks of MAR, Porter and Jacobs, together with systematic spatial econometric modeling techniques, contribute to understanding the relation between proximity, agglomeration and innovation intensity in the Dutch case.

From the descriptive analyses focusing on connected and national zoning spatial regimes we conclude that the distinction between industrial versus non-industrial economic activities and the spatial regimes themselves are potentially relevant segmentations for exploring spatial dependency in R&D intensity data over municipalities in the Netherlands. Industrial innovation *concentration* is in general concentrated outside the Randstad core region, while relative high values of industrial innovation *intensity* (per employee) are concentrated both inside and outside the Randstad region. Both non-industrial innovation concentration *and* intensity are predominantly found in the Randstad region. Industrial innovation concentration ratios do not vary much over the connectedness regimes, while industrial innovation intensity is found predominantly high in core municipalities and to a lesser extent in suburban locations, especially in the Randstad region. From the shift-share analyses, decomposing innovation intensity data into spatial and sector effects suggests that urban core and suburban locations in general show positive spatial effects. This metropolitan relationship is particularly strong in the Randstad region. While the sectoral structure of metropolitan (connected) municipalities is initially not favorable for enhanced chances of spatial innovation intensity, the *actual* innovation intensity indicates that spatial effects are on average positive. Peripheral locations do not confirm to this general notion: urban core and suburban typologies of locations scores show negative spatial effects on innovation intensity indicators despite their usually favorable sectoral composition. This notion strengthens the conclusion drawn on the relevance of urban and national zoning spatial regimes.

Concluding remarks on the spatial econometric models presented in section 7.3 are based on three themes. First we focus on spatial heterogeneity that was found significant in the research. Second we look at spatial proximity patterns of innovation. And thirdly we conclude upon the theoretical implications in terms of the agglomeration externalities framework developed in earlier chapters.

The labor market induced, metropolitan spatial regime of connectedness appears highly significant as a spatial heterogeneous, structuring modeling element for municipal industrial as well as non-industrial innovation intensity. Labor is an important input factor for innovative firms (Frenkel 2001, Lambooy 2000, Malecki and Bradbury 1992). Location within metropolitan regions (either core locations or suburban ones) ensures the proximity of reservoirs of high-skilled workers. This research outcome is quite interesting in the sense that it has not been reached upon before in Dutch spatial innovation research. The national zoning regime concerning Randstad observations also appear relevant for capturing spatial heterogeneity in the model structures on industrial innovation intensity. This finding is consistent with work on innovation input and output performance of firms in the Netherlands, as analyzed by Brouwer *et al.* (1999). These authors conclude that their findings on innovative output are favorable to an urban hierarchy or filtering down hypotheses on the national level (see chapter 2 for an explanation of this theorem). The research results are however not consistent with the work of Kleinknecht and Poot (1992) who conclude upon the urban field character of the spatial distribution of innovation in the Netherlands[10].

Concerning the spatial (contiguity) proximity theses of innovation we tend to confirm the Anglo-Saxon research tradition focusing on the limited reach of R&D spillovers. In the empirical models presented in this chapter, spatial lag specifications of agglomeration variables were not included in the parsimonious versions of the models. This omission implies that regional versions of the agglomeration externality induced variables as used throughout this dissertation are not related to municipal innovation intensity data. Only local versions of the agglomeration variables turned out significant. In the equations presented for industrial innovation intensity using the connected spatial regime, the estimation results indicate the significance of a spatial lag model for labor-intensive industrial innovation intensity and for non-industrial innovation intensity conditioned by the connected spatial regime. Although there is a strong indication of positive spatial lag autocorrelation in these innovation intensity (explained) variables (as was envisaged in chapter 4), its incorporation in the model does not alter substantially the evidence on regional heterogeneity nor individual agglomeration variables. There is little change between the interpretation of the models with and without

---

[10] These general observations are conditioned by important conceptualizations. One of those concerns the control of individual firm characteristics, which is not implemented in our models (as is for instance in Harrison *et al.* 1997). Another concerns the distinction of process and product innovations, a segmentation we could not focus on using the Senter database (as is the case in for instance Oerlemans *et al.* 2001b and in Poot *et al.* 1997).

spatial autocorrelation of the dependent variable. Usually, the main effect of the spatial lag autocorrelation is on the precision of the estimates, but in the cases presented in this chapter this is not sufficient to alter any of the indications of significance of the regimes nor the individual explanatory variables. Model outcomes of sectoral more detailed segments of industrial activities resemble a great deal the overall industrial innovation intensity model, indicating the robustness of the relationship between agglomeration variables and the spatial relations found for industrial innovation patterns in the Netherlands. We conclude that heavily localized innovation intensity patterns are caused by a few 'hot spots' of large, dominant firms creating a spatial concentration of innovation intensity

Concerning the theoretical hypotheses established by Jacobs, MAR and Porter, the model estimates do not conclude upon a single dominance of any of their theories on agglomeration economies. For industrial innovation intensity models we find that lack of concentration and industry diversity foster innovation intensity. That both concentration (negative) and diversity (positive) indicators show a significant relation to innovation intensity is not uncommon in empirical research (compare Harrison *et al.* 1997 and Paci and Usai 1999) and indicates the relevance of Jacobs-induced agglomeration hypotheses. The absence of small firm competitive power (as large firms dominate the local scenes of innovation) though, favors Porter and MAR hypotheses of competitive agglomeration. Agglomeration models on innovation intensity appear quite different from employment growth spatial externality analyses, but one conclusion can be firmly made: the localized ('hot spots') clustering of innovative firms and the significance of connected and national zoning spatial regimes indicate that innovation intensity is not distributed randomly over space. Urban field hypotheses of innovation patterns in the Netherlands thus prove to be less apparent than often suggested.

Chapter 8

Summary and Conclusions

8.1   Research Questions

As became clear in the literature overview in chapter 2 of this dissertation, according to endogenous growth and innovation diffusion theory, knowledge and knowledge spillovers potentially give rise to external economies of scale in production. However, the empirical literature (using predominantly US employment and innovation data in urban contexts) does not reach a clear conclusion as to the geographical, and especially agglomeration circumstances under which knowledge is most easily transferred. Does knowledge spill over predominantly between firms within the same sector or between firms in different sectors? Are economic growth and innovation diffusion processes in a framework of spatial externalities predominantly intra- or inter-urban in character? What role do regional circumstances play for local developments? And what is the role of competition in the growth and innovation process? In the agglomeration framework outlined in chapter 2, these theoretical and empirical aspects stress localization and urbanization economies in a dynamic, endogenous growth framework. Founded on Romer (1986) and Lucas (1988), the theory of endogenous growth emphasizes the role in the growth process of both the stock of knowledge and the (planned or unplanned) transfer of knowledge between economic agents. For example, knowledge spills over between firms via informal contacts between employees, or because employees switch jobs and take their knowledge with them. Indeed, the most important type of knowledge that plays a role in the growth process is not necessarily path-breaking innovations, but may be learning opportunities for everyday people. Although intangible by nature, economic growth theory tries to measure knowledge externalities under different economic settings. Empirical tests on geographic dimensions of this theory have often looked at cities to identify settings in which these external factors most effectively foster growth and innovation. Results, however, have been sharply divided. On the one hand it is found that employment growth and innovation is enhanced by diversity of activity across a broad range of sectors. On the other hand, research concludes on faster (employment) growth when more activity is concentrated in a single sector. Spatial clustering (agglomerations) of firms, sectoral heterogeneity and its spatial configuration, as well as spatial heterogeneity (non-contiguous spatial relations), together make up a complex picture of spatial-economic growth and innovation diffusion. A large body of recent literature focuses on contiguous proximity models with sharp declining distance decays that describe most adequately empirical observations of spatial R&D intensity, innovation and employment growth. Another important strand of literature clearly finds evidence for hierarchical urban density regimes for growth and the supposed functioning of knowledge externalities. Hypotheses concerning the spatial-econometric circumstances fostering or retarding growth and innovation are contingent upon several crucial factors. The research presented in this book contributes to some of these factors. The focus is on economic, spatially dynamic and R&D externalities to the extent that they 'explain' (spatially co-vary with) economic patterns of firm and industry performance.

One of the most promising contributions in the recent literature towards an understanding of the nature and content of dynamic urban externalities is provided in the theoretical and empirical framework developed by Glaeser *et al.* (1992). In their seminal contribution, an endogenous growth framework based on employment growth patterns in mixtures of industries in US cities is developed using three theoretically 'contrasting' spatial causal concepts of agglomeration economies: local industry level specialization, local industry diversity and the degree of local competition. This framework builds on the well-known regional-economic concepts of localization (specialization) and urbanization (diversity) economies that differentiate between localized growth and innovation patterns. In short, the theoretical propositions of localization and urbanization economies in their framework are summarized by three important (groups of) authors. First, in the theoretical and empirical contributions developed by Marshall (1890), Arrow (1962) and Romer (1986) (MAR), focusing on localization economies, spillovers are thought to be most important when there is little prevailing local competition so that rents associated with sector-specific knowledge can be internalized. The MAR-theory from a dynamic point of view predicts that local monopoly is better for growth than local competition, because local monopoly restricts the flow of ideas to others and so allows innovator-internalization. Again, this is supposed to speed up growth and new innovation. The second important author, Michael Porter (1990) agrees with the existence of localization economies, also arguing that knowledge spillovers in specialized, geographically concentrated industries stimulate growth. On the relevant market form, however, Porter disagrees with the MAR-theory: he insists that local competition fosters the pursuit and rapid adoption of innovation. Both influential frameworks (Porter on competitive advantage and MAR on innovation monopoly and power) embrace the concept of localization economies, both in static as well as dynamic versions. The third element of agglomeration externality hypotheses (besides localization and competition economies) is proposed by Jacobs (1969) and appears generally accepted in the literature. She agrees with Porter that competition fosters growth, but contends that regional diversity in economic activity (as a measure of urbanization economies) results in higher growth and innovation rates as many ideas developed by one sector can also be fruitfully applied in other sectors.

In our study, static (R&D) and dynamic (growth) externalities are tested for their importance on firm- and industry-level innovation intensity and employment growth, using this Glaeser *et al.* (1992) framework as the initial starting point of analysis. Rather than emphasizing differences in empirical model outcomes, because of a focus on a (urban polynucleated) Western European country instead of the US, the research stresses the implications of theoretical and conceptual departures from the original framework. These departures are introduced (one by one) because they better capture important conceptual (multilevel) aspects concerning spatial scale and spatial composition. The present literature does not acknowledge the importance of these aspects generally, or once acknowledged, it does not make sufficient use of available measurement and econometric modeling techniques.

The central research question of our study is to what extent spatial economic externalities (agglomeration economies) are related to endogenous employment growth and innovation intensity of firms in the Netherlands. The Netherlands is a country that traditionally is highly urbanized, polycentred and (relatively) data-rich. Alongside conceptual and econometric research extensions, these Dutch traditions impose some important research advantages that set our study apart from the (growing) US-induced research output on the subject of spatial externalities. The advantages (and hence scientific contributions) that concern the research in this dissertation can be summarized into three, heavily interrelated dimensions (research subquestions): (1) the given natural context of a dense and polynucleated urban environment; (2) theoretical conceptualizations concerning heterogeneity in firms and sectors concerning spatial growth and innovation; and (3) empirical measurement issues and a full account of possibilities and limitations of formal spatial econometric modeling. Controversial research results in the literature concerning explanatory spatial circumstances that most favorably induce dynamic and innovative externalities (to a large extent) can probably be attributed to the lack of consistent spatial research designs that allow for multiple spatial scale and composition effects to be modeled. In a theoretical sense, the lack of consistent inclusion of life-cycle aspects of firms (age and connected growth potential) in the present mainstream literature on dynamic externalities arguably contributes to controversies in research outcomes. Furthermore, ignorance of spatial heterogeneous research designs *a priori* excludes spatial network relational frameworks as opposed to spatial clustered ones.

8.2   Research Results

Descriptive Analyses of Heterogeneous Employment Growth

Chapters 3 and 4 provide descriptive analyses of spatial employment growth patterns preceding econometric modeling in chapters 5 to 7. In *chapter 3*, employment growth in the Netherlands is described on macro-economic (zoning), a regional (connectedness) and a local level (zip codes in South Holland) bases. It appears important to use stable industry-classification schemes over time when analyzing economic growth. Three kinds of spatial-sectoral classifications are introduced: (1) spatial analyses for industry, distribution, producer service and consumer service sectors; (2) location-industries as flexible combinations of spatial and sectoral detailed functional components (introduced in Glaeser *et al.* 1992); and (3) dummy variables for certain industries or types of locations. None of these classifications is *a priori* superior to others, but some appear more suitable for certain analyses.

The literature on Dutch spatial economic developments, as discussed in chapter 3, reveals some common hypothetical trends. The first trend focuses on urban (size) hierarchical growth patterns, urban networks and systems of cities. Complementary cities are often supposed (but often relatively unconvincingly found) to inhabit conditions that facilitate organizational networks to flourish, especially concerning office accommodation and growth of consumer and producer services. The second trend concerns concentric diffusive growth, either by spatial patterns of connectedness (functional regions in terms of commuting) or macro-economic zoning. From economic concentrations outwards, spatial growth processes diffuse simultaneously over different spatial scales. The two most commonly observed patterns concern suburbanization from individual cities (but within urban agglomerations) and de-concentration from the Randstad core region towards neighboring regions (the so-called intermediate zone). A third spatial growth tendency noted in the literature concerns 'autonomous impulses'. When autonomous developments can take place anywhere in larger functional area with the same degree of possibility, Hoekveld (1999) and Louter (1999) argue that we can speak of an urban field development. However, when exactly developments are autonomous and to what extent (parts of) the Netherlands function as an urban field in which economic *growth* patterns level out, is not analyzed unambiguously.

Descriptive analyses on the datasets used in our study, as well the evaluation of national spatial regimes (non-contiguous urban conceptualizations) presented in chapter 3, confirm some of the logic of these spatial growth patterns. They do not, however, systematically reveal the causal (economic) processes of agglomeration externalities connected. As a result of the dense system of medium-sized and smaller cities in the Netherlands, it is often unclear in which (of the three) diffusion and growth trends (and hence spatial regimes) the observations most obviously fit. It is therefore suggested that many processes of growth originate at lower spatial levels than the macro- and meso-economic developments described. The study focuses in (spatial) detail on one region in the Netherlands to examine this, the province of South-Holland. It is believed that a finer spatial scale than metropolitan areas (in our case: zip codes in South-Holland, that can be aggregated into cities, municipalities and regions) might reveal insights on intra-urban spatial dependency when modeled adequately (compare Wallsten 2001, Cervero 2001). Detailed data availability in a longitudinal data-set comprising all individual firms present in the research area make analyses on a lower spatial scale possible. The last section of chapter 3 shows that firm dynamics in terms of entrants, relocations, dissolution and growth of firms constitutes a complex interplay in identifying life-cycle circumstances of firms and industries for explaining localized endogenous growth patterns in this region. Potentially, indications of business volatility (establishment turnover) embedded in localities can be helpful in testing theoretical hypotheses on the role of competition in local markets of production and consumption.

Employment growth and innovation intensity indicators are central (explained) variables in this dissertation, and a thorough insight to their spatial configuration is essential for their econometric modeling. In *chapter 4*, therefore, the study of the spatial distribution of local employment concentration (1997), innovation intensity (1999)[1], as well as employment growth (1988-97)[2] using exploratory spatial data analysis (ESDA), highlights the magnitude of spatial dependence. The analyses reveal positive global spatial autocorrelation, which is to a large degree persistent over time, for employment density, firm density, employment function, relative firm representation, employment growth and population growth at zip code level in the research area of South-Holland, as well on municipal level for the Netherlands. On the latter spatial scale, innovation intensity is also spatially autocorrelated to a significant degree.

Moran scatterplot maps reveal that urban locations show significantly higher degrees of density (as used in Combes 2000) *and* specialization values (the latter estimated by location quotients) of economic activity. Comparison of standardized values of Moran's *I* statistic over time reveal that economic activities in general become relatively less agglomerated over time. Besides employment and innovation structure, economic (employment) *growth* is our central focus. It appears that employment and population growth patterns (the latter introduced as a reference) are not spatially random distributed. Cross-section and dynamic specifications reveal a significant tendency for (economic) growth to cluster in space. Local indicators of spatial autocorrelation of employment growth show contradictory patterns when compared to those of employment density and function. Central urban areas are characterized by spatial autocorrelation of low growth values (compare Summers *et al.* 1999), whereas non-urban areas, still close to the Randstad region and urban areas in general ('borrowed size', compare Phelps *et al.* 2001), show spatial autocorrelation of high growth values[3]. Most significantly and robust, this result appears from Moran's *I* test statistics when broad economic sectors (industry, distribution, producer services and consumer services) are analyzed. The spatial contiguity based, proximate spatial dependency of employment (growth) and innovation concentrations reaches *over* zip code as well as municipal (city) boundaries. This finding is envisioned both in global terms (from the Randstad region towards and into the intermediate zone and national periphery) and in local terms (from urban centers towards connected suburban locations and medium-sized cities throughout the region and country) by the analyses in chapter 4. An additional relevant (causal) segmentation appears to be based on industry and firm life stages or positions in the business cycle. New firm formation and exit rates of firms, as well as their hypothesized job creation and destruction capacities, show significant degrees of spatial autocorrelation in the research area of South-Holland. High spatial autocorrelated values of both new and dissoluted firms are present in both central urban locations and in suburban locations and medium-seized cities. This finding suggests the relevance of the extended incubation theory as formulated in the literature. Since employment creation by new firms and firm exit is significantly spatially correlated with own

---

[1] Conclusions on ESDA analyses concerning innovation intensity are discussed in later in this section.

[2] Growth rates in the research area of South-Holland concern the period 1988-1997 and in the Netherlands 1991-1997.

[3] The concentration of low and high values of growth *both* indicate *positive* spatial autocorrelation.

(survival) and total employment growth, the hypothesis that explanations of endogenous employment growth in spatial contexts gain from controlling for these dynamics appears *a priori* a very relevant one.

The Location-Industry OLS Modeling Framework

Based on the empirical literature, *chapter 5* presents agglomeration and spatial externality indicators that were used in econometric modeling. By means of relative space-neutral (OLS) modeling first empirical evidence on the basis of Dutch data is provided concerning the influence of growth externalities. As null-models, analyses in chapter 5 are kept as close as possible to the Glaeser *et al.* (1992) and Henderson (2003) analytical frameworks on employment growth in cities and agglomeration externalities. The regression results using data on Dutch municipalities provide general support for Jane Jacobs' (1969) hypothesis that knowledge spills over between sectors and that competition fosters growth because of the necessity to innovate and survive. In table 8.1 this finding is indicated by the first two rows (location-industries: neth-all and sh-all). This table is helpful in summarizing the most important findings. In the upper part of this table, a comparison is made between the four broad sectors and the four most important agglomeration variables introduced in chapters 5, 6 and 7 on several populations of employment growth and innovation intensity. Reading the table vertically, the four variables on concentration (stressed in MAR and Porter conceptualizations), diversity (stressed in Jacobs conceptualizations) and local competition (measured as relative firm size and firm turnover) are given for 'own' and spatially lagged ('regional') specifications (assigned w_). Combinations of the original variable and its spatially lagged conversion (w_) indicate the presence of window averaged variables. Reading horizontally, the table shows the research population by sector (printed in italics), research area (South-Holland sh- or the Netherlands) for all and incumbent (old) establishments. The table shows significant signs of coefficients found in the models discussed in this chapter and the preceding two chapters. The figure '0' means that no significant relation was found. These coefficient signs are accompanied by significant, conditioning spatial regimes (spatial heterogeneity) in brackets (explanation below the table). The light and grey shadings in the table register the model coefficient outcomes according to the dominant theoretical conceptualization: either MAR/Porter (localization economies) or Jacobs (urbanization economies) respectively. These results clearly show that specific spatial and conceptual conditions, translated into empirical model and specifications and indicators, are reflected in the *econometric* nature of contextual dependencies in the data.

The results in chapter 5 are similar to those in the Glaeser *et al.* (1992) analysis of employment growth in US cities, and are in conflict with Henderson *et al.* (1995), who found that industrial concentration is more important than industrial diversity. However, the data set for the province of South-Holland, which covers a substantial part of the core economic region of the country, enables us to correct several flaws in the Netherlands municipality regressions. The availability of establishment level data for this province enables us to better define two crucial variables.

Table 8.1   Summarizing results of spatial econometric analyses of employment growth and innovation intensity

empl. growth	concentration		diversity		competition			
	conc	w_con	gini	w_gini	size	w_size	volatil	w_vol
loc.-industries								
neth – all (1404)	-	x	-	x	+	x	x	x
sh- all (1797)	- (14)	x	-	x	+ (14)	x	+	x
sh – old (1797)	- (14)	x	- (14)	x	+ (14)	x	-	x
manufacturing								
sh-all (416)	-	+	+ (16)	- (17)	0		+ (17)	0
sh- all (1797)	0	-	-	0	+		-	0
sh-old (457/1797)	-	x	-	x	+	x	-	x
neth (370/1404)	-	x	-	x	+	x	x	x
netherl. (580)	- (6,9,11)	+ (4,6,9)	- (5)	0	0	0	x	x
distribution								
sh-all (416)	- (15)	+ (14)	-	0	+ (14)	0	+	0
sh-old (416)	- (15)	- (14)	- (15)	0	0	0	- (14)	0
netherl. (580)	- (2,3)	+ (1,7)	+ (1,7)	-	+ (1,7)	- (1,7)	x	x
producer serv.								
sh-all (416)	- (14)	+ (14)	0	- (14)	+ (15)	0	+ (14)	0
sh-old (416)	0	-	0	+	0	0	-	0
netherl. (580)	+ (1,4,9)	- (3,11)	+ (1,4,6)	-	+	- (6, 11)	x	x
consumer serv.								
sh-all (416)	-	0	-	0	0	0	0	0
sh-old (416)	0	0	0	0	0	0	+	0
netherl. (580)	- (6)		- (6)	0	+ (6)	0	x	x

Innovation (580)	conc	w_con	gini	w_gini	size	w_size	volatil	w_vol
Industry I	0	x	-	x	-	x	x	x
Industry II	0	x	-	x	-	x	x	x
industry III	0	x	-	x	+ (4)	x	x	x
industry IV	-	x	-	x	-	x	x	x
Industry	- (3,12)	x	- (1,3,12)	x	- (1,3)	x	x	x
non-industry	+ (13)	x	- (12)	x	- (12)	x	x	x

Spatial regimes:

(1)	Randstad (n=580)	(10)	south-wing Randstad (n=580)
(2)	intermediate zone (n=580)	(11)	non-wing & outside Randstad (n=580)
(3)	national periphery (n=580)	(12)	connected (n=580)
(4)	large cities (n=580)	(13)	non-connected (n=580)
(5)	medium-sized cities (n=580)	(14)	urban (n=416)
(6)	small cities (n=580)	(15)	non-urban (n=416)
(7)	accessible (n=580)	(16)	workarea (n=416)
(8)	non-accessible (n=580)	(17)	non-workarea (n=416)
(9)	north-wing Randstad (n=580)		

■■■■ in line with Jacobs hypotheses (and Porter for competition)

light grey shade   in line with MAR/Porter hypotheses (Porter excluded for competition)

First, the dependent variable can be expressed as employment growth in establishments that already existed in the base year (third row in table 8.1: sh-old), rather than growth in all establishments including new establishments. As the theory of knowledge externalities and growth focuses on dynamic externalities rather than at location choice, the appropriate dependent variable in the analysis is employment changes in existing firms. Second, an (alternative and arguably theoretically stronger) measure of competition based on establishment turnover can be constructed (7th column in table 8.1: competition-volatility). The results are markedly different from the ones mentioned in the 'pure' Glaeser *et al.* (1992) framework. The results for regional composition in location-industry contexts (row 1, 2 and 3 in table 8.1) in general offer support to Jacobs' theory that knowledge is not necessarily sector-specific and that ideas conceived in one sector can fruitfully be applied in others. However, the fact that lack of regional competition (as measured by the turnover variable) is found to foster growth in *existing* firms gives support to the ideas of Marshall, Arrow, Romer and Porter that knowledge creation is stimulated by the possibility of rent capture. Hence, these outcomes do not give full support to any of the existing hypotheses concerning the spatial-economic circumstances that foster growth.

Extensions of Agglomeration Models for Employment Growth

Chapters 5 and 6 further bring together two strands of the empirical literature on the relationship between knowledge externalities and employment *growth*. The first strand tests for evidence of endogenous growth linked to agglomeration economies between economic agents *within* cities, and the second tests whether knowledge spills over between economic agents *in different locations, not necessarily being located in the same city*. The link between these two topics is made, through further extension of the modeling framework for the Dutch data. The purpose is to develop spatial econometric models that allow employment growth in one location to affect growth in other locations. Compared to the earlier analyses in chapter 5, more detailed focus is on determinants of *sectoral* employment growth at the municipal and zip code level and accompanying, proximate locations (contiguous spatial lag modeling), or locations unified in theoretical relevant spatial regimes. The focus is whether urban economic growth models improve over the 'null-model' when further conceptual extensions are introduced. A key finding is that local industrial diversity, rather than industrial concentration, tends to promote growth. This general conclusion is subject to revaluation when four *interrelated* spatial model extensions, discussed in the following sections, are also introduced.

The first model extension asks whether improvements occur when explicitly proximity-based spatial research designs are applied, either by spatial lag and window average specifications of explained and explaining variables. On the *intra-urban (zip code) level*, analyses on location-industries suggest that knowledge externalities (spillovers) between locations can occur *indirectly* through the growth process (spatial contiguous design of the *dependent* variable). In other words, increased spillovers (externalities) can lead to increased growth in one location that can in turn lead to increased growth elsewhere. Empirical estimates suggest that between 20 and 60 percent of the growth induced by agglomeration economies occurs locally, depending on whether the model allows for inter-industry linkages over space, or just intra-industry linkages over space (sectoral models by their definition and construction only focus on intra-industry linkages). These findings are particularly significant in light of the small size of the regions studied and suggests that areas with a relatively high knowledge generating capacity may be expected to grow faster than others, while proximate spillover effects are limited. This conclusion should be conditioned on the spatial transformation of *individual (explaining)* agglomeration variables (see the signs of w_ denoted significant variables in table 8.1). Spatially lagged indicators of specialization were found significant for all-firms specifications on zip code level of industrial, distribution and producer service models (together making up the economic basic activities). Compared to 'own' location coefficients, spatially lagged (neighboring) agglomeration variables often show *reversed* signs when related to employment growth. These findings stress that analyses on the level of zip codes in the South-Holland research area are sensitive to explicit spatial contiguous specifications to a larger degree than suggested by the OLS-based location-industry results. We also discovered that the introduction of spatially lagged agglomeration variables capturing regional externality circumstances in *municipal (city) analyses* significantly contribute to improved model fit. This finding concerns in particular the spatial analyses of industrial, distribution and producer services employment growth (the 'basic' economic activities). Regional localization and urbanization economies frequently interfere with local growth patterns, indicating the importance of multilevel-based analyses. Often, as in the zip code analyses, regionalized (spatially lagged) agglomeration indicators show *inverse* relations to employment growth compared to 'own' city relations.

The second model extension relates to sectoral interrelations captured in location-industry spatial weight matrices that allow for inter- as well as intra-('own') sectoral growth interchanges. A key finding following chapter 5 was that local industrial diversity, rather than industrial concentration, tends to promote growth. This outcome holds for most specifications presented for inter- as well as intra-industry specifications of the weight matrices in the spatial lag models for location industries (n=1797) and for individual sectoral models (n=416). The fact that no substantial change in performance of agglomeration variables occurred when changing from an inter- to an intra-industry specification, and the dominance of industrial diversity over industrial concentration in the models, suggest that urbanization economies are more important attributes for the growth process than localization economies. However, the choice of the dependent variable is found to be of crucial importance when determining the impact of competition on growth. If the dependent variable measures all employment growth, as is the case with Glaeser *et al.* (1992), competition is found to foster growth in the location-industry analyses as well as in the sectoral analyses for manufacturing, distribution, producer services and consumer services separately. If, on the other hand, only growth in (1988) existing establishments is analyzed, we find that competition is found to retard growth in location-industry analyses and in analyses on consumer services and manufacturing. Analyses for distribution and producer service activities reveal a positive influence of the competition variable for all-establishments specified models. Volatility measured competition further proved important for old-establishment consumer service growth and all-establishment industrial growth.

The third model extension asks whether separate sectoral models for industrial, distribution, producer and consumer service activities add value to location-industry mixed models. Some of the agglomeration based hypotheses in the spatial-economic literature focus explicitly on certain individual industries or broader sectors. As the models designed show considerable variation over sign, significance and magnitude of individual coefficients and spatial regime design (see table 8.1), it is clear that the aggregation of the data into the four broad sectors is relevant from both empirical and theoretical points of view. Building on Henderson *et al.* (1995) and Henderson (2003), we find that MAR-related theoretical hypotheses are more appropriate for describing the externality-patterns in the data.

The fourth model extension searches for the role of spatial heterogeneity when introduced in models by spatial regimes. An advantage of looking at the region of *South-Holland* is that it is small enough for location-specific factors, such as those related to cost, demand, and resource endowments, to not differ greatly between locations. As a consequence, the choice of this specific study area ameliorates an important objection to previous empirical analyses of the role of agglomeration economies in urban growth. South-Holland's small size potentially reduces the problem of unmeasured heterogeneity that has become an important issue in evaluating related studies of US metropolitan areas. In any case, spatial regimes still turned out to be highly relevant modeling attributes for the sectoral models (see table 8.1, significant spatial regimes in brackets throughout the table). Employment growth in manufacturing is fostered more by agglomeration variables in locations characterized as working areas. These areas are not all urban in character and indicate that a scattered spatial structure is underlying the spatial growth process of this sector in the research area. For distribution activities the non-urban regime (as opposed to urban) contributes significantly to the spatial externalities model and represents the data most adequately. Producer services growth on the contrary, captured in an urban regime, is closely related to intra-local development trajectories in the models presented. For young firms this aspect is more important than for old, incumbent firms. The spatial growth models on *the municipal level* are also conditioned by spatial heterogeneity (non-contiguous spatial dependence) patterns to a large degree. Growth of manufacturing activities for instance is conditioned by small urban (concentration and regionalized concentration), medium-sized urban (diversity), large urban (regionalized concentration) and the south-wing of the Randstad (negatively) spatial regimes respectively. See table 8.1 for all significant relations. The relevance of urban hierarchical, national zoning, subcity-level work-area zoning and accessibility spatial regimes for economic growth indicate that urban network theories on spatial dependence (as far as the spatial regimes introduced allow for such spatial network constellations) are at least as important as contiguous, proximate agglomeration circumstances.

Spatial Models for Innovation Intensity

From the agglomeration models on employment growth, it was concluded that correlation in *unobserved characteristics* that vary over space on a higher than zipcode or municipal scale might cause the results from spatial lag and error estimates to be reminiscent of OLS estimates. One of these unobserved aspects of economic growth processes and learning capacities in firms is innovation and innovative behavior. This important aspect, complementary to the indirect measurement of knowledge externalities by means of production function *input* (employment) growth, sheds light more directly on potential knowledge spillovers and economic *output* growth[4]. The hypothesis that agglomeration, proximity and spatial composition (heterogeneity) is important for the promotion of innovation, knowledge transfer and growth is central in this dissertation. *Chapter 7* focuses on firm specific research and development (R&D) patterns in a similar framework of economic agglomeration as with the growth analyses. A distinction in industrial and non-industrial innovation is made in the analysis. The data used stem from labor costs estimates related to R&D in Dutch firms. The main advantages of this dataset are its integral character and spatial detail. The level of analysis is that of 580 municipalities (in which the four largest cities are divided into three-digit zip codes). Recently, the Anglo-Saxon literature concludes on a very limited extent of spatial spillovers and a large degree of local clustering. In addition, a recent body of literature on the Dutch spatial configuration of innovation and high-technology firms predominantly stresses the supposed urban field character of the Dutch case: location and agglomeration aspects do not seem to have a systematic impact on the distribution of innovative activities over space. As is argued in chapter 7, many of these stylized conclusions depend heavily on definitions of R&D, innovation, research population, hypothesized functional relations over space and spillovers. The question central in chapter 7 was whether the testable hypotheses from the theoretical agglomeration frameworks of MAR, Porter and Jacobs, together with systematic spatial econometric modeling techniques, contribute to understanding the relation between proximity, agglomeration and innovation intensity in the Dutch case.

The technique of exploratory spatial data analysis (ESDA) was applied to the degrees of innovation intensity in Dutch municipalities in *chapter 4*. Moran's *I* statistics are presented for R&D levels in industries and technology groups. The definition of innovation intensity by nature shows the difference in spatially autocorrelated values of R&D expenditures when compared to employment density. Positive spatially autocorrelated values of innovation intensity are found *outside* the Randstad core region. Clearly, this spatial pattern of innovative intensity is different from the employment and population density functions. While both industrial and non-industrial innovation intensities are spatially autocorrelated, two differences become apparent. First, non-industrial innovation shows a higher degree of spatial autocorrelation than industrial. Second, except for the difference in magnitude of

---

[4] It should be noted that R&D expenditures as innovation indicator measures *input* to the innovation process as well.

correlation, the clustering of high values of positive spatial autocorrelation takes place in different regions. The intermediate zone on a macro scale and the north-wing of the Randstad (Amsterdam-Utrecht) are clusters of *industrial* innovation intensity. For *non-industrial* innovation intensity, the main density of positive values shifts towards the (south-wing) of the Randstad. From the descriptive analyses of connected and national zoning spatial regimes in chapter 4, we conclude that the distinction industrial versus non-industrial economic activities and the spatial regimes themselves are relevant segmentations for exploring spatial dependency in R&D intensity data over municipalities. Industrial innovation *concentration* is in general concentrated outside the Randstad core region, while relative high values of industrial innovation *intensity* (per employee) are concentrated both inside and outside the Randstad region. From a shift and share analysis in innovation intensity, decomposing innovation intensity data into spatial and sector effects, we conclude that urban core and suburban locations show positive spatial effects. This metropolitan relationship is especially strong in the Randstad region. Although the sectoral structure of metropolitan (connected) municipalities is not initially favourable for enlarged chances of spatial innovation intensity, the *actual* innovation intensity indicates that spatial effects are on average positive. In peripheral regions, urban core and suburban locations show negative spatial effects on innovation intensity indicators despite their usually favorable sectoral composition (a relative emphasis of high-tech industrial activities). A summary of the spatial econometric models on innovation intensity presented in chapter 7 focuses on three themes: first on significant spatial heterogeneity, second on significant spatial proximity patterns and third on the theoretical implications in terms of the agglomeration externalities framework developed in earlier chapters (see also the bottom rows in figure 8.1).

First, the labor market induced, metropolitan spatial regime of connectedness appears highly significant as a spatial heterogeneous, structuring modeling element for municipal industrial and non-industrial innovation intensity. Labor is an important input factor for innovative firms and location within metropolitan regions (either core locations or suburban ones) ensures proximity to reservoirs of high-skilled workers. This research outcome is quite interesting. It has not been reached upon before in Dutch spatial innovation research. The national zoning regime concerning Randstad observations also appear relevant for capturing spatial heterogeneity in the model structures on industrial innovation intensity. This finding is consistent with previous work on innovation performance of firms in the Netherlands, which favour urban hierarchy or filtering down hypotheses on the national level. However, it is not consistent with other, much cited work that concludes on an urban field character of the spatial distribution of innovation in the Netherlands.

Second, concerning the spatial (contiguity) proximity theses of innovation, we confirm the Anglo-Saxon research tradition focusing on the limited reach of R&D spillovers. In the empirical models presented in this chapter, spatial lag specifications of agglomeration variables were not included in the parsimonious versions of the models discussed. This exclusion implies that regional versions of the agglomeration externality induced variables, as used throughout this dissertation are not related to municipal innovation intensity data. Only local versions of the agglomeration variables turned out significant. In the equations presented for industrial innovation intensity (conditioned by the connected spatial regime), for labor-intensive industrial innovation intensity and for non-industrial innovation intensity (conditioned by the connected spatial regime), the estimation results indicate the significance of a spatial lag model. Although this is a strong indication of positive spatial autocorrelation in these innovation intensity (explained) variables, its incorporation in the model does not alter substantially the evidence on regional heterogeneity nor individual agglomeration variables. There is little change in interpretation of the models with and without spatial autocorrelation of the dependent variable. Model outcomes of more detailed segments of industrial activities resemble a great deal the overall industrial innovation intensity model, indicating the robustness of the relationship between agglomeration variables and the spatial relations found for industrial innovation patterns. We conclude that localized innovation intensity patterns are caused by a few 'hot spots' of large, dominant firms leading to spatial concentration of innovation intensity.

The model estimates presented do not conclude on a single dominance of any of the theoretical hypotheses on agglomeration economies postulated by Jacobs, MAR and Porter. For industrial innovation intensity models we find that lack of concentration and industry diversity foster innovation intensity. That both concentration and diversity indicators show this relation to innovation intensity indicates the relevance of Jacobs-induced agglomeration hypotheses. The absence of small firm competitive power (as large firms dominate the local scenes of innovation) however, favors Porter and MAR hypotheses of competitive agglomeration. Agglomeration models on innovation intensity appear quite different from (employment) growth spatial externality analyses. But one conclusion can be firmly made: the localized ('hot spot') clustering of innovative firms and the significance of connected and national zoning spatial regimes indicate that innovation intensity is not distributed randomly over space. Urban field hypotheses of innovation patterns in the Netherlands do not appear as dominant as often suggested.

8.3 Research Conclusions

The research in this thesis takes a few steps further towards a better understanding of the relationship between knowledge and growth spillovers and agglomeration economies, especially concerning spatial scale and composition effects. In chapter 1 a distinction is made in elements connected to the urban, historically grown setting, to firm-heterogeneity in economic theory and to measurement and econometric modeling (related to spatial scale and composition issues). We focus on these subjects now, one by one, although conclusions on spatial research designs in our study are simultaneously dependent on all three aspects.

The Natural Setting: Urban Agglomeration

The analyses presented in our study form a contribution to the literature that uses predominantly US employment and innovation data, in the sense that analyses outside the US confirm some important agglomeration hypotheses (as the study of Combes (2000) does for France). The specific spatial setting of urban development and agglomeration externalities in the Netherlands potentially deserves some creditability in its own right. It is often pointed out that the polycentric character of the urban structure in the Netherlands forms an ideal spatial-economic setting for urban sprawl, urban field and urban network conceptualizations. Although really large cities are not present, (parts of) the Netherlands are indeed urbanized to a degree that naturally gives rise to descriptions via a range of such conceptualizations. The present spatial constellation provides polynuclear circumstances that make the Randstad (the economic core region), or even the country as a whole, function as an *economic* entity, often labeled 'urban field'. Whether this urban configuration conforms to urban field conceptualization depends heavily on definitions and measurement. Spatial innovation patterns as measured by R&D intensity of firms in our study show a limited agglomerated spatial dependence and a conditioning on the connectedness (labor market) spatial regime. Spatial growth patterns also appeared relatively limited in their contiguous spatial dependence, although ESDA analyses showed overall positive values of spatial autocorrelation. Growth data are conditioned on intra-urban (work-area), national zoning (north-wing Randstad), accessibility and inter-urban (hierarchical) spatial heterogeneity. The relevance of the subcity-level spatial dependency found in the analysis is important, since it indicates that small-scale urban *functions*, rather than aggregated urban (municipal) observations should be the relevant focus of analysis. In a spatial sense, significant agglomeration economies are found but they are not predominantly contiguous in character. Spatial sprawl of growth and innovation are far from spatial homogeneous, but whether the urban and subcity-level irregularities (spatial discontinuity) are really attributable to small-scale, polycentric urban structures remains arguable (compare Anas *et al.* 1998). We conclude anyway, that urban field development, in the sense of equal conditions for growth and innovation performance over the country as often suggested in the literature should be rejected. The revealed spatial patterns of growth and innovation intensity are significantly different over heterogeneous spatial designs. The significant spatial heterogeneity designs applied, however, still predominantly emphasize urban functions. Testing for growth and innovation (knowledge) externalities should therefore focus on urban environments, as the literature predominantly takes for granted. Scale and composition effects of urban locations preferably deserve more consistent treatment though (see next section). As a result, the high degree of urbanization throughout the Netherlands (without being an 'urban field'), a conceptualization stressing *network* externalities could be applied to the observed spatial patterns. But it is *a priori* unclear whether the polycentric character of urbanization in the Netherlands contributes to this situation in any particular way. Here, a conceptual difficulty related to the type of research presented arises. Network externalities are defined in actor network frameworks. Only to a limited extent these (economic and social) networks form a print upon (urban) space. And it is the latter spatial outcomes we look (and test) for. When externalities are predominantly 'available' in urban environments (as argued above), then the polycentric character of the Dutch urban network (many medium-sized cities located close to each other) potentially contribute to ideal spatial spillover and externality circumstances. Little is actually known (yet) on the exact spatial configuration of network externalities. Acknowledging specific agglomeration circumstances of the polycentric urban landscape in the Netherlands is therefore difficult. A spatial research design using spatial regimes on relatively small spatial scales, as applied in this dissertation to US spatial (urban) externality research, would shed more light on the 'uniqueness' of the Netherlands in this respect.

Economic Heterogeneity and Life Cycles of Firms

It is important to note that when the research design of spatial externality models is equivalent to the Glaeser *et al.* (1992) framework, results are rather similar. Locational sectoral diversity (urbanization economies) rather than specialization (localization economies) is found to foster growth in a six largest location-industry OLS modeling framework, controlling for many important aspects. Two theoretically relevant additions to this modeling framework are age-determined research populations (often suggested but not much systematically explored because of data limitations) and an alternative definition of localized competition based on establishment turnover. Within the initial location-industry framework, the distinction in all and incumbent firm populations (the latter concerns firms that are and remain active throughout the research period) confirmed their independent significance, that already came to the fore in the descriptive analyses in chapters 3 and 4. Simultaneously, the alternative indicator of local competition defined as firm turnover (firm birth and death rates) is introduced, based on the recent industrial organization literature. Endogenous growth theory stresses growth potentials stemming from incumbent (representative) firms more than from new firms. From analysis in this dissertation it appears that focusing solely on these incumbent firms, the model interpretation of this local competition variable is quite different from the 'traditional' research outcomes (in which local sectoral competition is defined by average establishment size, a mainstream-economic accepted indicator of market and competitive structure). Employment growth in incumbent firms is enhanced by a *lack* of local competition, indicating that optimal competitive circumstances for these firms induce internal rent capturing. This finding is a first indication that the Jacobs-favoring research results become less robust when spatial and economic structures are modeled more adequately over relevant research populations. Changing the economic performance indicator from growth to innovation intensity (often regarded as sides of the same performance coin) in this dissertation showed considerable differences in research outcomes concerning the nature and extent of spatial externality hypotheses. While the alternative competition indicator and the distinction in age-determined research populations of firms are not exogenous to each other (they are both dependent on age-determined turnover rates of establishments), it forms an alternative for the dissatisfaction that prevails within the literature concerning indicators of local competition in economic models. We showed that theoretically justified changes in designs of research populations (growth, innovation, age-determined firm populations) and agglomeration indicators (in this case for local competition) to a large degree influence research outcomes. Life cycles of firms are thus found dominant in the interpretation of externality hypotheses, and theoretical and empirical research designs should incorporate this aspect more than is accepted in the present (representative-firm world) literature.

Modeling Spatial Scale, Contiguity and Composition

In the international literature, a strong debate prevails on the question which spatial circumstances most adequately reflect spatial externality circumstances that endogenously induce growth and innovation. Research by Henderson *et al.* (1995), Feldman and Audretsch (1999), Jaffe *et al.* (1993) and Henderson (2003) on the one hand stresses 'traditional', Marshallian industrial district theory. Glaeser *et al.* (1992), Bivand (1999) and Quigley (1998) on the other hand stress that dynamic externalities are predominantly fostered by a diversified production structure, especially in urban locations. Marshall envisioned regional development characterized by a business structure that is comprised of small, locally owned firms that make investment and production decisions locally. Dominated by conceptualizations such as localization economies (measured by local and regional specialization), clustering of vertically integrated production systems and flexible specialization, this strand of research focuses with renewed attention on own-industry proximity effects of local developments. The proximity thesis emphasized by Gleaser et al. (1992) stresses the importance of the endogenous growth and innovation context for intra-industry knowledge spillovers as the main attributes of spatial externalities. Both strands of research focus on urban and industrial agglomerations in determining (the spatial extent of) growth and innovation externalities. The theories are, despite the important role of the representative firm in neo-classical economic theory, rather ambiguous on the role of localized competition and market structure as a factor explaining growth and innovation processes. Firm- and industry-level internalization and externalization processes concerning power relations are the polarizing conceptualizations in the literature on this issue. Research outcomes in this dissertation confirm the crucial role of market structure and (localized) competition in terms of internalization and externalization conceptualizations in a spatial externalities framework.

Our research findings mainly show that no full support exists for any of these theories put forward in the agglomeration externality literature. This finding was summarized in table 8.1. Strict copying of the research design developed by Glaeser *et al.* (1992) resulted in research results similar to them concerning the role of agglomeration economies (mainly diversity) in the growth process of firms. Model extensions were explored to test whether they capture more systematically spatial (agglomeration) dependence in the employment growth and innovation data. Model extensions capturing spatial research designs focusing on localization economies (individual sector estimations and the introduction of regionalized specialization indicators) made clear that these conceptualizations indeed are important in the *same* urban context. In the light of the small size of the regions studied, the research outcomes suggest that areas with a relatively high knowledge generating capacity may expect to grow faster than others, while *proximate* spillover effects (measured by transboundary statistical relationships both in growth and innovation contexts) appear limited.

Regional localization and urbanization economies on the other hand frequently and simultaneously interfered with local growth patterns, indicating the importance of spatial multilevel analyses. It became clear that the spatial growth and innovation models are conditioned on spatial heterogeneity (*non-contiguous* spatial dependence) patterns to a large degree as well. Degrees of urbanization, labor market connectedness, physical accessibility and national zoning regimes appeared important for improving the (intra-) local and regional econometric model fit for growth and innovation equations. It is concluded that research designs based on spatial heterogeneity in addition to adjacency definitions of agglomeration are of utmost importance for adequate analysis of the (urban) growth and innovation contexts; research designs that ignore these aspects miss out relevant spatial structures beforehand. The introduction of different levels of spatial analyses in which locations, municipalities and labor market regions are nested, contributes strongly to the notion that no full support can be given for any of the (strictly local interpreted) theories put forward in the agglomeration externalities literature. The research results appear scale-dependent. The paradoxal statistical research outcomes (limited local spillovers coincide with far-reaching regional and spatial heterogenous relations) indicate that even if knowledge and economic relations stay close to home, economic (network) linkages in the growth and innovation process may spread its benefits (externalities) to other (types of) locations. This conclusion confirms space-contextual conceptualizations as presented in the geographical literature. Empirical multilevel research as presented by Harrison *et al.* (1997) reports significant effects of both localization and urbanization economies (with the latter relatively more important than the former in 'influencing' innovation). Markusen (1996) presents a contextual framework concerning Marshallian externalities and industrial districts (agglomerations) that stresses a prolonged 'stickiness' and 'spatial fix' of growth and innovation processes despite the growing 'slippery' (not pre-defined optimal and clear-cut) content of space. An exercise in distinguishing among types of 'sticky' places (as presented in Markusen 1996) illustrates that sticky places are complex products of multiple forces: corporate strategies, networks among (agglomerated) firms, industrial structure and resulting (industry and firm) internal and external market power, profit cycles and local and national politics. Some of these aspects concerning the (revisited) attention of the proximity thesis were explored econometrically in this dissertation. Due to data restrictions this exploration focuses on (spatial) outcomes and conditions of growth and innovation, rather than determining their accompanying processes. These different contextual circumstances (also remember the contingencies on innovation and growth externalities presented in figure 2.1) suggest that no blueprint for 'the' industrial district or agglomeration of economic activity can be given. Spatial discontinuities in the build-up of growth and innovation patterns occur when region-external (power) relations dominate over region-internal relations[5]. Static and dynamic urbanization and localization economies together form the contextual platform that fosters growth and innovation (Markusen 1996, p307: 'sticky mixes'). Our conclusions following the econometric analyses are that not one single spatial scale of analysis prevails over others and that spatial context (by contiguous and heterogeneous spatial research designs) makes up the complex spatial structure of dynamic externalities encountered in the Dutch data. The proposition of Paul Romer (1994, p.11) that 'many theories are consistent with the same small number of facts' should, after careful and consistent spatial model estimation, be preferably be inverted to 'not one single theory is consistent with a large number of facts'.

---

[5] This can be conceptualized using a network externalities approach, but this approach does not necessarily induce a *spatial* network in terms of spatial processes or even spatial structures. Recently, contributions by Anas *et al.* (1998), Batty (2001) and Cervero (2001) suggest that spatial form and configuration can be seen as the reflection of urban (polynucleated), entrepreneurial networks.

Appendix A

Data on Employment Dynamics

The data concerning employment dynamics in location-industries and (broad) sectors used in chapters 3 to 6 are based on several sources that have been used in combination. Several drawbacks of the original data were taken care of and limitations and clear shortcomings in the data were intensively checked and corrected. This appendix gives an overview of the data and the corrections applied. The first three sections handle with the construction of the explanatory variable in the national analysis: employment data on the local and industry and sector-specific level for 1991 and 1997. The main corrections were necessary for the employment data concerning 1991. In the first section, the original data stemming from the LISA-database are described. In the second section its verification on superior databases of aggregated employment data is explained. Thirdly, a description is given on how changes over industry coding are handled, and how industry and sector-specific data are exactly defined. The fourth section gives an overview of the sources and corrections made on the explaining variables in the national employment growth analysis. As far as the data structure used for the analysis on the regional level (South-Holland) differs from that of the national level, in the final section a brief description is given on the longitudinal data set for South-Holland in the period 1988-1997.

LISA as a Source for National Employment Data (1991-97)

The initial zip code specific data (n=3957, situation per 1-1-1998) on employment and number of firms stem from the LISA database. Final aggregation to municipalities and 3-digit zip codes within the four largest cities in the Netherlands resulted in 580 spatial observation units. Data suitable for longitudinal analysis of firm dynamics and employment change are scarce in the Netherlands, and those present are not always consistent in definitions and measurement over time and space. Combination of the datasets therefore turned out most fruitful (and time consuming) for empirical analysis. The starting point in this is the LISA-dataset. LISA is the 'National Information System of Employment'.

This database is collected by 18 (regional) organizations jointly. Its aim is to give an accurate cut through of the employment structure in Dutch industries[1]. Data are collected by a yearly questionnaire among all economic actors. Two other national data sources for employment and number of firms in the Netherlands are present: the database of the Chamber of Commerce (KVK) and the Central Business Register (ABR) of Statistics Netherlands. The database of the KVK has the important drawback that not every individual entrepreneur or government agency is obliged to subscribe in the KVK registers in the first place. Besides that, not every firm takes the effort to withdraw or change its information once bankrupt or moved. The third database, the ABR, has a main drawback for our research that it does not allow for too detailed local or industrial compositions because of its survey character.

The LISA database as source of information gives potentially the most complete and accurate picture. Besides those firms registered by the Chamber of Commerce (KVK), LISA registers entrepreneurs not obliged to subscribe in the KVK and governmental institutions. The strengths of the other data sources can be used to verify the LISA data even further, as we have done in combining the three sources in our research. In this research we do not distinguish a threshold for part-time jobs in the data. The LISA data used in this research are provided by the Spatial Planning Agency and are consistent with the Living Environment database (Woonmilieu database, WMD)[2]. The data concerning 1997 are judged as fairly accurate on the employment situation on 4-digit zip code level in the Netherlands. The original data concerning 1991 are incomplete in several respects. The corrections made within the Woonmilieu database project (see WMD 1999, p.31) only partly solved these deficiencies. Therefore, additional corrections and verifications were made upon these data, described in the next section (see Van Oort 2002a for a detailed explanation of the data corrections).

Verification on Superior Aggregated Data

The first replacement in the dataset concerns agriculture. LISA does not register this industry accurately, neither do the CBS and KVK databases. The poor quality of this industry in the data usually urges researchers to leave this industry out of their analyses. We estimated the number of firms and employees for this industry separately. Municipal data concerning firms and employed persons in agriculture

---

[1] The LISA-dataset does not turn out to be nationwide and longitudinal consistent for the data concerning 1991 and 1997. Administrative changes in registration occurred in the regions of Amsterdam, Gooi- en Vechtstreek, North-Holland North, Haaglanden (Delft) and Drechtsteden. The latter is not formerly represented by one of the 18 LISA-participants and because of its questionable quality excluded from analyses of the South-Holland data. We therefore preferable speak of the South-Holland research area.

[2] The initial 2-digit zip code level LISA data on firms and employment for 1991 and 1997 were provided by the National Spatial Planning Agency (RPD) in The Hague. In the Living Environment Database (WMD), provided by ABF Research in Delft, six broad industries are available per 4-digit zip code for 1991 and 1997 (see Brouwer and Willems 1999). The latter data were used as (one of the) forcing conditions on the localized LISA data because of their superior quality on the (broad) sectoral level.

were verified (see for handling changes in municipal boundaries section A3) and simulated into 4-digit zip codes (that aggregate to municipalities present in 1998) by using the surface of land in use by agriculture and horticulture[3]. Those localities within a municipality containing most arable land are supposed to contain most firms (farms) and employment. The distribution of employment resulting from this estimation showed a spatial correlation with the original distribution of employment in the LISA data of 0.87 (n=3957), although the number of employees per municipality on average tripled in absolute terms. The size effect therefore did not coincide with a changing *spatial* distribution of the agricultural employment.

Five more conditioning sources of data were used for verifying the 1991 LISA-data. First the data were verified on municipal distribution according to a data set from the Chamber of Commerce. This dataset was acquired, maintained and corrected by the former Economic Geographical Institute (EGI) of the Erasmus University Rotterdam (see Bleichrodt *et al.* 1992 for a description and commentary on this database). These micro-data were used to verify the spatial distribution of employment among municipalities. The EGI data concern 1990 and have SBI74 industries as measuring units (see section A3). Second, the regional distribution of employment as present in CBS-statistics has been taken as a solid point of reference[4]. Third, for non-basic industries (those activities that depend on carrying capacity of population, like retailing and caring services), the distribution over 2-digitindustries in 1997 was used as reference when endogenous growth figures within this industry turned out not plausible[5]. Fourth, the distribution of employment over six broad industries per 4-digit zip code as distinguished in Brouwer and Willems (1999) was used as forcing condition as well. Finally, the data concerning localities in South-Holland were verified according to the longitudinal data available in the BRZ Firm Register South-Holland (see section A5).

---

[3] Sources: *Municipal data for agriculture and horticulture in the Netherlands*, Landbouwtelling (LT) LEI/CBS (1991/1997). The definition of employed persons in this survey comprises family workers and regular but non-family workers in this industry. The percentage of land surface in use by agriculture and horticulture per 4-digit zip code stems from the National Soil Statistic (Bodemstatistiek, CBS, 1993).

[4] The statistics are RARBON/JWL (Annual Employment and Wages Survey) and AR (Labor Accounts) for 1991 and 1997, concerning 40 COROP (nodal) regions in the Netherlands (for descriptions and definitions see Leunis and Verhage 1999). Their longitudinal robustness is an advantage in its own right, although the 1991 data had to be transformed because of the change in industry codes in 1993 (see section A3). As the LISA-data applied in our research, no threshold for part-time work is distinguished in the CBS-data.

[5] For certain regions, small firms are misrepresented in the original 1991 LISA-file. This concerned especially two groups of firms: small retailing/free practitioners and small business services. While the latter was 'corrected' by means of the Chamber of Commerce micro data (KVK), the former is not represented well in the KVK data. The deviating growth patterns of these industries was noticed when observing 4-digit zip code maps for all 57 2-digit growth rates. Therefore we used the distribution in 1997 over particular industries within the general development in non-basic industries between 1991-1997 (together constituting one of the six broad industries applied in Brouwer and Willems 1999). This hypothesized that the *subdivision* over certain consumer services did not change alongside the general development of these services. For the region of North-Holland North, corrections were further needed for business services in 1991 (SBI93-codes 67, 70, 71 and 74).

Industry Definitions

In 1993 the Statistics Netherlands (CBS) changed the standard industrial classification for business and firms (into SBI93). The classification prior to 1993 is referred to as the 1974-classification (SBI74)[6]. The SBI93 classification allows optimal comparison to the ISIC(3)-level and NACE industrial classifications. Table A1 gives an overview of the 49 industries distinguished and used in this book. A key of fractions from 2-digit SBI74 to 2-digit SBI93 has been used in this study for transforming the 1991 LISA- and KVK-data, both administrating in SBI74-industries. This key has been constructed making use of two datasets: the micro-data for South-Holland concerning the period 1988-1997 (10,685,912 employed persons) as described in Van Oort *et al.* (2000) and a 3-digit data set for the province of North-Brabant in 1996 (854,693 employed persons)[7]. From these two databases fractions were distracted with a minimum threshold of 2.5%[8].

It is *a priori* useful to identify a classification of economic activities as meant with neither too many separate industries nor too little, taking into account theoretical considerations of plausibility and functionality. Many hypotheses concerning economic growth and innovation intensity (as central in this dissertation) are more appropriate for certain sectors than for other. The industrial classification of the Dutch and the South-Holland data used in this study is initially very detailed (see table A1). This makes it possible to apply the concept of location-industries as developed by Glaeser *et al.* (1992), as well as industrial branch classifications for broader sectors. A sectoral distinction initially applied in this study stems from Louter (1992) and Louter and Van Oort (1992). The classification consists of a typology of sixteen complementary economic sectors that can be distinguished in modern western economies. For distinguishing sixteen types of industrial activities, societal linkages between the different industrial branches are regarded crucial. Economic activities contribute to material and immaterial welfare of people by performing tasks of producing and delivering goods and services by means of transforming labour and capital into clusters of the production process (Heilbronner 1962, Malecki 1997). Besides obvious production activities, distribution, co-ordinating and facilitating activities can be distinguished.

---

[6] Initial source and explanation of the transformation SBI74 into SBI93: Statistics Netherlands (CBS), *Standaard Bedrijfs Indeling 1993. Overzicht en schakelschema's.* Although all source and destination codes are listed in this publication, no fractions concerning the transformations are published.

[7] The data for North-Brabant have been used in co-operation with Peter Louter and Siwert de Groot (TNO Inro, Delft).

[8] Because of the complex character of split-up, special attention was given to basic metal industry (SBI74 33), electronic industry (36), transportation industry (37) and aviation (75).

Table A1   **2-digit industries (49) in employment data[1] and aggregation into sixteen[2] detailed and four[3] broad sectors**

01	Agriculture & fishery	RA	X		40	Electr. & water supply	PI	D
11	Natural resources	RM	X		45	Building & construction	PI	D
15	Food & beverage ind.	PC	I		51	Wholesale trade	DA	D
16	Tobacco industry	PC	I		52	Retail	CA	C
17	Textile industry	PL	I		55	Hospitality industry	WL	C
18	Clothing industry	PL	I		60	Distribution over land	DP	D
19	Leather goods industry	PL	I		61	Distribution over water	DP	D
20	Timber industry	PL	I		62	Distribution by air	DP	D
21	Paper industry	PC	I		63	Distribution services	DP	D
22	Publishing & reprod.	IK	P		64	Telecom. and post	PI	D
23	Oil processing industry	PP	I		65	Banks	IC	P
24	Chemical industry	PP	I		66	Financial services	IC	P
25	Synthetic & rubber ind.	PC	I		70	Real estate intermediates	IK	P
26	Glass and ceramic ind.	PC	I		71	Movable est. intermed.	IK	P
27	Primary metal industry	PP	I		72	Computer-services	IK	P
28	Metal prod. industry	PL	I		73	Research and developm.	IK	P
29	Machinery industry	PK	I		74	Other business services	IK	P
30	Computer industry	PK	I		75	Government	II	C
31	Electronics industry	PK	I		80	Education	IE	C
32	Audio & telecom. Ind.	PK	I		85	Health care	WH	C
33	Medical instr. industry	PK	I		90	Environmental services	WH	C
34	Car industry	PK	I		91	Unions (employe- e/r)	II	C
35	Transport ind. (- cars)	PK	I		92	Culture, sports & recr.	WL	C
36	Furniture industry	PL	I		93	Personal services	WL	C
37	Recycling industry	PL	I					

[1] SBI93-coding.

[2] PL= Labor-intensive production, PC= Capital-intensive production, PP= Knowledge-intensive process industry, PK= Knowledge-intensive production, DA= Administrative distribution, DP= Physical distribution, IC= Information activities: coordinating, IK= Information activities: knowledge services, RM= Resource-based activities: minerals, RA= Resource-based activities: agriculture, CA= Consumer-based activities, II= Information infrastructure: institutions, IE= Information infrastructure: education, PI= Physical infrastructure, WH= Well-being: health care, WL= Well-being: leisure.

[3] I = Industrial Production, D = Distribution Activities, P = Producer Services, C = Consumer Services, X = not assigned.

This production-function kind of distinguishing of related activities not only holds on individual firm level, but also and especially at industry, national and regional levels of analyses (Caballero and Lyons 1990)[9]. Table A1 shows how the originally 49 2-digit industries of the Dutch and South-Holland data have been aggregated into respectively 16 and 4 sectors of economic production. The 16 categories are used in exploratory spatial dependence analysis in chapter 4. From this analysis, and from previous literature on Dutch employment dynamics (especially Louter

---

[9] In the economic-geographical literature, several attempts for categorizing economic activities according to their function in a societal context have been made. Most notably are Törnqvist's (1978) division in economic functions, Dicken's (1992) distinction in production chains and system of linked production chains and Porter's (1990) value chain and value system concepts.

1997) it becomes clear that econometric spatial agglomeration analyses on the national and regional level (in chapters 5 and 6) should focus on four distinctive (broad) sectors (that can be aggregated from both the 16 sectors and 49 industries): production activities, distribution activities, producer services and consumer services.

Production activities are aggregated from four sub-categories. The distinction in these four appears initially important for especially the innovation (R&D) analyses (chapter 7) that are predominantly industrial in character. Two dimensions are used to categorize the four initial industrial branches: their respective degree of knowledge- and capital intensity (Louter 1992). First, labour-intensive production shows low scores on either two indicators. Firms in these industries are characterised as traditional and craft oriented. Second, capital-intensive industries transform large amounts of physical inputs into products, using large-scale and capital intensive production processes. Usually, firms in these categories are large space consumers and dependent on physical delivery of inputs (and thus infrastructure). Third, knowledge-intensive process industry has the same characteristics but at the same time has a large tendency towards technological dependency and innovation. The petrochemical industries in the Rotterdam harbour area form important examples of this category of firms in the South-Holland region. Fourth, knowledge-intensive production incorporates modern, medium- to high-technology firms in which knowledge, qualified employees and research and development form important ingredients for the production process.

Distribution activities move goods and people from one part of the production process to other parts. Optimal logistics enable efficient physical distribution. Wholesale trade activities initially are distinguished separately because they also comprise office-bound activities that in general consume less space. The category of activities labelled physical infrastructure, comprising building, construction and exploitation activities, including energy and water supply, is also gathered in the distribution activities sector.

Within *producer service activities* several sub-sectors are initially distinguished. Information activities mainly focus on the generation, gathering, handling, transformation and provision of information, used in other sectors. One part of these activities comprises typical co-ordinating activities (banks, insurance and head office locations of multi-establishment firms). Other parts focus on knowledge services as such, mainly comprising business services, research and development agencies and ICT-service firms. Information activities show in general an urban locational preference because of their dependency on (concentrations of) other firms and customers.

Consumer-based services contain several sub-sectors, the largest being retail firms. Those firms are by tradition naturally located in or near large concentrations of population. Further elements of consumer services are activities that concentrate on the information infrastructure: institutions (governmental and employee/ers organisations) and education. Central government activities in the Netherlands are concentrated in the region of The Hague. Universities in the Netherlands are located in a few larger cities[10]. High-schools are concentrated in provincial capital cities. Consumer service activities in the category well-being finally comprise of health-care and leisure activities. Several empirical studies revealed the growing economic importance of consumer services in the Netherlands (especially Klomp 1996). A remaining category comprises *resource-based activities*: agriculture and mineral based resource firms (gas and oil winning). This category of activities is not assigned to any of the four broad sectors.

Construction of Explaining Variables

Most of the explaining variables are related to the data on employment and firms described in the previous sections. The variables concerning specialization, local diversification, national growth rates, competition and employment stock at the beginning of the period are constructed from these data (see Van Oort 2002a). The dynamics of population was determined between 1991 and 1997 using the CBS zip code database, with verification to the CBS municipal aggregates[11]. The index and dummy variable of 4-digit zip codes characterized by more than average issuing of new business premises is constructed making use of the IBIS database (RPD 1998). The functional distinctions urban and non-urban in conjunction with living, working or mixed localities are constructed from the WMD-database (WMD 1999). The distinction urban-non urban is based on the density of addresses as registered by Statistics Netherlands (CBS), using a potential function for its final estimation. The distinction in activity dominance per locality is based on the employment and residential functions, as well as the provision and accessibility of (daily) services (retail-shops, recreation, health-care, administrative functions and public transportation). This indicator bears strong resemblance to the Beale indicator of urbanization in the US (access to diverse economic and social resources) as used in Harrison *et al.* (1997). The measurement of urban form by occupation functions using GIS-facilities as applied in this research resembles the procedures as outlined by Longley and Mesev (2000). Accessibility of locations is measured by physical distances to highway-enters and exits as well as train stations. All variables directly or indirectly embodying physical distances were constructed making use of AtlasGIS, ArcInfo and ArcView geographical information systems, as well as internal calculations (of distance and weight matrices) in the statistical package SpaceStat (Anselin 1995a).

---

[10] Amsterdam, Delft, Eindhoven, Enschede, Groningen, Leiden, Maastricht, Nijmegen, Rotterdam, Tilburg, Utrecht and Wageningen.

[11] For 1991 the municipal aggregates were distributed along the zip codes according to the detailed 1993 CBS distribution of population (1993 is the first year of publication of population data on the detailed 4-digit zip code level).

The BRZ Longitudinal Micro-data for South-Holland (1988-97)

The data used for the analysis in South-Holland stem from a longitudinal data set containing all establishments with employees present in the province during the period 1988-1997, the Firm Register South-Holland (BRZ)[12]. Figure A.1 shows the research area, decomposed in zip code (416), municipality (69) and registration area (3) spatial units. Movement of firms is traceable only within the three registration areas. Inputs for this data set are information provided by the Chamber of Commerce, insurance companies and industrial sector associates. This information is checked and modified in many ways, resulting in a questionnaire of the BRZ sent every year to all addresses. The response of this questionnaire is after intensive checking and recalling finally 96%. Besides this questionnaire, the register is updated and validated by visual verification of the establishments, a region-specific registration of newspaper advertisements (announcements of bankruptcy and newly established firms) and the telephone and Golden-Guide books and CDs. In cases of doubt on information on establishments, verification by time-series analysis and telephonic checking were applied.

Every establishment is traceable through time and space (within the three jurisdictions of observation) by an individual identification number. The establishment data most useful for our study are: unique identification number, zip code (4-digit, allows aggregation to higher spatial levels of observation), SBI74-code (4-digit), SBI93-code (5-digit, comparable with SIC-codes), year of observation (1988-1997 if present) and employment by gender and hours of work (full-time/part-time). The results of the questionnaires are (made) consistent for the period of observation in terms of employment, exact location and five-digit activity code (SBI93). Despite this relatively high level of initial accuracy, corrections needed to be made for changes over time in the composition of the three main jurisdictions of observation within the observation area, changes in municipal boundaries and alternative codes due to changing industry coding. As with the national dataset described in the previous sections, data were scaled according to CBS and KVK data on national employment levels. The data of the BRZ form input for most of the explanatory variables in the regional analyses. The analysis concerning surviving (incumbent) firms (1988-1997) as well as the spatial-industry specific volatility indices of firm dynamics, both explicitly make use of the longitudinal character of the dataset.

---

[12] In the analysis we will simultaneously use the terms establishment and firm, while only the former is actually observed. The initial micro-data were provided by Ron Houterman, Gabriël Janssen (Province of South-Holland) and Chris Nonnekes (BRZ).

Figure A1　　The research area of South-Holland decomposed by zip code (416), municipality (69) and registration area (3)

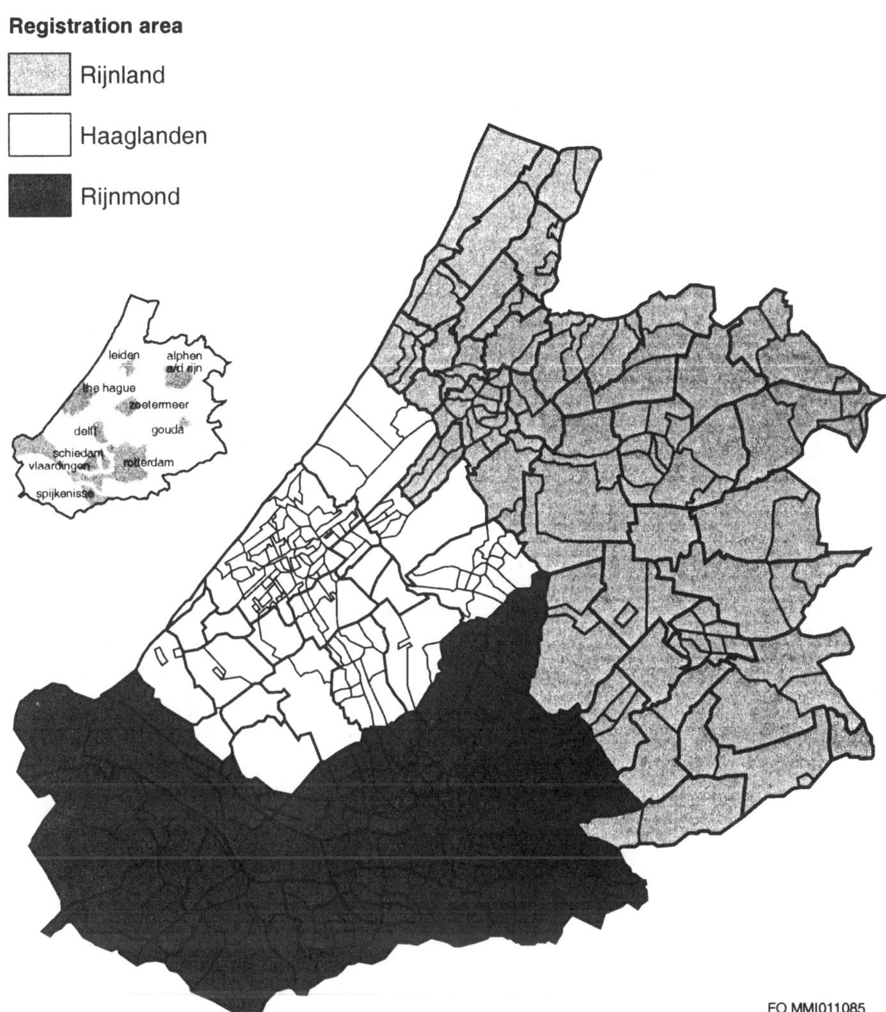

The explaining variables not stemming from the BRZ data set itself are constructed as a regional subset of the national data sources (see section A4). Additionally, the variables on *REGWAGE* concern a regionalized version of wage levels per 2-digit industry, based on national economic accounts (CBS 1999c). This statistic allows a spatial detail that is more refined than the *WAGE* variables, which are industry-specific but national in character. The industry-specific *REGWAGE* variable has been calculated for 40 so-called COROP-regions in the Netherlands. These regions function as labor market areas with one relatively central place and numerous suburban and rural municipalities surrounding it. See for recent research on labor market relations on this spatial level Van der Knaap *et.al.* (1995). The South-Holland research region comprises five of the 40 national COROP-regions: agglomeration Leiden, the Haaglanden region, the Delft region, the Green Heart region and the Rijnmond Region. Figure A2a shows the average regional variations in average wage level in the period 1988-1997 over the 40 regions. Figure A2b shows the increase in wage levels over the 40 regions in the period 1988-1997[13]. It should be noticed that the distribution of observations over the classes assigned indicates little variation[14]. The average regional wage level circles closely around the national average in both 1988 and 1996 (43.544 and 58.456 respectively), and the growth rates circles around the national (1.324%) growth rate[15]. This indicates that the absolute magnitude of wage levels is of little (spatial-) institutional economic importance in the Dutch regional labour market. If any regional patterns come to the surface, it is that more urbanized regions (especially in the Randstad region) show slightly higher average wage levels, and that the Intermediate Zone of Gelderland and Noord-Brabant shows slightly higher growth rates in the period 1988-1997. Over industries the variation in wage levels and growth in wage levels differs to a much larger degree, the averaged regional patterns presented in figure A2 level out the developments in the 49 individual industries.

---

[13] Corrected for average price developments.

[14] A quintile division (5 classes of 8 observations) has been applied.

[15] Wage levels in thousands of guilders, growth rate is wage level 1997 divided by wage level 1988.

Figure A2 **(a) Wage levels in 40 regions in the Netherlands (average 1988-1997) and (b) change in average wage levels (1988-1997)**

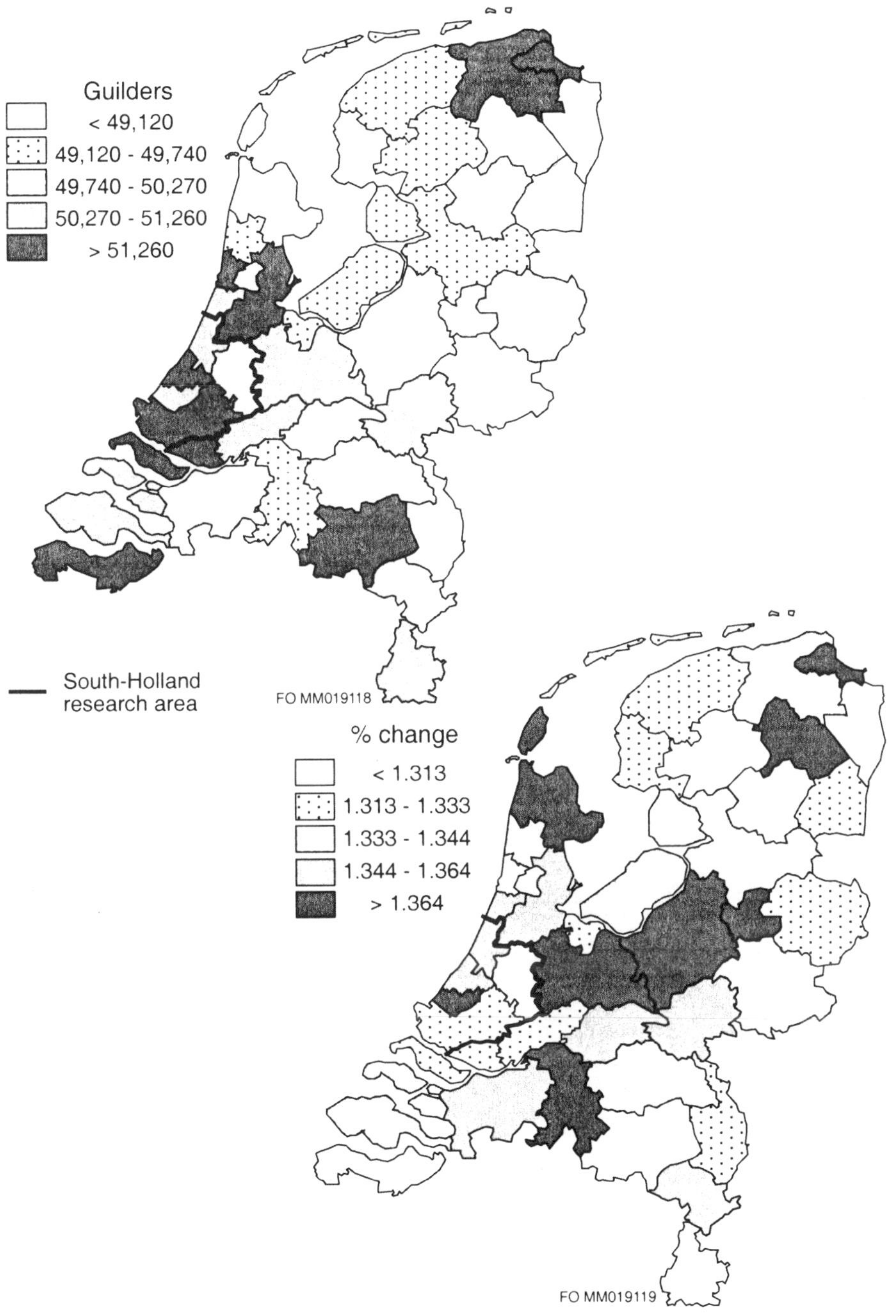

Appendix B

Data on Innovation Intensity

Description of the Senter Database

The analyses on innovation intensity in chapters 4 and 7 are based on firm-level wage expenditures spent on research and development activities. These data stem from the so-called Senter R&D database on technology subsidies. Senter is a governmental organization that collects, guards, checks and analyses all project based subsidies that the ministry of Economic Affairs grants to individual firms. For 1999 in total around 52,000 projects, concentrated in approximately 12,000 firms, are present in the Senter database. Of all projects, the following data are registered: the wage expenditures concerning R&D activities[1], the exact 6-digit zip code location of the establishment where the project is carried out, the SBI activity code of the firm (see appendix A), the technology (BSI) code of the project, the total wage costs of the firm and the number of employees of the firm. The BSI technology codes are presented in table B1. The original Senter dataset is build up by data concerning four individual subsidies:

(1) The WBSO subsidy (Law on Stimulating Research and Development). This concerns a fiscal arrangement for firms and entrepreneurs that apply R&D wage costs. These costs can be deducted from wage-tax regulations. This category of subsidies makes up most of the Senter database. A thorough economic analysis of this subsidy is in Cornet (2001). This is actually the sole subsidy used in this study.

(2) The BTS subsidy (Firm-level Technological Cooperation). This is generic subsidizing arrangement for firms and research institutions (also universities) co-operating in R&D. Projects have to be marked 'fundamental' for a minimum of 50 percent.

(3) The EET program (Program on Economy, Ecology and Technology). EET is a joint program of the ministry of Housing, Spatial Planning & the Environment and the ministry of Economic Affairs. It stimulates large-scale projects that in the long term potentially contribute to a more environmental friendly and durable economy.

(4) The SMO program (Resolution on Subsidies on Maritime Research). This resolution aims at knowledge exchange and spillovers between firms operating in the maritime sector. At least 50 percent of project expenditures needs to be subcontracted to non-commercial institutions.

---

[1] Senter calculates average wage expenditures for projects of the self-employed based on the R&D hours given and the average R&D-wage.

Table B1   BSI-technology fields (aggregated into 5 classes[1])

Measuring and instruments	2	Military	3
Sciences (mathematics)	5	Production technology	3
Chemical science	1	Transportation	3
Biology and geology	5	Construction	3
Medical	5	Minerals	1
Environment & safety	5	Materials	3
Agriculture	4	Metallurgy	3
Food processing	4	Chemical technology	1
Energy	3	Paper and textile	5
Electronics	3	Consumer products	5
Information & communication	2	Administrative	5
Computer	2	Social sciences	5
Engineering	3		

[1] 1=chemical technology, 2=communication and computer technology (ict), 3=production technology, 4=agricultural and food technology, 5=scientific technology.

Before analyzing the data, they were intensively checked and screened on irregularities. Corrections and additional estimates ware introduced concerning (Schmitz and Heijs 2001, p.17) firms having a *total* wage sum less than 5000 guilders a year; firms with an average wage level *per person* higher than 500,000 guilders; firms where the R&D wage sum exceeded the total firm-level wage sum; firms with wage information data stemming from 1997 or before (corrected for inflation); the determining of exact location of R&D activities in multi-plant firms; non-existent zip code registrations; SBI activity codification and numbers of employed persons. In 1999 for the total amount of 4,179 million guilders on R&D were subsidized. This concern R&D related wage costs that were deducted from tax payments. The CBS-database estimates the total R&D wage sum in 1999 on 4,492 million guilders[2].

Almost half of all R&D wage costs are spend in the top five sectors: chemical industry (14% of all wages), electronic industry (12%), machinery industry (12%), food-processing industry (8%) and metal products industry (7%). 85 percent of the R&D wage sums in the Senter database are attributable to industrial industries and approximately 15% in the service industries (Schmitz and Heijs 2001, p.19). Besides the sectoral industry-code, the Senter database administrates the dominant technology code relevant for the project. Partly, the industry and technology codes can be unified. In chemical industries for instance, the R&D expenditures are mainly

---

[2] Including material investments in R&D, Statistics Netherlands (CBS) estimates total R&D expenditures in 1998 in the Netherlands on 8,199 million guilders (CBS 1999b).

on chemical technologies (in total accounting for 12% in the R&D wage sum). A major difference though concerns the information, communication and technology activities (ICT). In terms of industry, this sector only plays a minor role, but as a leading technology it comes second. Many industries thus use ICT in R&D activities. Finally, it should be emphasized that the 4,179 million guilders wage sum on R&D activities is biased towards relatively large firms. Approximately 37 percent of the R&D wages is to be found in firms with more than 1,000 employees. Approximately 45 percent is in small and medium-sized firms (less than 250 employees). This distribution is important in the sense that it partly determines the geography of R&D expenditures in the Netherlands (Schmitz and Heijs 2001, p.20).

Comparability with Other Dutch Sources of Innovation Data

Research into the spatial distribution of innovative firms in the Netherlands has a longstanding tradition. In general, three mainstream groups of publications on spatial R&D in the Netherlands can be distinguished. First are the publications by SEO and Kleinknecht and others based on questionnaires. Several contributions in Molle (1985) concentrate on R&D presence and development in spatial contexts, thus being forerunners of this strand of literature. For the ministry of Economic Affairs, Kleinknecht and others investigated the spatial dimension of research and development in the Netherlands by means of (SEO) questionnaires in 1987, 1992 and 1997 (Kleinknecht 1987, Kleinknecht and Poot 1992, Poot *et al.* 1997, Ouwersloot and Rietveld 2000). The second source of information on spatial innovation patterns more recently stems from Statistics Netherlands (CBS), who published on regional innovation patterns in the Netherlands based on an innovation questionnaire (CBS 1999a, 1999b). A third source of the geography of innovation stems from indirect measurement of innovation and technological potential. Industries that in general are found to be innovative and R&D intensive are investigated on their relative specialization and growth in spatial contexts. As such, only share (and not differential) effects of industrial composition and its growth patterns are determining in this strand of research. A related indirect, albeit different, research setup refers to the spatial distribution of new product announcements (Brouwer *et al.* 1999).

The Senter database has some advantages over these other three sources of R&D information (Schmitz and Heijs 2001, p. 12-13). First, the data do not stem from questionnaires (with restricted population characteristics), but from all actual projects subsidized by the ministry of Economic Affairs. All projects are individually validated, and therefore probably more robust and reliable than questionnaire data. Second, the initial detail of the information at the micro (project) level is a real advantage. Information on the geographical position of the establishment (on 6-digit zip code level) and the BSI and SBI classifications are extremely detailed. Reliable aggregations from the basic data therefore can (and were) constructed. A disadvantage of the Senter database is the emphasis on industrial innovation (compared to the service-based innovation also included in the two questionnaire sources). Also, innovative R&D activity carried out without subsidies from the ministry of Economic Affairs are possible[3]. In general it should be emphasized that the Senter database is *complementary* to earlier studies by the Kleinknecht and others research groups and Statistics Netherlands (CBS). The overview of CBS research results can be complemented with detailed spatial insights from the Senter database.

---

[3] Since all requests for fiscal tax deductions concerning R&D wages are usually met, there is a very strong incentive for firms to apply for the deduction.

Bibliography

Abdel-Rahman, H. (1988), 'Product differentiation, monopolistic competition and city size', *Journal of Urban Economics*, 18, pp. 69-86.

Acemoglu, D. (1996), 'A microfoundation for social increasing returns in human capital accumulation', *The Quarterly Journal of Economics*, vol. 111, pp. 779-804.

Acs, Z.J., D.B. Audretsch and M.P. Feldman (1994), 'R&D spillovers and innovative activity', *Managerial and Decision Economics*, 15, pp. 131-38.

Acs, Z.J. (2002), *Innovation and the growth of cities*, Cheltenham: Edward Elgar.

Ades, A.F. and E.L. Glaeser (1995), 'Trade and circuses: explaining urban giants', *The Quarterly Journal of Economics*, 110, pp. 195-258.

Aghion, P. and P. Howitt (1998), *Endogenous growth theory*, Cambridge, Mass.: The MIT Press.

Alker, H.R. (1969), 'A typology of ecological fallacies', in M. Dogan and S. Rokkan (eds.), *Quantitative ecological analysis in the social sciences*, Cambridge Mass.: The MIT Press, pp. 69-86.

Alonso-Villar, O. and J.M. Chamorro-Rivas (2001), 'How do producer services affect the location of manufacturing firms? The role of information accessibility', *Environment and Planning*, 33, pp.1621-42.

Alperovich, G. and J. Deutsch (2002), 'An application of a switching regime regression to the study of urban structure', *Papers in Regional Science*, 81, pp.83-98.

Amin, A. (1999), 'An institutionalist perspective on regional economic development', *International Journal of Urban and Regional Research*, pp. 365-78.

Amin, A. and N. Thrift (2002), *Cities. Reimagining the urban*, Cambridge: Polity Press.

Amin, A. and N. Thrift (1992), 'Neo-Marshallian nodes in global networks', *International Journal of Urban and Regional Research*, 16, pp. 571-87.

Anas, A., R. Arnott and K.A. Small (1998), 'Urban spatial structure', *Journal of Economic Literature*, 36, pp. 1426-64.

Anselin, L. (1988), *Spatial econometrics: methods and models*, Dordrecht: Kluwer.

Anselin, L. (1995a), *SpaceStat. A software program for the analysis of spatial data (version 1.80)*, Morgantown: Regional Research Institute, West Virginia University.

Anselin, L. (1995b), 'Local indicators of spatial association - LISA', *Geographical Analysis*, 27, pp. 93-115.

Anselin, L. (1996), 'The Moran scatterplot as an ESDA tool to assess local instability in spatial association', in M. Fisher, H.J. Scholten and D. Unwin (eds.), *Spatial analytical perspectives on GIS*, London: Taylor & Francis.

Anselin, L., A.K. Bera, R. Florax and M.J. Yoon (1996), 'Simple diagnostic tests for spatial dependence', *Regional Science and Urban Economics*, 26, pp. 77-104.

Anselin, L., A. Varga and Z.J. Acs (1997), 'Local geographic spillovers between university research and high technology innovations', *Journal of Urban Economics*, 42, pp. 422-48.

Anselin, L., A. Varga and Z.J. Acs (2000), 'Geographic and sectoral characteristics of academic knowledge externalities', *Papers in Regional Science*, 79, pp.435-43.

Arbia, G. (2001), 'Modelling the geography of economic activities on a continuous space', *Papers in Regional Science*, 80, pp.411-24.

Argewal, R. and D.B. Audretsch (1999), 'The two views of small firms in industry dynamics: a reconciliation', *Economics Letters*, 62, pp.245-51.

Arrow, K.J. (1962), 'The economic implications of learning by doing', *Review of Economic Studies*, 29, pp. 155-73.

Arthur, B. (1989), 'Competing technologies, increasing returns and lock-in by historical events', *The Economic Journal*, 99, pp. 116-31.

Arthur, B. (1994), *Increasing returns and path dependence in the economy*, Ann Arbor: The University of Michigan Press.

Ashcroft, B. and J.H. Love (1996), Firm births and employment change in the British counties: 1981-89, *Papers in Regional Science*, 75, pp. 483-500.

Atzema, O. and J. Lambooy (1999), 'Economic evolution within the Netherlands' polycentric urban system', in E. Wever, ed., *Cities in perspective I. Economy, planning and the environment*, Assen: Van Gorcum, pp. 11-28.

Audretsch, D.B. (1998), 'Agglomeration and the location of economic activity' *Oxford Review of Economic Policy*, 14, pp.18-29.

Audretsch, D.B. and M.P. Feldman (1996), 'R&D spillovers and the geography of innovation and production', *The American Economic Review*, 86, pp. 630-40.

Audretsch, D.B., L. Klomp and A.R. Thurik (1999), 'Do services differ from manufacturing? The post-entry performance of firms in Dutch services', in D. B. Audretsch and R. Thurik (eds.), *Innovation, industry evolution and employment*, Cambridge: University Press.

Bailey, T. and A.C. Gatrell (1995), '*Interactive spatial data analysis*', Harlow: Longman.

Baldwin, R.E. and R. Forslid (1997), *The core-periphery model and endogenous growth*, CEPR Working Paper no. 1749, London.

Baptista, R. (2000), 'Do innovations diffuse faster within geographical clusters?', *International Journal of Industrial Organisation*, 18, pp. 515-35.

Baptista, R. and P. Swann (1998), 'Do firms in clusters innovate more?', *Research Policy*, 27, pp. 525-40.

Barnes, T.J. and M.S. Gertler (1999), *The new industrial geography: regions, regulation and institutions*, London: Routledge.

Barro, R.J. and X. Sala-i-Martin (1995), *Economic growth*, Cambridge, Mass.: The MIT Press.

Barkley, D., M. Henry and S. Bao (1996), 'Identifying spread versus backwash effects in regional economic areas: a density functions approach', *Land Economics*, 72, pp. 336-57.

Batten, D.F. (1995), 'Network cities: creative urban agglomerations for the 21st century', *Urban Studies*, 32, pp. 313-27.

Batty, M. (2001), 'Polynucleated urban landscapes', *Urban Studies*, 38, pp.635-55.

Beardsell, M. and V. Henderson (1999), 'Spatial evolution of the computer industry in the USA, *European Economic Review*, 43, pp. 431-56.

Bennett, R.J. and C. Smith (2002), 'The influence of location and distance on the supply of business advice', *Environment and Planning A*, 34, pp. 251-70.

Berliant, M. and H. Konishi (2000), 'The endogenous formation of a city: population agglomeration and market places in a location-specific production economy', *Regional Science and Urban Economics*, 30, pp.289-324.

Birch, D.L. (1979), *The job generation process*, Cambridge Mass.: University Press.

Bivand, R.S. (1999), 'Dynamic externalities and regional manufacturing development in Poland', *Tijdschrift voor Economische en Sociale Geografie*, 90, pp.347-62.

Black, D. and J.V. Henderson (1999a), 'Spatial evolution of population and industry in the United States', *American Economic Review*, 89, pp. 321-27.

Black, D. and J.V. Henderson (1999b), 'A theory of urban growth', *Journal of Political Economy*, 107, pp. 252-84.

Blackley, P.R. (1985), 'The demand for industrial sites in a metropolitan area: theory, empirical evidence and policy implications', *Journal of Urban Economics*, 17, pp. 247-61.

Blanchard, O.J. and L.F. Katz (1992), 'Regional evolutions', *Brookings Papers on Economic Activity*, pp. 1-76.

Bleichrodt, H., P.J. Louter and W.F. Sleegers (1992), *Jonge bedrijven in Nederland*, EGI-onderzoekspublikatie 02, Rotterdam: Erasmus Universiteit.

Boarnet, M.G. (1994), 'The monocentric model and employment location', *Journal of Urban Economics*, 36, pp. 79-97.

Boggs, J.S. and N.M. Rantisi (2003), 'The 'relational turn' in economic geography', *Journal of Economic Geography*, 3, pp.109-16.

Boschma, R.A. and J.G. Lambooy (1999), 'Evolutionary economics and economic geography', *Journal of Evolutionary Economics*, 9, pp. 411-29.

Bostic, R.W., J.S. Gans and S. Stern (1997), 'Urban productivity and factor growth in the late nineteenth century', *Journal of Urban Economics*, 41, pp. 38-55.

Boudeville, J.R. (1966), *Problems of regional economic planning*, Edinburgh: University Press.

Von Böventer, E. (1975), 'Regional growth theory', *Urban Studies*, 12, pp. 1-29.

Braczyk, H.J., P. Cooke and M. Heidenreich (eds.) (1998), *Regional innovation systems. The role of governance in a globalized world*, London: UCL Press.

Bradburd, R.M. and D.R. Ross (1989), 'Can small firms find and defend strategic niches?', *Review of Economics and Statistics*, 71, pp. 258-62.

Brakman, S., H. Garretsen and C. van Marrewijk (2001), *An introduction to geographical economics*, Cambridge: University Press.

Breschi, S. (2000), 'The geography of innovation: a cross-sector analysis', *Regional Studies*, 34, pp. 213-29.

Breschi, S. and F. Lissoni (2001), 'Localised knowledge spillovers vs. innovative milieux: knowledge "tacitness" reconsidered', *Papers in Regional Science*, 80, pp.255-73.

Bröcker, J. (1989), 'How to eliminate certain defects of the potential formula', *Environment and Planning A*, 21, pp. 817-30.

Broersma, L. and P. Gautier (1997), 'Job creation and job destruction by small firms: an empirical investigation for the Dutch manufacturing sector', *Small Business Economics*, 9, pp. 211-24.

Brouwer, E., H. Budil-Nadvornikova and A. Kleinknecht (1999), 'Are urban agglomerations a better breeding place for product innovation? An analysis of new product announcements', *Regional Studies*, 33, pp. 541-49.

Brouwer, J., L. Mattemaker and H. Heijda (2001), *Ruimtevraag wonen, werken en voorzieningen*, Delft: ABF Onderzoek.

Brouwer, J. and J. Willems (1999), *Ruimtelijke transformaties van productiemilieus*, Delft: ABF Onderzoek.

Brown, L.A. (1981), *Innovation diffusion: a new perspective*, London: Methuen.

Brown, L.A. and J. Holmes (1971), 'The delimitation of functional regions, nodal regions and hierarchies by functional distance approaches', *Journal of Regional Science*, 11, pp. 57-71.

Brueckner, J.K., J.F. Thisse and Y. Zenou (1999), 'Why is central Paris rich and downtown Detroit poor? An amenity-based theory', *European Economic Review*, 43, pp. 91-107.

Bruinsma, F.R., R.J.G.M. Florax, F.G. van Oort and M. Sorber (2002), *Volgt wonen werken of werken wonen?*, Research Memorandum 2002-15, Amsterdam: Vrije Universiteit.

Buettner, T. (1999), *Agglomeration, growth and adjustment. A theoretical and empirical study of regional labor markets in Germany*, Heidelberg: Physica Verlag.

Buettner, T. (1999), 'The effect of unemployment, aggregate wages and spatial contiguity on local wages: an investigation with German district level data', *Papers in Regional Science*, 78, pp. 47-67.

Button, K. (2000), 'New approaches to spatial economics', *Growth and Change*, 31, pp.480-500.

Burke, G.L. (1956), *The making of Dutch towns. A study in urban development from the tenth to the seventeenth centuries*, London: Cleaver-Hume Press.

Caballero, R. and R. Lyons (1990), 'Internal versus external economies in European industry', *European Economic Review*, 34, pp. 805-30.

Caniëls, M. (1999), *Regional growth differentials. The impact of locally bounded knowledge spillovers*, Dissertation, Maastricht University.

Carree, M. and R. Thurik (1999), 'Industrial structure and economic growth', in D.B. Audretsch and A.R. Thurik (eds.), *Innovation, industry evolution and employment*, Cambridge: University Press, pp. 86-110.

Carrincazeaux, C., Y. Lung and A. Rallet (2001), 'Proximity and localisation of corporate R&D activities', *Research Policy*, 30, pp. 777-89.

Carlaw, K.I. and R.G. Lipsey (2002), 'Externalities, technological complementarities and sustained economic growth', *Research Policy*, 31, pp.1305-15.

Carlton, D.W. (1982), 'The location and employment choices of new firms: an econometric model with discrete and continuous endogenous variables', *The Review of Economics and Statistics*, 27, pp. 440-49.

Caroll, G. (1982), 'National city size distributions: what do we know after 67 years of research?', *Progress in Human Geography*, 6, pp. 1-43.

Caroll, G.R. and M.T. Hannan (2000), *The demography of corporations and industries*, Princeton, New Jersey: Princeton University Press.

Castells, M. (1989), *The informational city. Information technology, economic restructuring and the urban-regional process*, Oxford: Blackwell.

CBS (1999a), *Innovatie en provincie 1999. Regionale innovatieprofielen van het MKB in Nederland*, Voorburg: Statistics Netherlands (CBS) and IPO.

CBS (1999b), *Kennis en economie 1999. Onderzoek en innovatie in Nederland*, Voorburg: Statistics Netherlands (CBS) and Elsevier.

CBS (1999c), *Regionale economische jaarcijfers 1997*, Voorburg: Statistics Netherlands (CBS).

Cervero, R. (2001), 'Efficient urbanisation: economic performance and the shape of the metropolis', *Urban Studies*, 38, pp.1651-71.

Chamberlin, E.H. (1933), *The theory of monopolistic competition*, Cambridge Mass.: Harvard University Press.

Champernowne, D.G. (1974), 'A comparison of measures of inequality of income distribution', *The Economic Journal*, pp. 787-816.

Chapman, K. and D.F. Walker (1991), *Industrial location. Principles and policies*, Oxford: Blackwell.

Chevassus-Lozza, E. and D. Gailliano (2003), 'Local spillovers, firm organization and export behaviour: evidence from the French food industry', *Regional Studie*, 37, pp.147-58.

Chinitz, B.J. (1961), 'Contrasts in agglomeration: New York and Pittsburgh', *The American Economic Review*, 51, pp. 279-89.

Clark, G.L. (1997), 'Stylised facts and close dialogue: methodology in economic geography', *Annals of the Association of American Geographers*, 88, pp. 73-87.

Clark, G.L. and N. Wrigley (1995), 'Sunk costs: a framework for economic geography', *Transactions of the Institute of British Geographers*, 20, pp. 204-23.

Cliff, A.D. and J.K. Ord (1973), *Spatial autocorrelation*, London: Pion.

Cliff, A.D. and J.K. Ord (1981), *Spatial processes: models and applications*, London: Pion.

Coe, N.M. and A.R. Townsend (1998), 'Debunking the myth of localized agglomerations: the development of a regionalized service economy in South-East England', *Transactions of the Institute of British Geographers*, 23, pp. 385-404.

Coffey, W.J., R. Drolet and M. Polèse (1996), 'The intrametropolitan location of high order services: patterns, factors and mobility', *Papers in Regional Science*, 75, pp. 293-323.

Combes, P.P. (2000), 'Economic structure and local growth: France 1984-1993', *Journal of Urban Economics*, 47, pp. 329-55.

Cooper, D.P. (2001), 'Innovation and reciprocal externalities: information transmission via job mobility', *Journal of Economic Behavior and Organization*, 45, pp.403-25.

Cornet, M. (2001), *De maatschappelijke kosten en baten van technologiesubsidies zoals de WBSO*, CPB Research Memorandum 008, 's-Gravenhage.

Cortright, J. and H. Mayer (2001), 'High tech specialization: a comparison of high technology centres', *The Brookings Institution Surveys*, pp. 1-13.

CPB (1997), *Bedrijfslocatiemonitor. Terreinverkenning*, Den Haag: Centraal Planbureau.

Crihfield, J.B. (1989), 'A structural empirical analysis of metropolitan labor demand', *Journal of Regional Science*, 29, pp. 347-71.

Cronon, W. (1991), *Nature's metropolis. Chicago and the Great West*, New York: Norton.

Curran, J. and R. Blackburn (1994), *Small firms and local economic networks. The death of the local economy?*, London: Paul Chapman Publishing.

Daniels, P.W. (1991), *Services and metropolitan development*, London: Routledge.

Daniels, P.W. and F. Moulaert (1991), eds., *The changing geography of advanced producer services*, New York: Belhaven Press.

Davelaar, E.J. (1989), *Incubation and innovation; a spatial perspective*, dissertation, Free University Amsterdam.

Davis, S.J., J.C. Haltiwanger and S. Schuh (1996), *Job creation and destruction*, Cambridge, Mass.: The MIT Press.

Desrochers, P. (2001), 'Local diversity, human creativity and technological innovation', *Growth and Change*, 32, pp. 369-94.

Dicken, P. (1992), *Global shift. The internationalization of economic activity*, London: Paul Chapman Publishing.

Dicken, P. and P. Lloyd (1990), *Location in space. Theoretical perspectives in Economic Geography*, New York: Harper & Row.

Van Dijk, J. and P. H. Pellenbarg (2000), 'Firm relocation decisions in The Netherlands: an ordered logit approach', *Papers in Regional Science*, 79, pp. 191-219.

Van Dinteren, J.H.J. (1989), *Zakelijke diensten en middelgrote steden*, dissertation, Katholieke Universiteit Nijmegen.

Dixit, A.K. and J.E. Stiglitz (1977), 'Monopolistic competition and optimum product diversity', *The American Economic Review*, 67, pp. 297-308.

Dobkins, L.M. and Y.M. Ioannides (2001), 'Spatial interactions among US cities: 1900-1990', *Regional Science and Urban Economics*, 31, pp.701-31.

Dosi, G. (1988), 'Sources, producers and microeconomic effects of innovation', *Journal of Economic Literature*, 26, pp. 1120-71.

Dosi, G., F. Malerba, O. Marsili and L. Orsenigo (1997), 'Industrial structures and dynamics: evidence, interpretations and puzzles', *Industrial and Corporate Change*, 6, pp. 3-24.

Drennan, M.P. (1999), 'National structural change and metropolitan specialization in the United States', *Papers in Regional Science*, 78, pp. 297-318.

Dumais, G., G. Ellison and E.L. Glaeser (2002), 'Geographic concentration as a dynamic process', *The Review of Economics and Statistics*, 84, pp.193-204.

Duranton, G. (1999), 'Distance, land and proximity: economic analysis and the evolution of cities', *Environment and Planning A*, 31, pp. 2169-88.

Duranton, G. and D. Puga (2000), 'Diversity and specialisation in cities: why, where and when does it matter?', *Urban Studies*, 37, pp. 533-55.

Dymski, G.A. (1996), 'On Krugman's model of economic geography', *Geoforum*, 27, pp. 439-52.

Eaton, J. and Z. Eckstein (1997), 'Cities and growth: theory and evidence from France and Japan', *Regional Science and Urban Economics*, 27, pp. 443-74.

Echeverri, E.L. and W. Brennan (1999), 'Are innovation networks bounded by proximity?', in M.M. Fischer, L. Suarez-Villa and M. Steiner (eds.), *Innovation networks and localities*, Berlin: Springer Verlag.

Eliasson, G. (2000), 'Industrial policy, competence blocs and the role of science in economic development', *Journal of Evolutionary Economics*, 10, pp.217-41.

Ellison, G. and E.L. Glaeser (1999), 'The geographic concentration of industry: does natural advantage explain agglomeration?', *The American Economic Review*, 89, pp. 311-16.

Encaouda, D. and A. Jacquemin (1980), 'Degree of monopoly, indices of concentration and threat of entry', *International Economic Review*, 21, pp. 87-105.

Englmann, F.C. and U. Walz (1995), 'Industrial centers and regional growth in the presence of local inputs', *Journal of Regional Science*, 35, pp. 3-27.

Erickson, R.A. (1983), 'The evolution of the suburban space economy', *Urban Geography*, 4, pp.95-121.

Esparza, A. and A.J. Krmenec (1996), 'The spatial extent of producer service markets: hierarchical models of interaction revisited', *Papers in Regional Science*, 75, pp. 375-95.

Esparza, A.X. and A.J. Krmenec (2000), 'Large city interaction in the US urban system', *Urban Studies*, 37, pp. 691-709.

Evans, D.S. (1987), 'Tests of alternative theories of firm growth', *Journal of Political Economy*, 95, pp. 657-74.

Feige, E. and H. Watts (1972), 'An investigation of the consequences of partial aggregation of micro-economic data', *Econometrica*, 15, pp. 343-60.

Feldman, M.P. (1994), *The geography of innovation*, Boston: Kluwer Academic Publishers.

Feldman, M.P. (1999), 'The new economics of innovation, spillovers and agglomeration: a review of empirical studies', *Economics of Innovation and New Technology*, 8, pp.5-25.

Feldman, M.P. and D.B. Audretsch (1999), 'Innovation in cities: science based diversity, specialization and localized competition', *European Economic Review*, 43, pp. 409-29.

Feldman, M.P. and R. Florida (1994), 'The geographic sources of innovation: technological infrastructure and product innovation in the United States', *Annals of the Association of American Geographers*, 84, pp.210-229.

Feser, E.J. (2001), 'A flexible test for agglomeration economies in two US manufacturing industries', *Regional Science and Urban Economics*, 31, pp. 1-20.

Feser, E.J. (2002), 'Tracing the sources of local external economies', *Urban Studies*, 39, pp.2485-2506.

Feser, E.J. and E.M. Bergman (2000), 'National industry cluster templates: a framework for applied regional cluster analysis', *Regional Studies*, 34, pp. 1-19.

Fingleton, B. (2000), 'Spatial econometrics, economic geography, dynamics and equilibrium: a 'third way'?', *Environment and Planning A*, 32, pp.1481-98.

Florax, R. and H. Folmer (1992), 'Knowledge impacts of universities on industry: an aggregate simultaneous investment model', *Journal of Regional Science*, 32, pp. 437-66.

Florida, R. (2001), 'Technology and tolerance: the importance of diversity to high-technology growth', *The Brookings Institution Survey Series*, pp. 1-12.

Florida, R. (2002), *The rise of the creative class*, New York: Basic Books.

Frenkel, A. (2001), 'Why high-technology firms choose to locate in or near metropolitan areas', *Urban Studies*, 38, p.1083-1101.

Frenkel, A. and D. Shefer (1996), 'Modeling regional innovativeness and innovation', *The Annals of Regional Science*, 30, pp.31-54.

Friedmann, J. (1978), 'The urban field as human habitat', in L.S. Bourne and J.W. Simmond, (eds.), *Systems of cities. Readings on structure, growth and policy*, Oxford: University Press, pp.42-52.

Friedmann, J. and J. Miller (1965), 'The urban field', *Journal of the American Institute of Planners*, 31, pp. 312-19.

Fritsch, M. (1997), 'New firms and regional employment change', *Small Business Economics*, 9, pp. 437-48.

Frost, M.E. and N.A. Spence (1995), 'The rediscovery of accessibility and economic potential: the critical issue of self-potential', *Environment and Planning A*, 27, pp.1833-48.

Fujita, M. (1989), *Urban economic theory. Land use and city size*, Cambridge: University Press.

Fujita, M. (1996), 'On the self-organization and evolution of economic geography', *The Japanese Economic Review*, 47, pp. 34-61.

Fujita, M., P. Krugman and T. Mori (1999), 'On the evolution of hierarchical urban systems', *European Economic Review*, 43, pp. 209-51.

Fujita, M., P. Krugman and A. Venables (2000), *The spatial economy. Cities, regions and international trade*, Cambridge, Mass.: The MIT Press.

Fujita, M. and J.F. Thisse (2002), *Economics of agglomeration. Cities, industrial location, and regional growth*, Cambridge: University Press.

Le Gallo, J. and C. Ertur (2003), 'Exploratory spatial data analysis of the distribution of regional per capita GDP in Europe 1980-1995', *Papers in Regional Science*, 82, pp.175-201.

Van Geenhuizen, M.S. (1993), *A longitudinal analysis of the growth of firms. The case of the Netherlands*, dissertation, Erasmus University Rotterdam.

Geroski, P.A. (1991), *Market dynamics and entry*, Oxford: Basil Blackwell.

Gersbach, H. and A. Schmutzler (1999), 'External spillovers, internal spillovers and the geography of production and innovation', *Regional Science and Urban Economics*, 29, pp. 679-96.

Gertler, M.S. (1988), 'The limits of flexibility: comments on the Post-Fordist vision of production and its geography', *Transactions of the Institute of British Geographers*, 13, pp. 419-32.

Gertler, M.S. (2003), 'Tacit knowledge and the economic geography of context, or: The undefinable tacitness of being (there)', *Journal of Economic Geography*, 3, pp.75-99.

Gianmarco, I., P. Ottaviano and J.F. Thisse (2001), 'On economic geography in economic theory: increasing returns and pecuniary externalities', *Journal of Economic Geography*, 1, pp.153-79.

Glaeser, E.L. (1998), 'Are cities dying?', *Journal of Economic Perspectives*, 12, pp. 139-60.

Glaeser, E.L. (1999), 'Learning in cities', *Journal of Urban Economics*, 46, pp. 254-77.

Glaeser, E.L. (2000), 'The future of urban research: nonmarket interactions', *Brookings-Wharton Papers on Urban Affairs*, pp. 101-149.

Glaeser, E.L., H.D. Kallal, J.A. Scheinkman and A. Schleifer (1992), 'Growth in cities', *Journal of Political Economy*, 100, pp. 1126-52 .

Glaeser, E.L., J.A. Scheinkman and A. Schleifer (1995), 'Economic growth in a cross-section of cities', *Journal of Monetary Economics*, 36, pp. 117-43.

Goldstein, H. (1995), *Multilevel statistical models*, London: Arnold.

Goodchild, M.F. (1986), *Spatial autocorrelation*. Concepts and Techniques in Modern Geography (CATMOG) no. 47, London: Institute of British Geographers.

Gordon, I.R. and P. McCann (2000), 'Industrial clusters: complexes, agglomeration and/or social networks?', *Urban Studies*, 37, pp. 513-32.

Gottmann, J. (1983), *The coming of the transactional city*, Maryland: University of Maryland.

Graham, S. and S. Marvin (2001), *Splintering urbanism. Networked infrastructures, technological mobilities and the urban condition*, London: Routledge.

Greene, W.H. (1997), *Econometric analysis*, New Jersey: Prentice-Hall.

Griffith, D. and F. Lagona (1998), 'On the quality of likelihood-based estimators in spatial autoregressive models when the data dependence structure is misspecified', *Journal of Statistical Planning and Inference*, 69, pp.153-174.

Griliches, Z. (1985), 'Issues in assessing the contribution of research and development to productivity growth', *The Bell Journal of Economics*, 10, pp. 92-116.

Griliches, Z. (1990), 'Patent statistics as economic indicators: a survey', *Journal of Economic Literature*, 28, pp. 1661-707.

Griliches, Z. (1992), 'The search for R&D spillovers', *Scandinavian Journal of Economics*, 94, pp. 29-47.

Grossman, G.M. and E. Helpman (1992), *Innovation and growth in the global economy*, Cambridge Mass.: MIT Press.

Grossman, G.M. and E. Helpman (1994), 'Endogenous innovation in the theory of growth', *Journal of Economic Perspectives*, 8, pp. 23-44.

Haggett, P., A.D. Cliff and A. Frey (1977), *Locational analysis in human geography. Volume II: locational methods*, London: Edward Arnold.

Hägerstrand, T. (1966), *Innovation and diffusion as a spatial process*, Chicago: University Press.

Haining, R. (1990), *Spatial data analysis in the social and environmental sciences*, Cambridge: University Press.

Hall, P. (1977), *The world cities*, London: Weidenfeld and Nicolson.

Hall, P. (1998), *Cities in civilization. Culture, innovation and urban order*, London: Phoenix Giant.

Hall, P. (2000a), 'Creative cities and economic development', *Urban Studies*, 37, pp. 639-49.

Hall, P. (2000b), 'Work and the places to be', *Town and Country Planning*, pp. 78-9.

Van Ham, M., P. Hooimeijer and C.H. Mulder (2001), 'Urban form and job access: disparate realities in the Randstad', *Tijdschrift voor Economische en Sociale Geografie*, 92, pp. 231-46.

Hamermesh, D.S. (1996), *Labor demand*, Princeton: University Press.

Hannan, M.T. and J. Freeman (1989), *Organizational ecology*, Cambridge, Mass.: Harvard University Press.

Hanson, G.H. (2001), 'Scale economies and the geographic concentration of industry', *Journal of Economic Geography*, 1, pp.155-76.

Harrison, B. (1991), 'Industrial districts: old wine in new bottles?', *Regional Studies*, 26, pp.469-83.

Harrison, B. (1994), *Lean and mean. The changing landscape of corporate power in the age of flexibility*, New York: Basic Books.

Harrison, B., M.R. Kelley and J. Gant (1997), 'Innovative firm behavior and local milieu: exploring the intersection of agglomeration, firm effects, and technological change', *Economic Geography*, 72, pp. 233-58.

Hayter, R. (1997), *The dynamics of industrial location. The factory, the firm and the production system*, Chichester: Wiley.

Heilbronner, R.L. (1962), *The making of economic society*, Englewood Cliffs: Prentice-Hall.

Helsey, R.W. and W.C. Strange (1990), 'Matching and agglomeration economies in a system of cities', *Regional Science and Urban Economics*, 20, pp. 189-212.

Henderson, J.V. (1974), 'The sizes and types of cities', *The American Economic Review*, 64, pp. 640-56.

Henderson, J.V. (1986), 'Efficiency of resource usage and city size', *Journal of Urban Economics*, 19, pp. 47-70.

Henderson, J.V. (1996), 'Ways to think about urban concentration: neoclassical urban systems versus the new economic geography', *International Regional Science Review*, 19, pp.31-36.

Henderson, J.V. (1997a), 'Medium size cities', *Regional Science and Urban Economics*, 27, pp. 583-612.

Henderson, J.V. (1997b), 'Externalities and industrial development', *Journal of Urban Economics*, 42, pp. 449-70.

Henderson, J.V. (2000), *The effects of urban concentration on economic growth*, NBER Working Paper 7503, Cambridge Mass.

Henderson, J.V. (2003), 'Marshall's scale economies', *Journal of Urban Economics*, 53, pp.1-28.

Henderson, J.V., A. Kuncoro and M. Turner (1995), 'Industrial development in cities', *Journal of Political Economy*, 103, pp. 1067-85.

Hepworth, M.E. (1989), *Geography of the information economy*, London: Belhaven Press.

Hirschman, A.O. (1958), *The strategy of economic development*, New Haven: Yale University Press.

Hoare, A. (1992), 'Review of Krugman's Geography and Trade', *Regional Studies*, 26, p. 679.

Hoekveld, G.A. (1999), 'Een model voor een meerkernig gebied', *Geografie*, 8, pp. 28-33.

Hoover, E.M. (1937), *Location theory and the shoe and leather industries*, Cambridge: Harvard University Press.

Hoover, E.M. (1948), *The location of economic activity*, New York: McGraw-Hill.

Hopenhayn, H. (1992), 'Entry, exit and firm dynamics in long-run equilibrium', *Econometrica*, 60, pp. 1127-50.

Hornstein, A. and J. Praschnik (1997), 'Intermediate inputs and sectoral comovement in the business cycle', *Journal of Monetary Economics*, 40, pp.573-95.

Houston, D.B. (1967), 'The shift-share analysis of regional growth: a critique', *Southern Economic Journal*, 33, pp. 577-81.

Howells, J.R.L. (2002), 'Tacit knowledge, innovation and economic geography', *Urban Studies*, 39, pp.871-84.

Hunt, S. (1997), 'Resource-advantage theory', *Journal of Economic Issues*, 31, pp.59-78.

Huriot, J.M. and J.F. Thisse (2000) (eds.), *Economics of cities. Theoretical perspectives*, Cambridge: University Press.

Isard, W. (1956), *Location and space-economy. A general theory relating to industrial location, market areas, land use, trade and urban structure*, Cambridge, Mass.: MIT Press.

Isard, W. (1960), *Methods of regional analysis. An introduction to regional science*, Cambridge, Mass.: The MIT Press.

Isserman, A.M. (1996), 'It's obvious, it's wrong and anyway they said it years ago? Paul Krugman on large cities', *International Regional Science Review*, 19, pp.37-48.

Izraeli, O, and K.J. Murphy (2003), 'The effect of industrial diversification on state unemployment rate and per capita income', *The Annals of Regional Science*, 37, pp.1-14.

Jackson, R.W. (1984), 'An evaluation of alternative measures of regional industrial diversification', *Regional Studies*, 18, pp.103-12.

Jacobs, J. (1969), *The economy of cities*, New York: Vintage.

Jaffe, A.B. (1989), 'Real effects of academic research', *The American Economic Review*, 79, pp. 957-70.

Jaffe, A.B., M. Trajtenberg and R. Henderson (1993), 'Geographic localization of knowledge spillovers as evidenced by patent citations', *The Quarterly Journal of Economics*, 36, pp. 577-98.

Jones, C.I. (1995), 'R&D based models of economic growth', *Journal of Political Economy*, 103, pp. 759-84.

De Jong, M.W. (1987), *New economic activities and regional dynamics*, Amsterdam: Netherlands Geographical Studies.

Kaiser, U. (2002), 'Measuring knowledge spillovers in manufacturing and services: an empirical assessment of alternative approaches', *Research Policy*, 31, pp. 125-44.

Katz, M.L. and C. Shapiro (1985), 'Network externalities, competition and compatibility', *American Economic Review*, 75, pp.424-40.

Ke, S. and M.I. Luger (1996), 'Embodied technological progress, technology-related producer inputs and regional factors in a firm-level model of growth', *Regional Science and Urban Economics*, 26, pp. 23-50.

Kelley, M.R. and S. Helper (1999), 'Firm size and capabilities, regional agglomeration, and the adoption of new technology', *Economic Innovation and New Technology*, 8, pp. 79-103.

Kelly, M. and A. Hageman (1999), 'Marshallian externalities in innovation', *Journal of Economic Growth*, 4, pp. 39-54.

Kephart, G. (1988), 'Heterogeneity and the implied dynamics of regional growth rates', *Demography*, 25, pp. 99-113.

Kim, C., T. Phipps and L. Anselin (2000), 'Measuring benefits of air quality improvement: a spatial hedonic approach', Morgantown: West Virginia University (mimeo).

Kim, S. (1987), 'Diversity in urban labor markets and agglomeration economies', *Papers of the Regional Science Association*, 62, pp. 57-70.

Kim, S. (1999), 'Regions, resources and economic geography: sources of US regional comparative advantage 1880-1987', *Regional Science and Urban Economics*, 29, pp. 1-32.

Kim, Y., D.L. Barkley and M.S. Henry (2000), 'Industry characteristics linked to establishment concentrations in nonmetropolitan areas', *Journal of Regional Science*, 40,pp.231-59.

Kleinknecht, A. (1987), *Industriële innovatie in Nederland*, Assen: Van Gorcum.

Kleinknecht, A. and T.P. Poot (1992), 'Do regions matter for R&D?', *Regional Studies*, 26, pp. 221-32.

Klepper, S. (1997), 'Industry life cycles', *Industrial and Corporate Change*, 6, pp. 145-81.

Klomp, L. (1996), *Empirical studies in the hospitality sector*, dissertation, Erasmus University Rotterdam.

Van der Knaap, G.A. (1978), *A spatial analysis of the evolution of an urban system: the case of the Netherlands*, dissertation, Erasmus University Rotterdam.

Van der Knaap, G.A. (2002), *Stedelijke bewegingsruimte: over veranderingen in stad en land*, 's-Gravenhage: WRR.

Van der Knaap, G.A. and P.J. Louter (1986), *De middelgrote steden*. EGI-onderzoeks-publikaties 86-1, Rotterdam: Ersamus Universiteit.

Van der Knaap, G.A., F.G. van Oort and H. Scholten (1995), *Een multiregionaal arbeids-aanbodmodel voor Nederland (MURAM)*, EGI-onderzoekspublikatie 33, Rotterdam: Erasmus University.

Knol, H. and W. Manshanden (1990), *Functionele samenhang in de noordvleugel van de Randstad*, Utrecht: Nederlandse Geografische Studies.

Kooij, P. (1988), 'Peripheral cities and their regions in the Dutch urban system until 1900', *The Journal of Economic History*, 48, pp.357-71.

Krugman, P. (1991a), *Geography and trade*, Cambridge, Mass.: The MIT Press.

Krugman, P. (1991b), 'History and industry location. The case of the manufacturing belt', *The American Economic Review*, 81, pp. 80-83.

Krugman, P.R. (1991c), 'Increasing returns and economic geography', *Journal of Political Economy*, 99, pp. 483-99.

Krugman, P. (1992), 'First nature, second nature and metropolitan location', *Journal of Regional Science*, 33, pp. 129-44.

Krugman, P. (1993a), 'On the number and location of cities', *European Economic Review*, 37, pp. 293-98.

Krugman, P. (1993b), 'On the relationship between trade theory and location theory', *Review of International Economics*, 12, pp. 110-22.

Krugman, P. (1995a), *Development, geography and economic theory*, Cambridge, Mass.: The MIT Press.

Krugman, P. (1995b), 'Innovation and agglomeration: two parables suggested by city-size distributions', *Japan and the World Economy*, 7, pp. 371-90.

Krugman, P. (1996a), *The self-organizing economy*, Cambridge: Blackwell.

Krugman, P. (1996b), 'Urban concentration: the role of increasing returns and transport costs', *International Regional Science Review*, 19, pp.5-30.

Krugman, P. (1998), 'What's new about the new economic geography?', *Oxford Review of Economic Policy*, 14, pp.7-17.

Krugman, P. and A.J. Venables (1996), 'Integration, specialization and adjustment', *European Economic Review*, 40, pp. 959-67.

Kubo, Y. (1995), 'Scale economies, regional externalities and the possibility of uneven regional development', *Journal of Regional Science*, 35, pp. 29-42.

Kuiper, J.H. (1985), *Distributions of distances in pregeographical space*, dissertation, Erasmus University Rotterdam.

Van der Laan, L. (1998), 'Changing urban systems. An empirical analysis at two spatial levels', *Regional Studies*, 32, pp. 235-47.

Van der Laan, L. and F.G. van Oort (2003), 'Does ICT lead to anomalies in agglomeration theory? A survey of ICT impact on space and external economies'. Rotterdam: Erasmus University (mimeo).

Lamb, R. (1975), *Metropolitan impacts on rural America*, Research paper no. 162, Department of Geography. Chicago: University Press.

Lambert, A.M. (1985), *The making of the Dutch landscape. An historical geography of the Netherlands*, London: Academic Press.

Lambooy, J.G. (1990), 'Complexity, formations and networks', in M. de Smidt and E. Wever (eds.), *Complexes, formations and networks*, Amsterdam: Netherlands Geographical Studies, pp. 15-25.

Lambooy, J.G. (1998a), *Agglomeratievoordelen en ruimtelijke ontwikkeling: steden in het tijdperk van de kenniseconomie*, Oratie, Universiteit Utrecht.

Lambooy, J.G. (1998b), 'Polynucleation and economic development: the Randstad', *European PLanning Studies*, 6, pp. 457-66.

Lambooy, J. (2000), 'Learning and agglomeration economies: adapting to differentiating economic structures', in F. Boekema, K. Morgan, S. Bakess and R. Rutten (eds.), *Knowledge, innovation and economic growth*, Cheltenham: Edward Elgar, pp.17-37.

Lang, R.E. (2000), 'Office sprawl: the evolving geography of business', *The Brookings Institution Survey Series*, pp. 1-11.

Lawson, C. and E. Lorenz (1999), 'Collective learning, tacit knowledge and regional innovative capacity', *Regional Studies* 33, pp.305-317.

Leone, R.A. and R.J. Struyck (1976), 'The incubation hypothesis: evidence from five SMA's', *Urban Studies*, 13, pp. 325-31.

Leunis, W. and K. Verhage (1999), *Labour accounts in theory and practice. The Dutch experience*, Voorburg: Statistics Netherlands (CBS).

Leven, C.L. (1978), 'Growth and non-growth in metropolitan areas and the emergence of polycentric metropolitan form', *Papres of the Regeional Science Association*, 41, pp.101-12.

Lever, M.H.C. (1996), 'Firm size and employment determination in Dutch manufacturing industries', *Small Business Economics*, 8, pp. 389-396.

Lever, M. and H. Nieuwenhuijsen (1999), 'The impact of competition on productivity in Dutch manufacturing', in D.B. Audretsch and A.R. Thurik (eds.), *Innovation, industry evolution and employment*, Cambridge: University Press, pp. 111-128.

De Liso, N., G. Filatrella and N. Weaver (2001), 'On endogenous growth and increasing returns: modelling learning by doing and the division of labor', *Journal of Economic Behavior and Organization*, 46, pp.39-55.

Lösch, A. (1954), *The economics of location*, (originally published in German in 1939), New Haven: Yale University Press.

Longley, P.A. and V. Mesev (2000), 'On the measurement and generalisation of urban form', *Environment and Planning A*, 32, pp. 473-88.

Louter, P.J. (1992), *Economische structuurverandering en regionale specialisatie*, EGI-onderzoekspublikatie 04, Rotterdam: Erasmus Universiteit.

Louter, P.J. (1997), *De economische kaart van Nederland in 2015*, Delft: TNO Inro.

Louter, P.J. (1999), *De economie van steden en stadsgewesten: verleden en toekomst*, Delft: TNO Inro.

Louter, P.J. and F.G. van Oort (1992), *Dynamiek in regionaal-economische specialisatie*, EGI-onderzoekspublikatie 08, Rotterdam: Erasmus Universiteit.

Lovering, J. (1999), 'Theory led by policy: the inadequacies of the New Regionalism', *International Journal of Urban and Regional Research*, 23, pp. 379-95.

Lucas, R.E. (1988), 'On the mechanics of economic development', *Journal of Monetary Economics*, 22, pp. 3-42.

Lucas, R.E. (1993), 'Making a miracle', *Econometrica*, 61, pp. 251-72.

De Lucio, J.J., J.A. Herce and A. Goicolea (2002), 'The effects of externalities on productivity growth in Spanish industry', *Regional Science and Urban Economics*, 32, pp.241-58.

Lyons, D. (2000), 'Embeddedness, milieu and innovation among high-technology firms', *Environment and Planning A*, 32, pp.891-908.

Malecki, E.J. (1997), *Technology and economic development. The dynamics of local, regional and national competitiveness*. Harlow: Longman.

Malecki, E.J. and S.L. Bradbury (1992), 'R&D facilities and professional labour: labour force dynamics in high technology', *Regional Studies*, 26, pp. 123-36.

Malmberg, A. (1996), 'Industrial geography: agglomeration and local milieu', *Progress in Haman Geography*, 20, pp. 392-403.

Malmberg, A. and P. Maskell (1997), 'Towards an explanation of regional specialisation and industry agglomeration', *European Planning Studies*, 5, pp. 25-41.

Malmberg, A. and P. Maskell (2002), 'The elusive concept of localization economies: towards a knowledge-based theory of spatial clustering', *Environment and Planning A*, 34, pp.429-49.

Malmberg, A., O. Sölvell and I. Zander (1996), 'Spatial clustering, local accumulation of knowledge and firm competitiveness', *Geografiska Annaler*, 78B, pp. 85-97.

Manshanden, W. (1996), *Zakelijke diensten en regionaal-economische ontwikkeling. De economie van nabijheid*, Amsterdam: Nederlandse Geografische Studies.

Markusen, A. (1985), *Profit cycles, oligopoly, and regional development*, London: MIT Press.

Markusen, A. (1994), 'Studying regions by studying firms', *The Professional Geographer*, 46, pp. 477-90.

Markusen, A. (1996), Sticky places in slippery space: a typology of industrial districts. *Economic Geography* 72, pp. 293-313.

Markusen, A. (1999), 'Fuzzy concepts, scanty evidence, policy distance: the case for rigor and policy relevance in critical regional studies', *Regional Studies*, 33, pp. 869-84.

Marshall, A. (1890), *Principles of economics*, New York: Prometheus Books.

Marshall, N.J. and P.A. Wood (1995), *Services and space. Key aspects of urban and regional development*, Harlow: Longman.

Martin, P. and J.P. Ottaviano (1996), *Growth and agglomeration*, CEPR discussion paper 1529. London: Center for Economic Policy Rsearch.

Martin, P. and J.P. Ottaviano (1999), 'Growing locations: industry location in a model of endogenous growth', *European Economic Review*, 43, pp.281-302.

Martin, R. (1999), 'The new 'geographical turn' in economics: some critical reflections', *Cambridge Journal of Economics*, 23, pp. 65-91.

Martin, R. and P. Sunley (1996), 'Paul Krugman's geographical economics and its implications for regional development theory: a critical assessment', *Economic Geography*, 72, pp. 259-92.

Martin, R. and P. Sunley (2003), 'Deconstructing clusters: chaotic concept or policy panacea?', *Journal of Economic Geography*, 3, pp.5-35.

Maskell, P., H. Eskelinen, I. Hannibalsson, A. Malmberg and E. Vatne (1998), *Competitiveness, localised learning and regional development*, London: Routledge.

Massey, D. (1984), *Spatial divisions of labour. Social structures and the geography of production*, Basingstoke: Macmillan.

Maurel, F. and B. Sédillot (1999), 'A measure of geographic concentration in French manufacturing industries', *Regional Science and Urban Economics*, 29, pp. 575-604.

McCann, P. (1995), 'Rethinking the economics of location and agglomeration', *Urban Studies*, 32, pp. 563-77.

Molle, W.T.M. (ed.) (1985), *Innovatie en regio*, 's-Gravenhage: Staatsuitgeverij.

Moomaw, R.L. (1985), 'Firm location and city size: reduced productivity advantages as a factor in the decline of manufacturing in urban areas', *Journal of Urban Economics*, 17, pp. 73-89.

Moomaw, R.L. (1988), 'Agglomeration economies: localization or urbanization?', *Urban Studies*, 25, pp. 150-61.

Moomaw, R.L. (1998), 'Agglomeration economics: are they exaggerated by industrial aggregation?', *Regional Science and Urban Economics*, 28, pp. 199-211.

Moulaert, F. and F. Sekia (2003), 'Territorial innovation models: a critical survey', *Regional Studies*, 37, pp.189-302.

Myrdal, G. (1957), *Economic theory and under-developed regions*, London: Duckworth.

Nelson, R.R. (1995), 'Recent evolutionary theory about economic change', *Journal of Economic Literature*, 33, pp. 48-90.

Nelson, R.R. and S.G. Winter (1983), *An evolutionary theory of economic change*, Cambridge, Mass.: The Belknap Press.

Nijkamp, P. and J. Poot (1998), 'Spatial perspectives on new theories of economic growth', *The Annals of Regional Science*, 32, pp. 7-37.

Nooteboom, B. (1999), 'Innovation, learning and industrial organisation', *Cambridge Journal of Economics*, 23, pp. 127-50.

O'Donoghue, D. (1999), 'The relationship between diversification and growth', *International Journal of Urban and Regional Research*, pp. 547-66.

O'Donoghue, D. (2000), 'Some evidence for the convergence of employment structures in the Britisch urban system from 1978 to 1991', *Regional Science and Urban Economics*, 34, pp.159-67.

Oerlemans, L.A.G., M.T.H. Meeus and F.W.M. Boekema (2001a), 'On the spatial embeddedness of innovation networks: an exploration of the proximity effect', *Tijdschrift voor Economische en Sociale Geografie*, 92, pp. 60-73.

Oerlemans, L.A.G., M.T.H. Meeus and F.W.M. Boekema (2001b), 'Firm clustering and innovation: determinants and effects', *Papers in Regional Science*, 80, pp. 337-56.

Ohlin, B. (1933), *Interregional and international trade*, Cambridge, Mass.: Harvard University Press.

OhUallachain, B. (1989), 'Agglomeration of services in American metropolitan areas', *Growth and Change*, 20, pp.34-49.

OhUallachain, B. (1999), 'Patent places: size matters', *Journal of Regional Science*, 39, pp.613-36.

Oinas, P. (1998), *The embedded firm? Prelude for a revived geography of enterprise*, dissertation , Helsinki School of Economics and Business Administration.

Oinas, P. (2000), 'Distance and learning: does proximity matter?', in F. Boekema, K. Morgan, S. Bakkers and R. Rutten (eds.), *Knowledge, innovation and economic growth*, Cheltenham: Edward Elgar, pp. 57-69.

Olsen, J. (2002), 'On the units of geographical economies', *Geoforum*, 33, pp.153-64.

Van Oort, F.G. (1994), *Regionale variaties in welvaart in Nederland*, EGI onderzoekspublicatie 31, Rotterdam: Erasmus Universiteit.

Van Oort, F.G. (2002a), *Agglomeration, economic growth and innovation. Spatial analysis of growth- and R&D externalities in the Netherlands*, dissertation. Rotterdam: Tinbergen Institute.

Van Oort, F.G. (2002b). 'Innovation and agglomeration economies in the Netherlands', *TESG Journal of Economic and Social Geography* 93, pp.344-360.

Van Oort, F.G. and O. Atzema (2003), 'On the conceptualization of agglomeration economies: the case of new firm formation in the Dutch ICT-sector', *Annals of Regional Science* (forthcoming).

Van Oort, F.G., G.A. van der Knaap and W.F. Sleegers (2000), 'New firm formation, employment growth and the local environment: empirical observations in South-Holland', in J. Van Dijk and P. Pellenbarg (eds.), *Spatial dynamics of firm behaviour*. Groningen: Netherlands Geographical Studies, pp. 173-203.

Openshaw, S. and P.J. Taylor (1979), 'A million or so correlation coefficients: three experiments on the modifiable areal unit problem', in N. Wrigley (ed.), *Statistical applications in the spatial sciences*, London: Pion, pp. 127-44.

Ottaviano, G.I.P. and D. Puga (1998), 'Agglomeration in the global economy: a survey of the new economic geography', *World Economy*, 21, pp.707-731.

Ottens, H.F.L. (1976), *Het groene hart binnen de Randstad. Een beeld van suburbanisatie in West-Nederland* , Assen: Van Gorcum.

Ouwersloot, H. and P. Rietveld (2000), 'The geography of R&D: tobit analysis and a Baysian approach to mapping R&D activities in the Netherlands', *Environment and Planning A*, 32, pp. 1673-88.

Paci, R. and S. Usai (1999), 'Externalities, knowledge spillovers and the spatial distribution of innovation', *GeoJournal*, 49, pp. 381-90.

Paci, R. and S. Usai (2000), 'Technological enclaves and industrial districts: an analysis of the regional distribution of innovative activity in Europe', *Regional Studies*, 34, pp.97-114.

Pack, H. (1994), 'Endogenous growth theory: intellectual appeal and empirical shortcomings', *Journal of Economic Perspectives*, 8, pp. 55-72.

Palivos, T. and P. Wang (1996), 'Spatial agglomeration and endogenous growth', *Regional Science and Urban Economics*, 26, pp. 645-69.

Parr, J.B. (1999a), 'Growth-pole strategies in regional economic planning: a retrospective view. Part 1: origins and advocacy', *Urban Studies*, 36, pp. 1195-216.

Parr, J.B. (1999b), 'Growth-pole strategies in regional economic planning: a retrospective view. Part 2: implementation and outcome', *Urban Studies*, 36, pp. 1247-69.

Parr, J.B. (2002), 'Agglomeration economies: ambiguities and confusions', *Environment and Planning A*, 34, pp.717-31.

Peck, J. (1996), *Work-place. The social regulation of labor markets*, New York: The Guilford Press.

Peneder, M. (2001), *Entrepreneurial competition and industrial location. Investigating the structural patterns and intangible sources of competitive performance*, Cheltenham: Edward Elgar.

Perloff, H.S., E.S. Dunn, E.E. Lampard and R.F. Muth (1960), *Regions, resources and economic growth*, Baltimore: John Hopkins Press.

Perroux, F. (1955), 'Note on the concept of growth poles', in D.L. McKee, R.D. Dean and W.H. Leahy (eds.), *Regional economics*, (1970, translated reprint), New York: The Free Press, pp. 93-103.

Phelps, N.A. (1992), 'External economies, agglomeration and flexible accumulation', *Transactions of the Institute of British Geographers*, 17, pp. 35-46.

Phelps, N.A.., R.J. Fallon and C.L. Williams (2001), 'Small firms, borrowed size and the urban-rural shift', *Regional Studies*, 35, pp.613-24.

Pinch, S. and N. Henry (1999), 'Paul Krugman's geographical economics, industrial clustering and the British motor sport industry', *Regional Studies*, 33, pp. 815-27.

Piore, M.J. and C.F. Sabel (1984), *The second industrial divide. Possibilities for prosperity*, New York: Basic Books.

Plewis, I. (1985), *Analysing change. Measurement and explanation using longitudinal data*, Chichester: John Wiley.

Plummer, P. and M. Taylor (2001), 'Theories of local economic growth: concepts, models and measurement', *Environment and Planning A*, 33, pp.219-36.

Poot, A.P., N.M. Brouwer, J. Ouwersloot and P. Rietveld (1997), *Innovatie en regio. Provinciale innovatieprofielen*, Den Haag: Ministerie van Economische Zaken.

Porter, M. (1990), *The competitive advantage of nations*, New York: Free Press.

Porter, M. (1996), 'Competitive advantage, agglomeration economies and regional policy', *International Regional Science Review*, 19, pp.85-90.

Porter, M. (1998), *On competition: competing across locations*, Cambridge (Mass.): Harvard Business School Press.

Pred, A.R. (1966), *The spatial dynamics of US urban-industrial growth 1800-1914: interspective and theoretical essays*, Cambridge, Mass.: The MIT Press.

Pred, A. (1973), *Urban growth and the circulation of information*, Cambridge Mass.: Harvard University Press.

Pred, A. (1977), *City-systems in advanced economies. Past growth, present processes and future development options*, London: Hutchinson.

Puga, D. and A. Venables (1996), 'The spread of industry: spatial agglomeration in economic development', *Journal of the Japanese and International Economies*, 10, pp. 440-64.

Quigley, J.M. (1998), 'Urban diversity and economic growth', *Journal of Economic Perspectives*, 12, pp. 127-38.

Rallet, A. and A. Torre (1999), 'Is geographical proximity necessary in innovation networks in the era of global economy?', *GeoJournal*, 49, pp. 373-80.

Rauch, J.E. (1993), 'Does history matter only when it matters little? The case of city-industry location', *The Quarterly Journal of Economics*, 20, pp. 843-67.

Reynolds, P. (1994), 'Autonomous firm dynamics and economic growth in the United States, 1986-1990', *Regional Studies*, 28, pp. 429-42.

Ricardo, D. (1817), *The principles of political economy and taxation*, London: J.M. Dent & Sons (reprint).

Richardson, H.W. (1973a), *The economics of urban size*, Westmead: Saxon House.

Richardson, H.W. (1973b), *Regional growth theory*, London: Macmillan.

Richardson, H.W. (1978), *Regional and urban economics*, Hindsdale: Dryden Press.

Richardson, H.W. (1988), 'Monocentric vs. polycentric models: the future of urban economics in regional science', *Annals of Regional Science*, 22, pp.1-12.

Richardson, H.W. (1995), 'Economies and diseconomies of agglomeration', in H. Giersch (ed.), *Urban agglomeration and economic growth*, Berlin: Springer Verlag, pp.123-55.

Rigby, D.L. and J. Essletzbichler (2000), 'Impacts of industry mix, technological change, selection and plant entry and exit on regional productivity growth', *Regional Studies*, 34, pp. 333-42.

Rigby, D.L. and J. Essletzbichler (2002), 'Agglomeration economies and productivity differences in US cities', *Journal of Economic Geography*, 2, pp.407-432.

Rivera-Batiz, F.L. (1988), 'Increasing returns, monopolistic competition and agglomeration economies in consumption and production', *Regional Science and Urban Economics*, 18, pp. 125-53.

Robinson, W.S. (1950), 'Ecological correlations and the behavior of individuals', *Sociological Review*, 15, pp. 351-57.

Robson, B.T. (1973), *Urban growth: an approach*, London: Methuen.

Romer, P.M. (1986), 'Increasing returns and long-run growth', *Journal of Political Economy*, 94, pp. 1002-37.

Romer, P.M. (1990), 'Endogenous technological change', *Journal of Political Economy*, 98, pp. S71-102.

Romer, P.M. (1994), 'The origins of endogenous growth', *Journal of Economic Perspectives*, 8, pp. 3-22.

Roper, S. (2001), 'Innovation, networks and plant location: some evidence from Ireland', *Regional Studies*, 35, pp. 215-28.

Rosenthal, S.S. and W.C. Strange (2001), 'The determinants of agglomeration', *Journal of Urban Economics*, 59, pp.191-229.

Rosenthal, S.S. and W.C. Strange (2002), 'Geography, industrial organization and agglomeration', *Review of Economics and Statistics* (forthcoming).

Rotemberg, J.J. and G. Saloner (2000), 'Competition and human capital accumulation: a theory of interregional specialization and trade', *Regional Science and Urban Economics*, 30, pp. 373-404.

RPD (1998), *Werklocaties 1998. Rapportage bedrijventerreinen en voorradige kantoorlocaties (IBIS)*, Den Haag: Rijksplanologische Dienst.

Sabel, C.F. (1994), 'Flexible specialisation and the re-emergence of regional economies', in A. Amin (ed.), *Post-Fordism*, Oxford: Blackwell, pp. 101-56.

Sassen, S. (1991), *The global city*, New Jersey: Princeton.

Saxenian, A. (1994), *Regional advantage. Culture and competition in Silicon Valley and Route 128*, Cambridge Mass.: Harvard University Press.

Schoenberger, E. (1998), 'Discourse and practice in human geography', *Progress in Human Geography*, 22, pp. 1-14.

Schmitz, P.M.P.F. and J.B.M. Heijs (2001), *Hot spots: ruimtelijke patronen van innovatie in Nederland*, Den Haag: Senter.

Schumpeter, J. (1934), *The theory of economic development*, Cambridge: Harvard University Press.

Schumpeter, J.A. (1942), *Capitalism, socialsm and democracy*, New York: HarperPerennial.

Schutjens, V.A.J.M. and E. Wever (2000), 'Determinants of new firm success', *Papers in Regional Science* , 79, pp.135-153.

Schwartz, S. (1994), 'The fallacy of the ecological fallacy: the potential misuse of a concept and the consequences', *American Journal of Public Health*, 84, pp. 819-823.

Scitovsky, T. (1954), 'Two concepts of external economies', *Journal of Political Economy*, 62, pp. 143-51.

Scott, A.J. (1988a), *Metropolis. From the division of labor to urban form*, Berkeley: University of California Press.

Scott, A.J. (1988b), *New industrial spaces. Flexible production organization and regional development in North America and Western Europe*, London: Pion.

Scott, A.J. (2000), 'Economic geography: the great half-century', *Cambridge Journal of Economics*, 24, pp.483-504.

Shelburne, R.C. and R.W. Bednarzik (1993), 'Geographic concentration of trade-sensitive employment', *Monthly Labor Review*, pp.3-13.

Siebert, H. (1969), *Regional economic growth: theory and policy*, Scranton: International Textbook Company.

Sivitanidou, R. and P. Sivitanides (1995), 'The intrametropolitan distribution of R&D activities: theory and empirical evidence', *Journal of Regional Science*, 35, pp. 391-415.

Simon, C.J. (1998), 'Human capital and metropolitan employment growth', *Journal of Urban Economics*, 43, pp. 223-43.

Sjöholm, F. (1996), 'International transfer of knowledge: the role of international trade and geographic proximity', *Weltwissenschaftliches Archiv*, 132, pp.97-115.

Smith, A. (1776), *Inquiry into the nature and causes of the wealth of nations*, New York: Reprint 1991, Prometheus Books.

Van Soest, D.P., S.D. Gerking and F.G. van Oort (2002), 'Knowledge externalities, agglomeration economies, and employment growth in Dutch cities', Tilburg University (mimeo).

Van Soest, D.P., S.D. Gerking and F.G. van Oort (2003), 'Knowledge transfer and the location of new establishments in the Dutch province of Zuid-Holland', *The International Journal of Entrepreneurship and Small Business* (forthcoming).

Solow, R.M. (1957), 'Technical change and the aggregate production function', *Review of Economics and Statistics*, 39, pp. 312-320.

Solow, R.M. (1970), *Growth theory*, Oxford: University Press.

Solow, R.M. (1994), 'Perspectives on growth theory', *Journal of Economic Perspectives*, 8, pp.45-54.

Steinnes, D.N. (1977), 'Causality and intraurban location', *Journal of Urban Economics*, 4, pp. 69-79.

Sternberg, R. (1999), 'Innovative linkages and proximity: empirical results from recent surveys of small & medium sized firms in German regions', *Regional Studies*, 33, pp.529-40.

Storper, M. (1995), 'The resurgence of regional economies, ten years later', *European Urban and Regional Studies*, 2, pp. 191-221.

Storper, M. (1997), *The regional world. Territorial development in a global economy*, New York: The Guildford Press.

Storper, M. and R. Walker (1989), *The capitalist imperative. Territory, technology and industrial growth*, Oxford: Basil Blackwell.

Summers, A., P. Cheshire and L. Senn (1999) (eds.), *Urban change in the United States and Western Europe: comparative analysis and policy*, Washington: Urban Institute Press.

Sutton, J. (1996), 'Technology and market structure', *European Economic Review*, 40, pp.511-30.

Sutton, J. (1997), 'Gibrat's legacy', *Journal of Economic Literature*, 35, pp. 40-59.

Sunley, P. (1996), 'Context in economic geography: the relevance of pragmatism', *Progress in Human Geography*, 20, pp. 338-55.

Sunley, M.R. (1998), 'Slow convergence? New endogenous growth theory and regional development', *Economic Geography*, 74, pp.201-27.

Taylor, M. and B. Asheim (2001), 'The concept of the firm in economic geography', *Economic Geography*, 77, pp.315-28.

Taylor, P.J. (1975), *Distance decay models in spatial interactions*. Concepts and Techniques in Modern Geography (CATMOG) no. 2, London: Institute of British Geographers.

Taylor, P.J. and D.R.F. Walker (2001), 'World cities: a first multivariate analysis of their service complexes', *Urban Studies*, 38, pp.23-47.

Thompson, W.R. (1968), 'Internal and external factors in the development of urban economics', in H.S. Perloff and L. Wingo (eds.), *Issues in urban economics*, Baltimore: John Hopkins Press.

Thorngren, B. (1970), 'How do contact systems affect regional development?', *Environment and Planning A*, 2, pp.409-27.

Thrift, N. and K. Olds (1996), 'Refiguring the economic in economic geography', *Progress in Human Geography*, 20, pp. 311-37.

Von Thünen, J.H. (1842), *Der Isolierte Staat*, in P. Hall (ed.), Von Thünen's Isolated State, London: Pergamon (1966).

Thurston, L. and A.M.J. Yezer (1994), 'Causality in the suburbanization of population and employment', *Journal of Urban Economics*, 35, pp. 105-18.

Törnqvist, G.E. (1968), *Flows of information and the location of economic activities*, Lund: Studies in Geography B, nr. 30..

Törnqvist, G.E. (1978), 'Swedish industry as a spatial system', in F.E.I. Hamilton (ed.), *Contemporary industrialisation*, London: Longman.

Torre, A. and J.P. Gilly (2000), 'On the analytical dimension of proximity dynamics', *Regional Studies*, 34, pp. 169-80.

Vaessen, P. (1993), *Small business growth in contrasting environments*. Nijmegen: Netherlands Geographical Studies.

Variyam, J.N. and D.S. Kraybill (1992), 'Empirical evidence on determinants of firm growth', *Economics Letters*, 38, pp.31-36.

Verspagen, B. (1992), 'Endogenous innovation in neo-classical growth models: a survey', *Journal of Macroeconomics*, 14, pp. 631-62.

Verspagen, B. (1997), 'Measuring intersectoral technology spillovers: estimates from the European and US Patent Office databases', *Economic Systems Research*, 9, pp. 47-66.

Verspagen, B. and B. Los (2000), 'R&D spillovers and productivity: evidence from US manufacturing microdata', *Empirical Economics*, 25, pp. 127-48.

Van der Vegt, C. and W. Manshanden (1996), *Steden en stadsgewesten. Economische ontwikkelingen 1970-2015*, Amsterdam: SEO, Universiteit van Amsterdam.

Venables, A.J. (1996), 'Equilibrium locations of vertically linked industries', *International Economic Review*, 37, pp. 341-59.

De Vries, J. (1984), *European urbanization 1500-1800*. Cambridge, Mass.: Harvard University Press.

Wallsten, S.J. (2001), 'An empirical test of geographic knowledge spillovers using geographic information systems and firm-level data', *Regional Science and Urban Economics*, 31, pp.571-99.

Webber, M.M. (1964), 'The urban place and the nonplace urban realm', in M.M. Webber (ed.), *Explorations into urban structure*, Philadelphia: University Press, pp. 79-153.

Weber, A. (1909), *Theory of the location of industries*, Chicago: University Press.

Weibull, J.W. (1976), 'An axiomatic approach to the measurement of accessibility', *Regional Science and Urban Economics*, 6, pp.357-79.

Wever, E. and E. Stam (1999), 'Clusters of high technology SME's: the Dutch case', *Regional Studies*, 33, pp.391-400.

Wheeler, J.O., Y. Aoyama and B. Warf (2000), *Cities in the telecommunications age. The fracturing of geographies*, London: Routledge.

Van der Wiel, H.P. (1999), *Firm turnover in Dutch business services. The effect on labour productivity*, CPB Research Memorandum 159, 's-Gravenhage.

Willeboordse, A.J. (1986), 'Towards a 'demography' of firms', *Netherlands Official Statistics. Quarterly Journal of the Central Bureau of Statistics*, 1, pp. 5-11.

Williamson, O.E. (1975), *Markets and hierarchies: analysis and antitrust implications*, New York: The Free Press.

Van Wissen, L. (2000), 'A micro-simulation model of firms: applications of concepts of the demography of the firm', *Papers in Regional Science*, 79, pp. 111-34.

WMD (1999), *Woonmilieudatabase 1998. Toelichting*, ABF-Onderzoek, Delft.

Wolff, E.N. (1997), 'Spillovers, linkages and technical change', *Economic Systems Research*, 9, pp. 9-23.

Van der Woud, A. (1987), *Het lege land. De ruimtelijke orde van Nederland 1798-1848*, Amsterdam: Meulenhoff.

Wozniak, G.D. and R.A. Babula (1992), 'Dynamic relationships among regional and nationwide manufacturing', *Growth and Change*, 23, pp. 16-36.

Wrigley, N. (1995), 'Revisiting the modifiable areal unit problem and the ecological fallacy', in A.D. Cliff, P.R. Gould and N.J. Thrift (eds.), *Diffusing geography*, Oxford: Blackwell, pp. 49-71.

Zanette, D.H. and C. Manrubia (1997), 'Role of intermittency in urban development: a model of large-scale city formation', *Physical Review Letters*, 79, pp.523-26.

Index

accessibility 82, 85
Acs, Z. 36, 49, 76
agglomeration, 1, 17
  economies 9, 14
    dynamic 14, 19, 31, 218
    static 14, 19, 28, 218
  regional 8, 205
amenities 24
Anas, A. 7, 145
Anselin, L. 73, 76, 148, 164, 241
Arrow, K.J. 10, 39
Arthur, B. 41
Audretsch, D.B. 51, 142

Von Böventer, E. 31

carrying capacity 97, 113, 146
central place theory 32
cities 2, 45, 170
  hierarchy of cities 48, 228
  system of cities 2, 230
city-industries 64, 73, 222
clusters 24, 217
Combes, P. 5, 69, 141, 172
commuting 90
competition 3, 96, 143
  size of firms 97, 145, 160
  turbulence (volatility) 7, 98, 146, 224
components of employment change 99
conceptualization 13-19
  contingencies 17
congestion costs 1
consumer services 68, 115, 180, 189, 240
consumer surplus 145
corridors 80
cumulative causation 16, 32, 35, 56, 99

daily urban system 78
data 235-50
  BRZ South-Holland 242
  on employment 235-46
  on innovation 247-50

longitudinal 11, 235
  variables construction 143
  Senter innovation data 247
distance decay 86
distance weights 8, 86
  matrix 108
  row-standardization 108
  stochastic assumptions 108
distribution activities 68, 175, 183, 240
diversity 3, 51, 146

ecological fallacy 66
economies of scale 1, 23, 145
  diseconomies of scale 1
edge-cities 92
embeddedness 52
employment 65, 111
  density 111, 129, 221
  function 116, 129, 221
endogenous growth 2, 7, 14, 195
equilibrium models 2
evolutionary economics 2, 40
exploratory spatial data analysis 107, 221
externalities 1, 9
  MAR 58, 218
  Marshallian 23
  pecuniary (rent) 1, 23, 36
  technological (pure) 23, 197

Feldman, M.A. 51, 142
filtering down theory 45, 99, 228
firm migration 99
flexible specialization 54
Friedmann, J. 5, 80
Fujita, M. 34, 40

Gini coefficient 147
Glaeser, E.L. 3, 19, 60-64, 141, 222, 232
Gottmann, J. 30, 47
Griliches, Z. 196
gravity model 8, 85

growth 1, 7
  employment growth 3, 65, 120
growth pole 43

Hall, P. 1, 79
Hammermesh, D.S. 6
Heckscher-Ohlin theory 33
Henderson, J.V. 2, 4, 27, 60, 147, 232
Hirschman-Herfendahl index 147
Hoover, E.M. 26
hot spots 107, 229
human capital 29, 40

imperfect competition 23
increasing returns to scale 23, 26, 32
incubation function 46, 99
incumbent firms 10, 105, 157, 179, 222
industrial districts 44, 56
industrial sites 82, 85
information and communication
  technology 16
innovation 1, 7
  diffusion 43
  intensity 133, 195, 227
input-output relations 197
institutional theory 14, 53
institutions 2, 52, 54
  non-market 42
Isard, W. 26, 30

Jacobs, J. 10, 28, 58, 218
Jaffe, A.B. 2, 49, 164

knowledge 29, 40
  tacit knowledge 195
knowledge spillovers 1, 20, 37, 50
Krugman, P. 16, 31, 34

labor market matching 30
labor mobility 26, 197
Lambooy, J.G. 21, 38, 41, 153
land rents 22
learning 195
life-cycles 3, 220, 231
  of firms 3, 65, 96
  of products 45
  of sectors, 96
localization economies 2, 26, 58, 67, 143
location quotient 94, 143, 198
lock-in 41

Lucas, R.E. 2, 39, 61

Malmberg, A. 28, 53, 64
manufacturing 68, 172, 181, 240
market power 6, 145
MAR-externalities 58
Marshall, A. (MAR) 10, 22
measurement units 73
  city-industries 63, 67
  inter- and intra sectoral 160, 225
  location-industries 10, 65, 141
  manufacturing industries 63, 148, 163
  sectoral 65, 67, 169, 226
metropolitan regions 13, 205, 244
Miller, J. 5, 80
modifiable areal unit problem (MAUP) 7,
  73, 154
Moomaw, R.L. 67
Moran's *I* test statistic 10, 108, 221
  Moran scatterplot 109
  Moran scatterplot map 110, 221
Monopolistic competition 32
multilevel analysis 7, 73, 233
multipliers (spatial) 43, 164
Myrdal, G. 34

Nelson, R.R. 41
network theory 41, 47, 230
new firm formation 6, 98, 124
New Growth theory 21, 36
New Trade theory 21, 32

organizational ecology 146

Parr, J.B. 3, 8, 44
patents (citation) 50
path-dependency 41
Perroux, F. 43
Piore, M.J. 55
policentricity 3, 92, 219
Porter, M. 10, 27, 59, 218
Pred, A.R. 34, 47
producer services 68, 177, 185, 240
productivity 14, 62, 146
proximity 24

Quigly, J.M. 29, 58, 232

Randstad Holland 78
regional labor markets 8, 214

representative firm 6, 66, 232
research and development (R&D) 37, 195
    industrial 134, 198, 206
    non-industrial 134, 200, 212
    R&D wage sum 134, 195, 249
    spillovers 196
Richardson, H.W. 1, 21, 26, 31, 47
Romer, P.M. 2, 10, 39, 61
routines 41

Sabel, C.F. 55
Schumpeter, J. 27, 38
Scitovsky, T. 23
Scott, A.J. 28, 49
search costs 23
sectoral interdependencies 9
shift and share analysis 74, 203
Smith, A. 22
Solow, R.M. 38
South-Holland 7, 68
spatial autocorrelation 107
    global 108
    local 109
spatial configuration 3
    contiguous 3, 8
    non-contiguous 3, 8
spatial dependence 8
spatial error modeling 74
spatial heterogeneity 3, 77, 191, 226
    connectedness 90, 214
    degree of urbanization, 82, 85
    intra-urban 7, 80, 170, 220
    national zoning 85
    north/southwing Randstad 88

spatial lag modeling 74
spatially lagged variable 76, 109, 225
spatial regimes 77, 169, 220
spatial scale 3, 233
spatial policy 1, 16
splintering urbanism 16
Storper, M. 13, 48, 53
stylized facts 13, 17, 55
suburbanization 79, 220
sunk costs 41

technology fields (BSI) 248
technology flow matrix 197
Von Thunen, J.H. 22
trade sensitive firms 6
transaction costs 56
transport costs 25, 36

urban field 5, 16, 80, 196, 220, 230
urban system 6
urbanization (degree of) 8, 79, 82, 85
    medium-sized cities 79, 188
urbanization economies 2, 26, 59, 67

variety 23, 33
Venables, A. 37

wages 34, 62, 134, 244
Weber, A. 25
Winter, S.G. 41

zip codes 82, 224, 237